NOBUAKI ENOKI

The inside of my head is always chock-full of exciting ideas! Fantasizing is one thing, but giving form to those ideas is a whole different ball game. I hope that one day I'll be able to put lots of time and love into putting those ideas down on paper and into the hearts of others again.

Nobuaki Enoki received the Jump Treasure New Cartoonist Prize in April 2009 for his work *Rikuo*. *School Judgment: Gakkyu Hotei* was his first work to be serialized in *Weekly Shonen Jump*.

TAKESHI OBATA

Takeshi Obata was born in 1969 in Niigata, Japan, and first achieved international recognition as the artist of the wildly popular *Shonen Jump* title *Hikaru no Go*, which won the 2003 Tezuka Osamu Cultural Prize: Shinsei "New Hope" Award and the 2000 Shogakukan Manga Award. He went on to illustrate the smash hit *Death Note* as well as the hugely successful manga *Bakuman。* and *All You Need Is Kill*.

Congratulations on your graduation, class 6-3 students! Please keep stirring up trouble and pestering Inugami as middle schoolers!!

School Judgment
GAKKYU HOTEI

SHONEN JUMP MANGA EDITION

3

STORY BY Nobuaki Enoki
ART BY Takeshi Obata

TRANSLATION Mari Morimoto
TOUCH-UP ART & LETTERING James Gaubatz
DESIGN Shawn Carrico
WEEKLY SHONEN JUMP EDITOR Alexis Kirsch
GRAPHIC NOVEL EDITOR Marlene First

GAKKYU HOTEI © 2014 by Nobuaki Enoki, Takeshi Obata
All rights reserved. First published in Japan in 2014 by SHUEISHA Inc., Tokyo.
English translation rights arranged by SHUEISHA Inc.

Printed in the U.S.A.

Published by VIZ Media, LLC
P.O. Box 77010
San Francisco, CA 94107

10 9 8 7 6 5 4 3 2 1
First printing, June 2016

www.viz.com

www.shonenjump.com

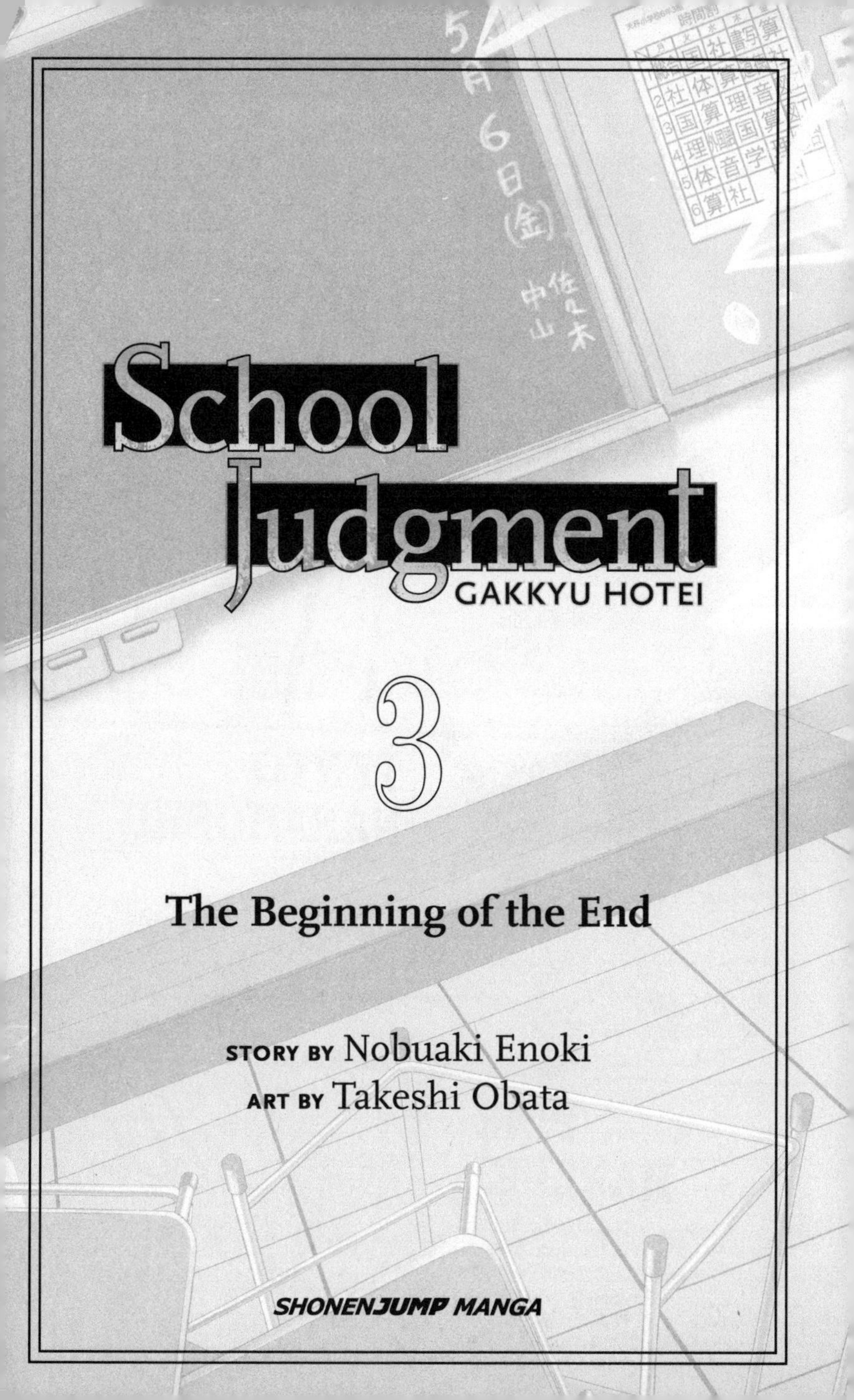

School Judgment

GAKKYU HOTEI

3

The Beginning of the End

STORY BY Nobuaki Enoki
ART BY Takeshi Obata

SHONENJUMP MANGA

C H A R A C T E R S

School Judgment
GAKKYU HOTEI

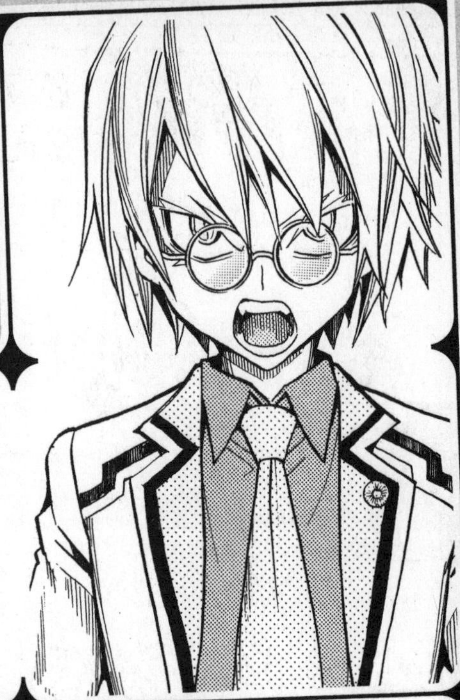

ABAKU INUGAMI

An elementary school attorney who transferred into Tenbin Elementary class 6-3. His hobby is *ronpa*. He is one of the Three Tongues. He previously attended the grade-schoolers' penitentiary Onigashima Elementary, but now...?!

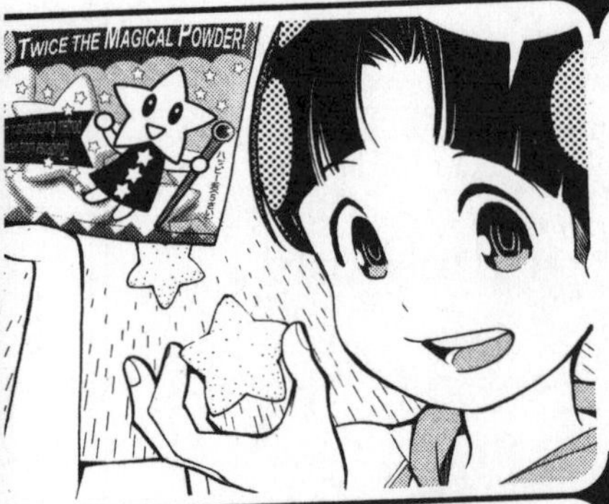
TWICE THE MAGICAL POWDER!

TENTO NANAHOSHI

Tenbin Elementary class 6-3 student. Was defended by Abaku in the Suzuki Murder Case and subsequently started assisting him with his work as a lawyer. A fan of fellow classmate Airin.

PINE HANZUKI

A pretty prosecutor who transferred into Tenbin Elementary at the same time as Abaku. She is the daughter of the head of the Hanzuki Conglomerate, which is famous in the legal world. She has nicknamed Abaku "Puppy-gami" and is always at odds with him.

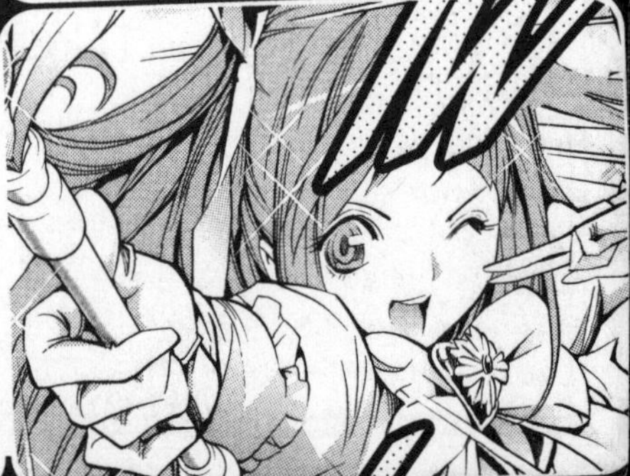

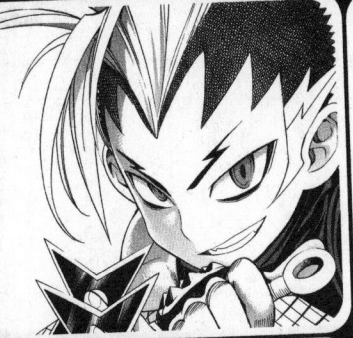

KOTARO SARUTOBI

An attorney who transferred into Class 6-3. Another of the "Three Tongues" and a (self-proclaimed) ninja. His speciality is making use of his ninja arts to collect evidence. Former Onigashima Elementary student along with Abaku.

CLASS 6-3 CLASSMATES

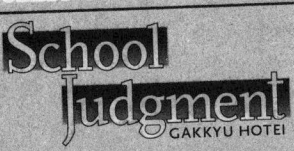

School Judgment
GAKKYU HOTEI

AIRIN TAKANASHI
SHUICHI HIGASHIDE
REIKO SHIRATORI
EISUKE UOZUMI

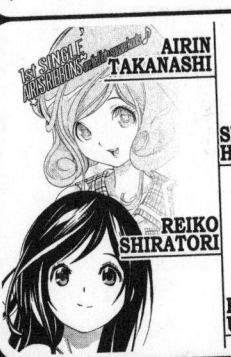

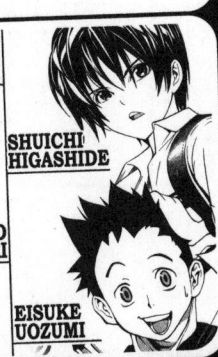

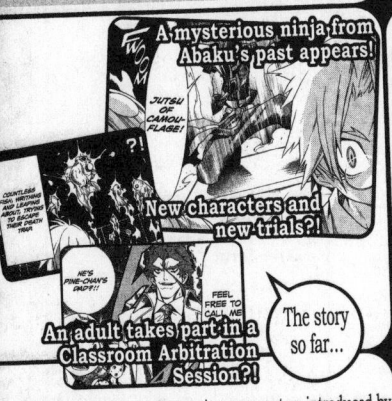

A mysterious ninja from Abaku's past appears!
FWOOM
JUTSU OF CAMOUFLAGE!
?!
COUNTLESS FISH, WRITHING AND LEAPING ABOUT, TRYING TO ESCAPE THEIR DEATH TRAP
New characters and new trials?!
HE'S PINE-CHAN'S DAD?!!
FEEL FREE TO CALL ME
An adult takes part in a Classroom Arbitration Session?!
The story so far...

STORY

School Judgment
GAKKYU HOTEI

The School Judgment System is a new system introduced by the government to resolve problems, such as bullying and punishment in schools.
It is a new form of Classroom Arbitration presided over by children who have answered the call to action to seek the truth under the law. Abaku Inugami, who transferred into Himawari Municipal District's Tenbin Elementary School, has a hard time fitting in with his class due to his difficult personality and occupation. However, as he works on various cases as an attorney, he starts to develop deep bonds with his classmates.
And today, once again, Abaku is approached to defend someone in this next case...

CLASS SCHEDULE

	MON	TUE	WED	THU	FRI
1		**School Judgment** GAKKYU HOTEI			**3**
2	**Chapter 17** The Beginning of the End p. 7	Phys Ed	**Chapter 21** Where the Ogre Dwells p. 87	Ethics	Social Studies
3	Language	**Chapter 19** I'm Not Afraid p. 47	Science	**One-Shot** Part A: Case Arc p. 139	Art
4	**Chapter 18** Dog vs. Pheasant p. 27	Foreign Language	**Finale** The Session That Started It All p. 107	Math	Art
5	Phys Ed	**Chapter 20** The Key p. 67	Classroom Arbitration	**One-Shot** Part B: Courtroom Arc p. 171	General Studies
6	Math	Social Studies		Phys Ed	**Glossary** p. 208

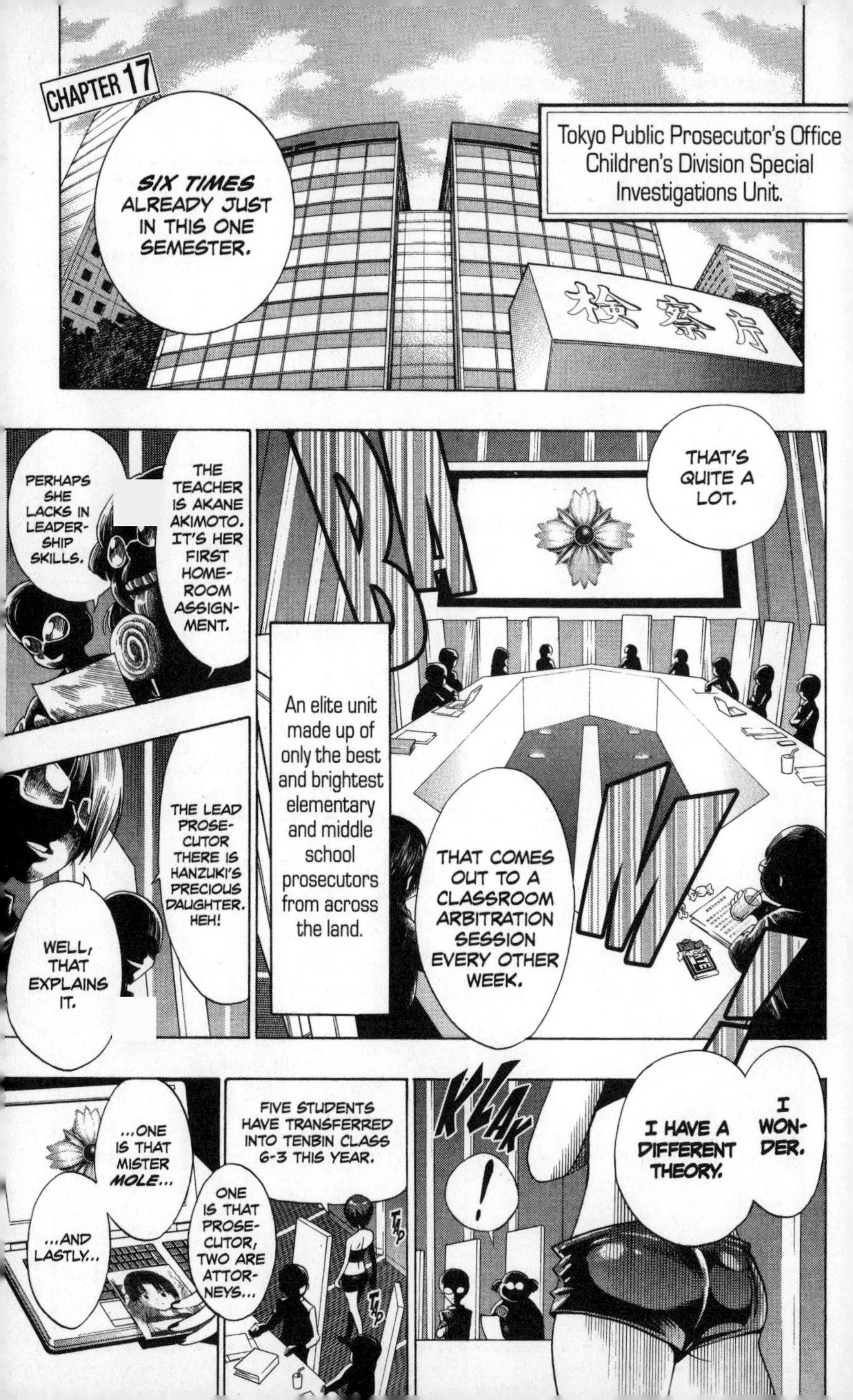
CHAPTER 17
Tokyo Public Prosecutor's Office Children's Division Special Investigations Unit.
SIX TIMES ALREADY JUST IN THIS ONE SEMESTER.
検察庁
THAT'S QUITE A LOT.
An elite unit made up of only the best and brightest elementary and middle school prosecutors from across the land.
THAT COMES OUT TO A CLASSROOM ARBITRATION SESSION EVERY OTHER WEEK.
THE TEACHER IS AKANE AKIMOTO. IT'S HER FIRST HOMEROOM ASSIGNMENT.
PERHAPS SHE LACKS IN LEADERSHIP SKILLS.
THE LEAD PROSECUTOR THERE IS HANZUKI'S PRECIOUS DAUGHTER. HEH!
WELL, THAT EXPLAINS IT.
I WONDER.
I HAVE A DIFFERENT THEORY.
K'LAK
!
TAP
TAP
FIVE STUDENTS HAVE TRANSFERRED INTO TENBIN CLASS 6-3 THIS YEAR.
ONE IS THAT PROSECUTOR, TWO ARE ATTORNEYS...
...ONE IS THAT MISTER MOLE...
...AND LASTLY...

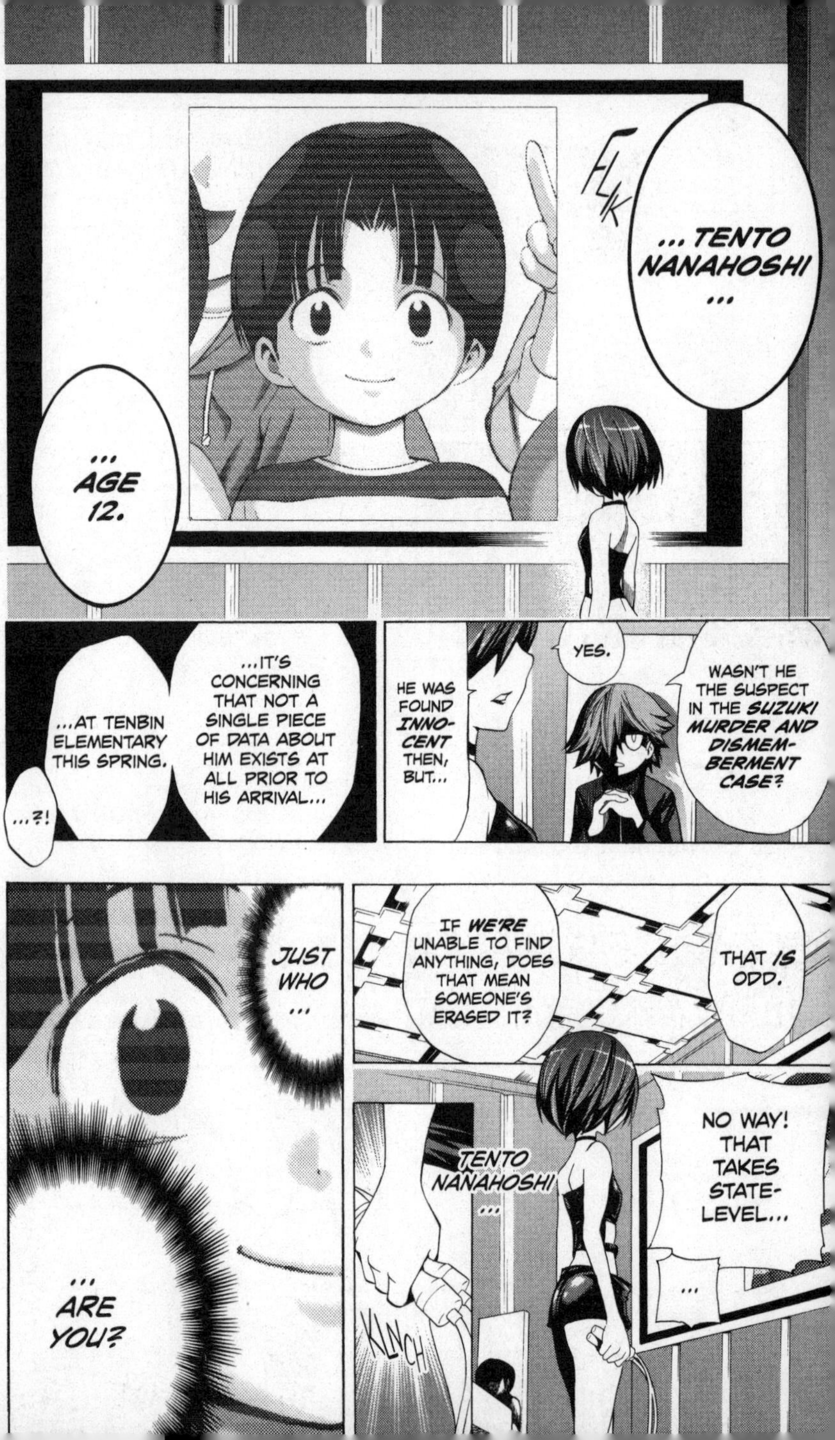
...TENTO NANAHOSHI...
FLIK
...AGE 12.
WASN'T HE THE SUSPECT IN THE SUZUKI MURDER AND DISMEMBERMENT CASE?
YES.
HE WAS FOUND INNOCENT THEN, BUT...
...IT'S CONCERNING THAT NOT A SINGLE PIECE OF DATA ABOUT HIM EXISTS AT ALL PRIOR TO HIS ARRIVAL...
...AT TENBIN ELEMENTARY THIS SPRING.
...?!
THAT IS ODD.
IF WE'RE UNABLE TO FIND ANYTHING, DOES THAT MEAN SOMEONE'S ERASED IT?
NO WAY! THAT TAKES STATE-LEVEL...
...
TENTO NANAHOSHI...
KLINCH
JUST WHO...
...ARE YOU?

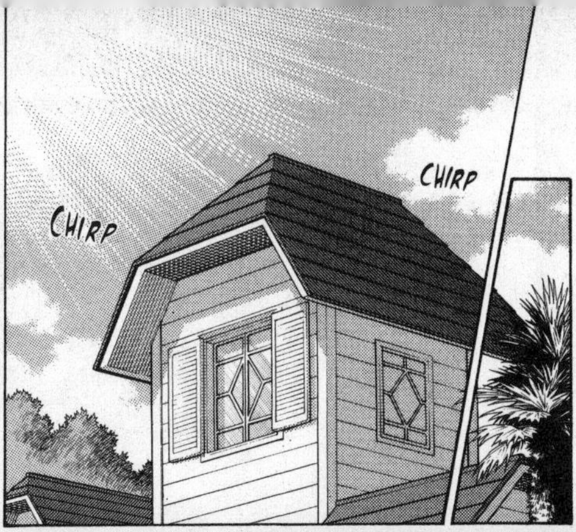
CHIRP
CHIRP
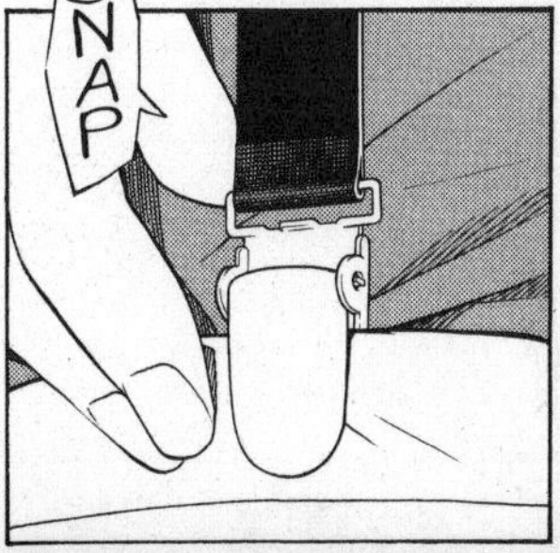
SNAP

CHAPTER 17:

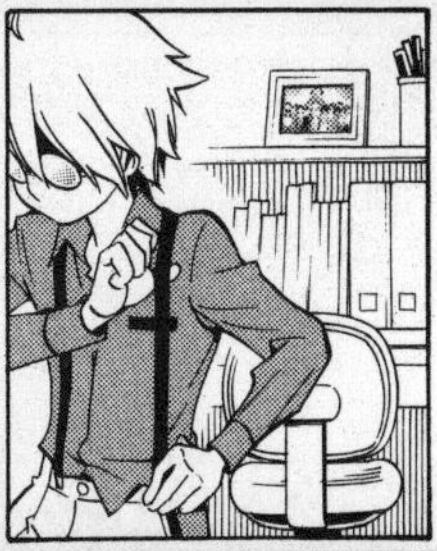
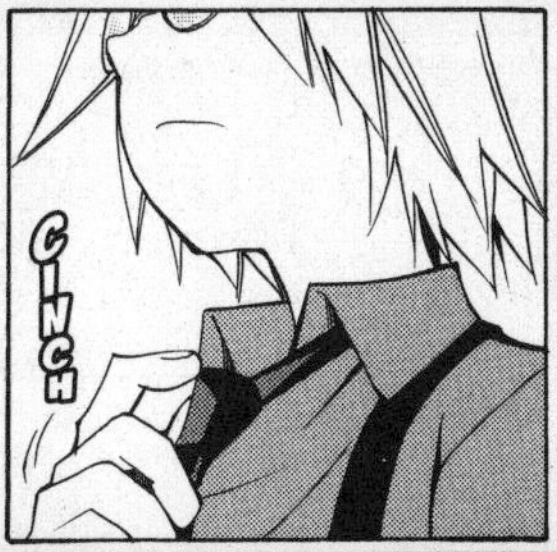
CINCH
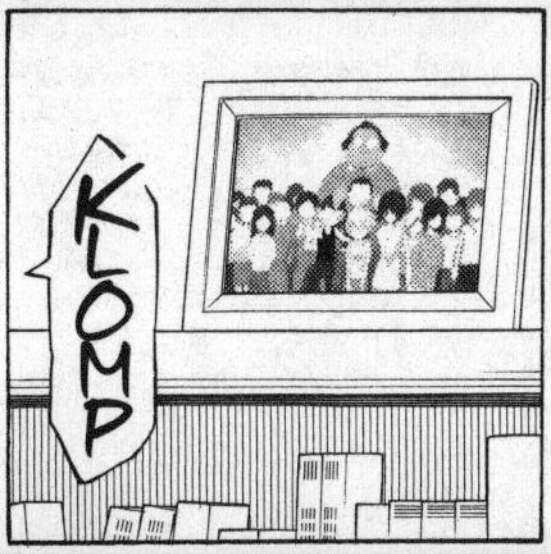
KLOMP

THE BEGINNING OF THE END

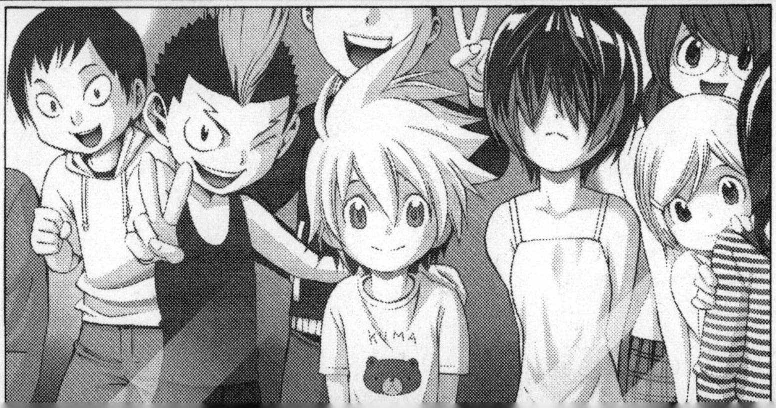
KUMA

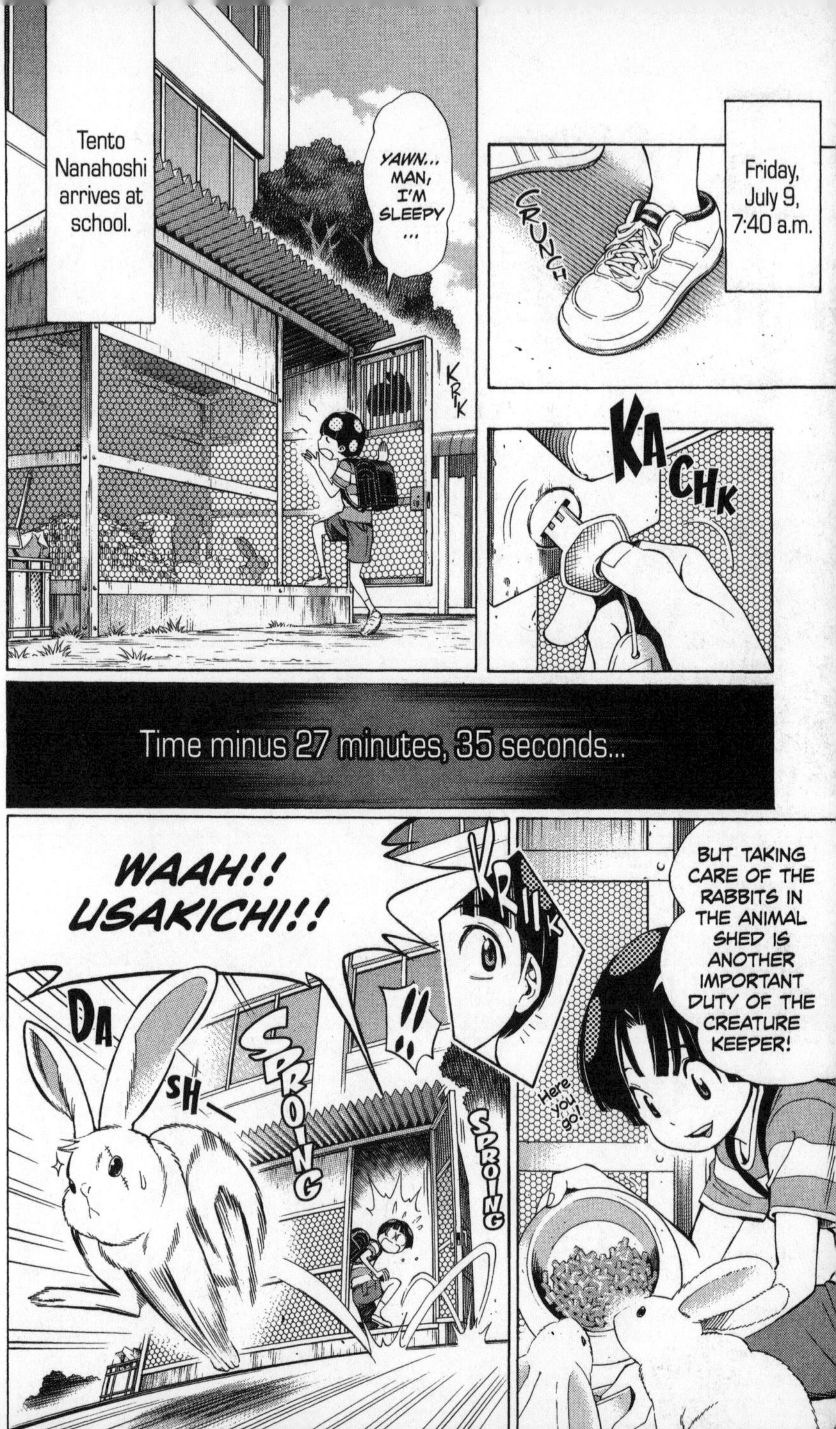
Friday, July 9, 7:40 a.m.
CRUNCH
KACHK
Tento Nanahoshi arrives at school.
YAWN... MAN, I'M SLEEPY...
KRIK
Time minus 27 minutes, 35 seconds...
BUT TAKING CARE OF THE RABBITS IN THE ANIMAL SHED IS ANOTHER IMPORTANT DUTY OF THE CREATURE KEEPER!
Here you go!
KRIIK
!!
WAAH!! USAKICHI!!
DASH
SPROING
SPROING

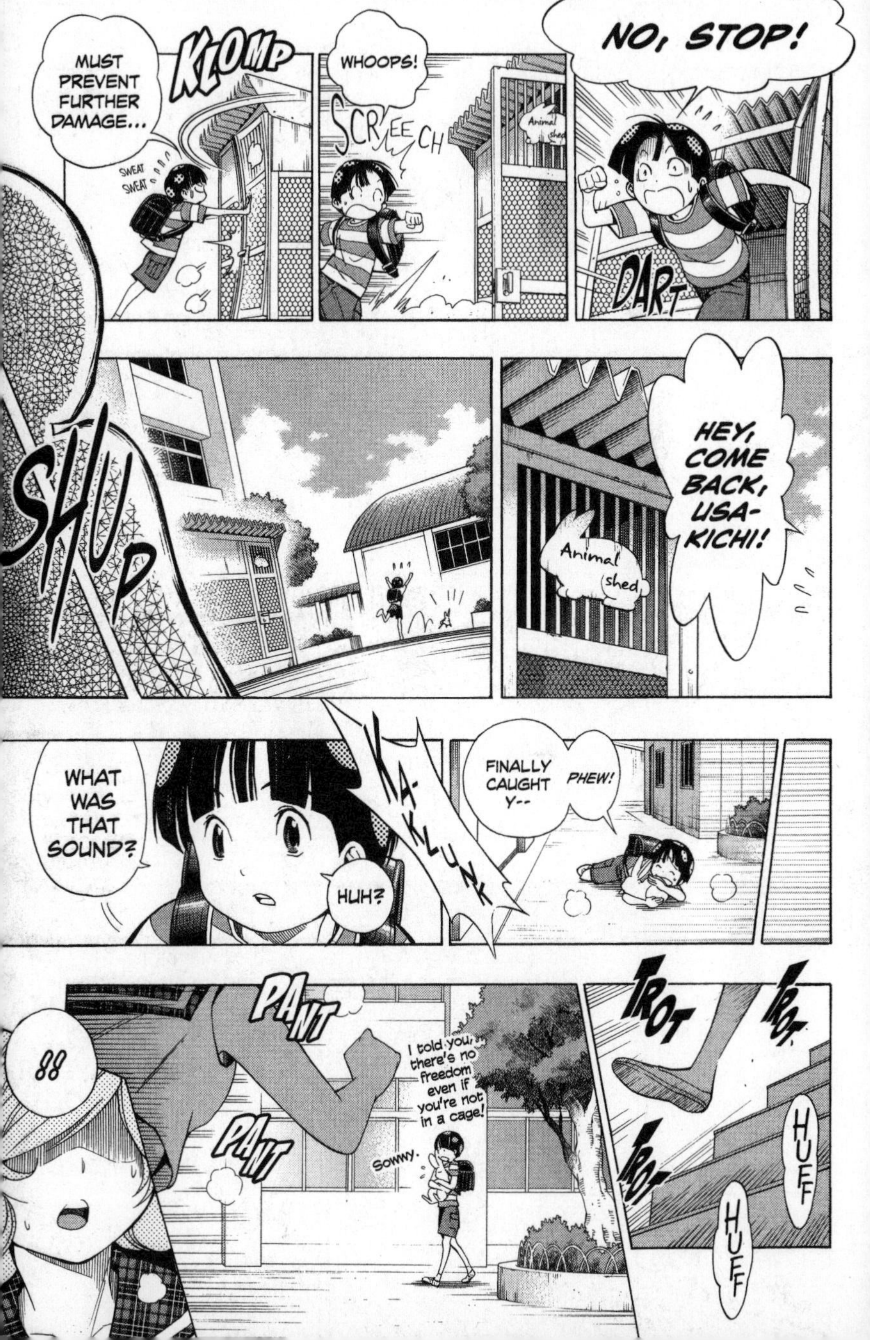
NO, STOP!
DART
WHOOPS!
SCREECH
Animal shed
MUST PREVENT FURTHER DAMAGE...
KLOMP
SWEAT SWEAT
HEY, COME BACK, USA-KICHI!
Animal shed
SHUP
FINALLY CAUGHT Y--
PHEW!
WHAT WAS THAT SOUND?
HUH?
KA-KLUNK
TROT
TROT
TROT
HUFF
HUFF
PANT
PANT
I told you, there's no freedom even if you're not in a cage!
Sowwy.

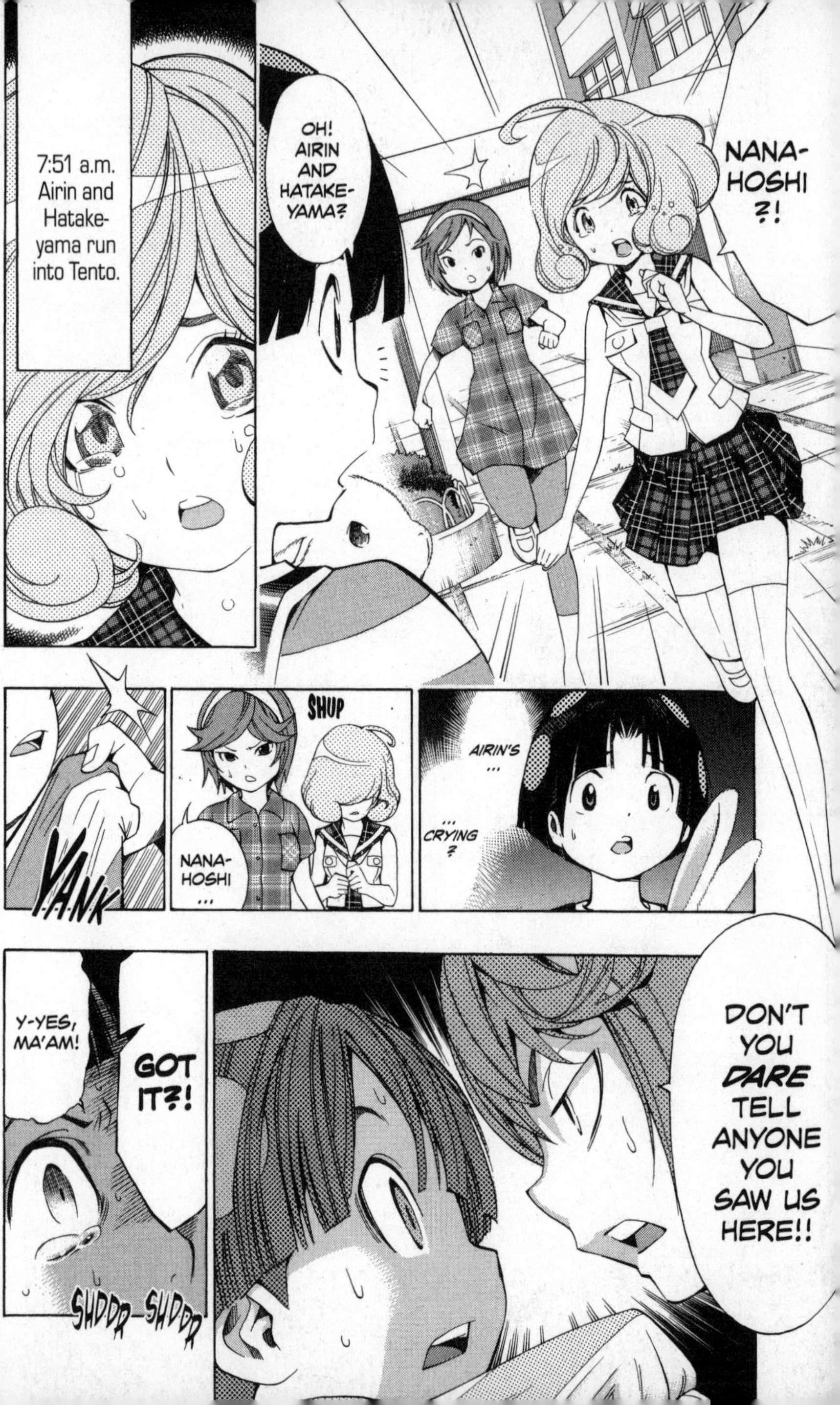
NANA-HOSHI ?!
OH! AIRIN AND HATAKE-YAMA?
7:51 a.m. Airin and Hatake-yama run into Tento.
AIRIN'S ...
... CRYING ?
SHUP
NANA-HOSHI ...
YANK
DON'T YOU DARE TELL ANYONE YOU SAW US HERE!!
GOT IT?!
Y-YES, MA'AM!
SHDDR-SHDDR

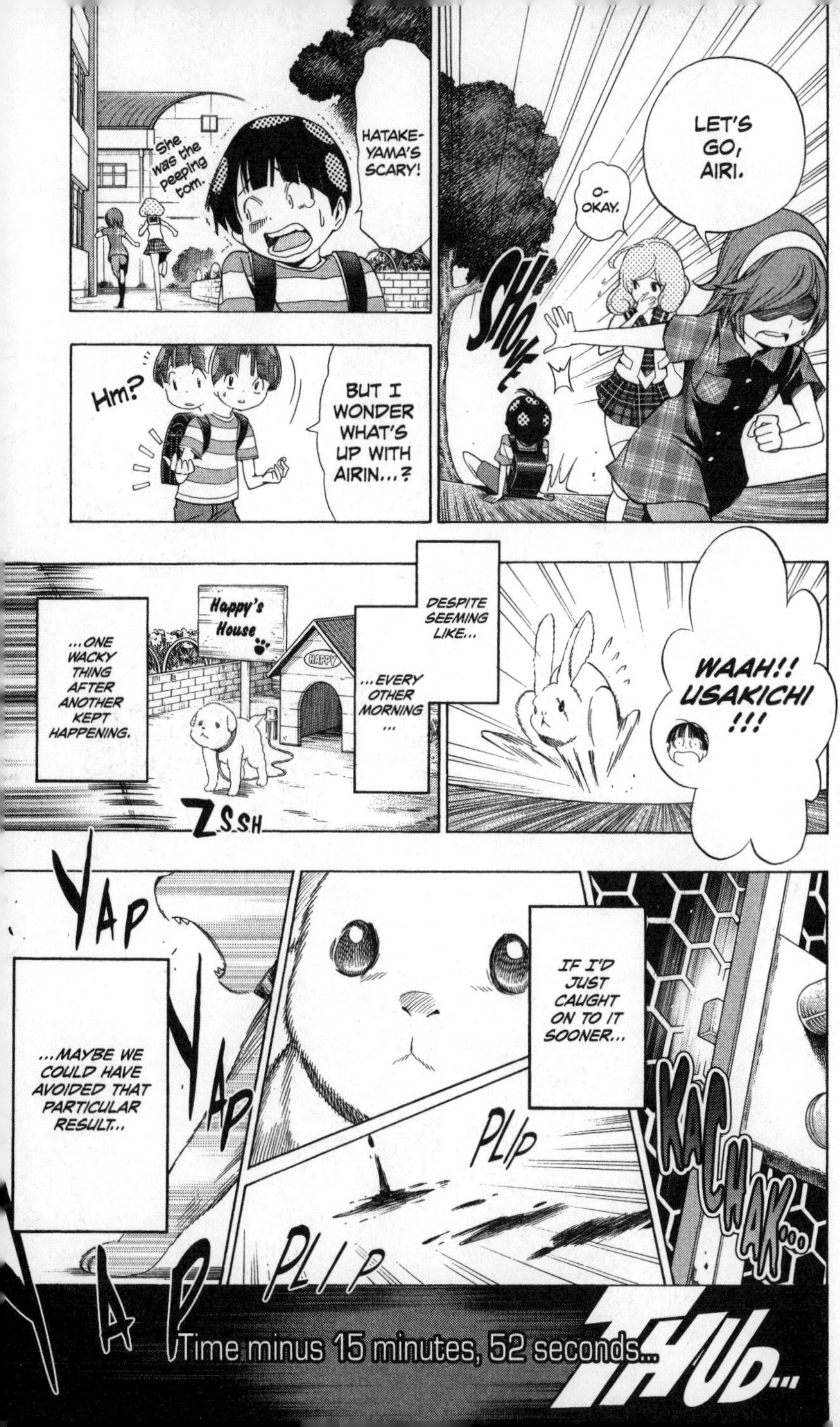
LET'S GO, AIRI.
O-OKAY.
HATAKE-YAMA'S SCARY!
She was the peeping tom.
BUT I WONDER WHAT'S UP WITH AIRIN...?
Hm?
WAAH!! USAKICHI !!!
DESPITE SEEMING LIKE...
...EVERY OTHER MORNING ...
...ONE WACKY THING AFTER ANOTHER KEPT HAPPENING.
Happy's House
HAPPY
ZSSH
KACHAK...
IF I'D JUST CAUGHT ON TO IT SOONER...
PLIP
...MAYBE WE COULD HAVE AVOIDED THAT PARTICULAR RESULT...
YAP
YAP
PLIP
YAP
Time minus 15 minutes, 52 seconds...
THUD...

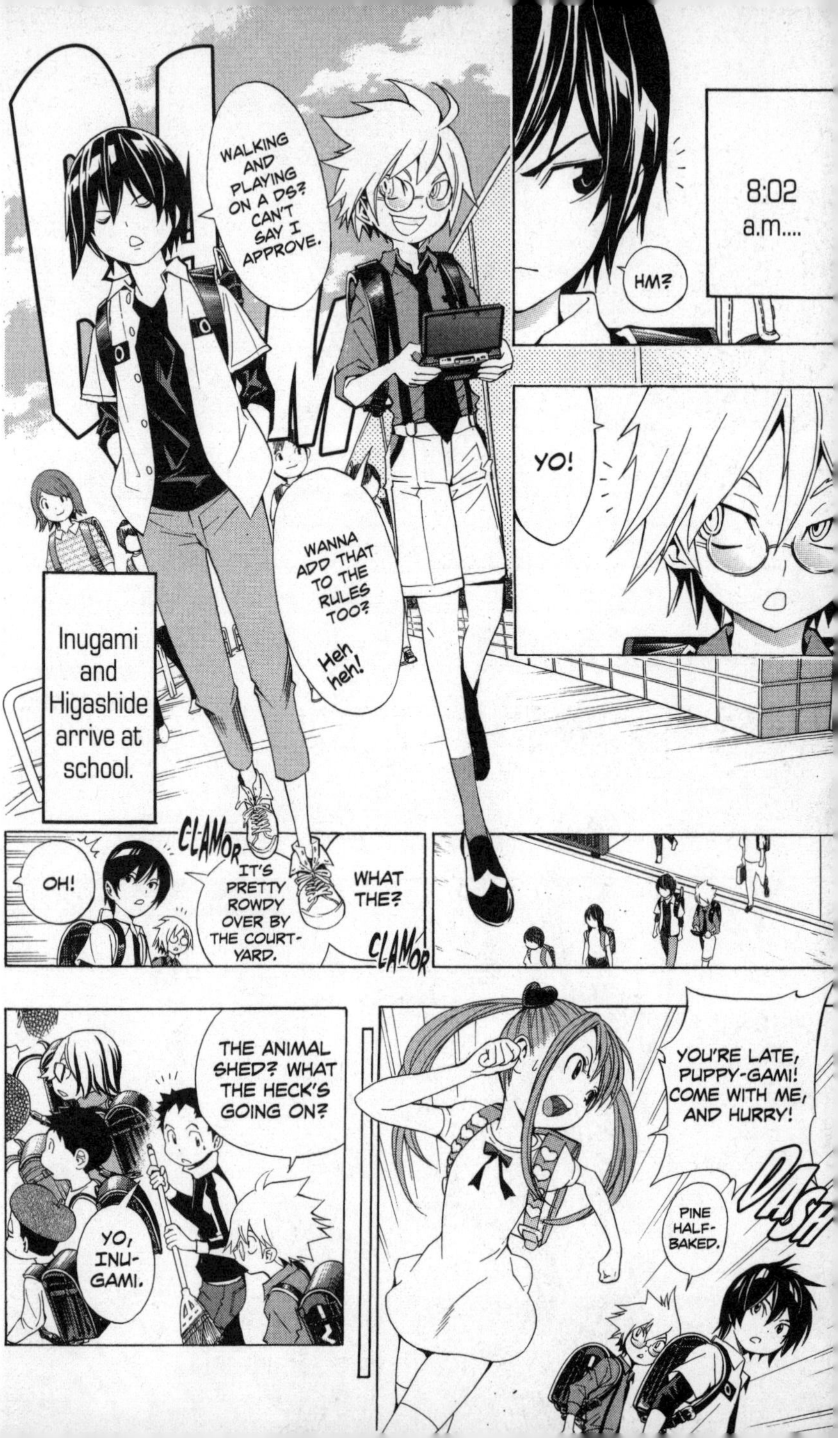
8:02 a.m....
HM?
YO!
WALKING AND PLAYING ON A DS? CAN'T SAY I APPROVE.
WANNA ADD THAT TO THE RULES TOO?
Heh heh!
Inugami and Higashide arrive at school.
CLAMOR
WHAT THE?
IT'S PRETTY ROWDY OVER BY THE COURTYARD.
OH!
CLAMOR
YOU'RE LATE, PUPPY-GAMI! COME WITH ME, AND HURRY!
DASH
PINE HALF-BAKED.
THE ANIMAL SHED? WHAT THE HECK'S GOING ON?
YO, INUGAMI.

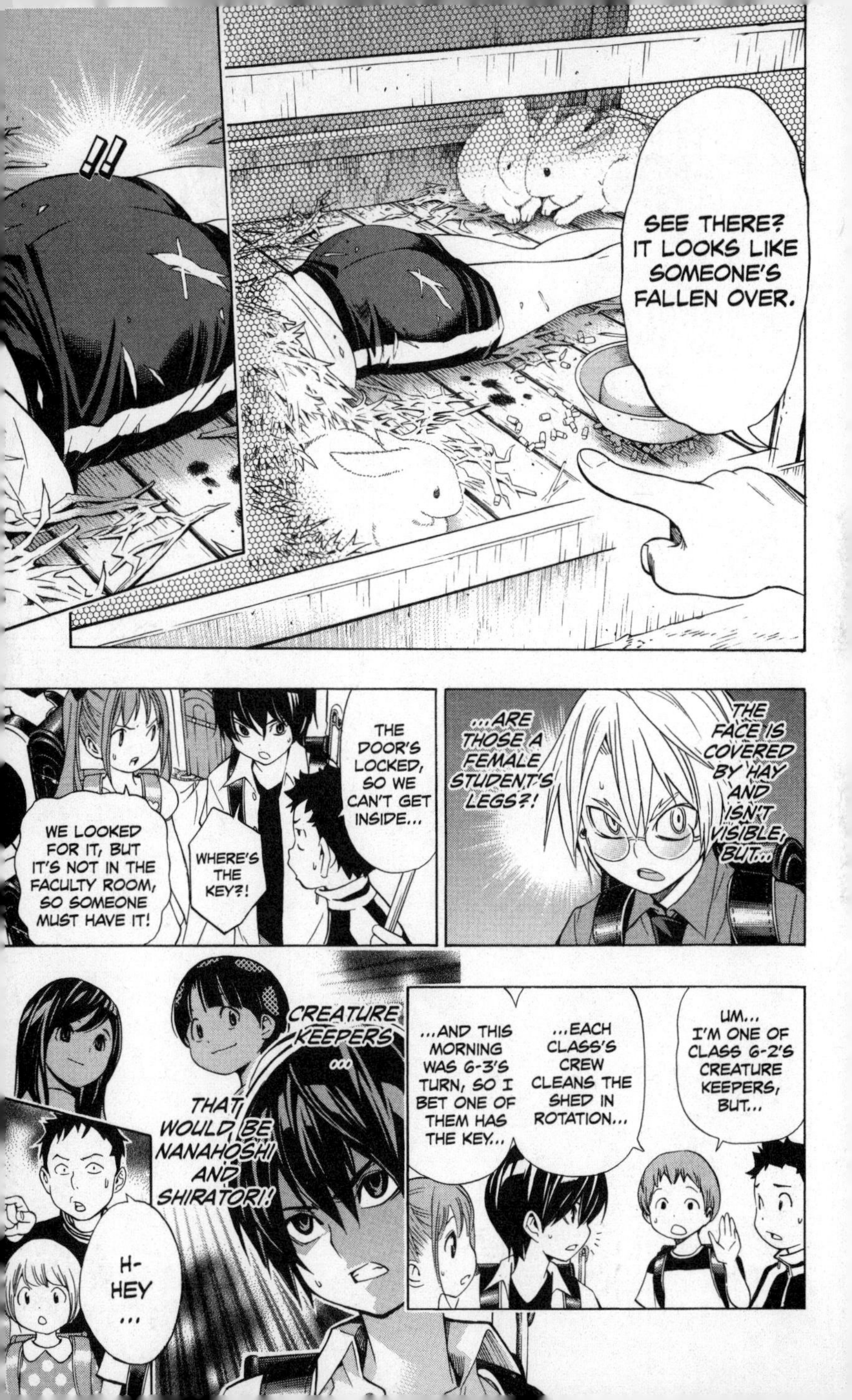
SEE THERE? IT LOOKS LIKE SOMEONE'S FALLEN OVER.
!!
THE FACE IS COVERED BY HAY AND ISN'T VISIBLE, BUT...
...ARE THOSE A FEMALE STUDENT'S LEGS?!
THE DOOR'S LOCKED, SO WE CAN'T GET INSIDE...
WHERE'S THE KEY?!
WE LOOKED FOR IT, BUT IT'S NOT IN THE FACULTY ROOM, SO SOMEONE MUST HAVE IT!
UM... I'M ONE OF CLASS 6-2'S CREATURE KEEPERS, BUT...
...EACH CLASS'S CREW CLEANS THE SHED IN ROTATION...
...AND THIS MORNING WAS 6-3'S TURN, SO I BET ONE OF THEM HAS THE KEY...
CREATURE KEEPERS...
THAT WOULD BE NANAHOSHI AND SHIRATORI!
H-HEY...

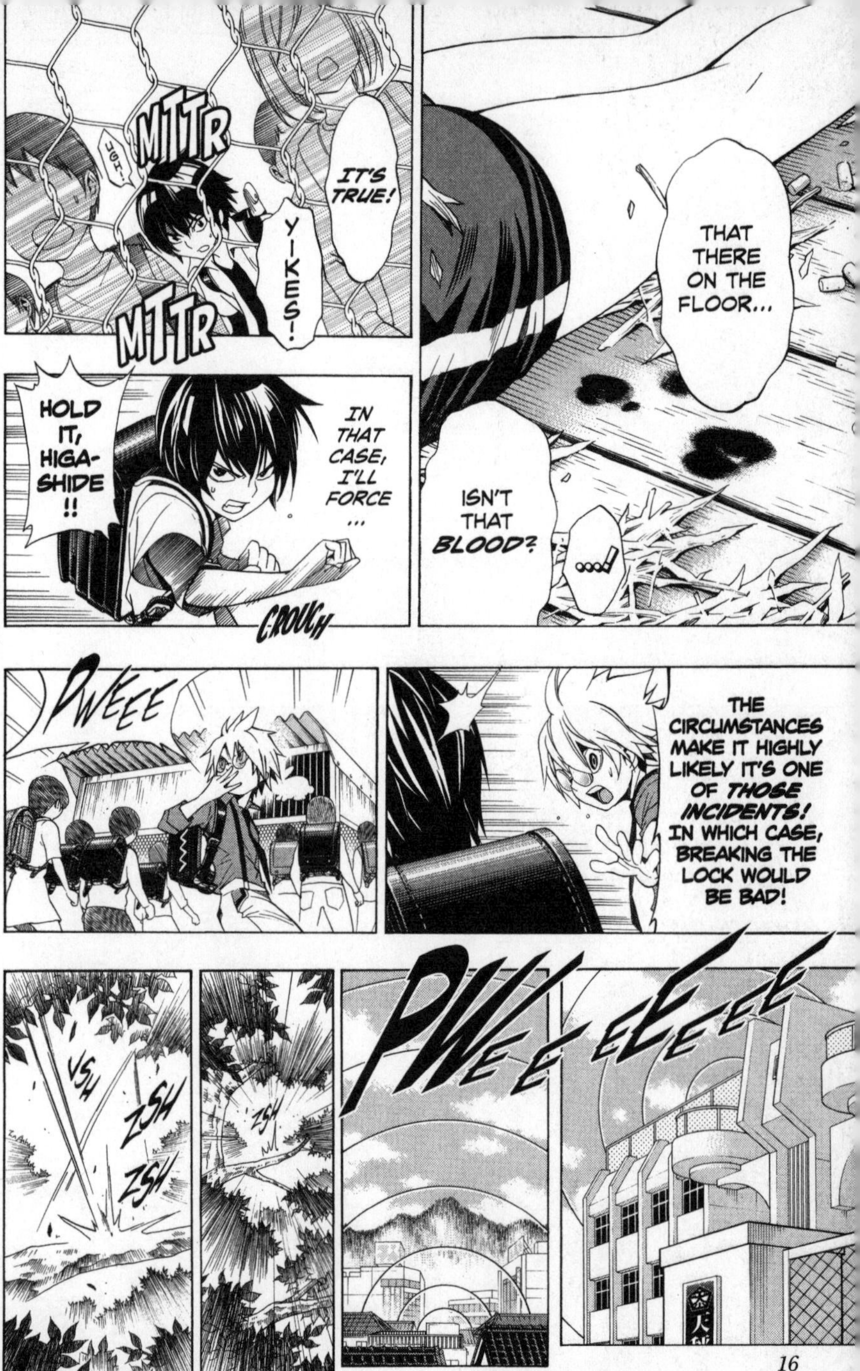
THAT THERE ON THE FLOOR...
ISN'T THAT *BLOOD?*
...!
IT'S TRUE!
YIKES!
UGH!
MTTR
MTTR
IN THAT CASE, I'LL FORCE...
HOLD IT, HIGA-SHIDE!!
CROUCH
THE CIRCUMSTANCES MAKE IT HIGHLY LIKELY IT'S ONE OF *THOSE INCIDENTS!* IN WHICH CASE, BREAKING THE LOCK WOULD BE BAD!
PWEEE
PWEEEEEEE
ZSH
VSH
ZSH
ZSH

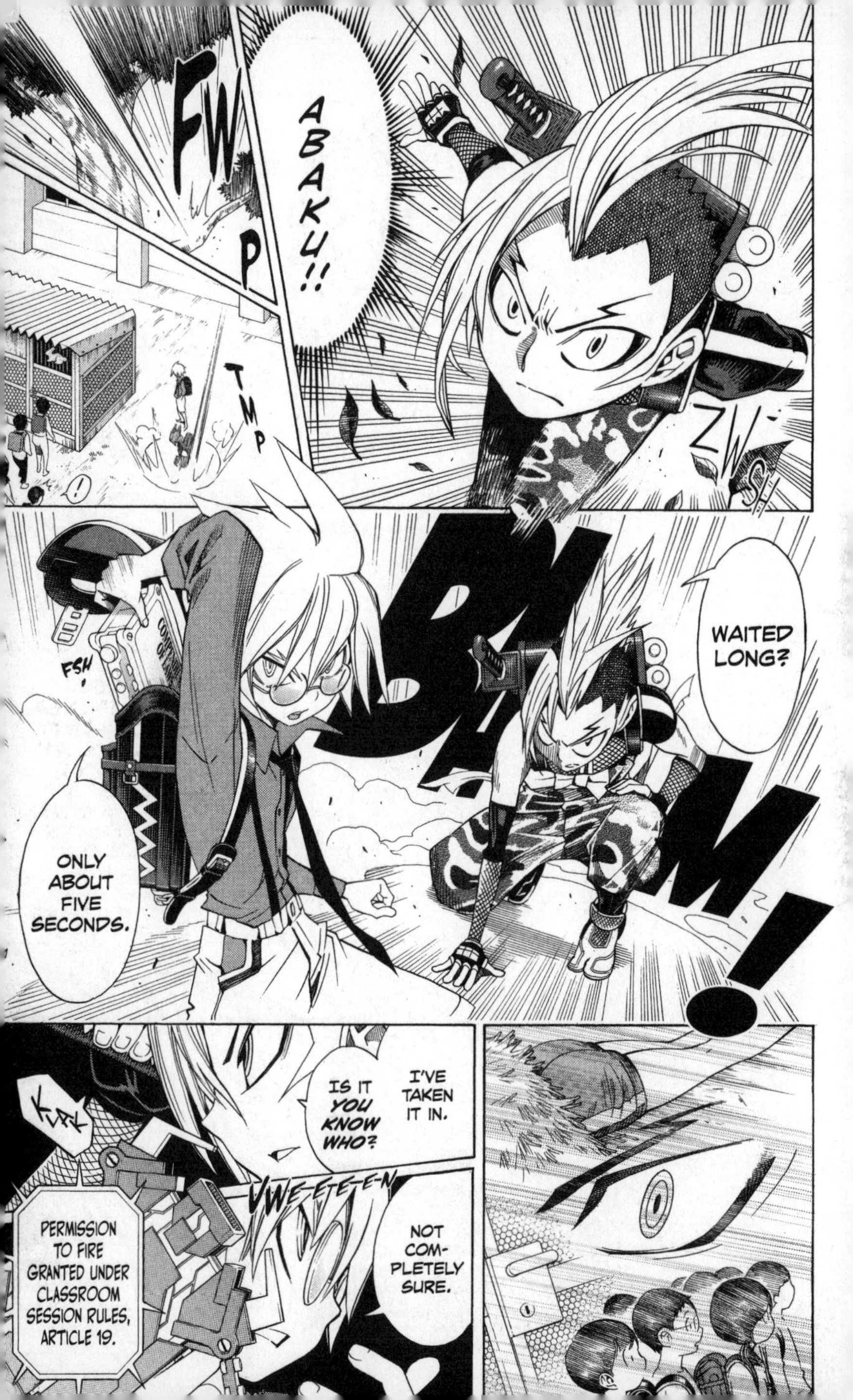
ABAKU!!
FWP
TMP
!
ZWSH
BAM!
WAITED LONG?
FSH
ONLY ABOUT FIVE SECONDS.
I'VE TAKEN IT IN.
IS IT *YOU KNOW WHO?*
KLIK
VWE-E-E-E-N
NOT COM-PLETELY SURE.
PERMISSION TO FIRE GRANTED UNDER CLASSROOM SESSION RULES, ARTICLE 19.

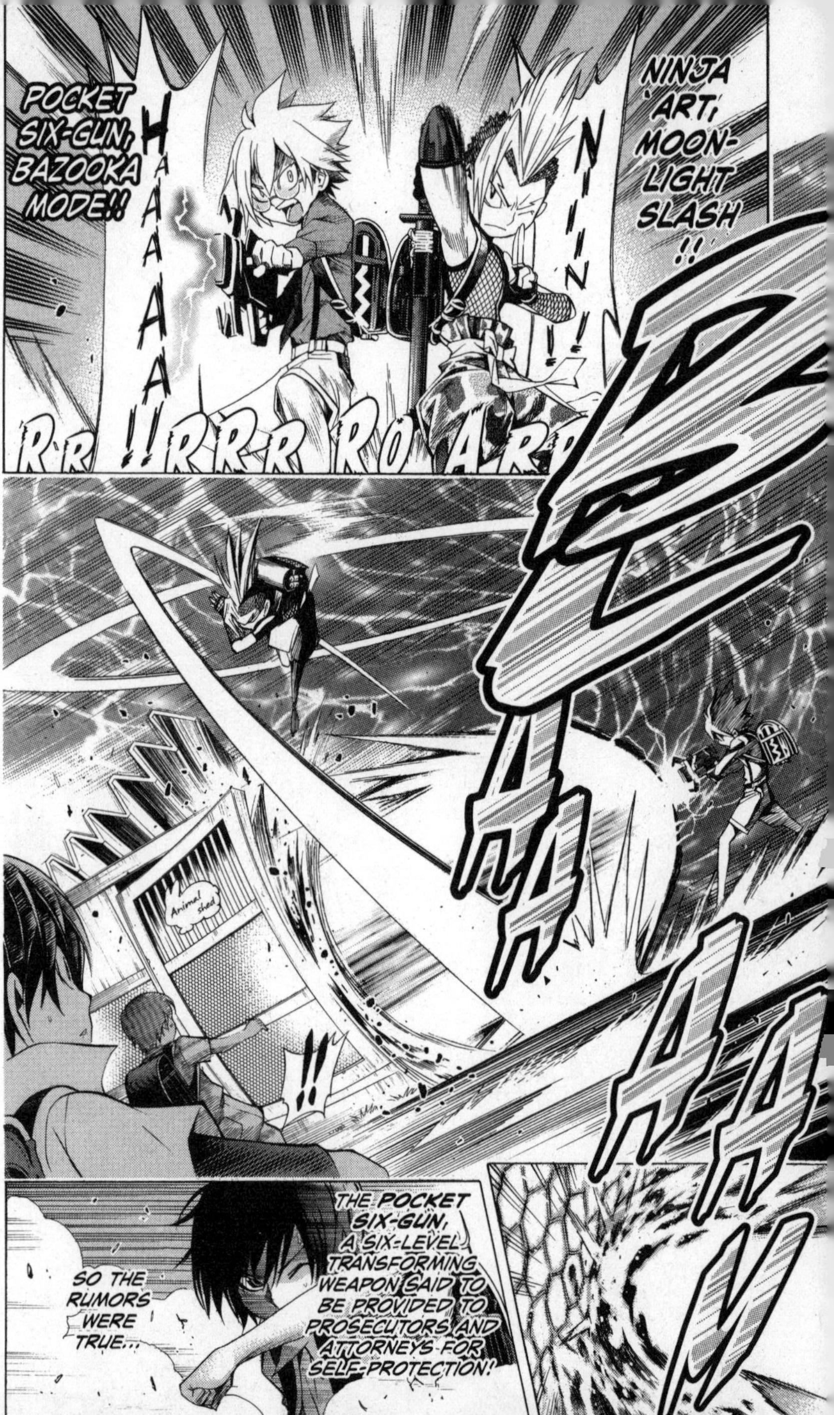
NINJA ART, MOONLIGHT SLASH!!
NIIIN!!
POCKET SIX-GUN, BAZOOKA MODE!!
HAAAAA!!
RRRRRR ROAR
Animal shed
!!
THE POCKET SIX-GUN, A SIX-LEVEL TRANSFORMING WEAPON SAID TO BE PROVIDED TO PROSECUTORS AND ATTORNEYS FOR SELF-PROTECTION!
SO THE RUMORS WERE TRUE...

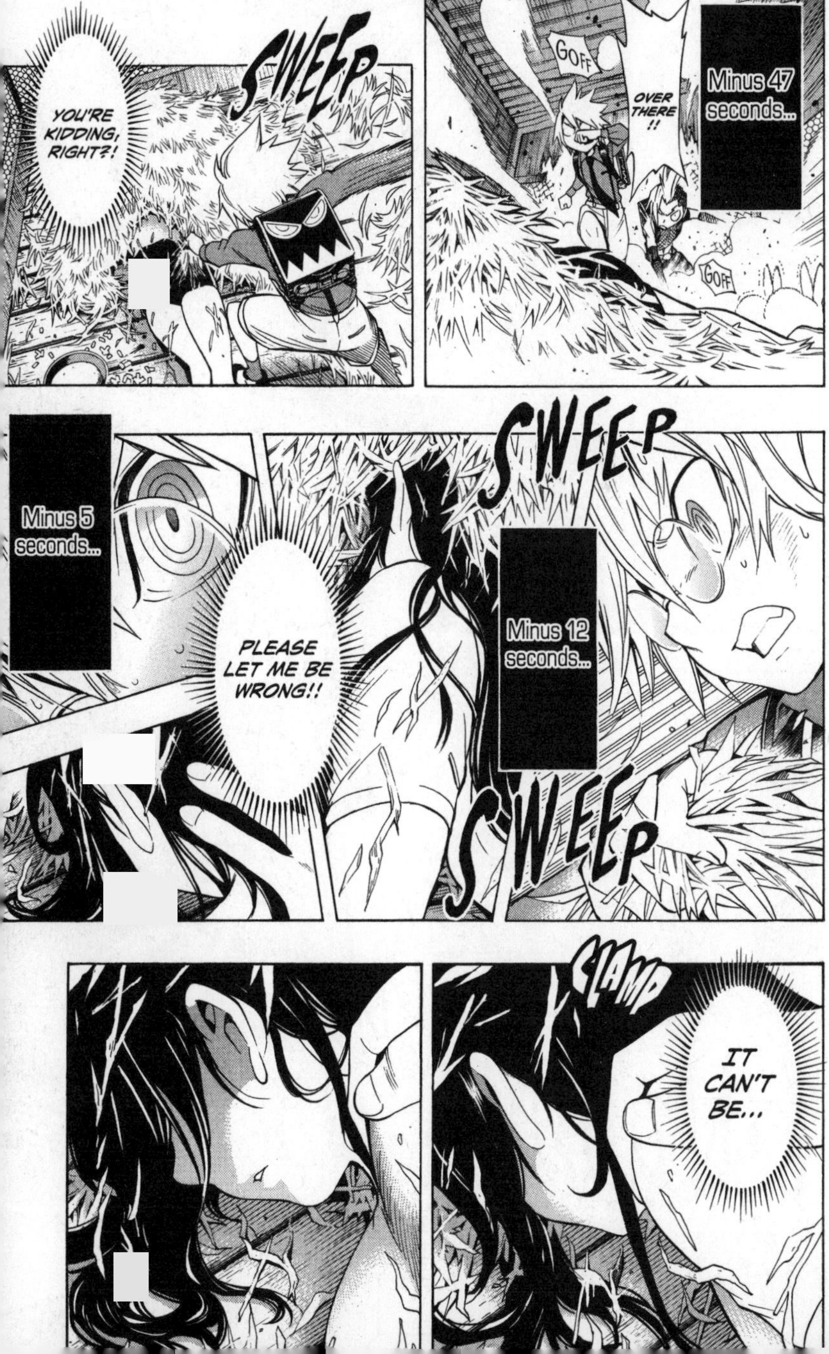
Minus 47 seconds...
GOFF
OVER THERE!!
GOFF
SWEEP
YOU'RE KIDDING, RIGHT?!
SWEEP
Minus 12 seconds...
SWEEP
Minus 5 seconds...
PLEASE LET ME BE WRONG!!
CLAMP
IT CAN'T BE...

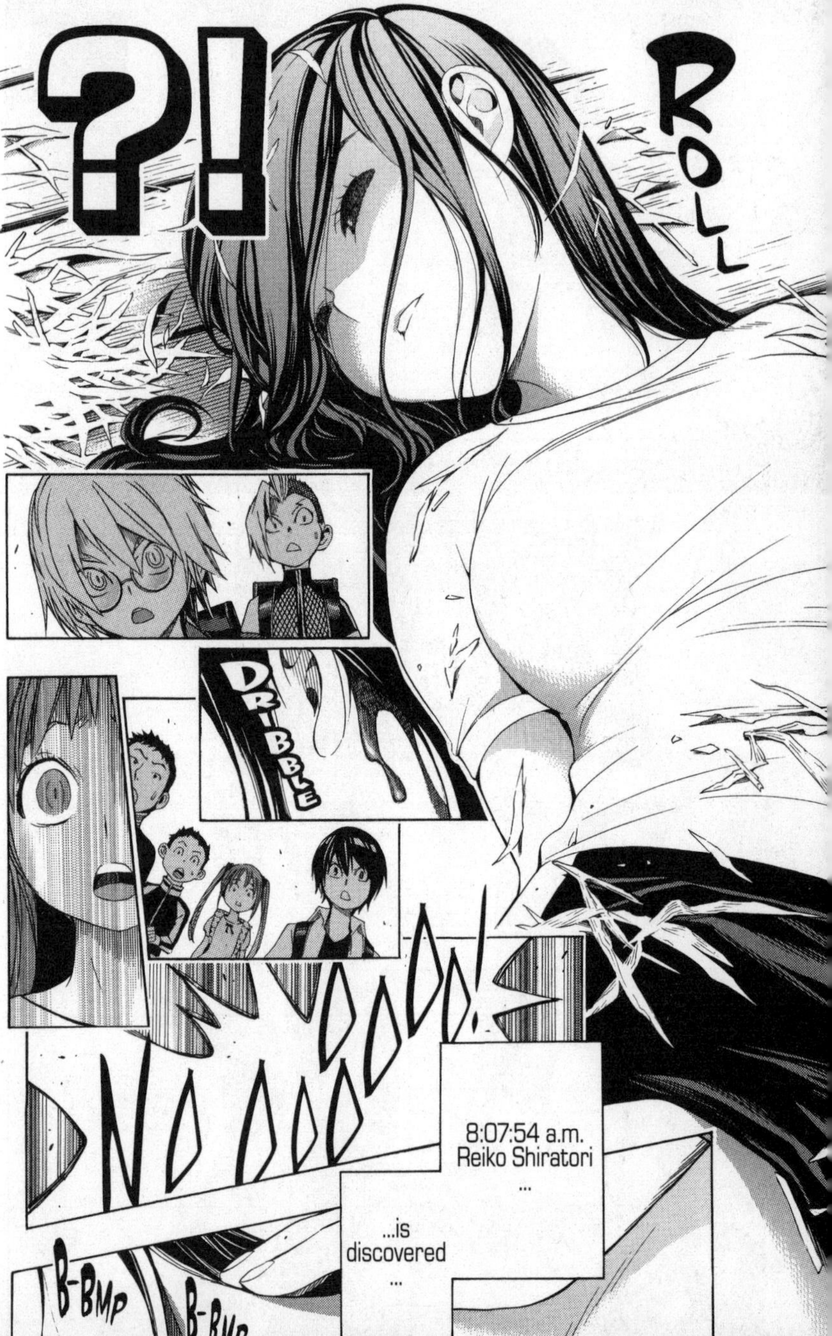
ROLL
?!
DRIBBLE
NOOOOOOOO!
8:07:54 a.m. Reiko Shiratori ...
...is discovered ...
B-BMP
B-BMP

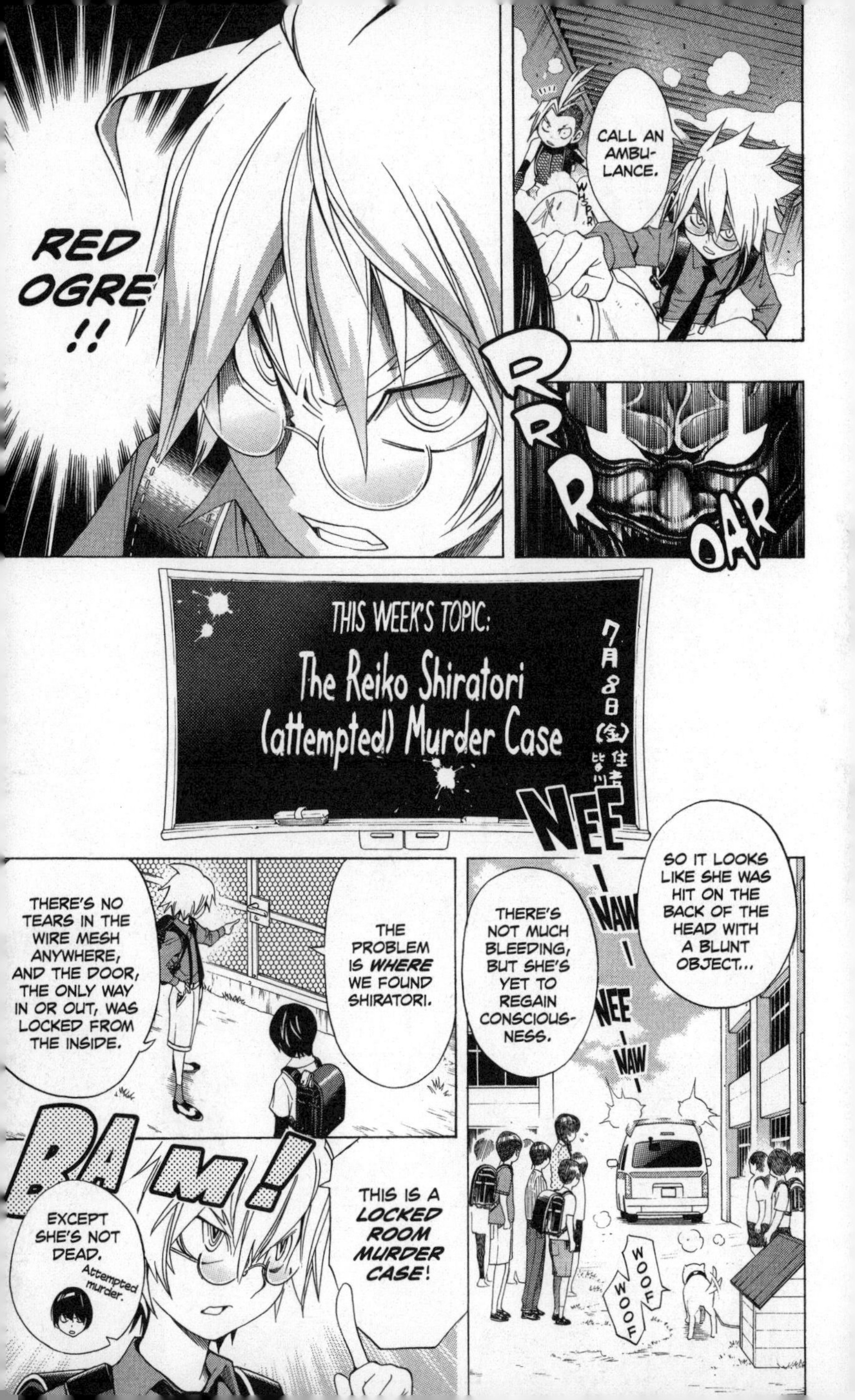
CALL AN AMBULANCE.
WHISPR
RRR
OAR
RED OGRE!!
THIS WEEK'S TOPIC:
The Reiko Shiratori (attempted) Murder Case
7月8日(金)
NEE NAW NEE NAW
SO IT LOOKS LIKE SHE WAS HIT ON THE BACK OF THE HEAD WITH A BLUNT OBJECT...
THERE'S NOT MUCH BLEEDING, BUT SHE'S YET TO REGAIN CONSCIOUSNESS.
WOOF WOOF
THE PROBLEM IS *WHERE* WE FOUND SHIRATORI.
THERE'S NO TEARS IN THE WIRE MESH ANYWHERE, AND THE DOOR, THE ONLY WAY IN OR OUT, WAS LOCKED FROM THE INSIDE.
THIS IS A *LOCKED ROOM MURDER CASE*!
BAM!
EXCEPT SHE'S NOT DEAD.
Attempted murder.

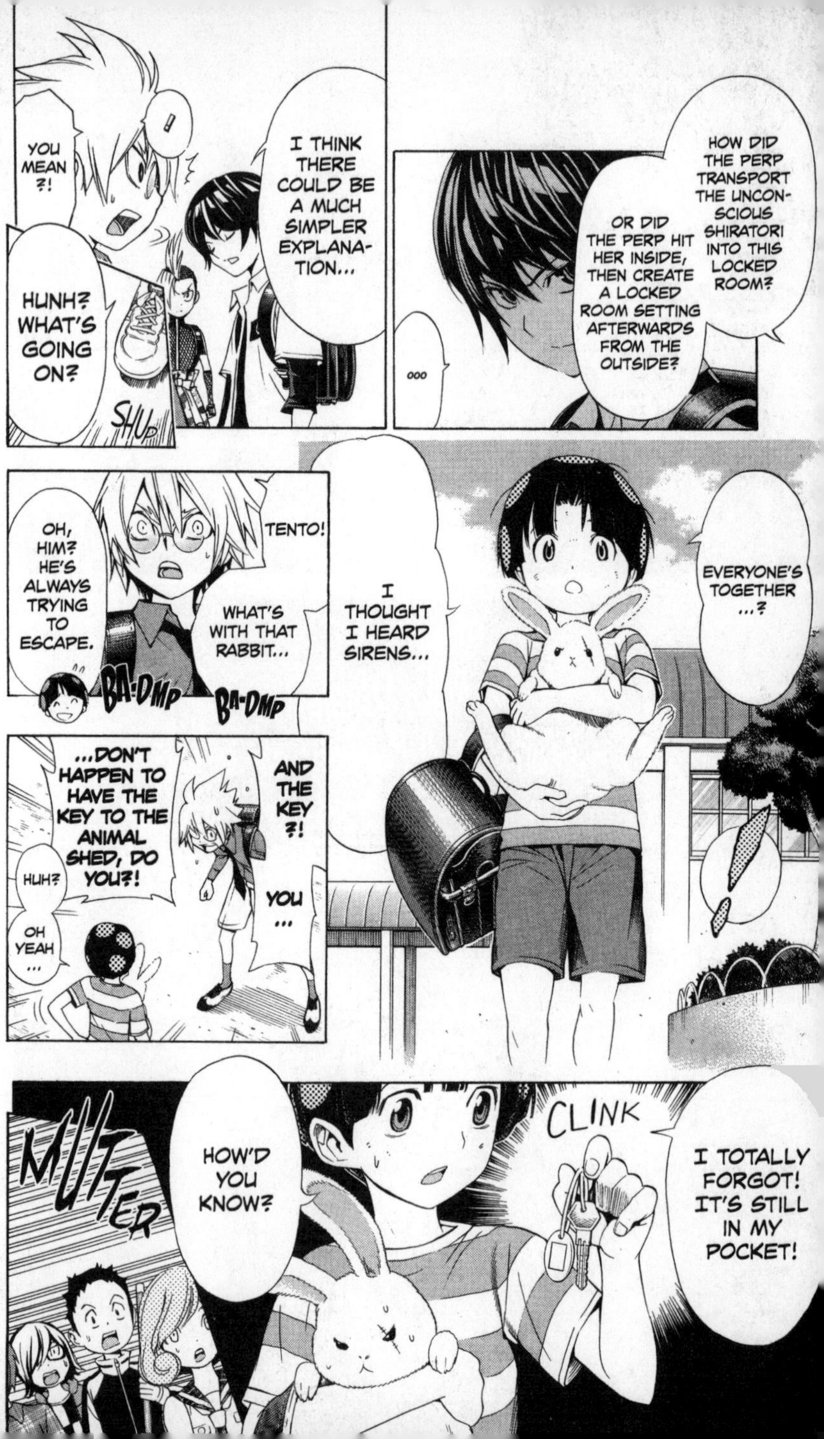
HOW DID THE PERP TRANSPORT THE UNCONSCIOUS SHIRATORI INTO THIS LOCKED ROOM?
OR DID THE PERP HIT HER INSIDE, THEN CREATE A LOCKED ROOM SETTING AFTERWARDS FROM THE OUTSIDE?
ooo
I THINK THERE COULD BE A MUCH SIMPLER EXPLANATION...
!
YOU MEAN ?!
HUNH? WHAT'S GOING ON?
SHUP
EVERYONE'S TOGETHER ...?
!
I THOUGHT I HEARD SIRENS...
TENTO!
WHAT'S WITH THAT RABBIT...
OH, HIM? HE'S ALWAYS TRYING TO ESCAPE.
BA-DMP
BA-DMP
AND THE KEY?!
YOU...
...DON'T HAPPEN TO HAVE THE KEY TO THE ANIMAL SHED, DO YOU?!
HUH?
OH YEAH...
I TOTALLY FORGOT! IT'S STILL IN MY POCKET!
CLINK
HOW'D YOU KNOW?
MUTTER

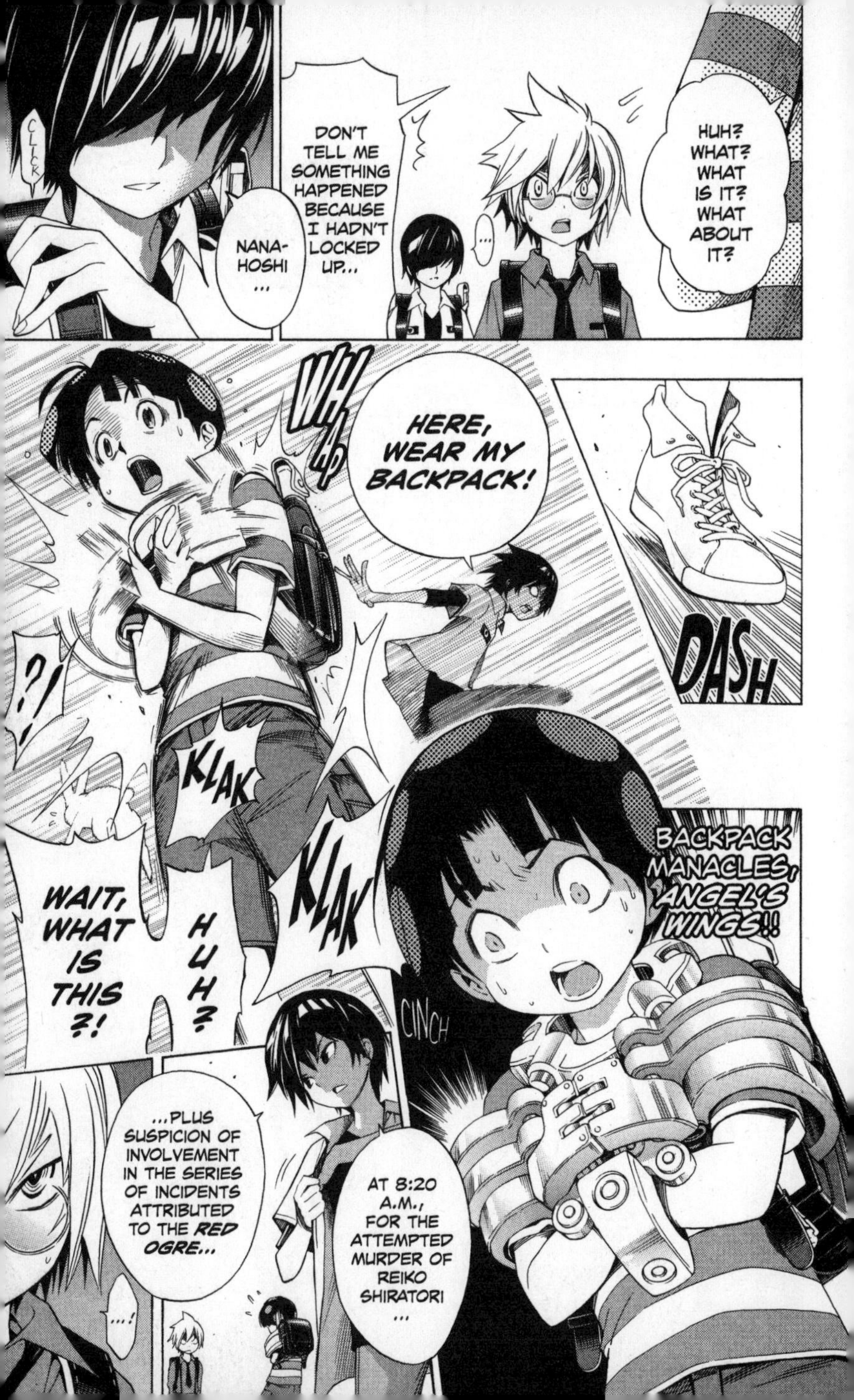
HUH? WHAT? WHAT IS IT? WHAT ABOUT IT?
...
DON'T TELL ME SOMETHING HAPPENED BECAUSE I HADN'T LOCKED UP...
NANA-HOSHI ...
CLICK
DASH
HERE, WEAR MY BACKPACK!
WHUP
?!
KLAK
KLAK
BACKPACK MANACLES, ANGEL'S WINGS!!
HUH?
WAIT, WHAT IS THIS ?!
CINCH
AT 8:20 A.M., FOR THE ATTEMPTED MURDER OF REIKO SHIRATORI ...
...PLUS SUSPICION OF INVOLVEMENT IN THE SERIES OF INCIDENTS ATTRIBUTED TO THE RED OGRE...
...!

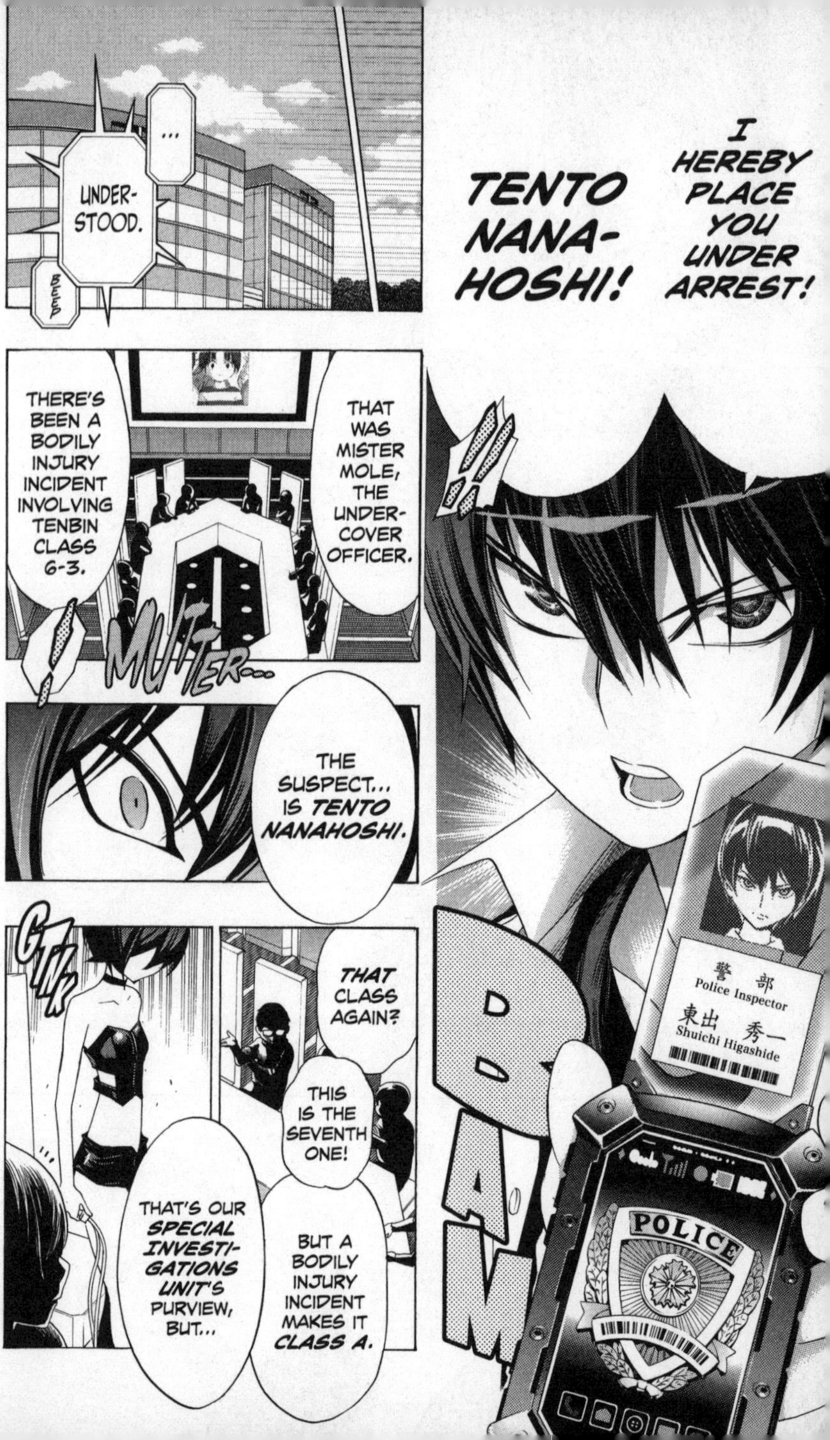
I HEREBY PLACE YOU UNDER ARREST!
TENTO NANA-HOSHI!
BAM
警 部
Police Inspector
東出 秀一
Shuichi Higashide
POLICE
...
UNDER-STOOD.
BEEP
THAT WAS MISTER MOLE, THE UNDER-COVER OFFICER.
THERE'S BEEN A BODILY INJURY INCIDENT INVOLVING TENBIN CLASS 6-3.
MUTTER...
THE SUSPECT... IS *TENTO NANAHOSHI*.
THAT CLASS AGAIN?
THIS IS THE SEVENTH ONE!
BUT A BODILY INJURY INCIDENT MAKES IT *CLASS A*.
THAT'S OUR *SPECIAL INVESTI-GATIONS UNIT*'S PURVIEW, BUT...
GTINK
...

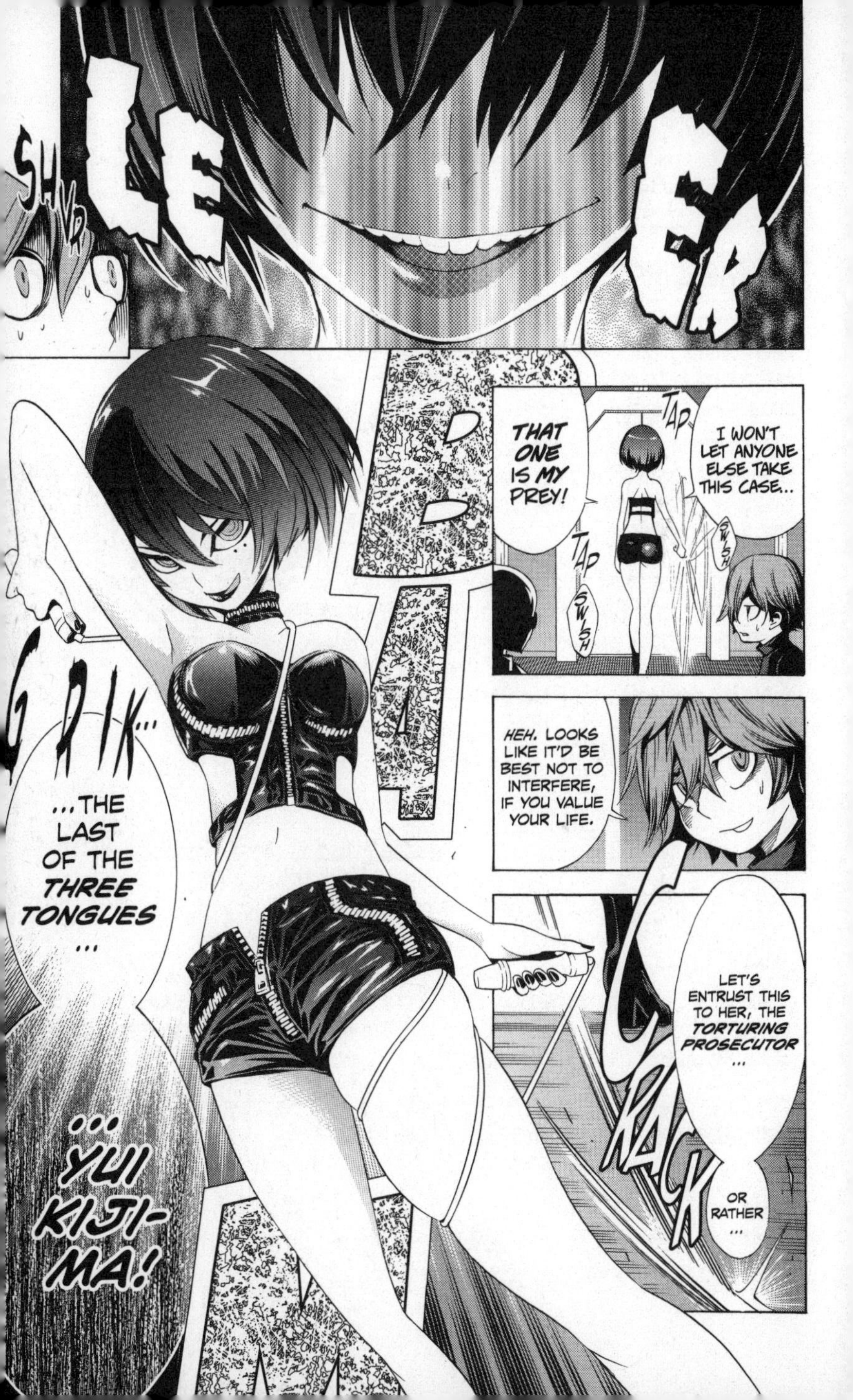
I WON'T LET ANYONE ELSE TAKE THIS CASE...
TAP
THAT ONE IS MY PREY!
TAP
SWISH
SWISH
HEH. LOOKS LIKE IT'D BE BEST NOT TO INTERFERE, IF YOU VALUE YOUR LIFE.
LET'S ENTRUST THIS TO HER, THE TORTURING PROSECUTOR...
OR RATHER...
GRIK...
...THE LAST OF THE THREE TONGUES...
...YUI KIJI-MA!

☆THE MAKING OF THE MANGA☆

① Meeting

When one case comes to a close, I meet with my editor to hash out the idea for the next one. The location for the meeting is often a family restaurant or a café. We used to meet at my house, but we stopped because it's messy.

The meetings where I've thought of the twist or plot ahead of time proceed smoothly. We settle on the direction and finish quickly.

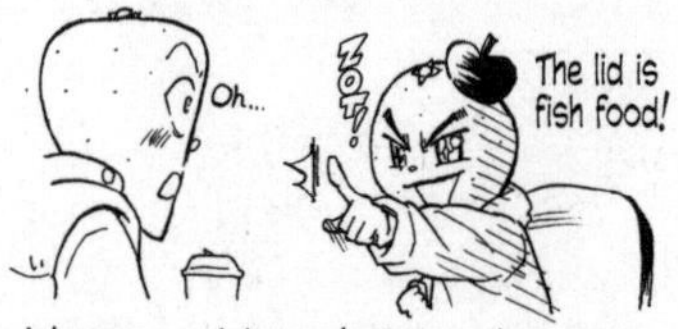
Oh...
The lid is fish food!

However, if the twist or plot is boring or I have no idea what to do next, it's a big ordeal. Silence looms over us. Time passes, and we go back and forth to the drink bar without exchanging words. As soon as my editor starts searching and muttering "Sealed room trick, sealed room trick..." we've reached dangerous territories. Let's start fresh another day!

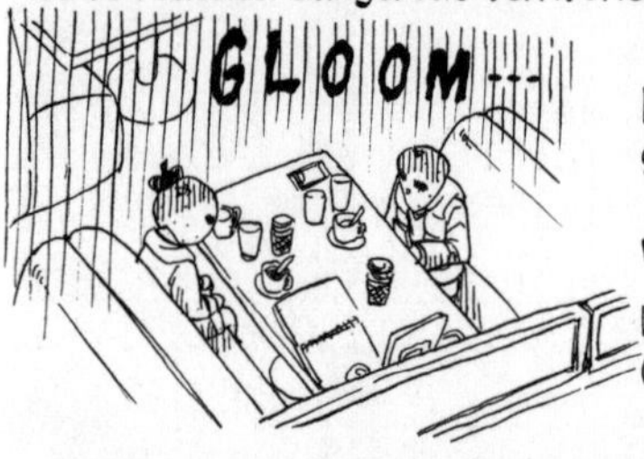
GLOOM---

My editor likes mystery books a lot, so I trust him.

"Perhaps I read all those whodunits up until now for this reason... Give me a day."

Despite his cool declaration, there are times when my editor ***doesn't*** come up with anything the next day. There are also times that young people sitting near us start discussing "that new series in this week's *Shonen Jump*..." and I get scared.

When our meeting reaches the end of its rope, we almost always conclude that *Case Closed*'s Aoyama Sensei is a beast.

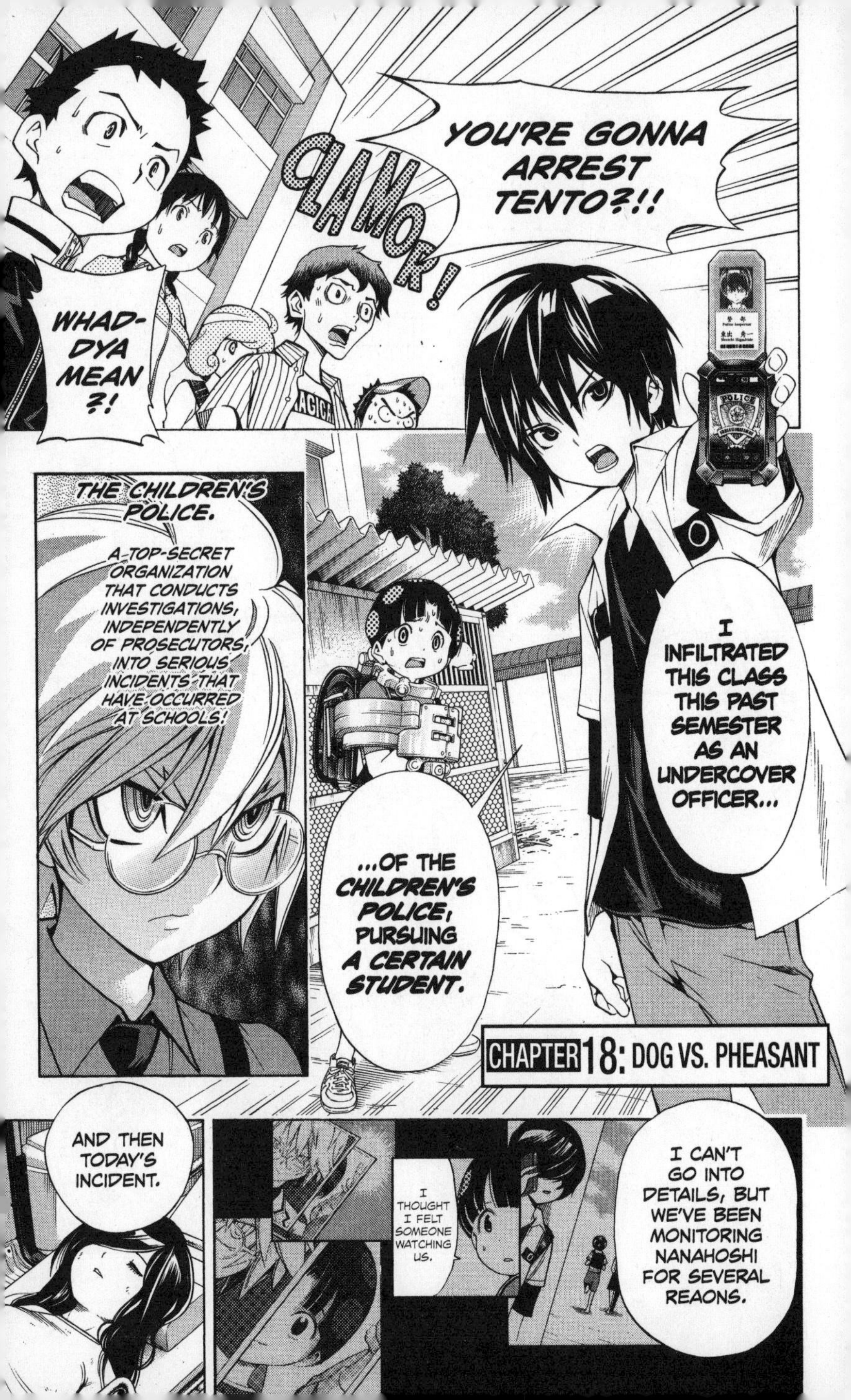
YOU'RE GONNA ARREST TENTO?!!
CLAMOR!
WHAD-DYA MEAN?!
I INFILTRATED THIS CLASS THIS PAST SEMESTER AS AN UNDERCOVER OFFICER...
...OF THE CHILDREN'S POLICE, PURSUING A CERTAIN STUDENT.
CHAPTER 18: DOG VS. PHEASANT
THE CHILDREN'S POLICE.
A TOP-SECRET ORGANIZATION THAT CONDUCTS INVESTIGATIONS, INDEPENDENTLY OF PROSECUTORS, INTO SERIOUS INCIDENTS THAT HAVE OCCURRED AT SCHOOLS!
I CAN'T GO INTO DETAILS, BUT WE'VE BEEN MONITORING NANAHOSHI FOR SEVERAL REAONS.
I THOUGHT I FELT SOMEONE WATCHING US.
AND THEN TODAY'S INCIDENT.

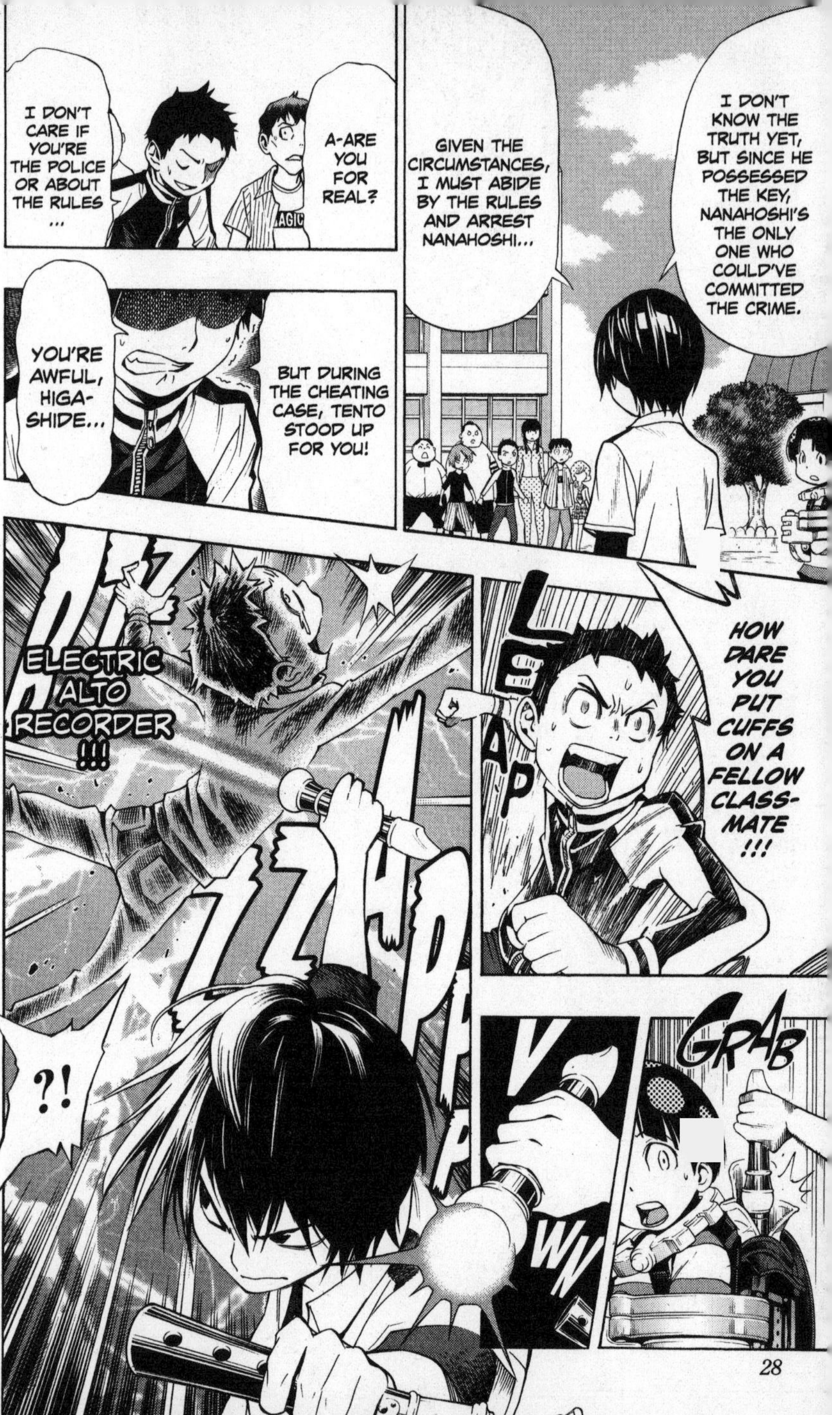
I DON'T KNOW THE TRUTH YET, BUT SINCE HE POSSESSED THE KEY, NANAHOSHI'S THE ONLY ONE WHO COULD'VE COMMITTED THE CRIME.
GIVEN THE CIRCUMSTANCES, I MUST ABIDE BY THE RULES AND ARREST NANAHOSHI...
A-ARE YOU FOR REAL?
I DON'T CARE IF YOU'RE THE POLICE OR ABOUT THE RULES ...
BUT DURING THE CHEATING CASE, TENTO STOOD UP FOR YOU!
YOU'RE AWFUL, HIGA-SHIDE...
HOW DARE YOU PUT CUFFS ON A FELLOW CLASS-MATE !!!
LEAP
ELECTRIC ALTO RECORDER !!!
GRAB
?!

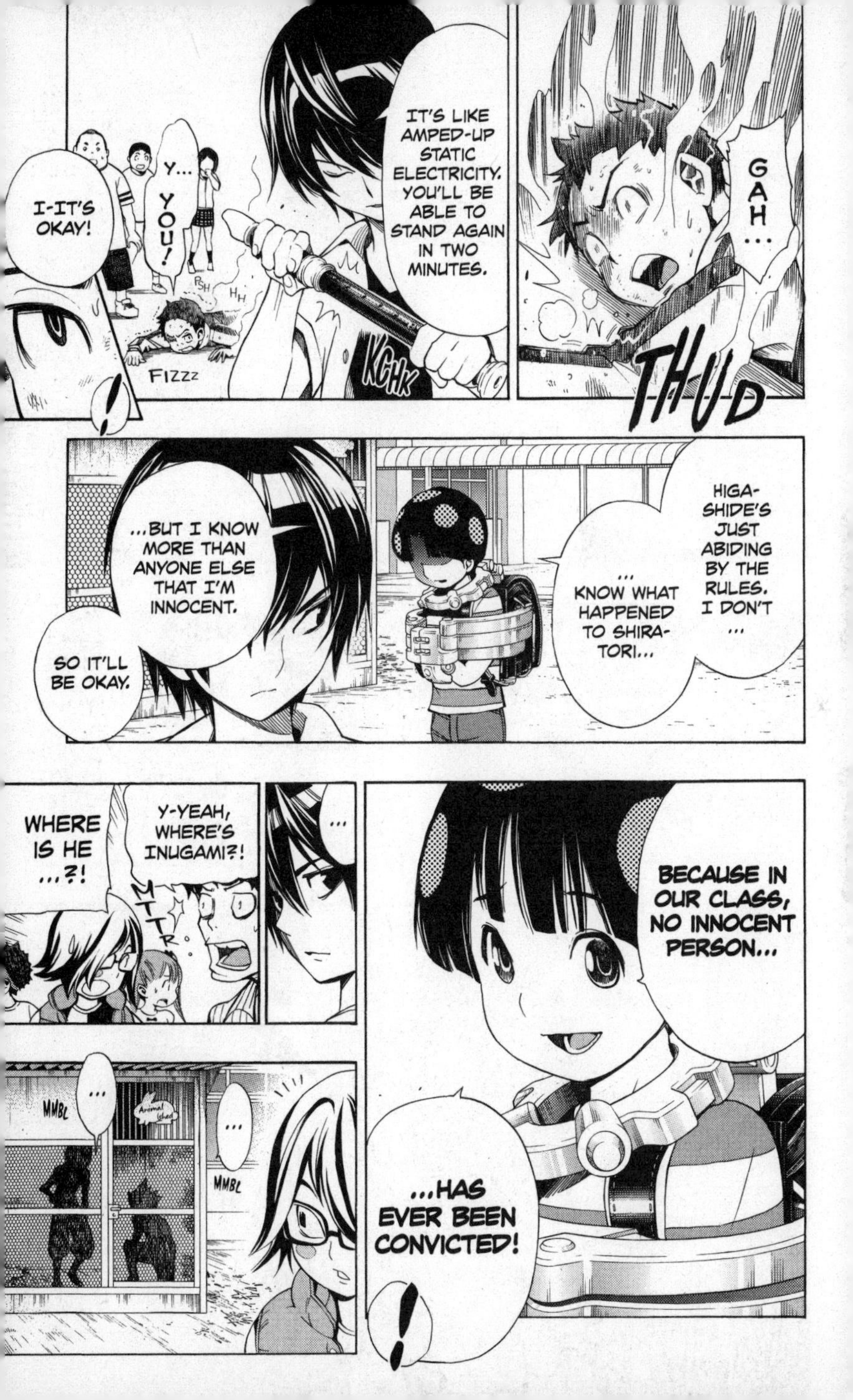
GAH...
THUD
IT'S LIKE AMPED-UP STATIC ELECTRICITY. YOU'LL BE ABLE TO STAND AGAIN IN TWO MINUTES.
KCHK
Y... YOU!
PSHHH
FIZZZ
I-IT'S OKAY!
!
HIGA-SHIDE'S JUST ABIDING BY THE RULES. I DON'T ...
... KNOW WHAT HAPPENED TO SHIRA-TORI...
...BUT I KNOW MORE THAN ANYONE ELSE THAT I'M INNOCENT.
SO IT'LL BE OKAY.
BECAUSE IN OUR CLASS, NO INNOCENT PERSON...
...HAS EVER BEEN CONVICTED!
!
...
Y-YEAH, WHERE'S INUGAMI?!
MTTR
WHERE IS HE ...?!
...
MMBL
...
Animal Shed
MMBL

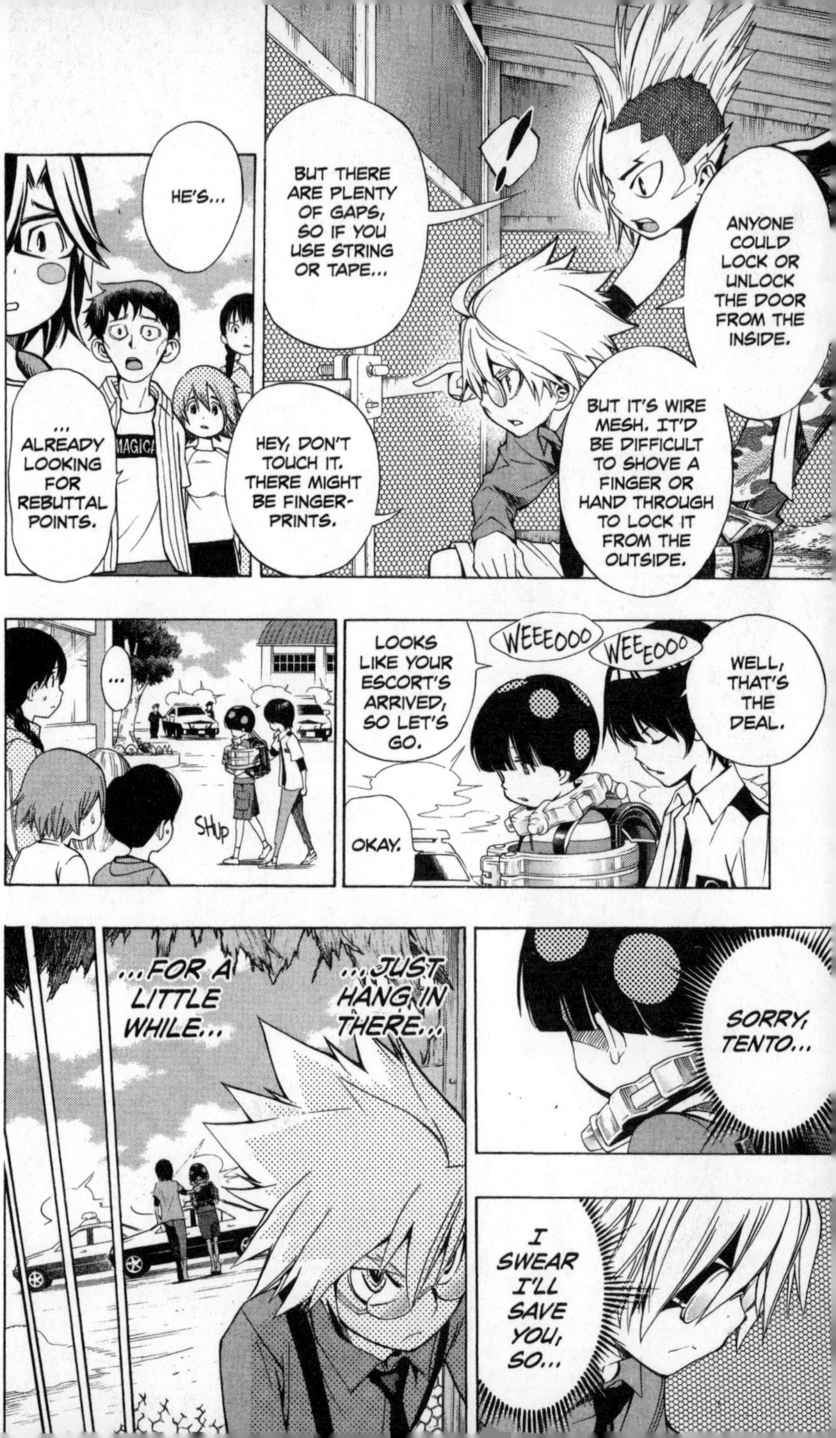
!
ANYONE COULD LOCK OR UNLOCK THE DOOR FROM THE INSIDE.
BUT IT'S WIRE MESH. IT'D BE DIFFICULT TO SHOVE A FINGER OR HAND THROUGH TO LOCK IT FROM THE OUTSIDE.
BUT THERE ARE PLENTY OF GAPS, SO IF YOU USE STRING OR TAPE...
HEY, DON'T TOUCH IT. THERE MIGHT BE FINGER-PRINTS.
HE'S...
...ALREADY LOOKING FOR REBUTTAL POINTS.
WEEEOOO
WEEEOOO
WELL, THAT'S THE DEAL.
LOOKS LIKE YOUR ESCORT'S ARRIVED, SO LET'S GO.
OKAY.
...
SHUP
SORRY, TENTO...
I SWEAR I'LL SAVE YOU, SO...
...JUST HANG IN THERE...
...FOR A LITTLE WHILE...

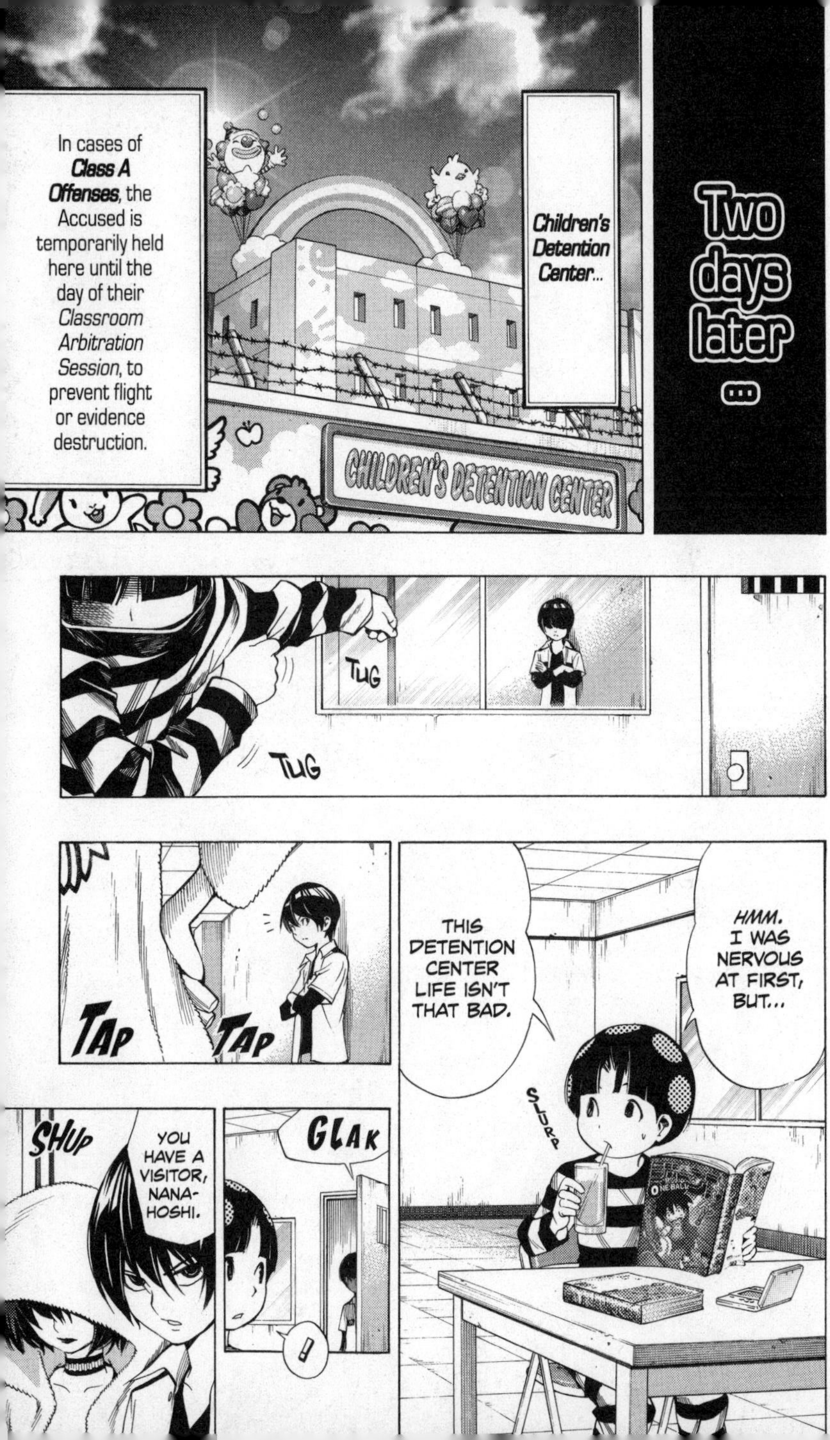
Two days later...
Children's Detention Center...
In cases of ***Class A Offenses***, the Accused is temporarily held here until the day of their *Classroom Arbitration Session*, to prevent flight or evidence destruction.
CHILDREN'S DETENTION CENTER
TUG
TUG
HMM. I WAS NERVOUS AT FIRST, BUT...
THIS DETENTION CENTER LIFE ISN'T THAT BAD.
SLURP
TAP
TAP
GLAK
YOU HAVE A VISITOR, NANA-HOSHI.
!
SHUP

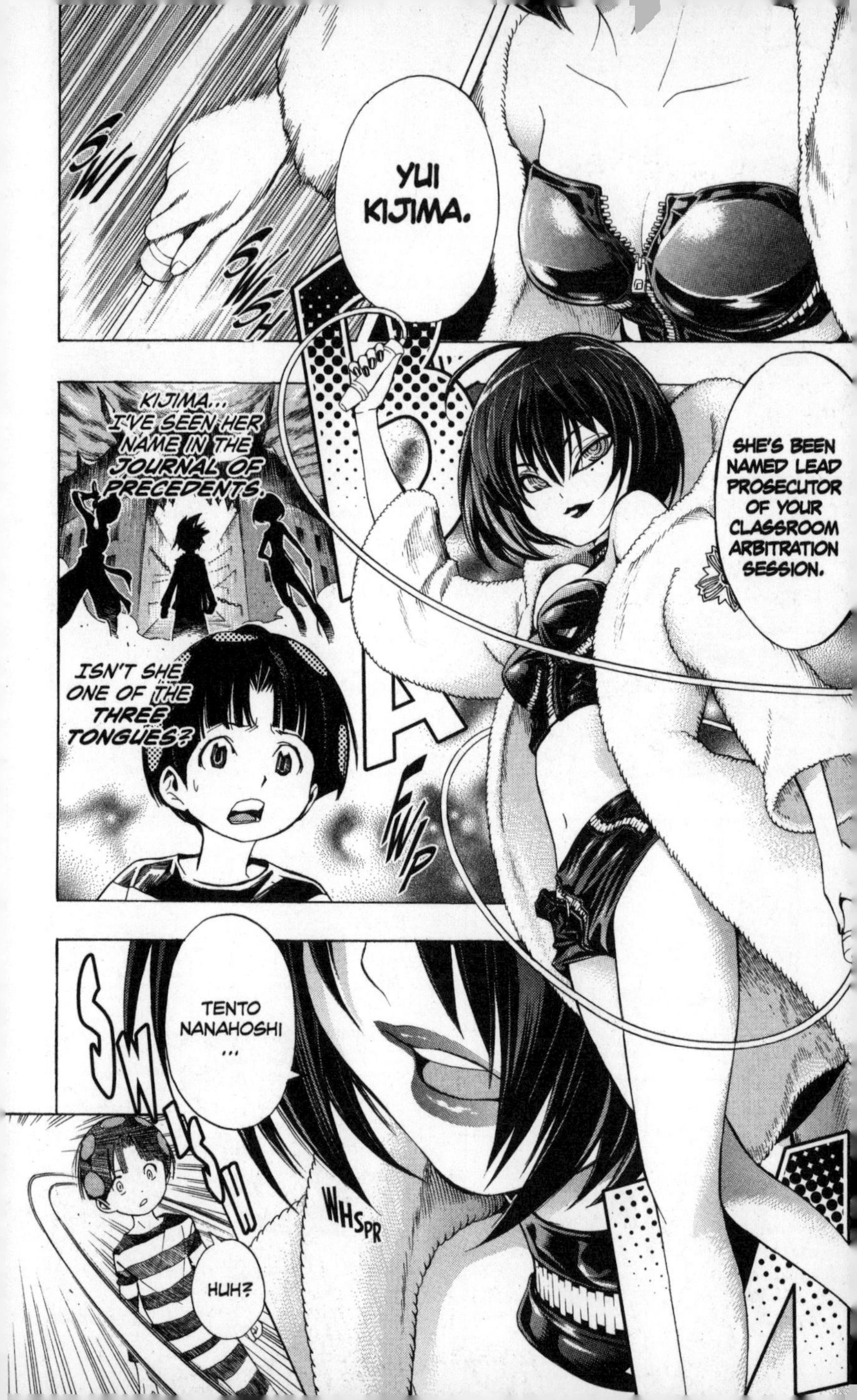
YUI KIJIMA.
SWISH
SHE'S BEEN NAMED LEAD PROSECUTOR OF YOUR CLASSROOM ARBITRATION SESSION.
KIJIMA... I'VE SEEN HER NAME IN THE JOURNAL OF PRECEDENTS.
ISN'T SHE ONE OF THE THREE TONGUES?
FWIP
TENTO NANAHOSHI ...
WHSPR
HUH?

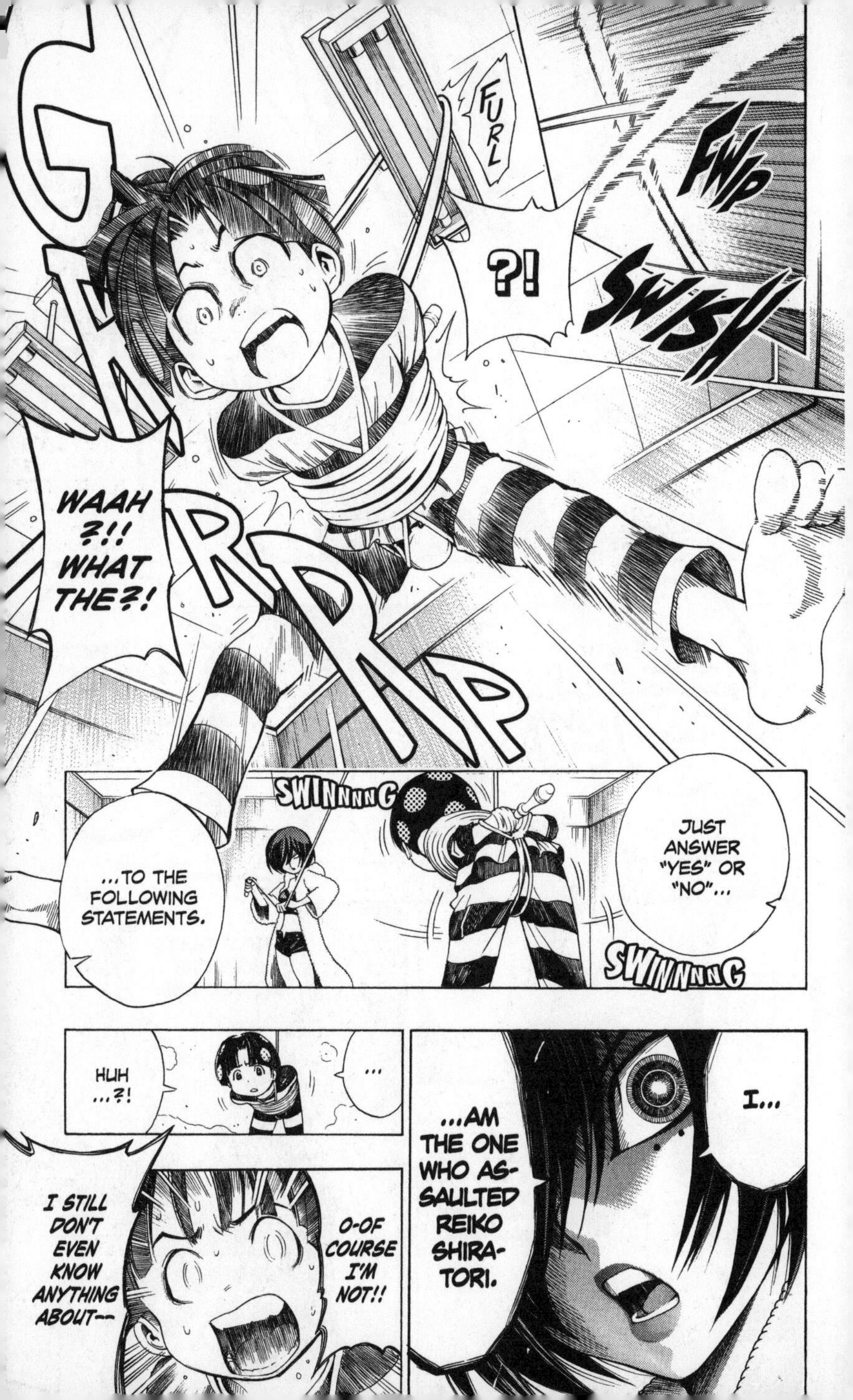
FWIP
SWISH
?!
FURL
WAAH ?!! WHAT THE?!
JUST ANSWER "YES" OR "NO"...
SWINNNNG
SWINNNNG
...TO THE FOLLOWING STATEMENTS.
I...
...AM THE ONE WHO AS-SAULTED REIKO SHIRA-TORI.
...
HUH ...?!
O-OF COURSE I'M NOT!!
I STILL DON'T EVEN KNOW ANYTHING ABOUT--

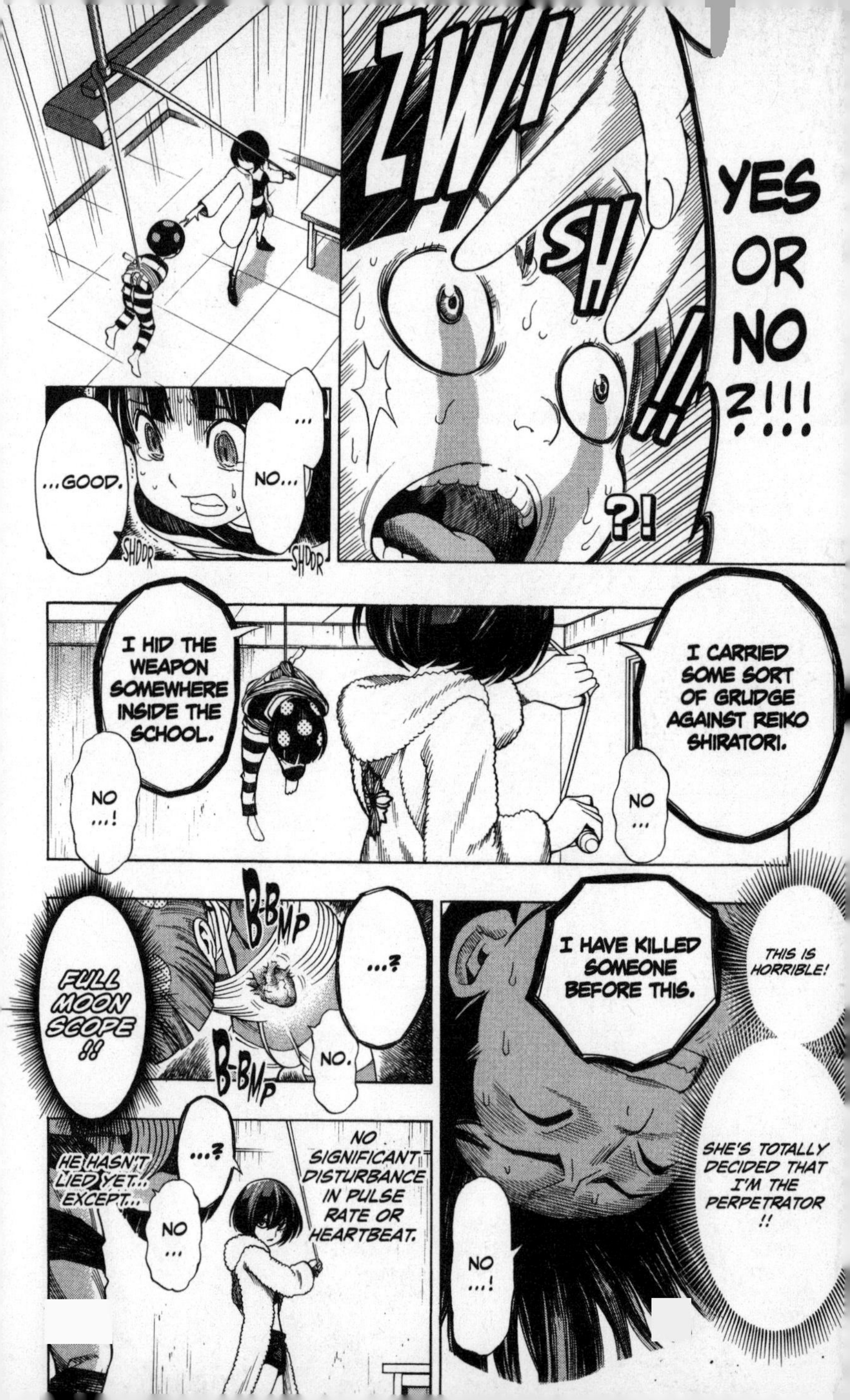
ZWA
SH!!
YES OR NO ?!!!
?!
...
NO...
...GOOD.
SHDDR
SHDDR
I CARRIED SOME SORT OF GRUDGE AGAINST REIKO SHIRATORI.
NO ...
I HID THE WEAPON SOMEWHERE INSIDE THE SCHOOL.
NO ...!
I HAVE KILLED SOMEONE BEFORE THIS.
THIS IS HORRIBLE!
SHE'S TOTALLY DECIDED THAT I'M THE PERPETRATOR !!
NO ...!
...?
B-BMP
FULL MOON SCOPE !!
NO.
B-BMP
NO SIGNIFICANT DISTURBANCE IN PULSE RATE OR HEARTBEAT.
...?
NO ...
HE HASN'T LIED YET... EXCEPT...

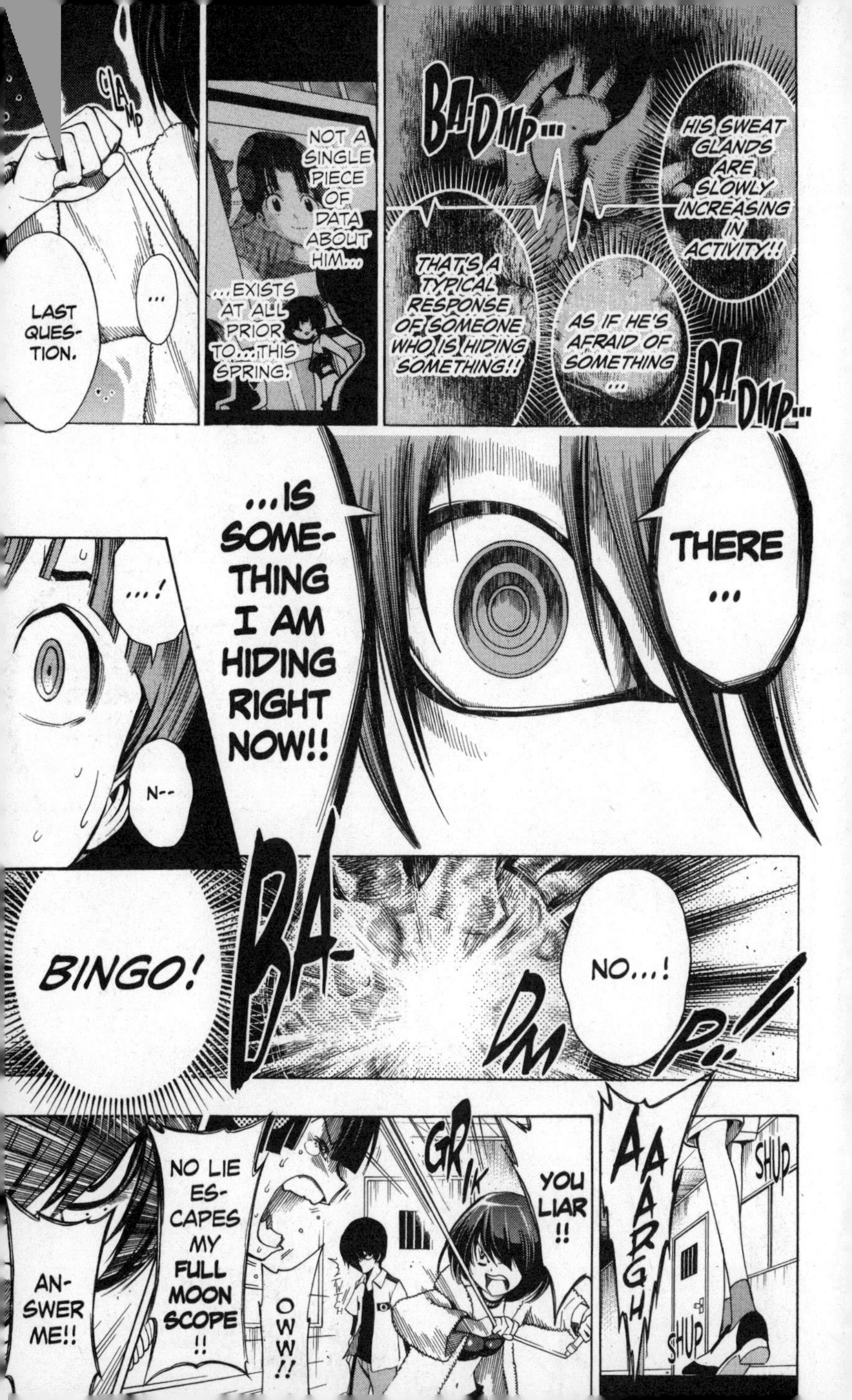
BADMP...
HIS SWEAT GLANDS ARE SLOWLY INCREASING IN ACTIVITY!!
THAT'S A TYPICAL RESPONSE OF SOMEONE WHO IS HIDING SOMETHING!!
AS IF HE'S AFRAID OF SOMETHING...
BADMP...
NOT A SINGLE PIECE OF DATA ABOUT HIM...
...EXISTS AT ALL PRIOR TO...THIS SPRING.
CLAMP
...
LAST QUES-TION.
THERE...
...IS SOME-THING I AM HIDING RIGHT NOW!!
...!
N--
BA-DMP!!
NO...!
BINGO!
SHUP
AAARGH
SHUP
GRIK
YOU LIAR!!
OWW!!
NO LIE ES-CAPES MY FULL MOON SCOPE!!
AN-SWER ME!!

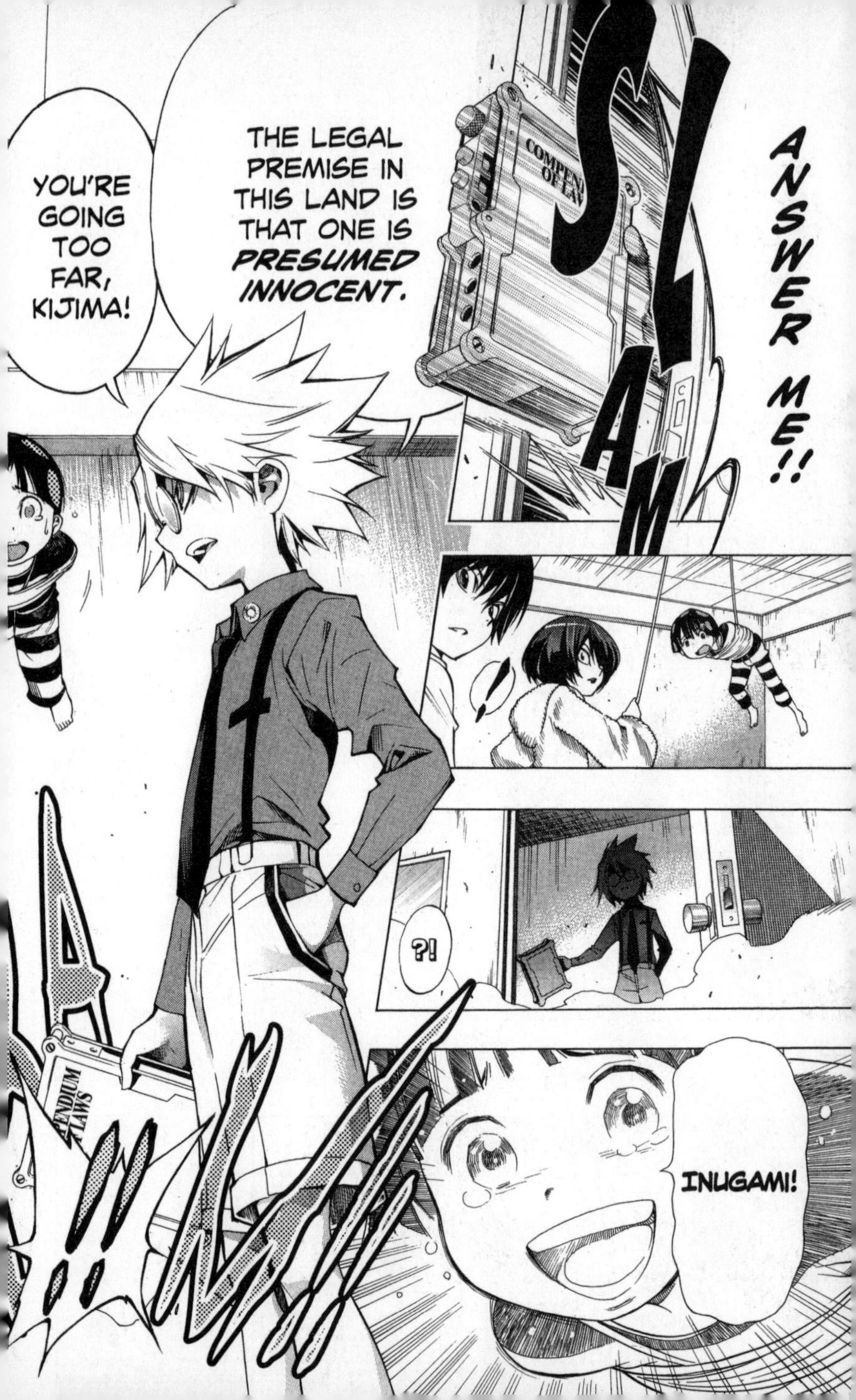
ANSWER ME!!
SLAM
THE LEGAL PREMISE IN THIS LAND IS THAT ONE IS PRESUMED INNOCENT.
YOU'RE GOING TOO FAR, KIJIMA!
!
?!
INUGAMI!

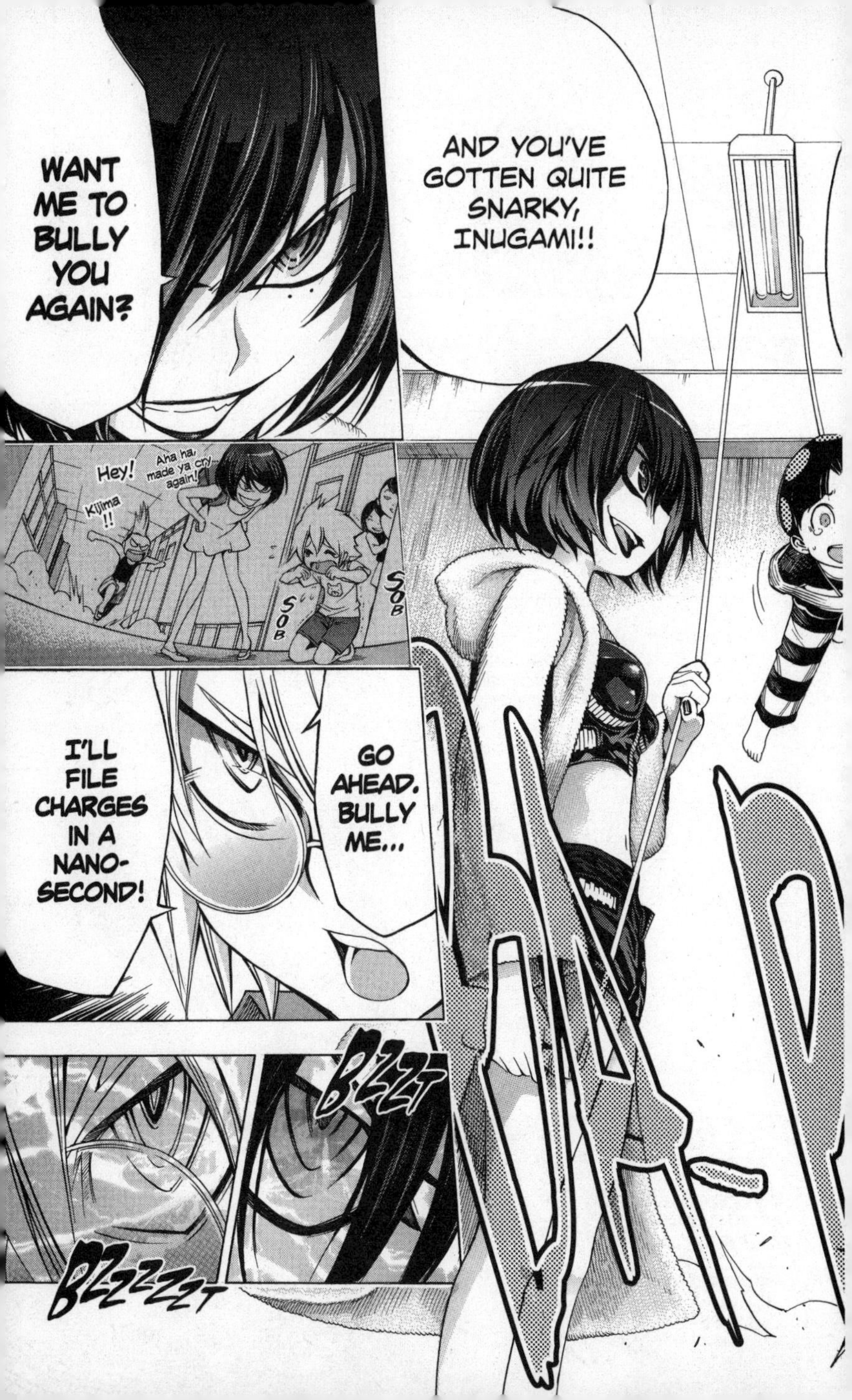
AND YOU'VE GOTTEN QUITE SNARKY, INUGAMI!!
WANT ME TO BULLY YOU AGAIN?
Aha ha, made ya cry again!
Hey!
Kijima!!
SOB SOB
GO AHEAD. BULLY ME...
I'LL FILE CHARGES IN A NANO-SECOND!
BZZT
BZZZZZZT

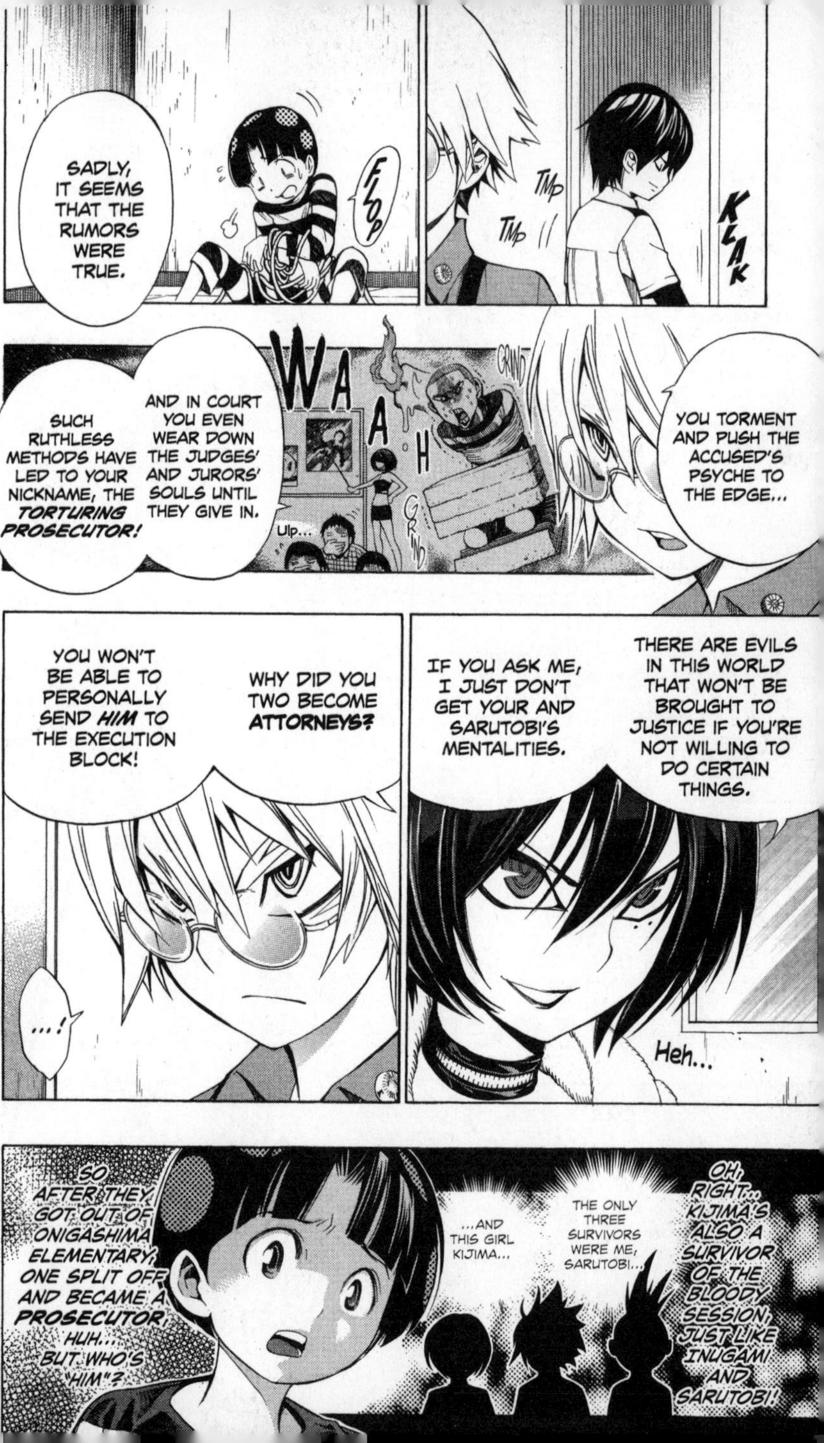
KLAK
TMP
TMP
FLOP
SADLY, IT SEEMS THAT THE RUMORS WERE TRUE.
YOU TORMENT AND PUSH THE ACCUSED'S PSYCHE TO THE EDGE...
GRIND
WAAAH
GRIND
AND IN COURT YOU EVEN WEAR DOWN THE JUDGES' AND JURORS' SOULS UNTIL THEY GIVE IN.
SUCH RUTHLESS METHODS HAVE LED TO YOUR NICKNAME, THE TORTURING PROSECUTOR!
Ulp...
THERE ARE EVILS IN THIS WORLD THAT WON'T BE BROUGHT TO JUSTICE IF YOU'RE NOT WILLING TO DO CERTAIN THINGS.
IF YOU ASK ME, I JUST DON'T GET YOUR AND SARUTOBI'S MENTALITIES.
Heh...
WHY DID YOU TWO BECOME ATTORNEYS?
YOU WON'T BE ABLE TO PERSONALLY SEND HIM TO THE EXECUTION BLOCK!
...!
OH, RIGHT... KIJIMA'S ALSO A SURVIVOR OF THE BLOODY SESSION, JUST LIKE INUGAMI AND SARUTOBI!
THE ONLY THREE SURVIVORS WERE ME, SARUTOBI...
...AND THIS GIRL KIJIMA...
SO AFTER THEY GOT OUT OF ONIGASHIMA ELEMENTARY, ONE SPLIT OFF AND BECAME A PROSECUTOR, HUH... BUT WHO'S "HIM"?

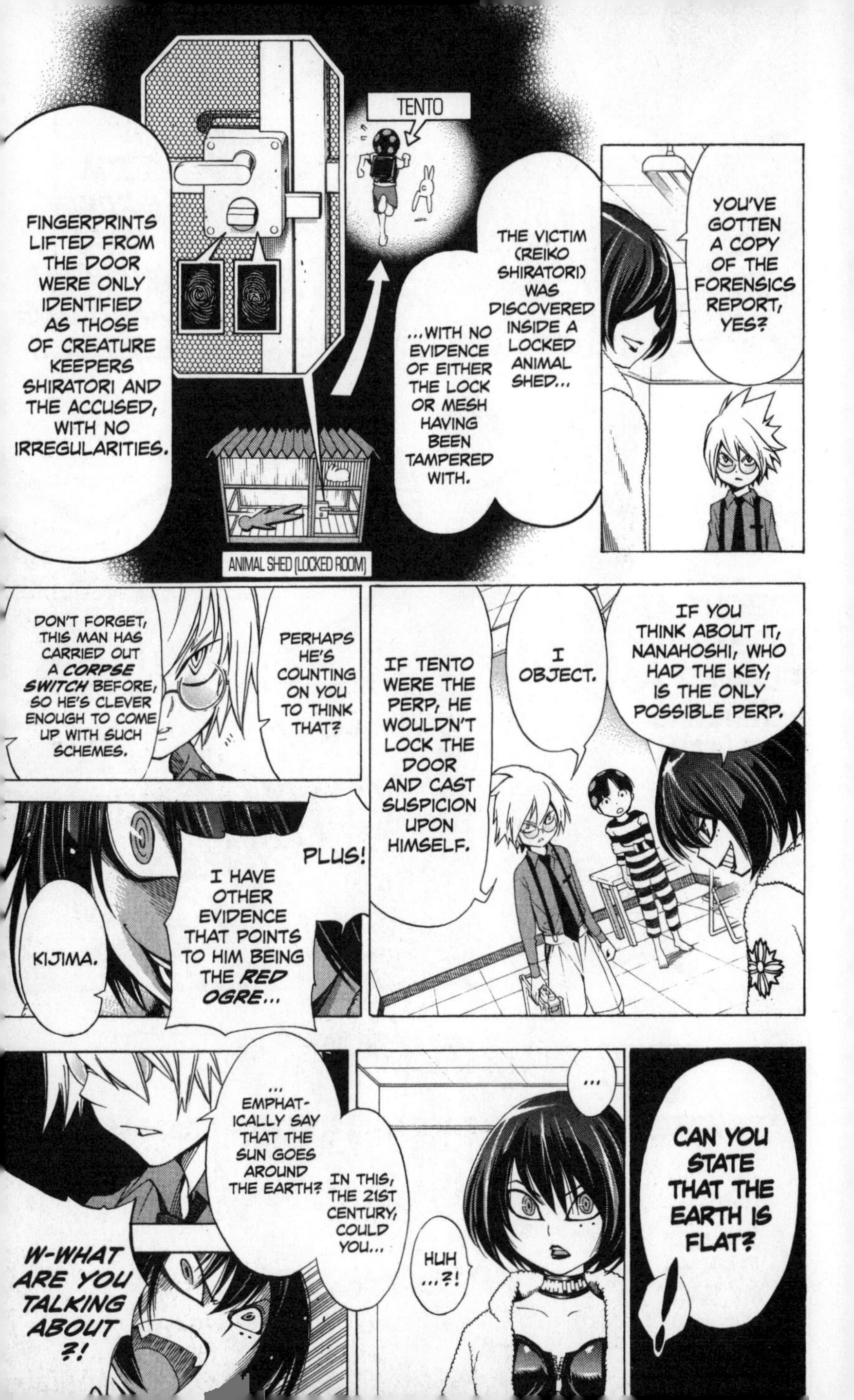
YOU'VE GOTTEN A COPY OF THE FORENSICS REPORT, YES?
THE VICTIM (REIKO SHIRATORI) WAS DISCOVERED INSIDE A LOCKED ANIMAL SHED...
...WITH NO EVIDENCE OF EITHER THE LOCK OR MESH HAVING BEEN TAMPERED WITH.
TENTO
FINGERPRINTS LIFTED FROM THE DOOR WERE ONLY IDENTIFIED AS THOSE OF CREATURE KEEPERS SHIRATORI AND THE ACCUSED, WITH NO IRREGULARITIES.
ANIMAL SHED (LOCKED ROOM)
IF YOU THINK ABOUT IT, NANAHOSHI, WHO HAD THE KEY, IS THE ONLY POSSIBLE PERP.
I OBJECT.
IF TENTO WERE THE PERP, HE WOULDN'T LOCK THE DOOR AND CAST SUSPICION UPON HIMSELF.
PERHAPS HE'S COUNTING ON YOU TO THINK THAT?
DON'T FORGET, THIS MAN HAS CARRIED OUT A *CORPSE SWITCH* BEFORE, SO HE'S CLEVER ENOUGH TO COME UP WITH SUCH SCHEMES.
PLUS!
I HAVE OTHER EVIDENCE THAT POINTS TO HIM BEING THE *RED OGRE*...
KIJIMA.
CAN YOU STATE THAT THE EARTH IS FLAT?
...
HUH ...?!
IN THIS, THE 21ST CENTURY, COULD YOU...
... EMPHAT-ICALLY SAY THAT THE SUN GOES AROUND THE EARTH?
W-WHAT ARE YOU TALKING ABOUT ?!

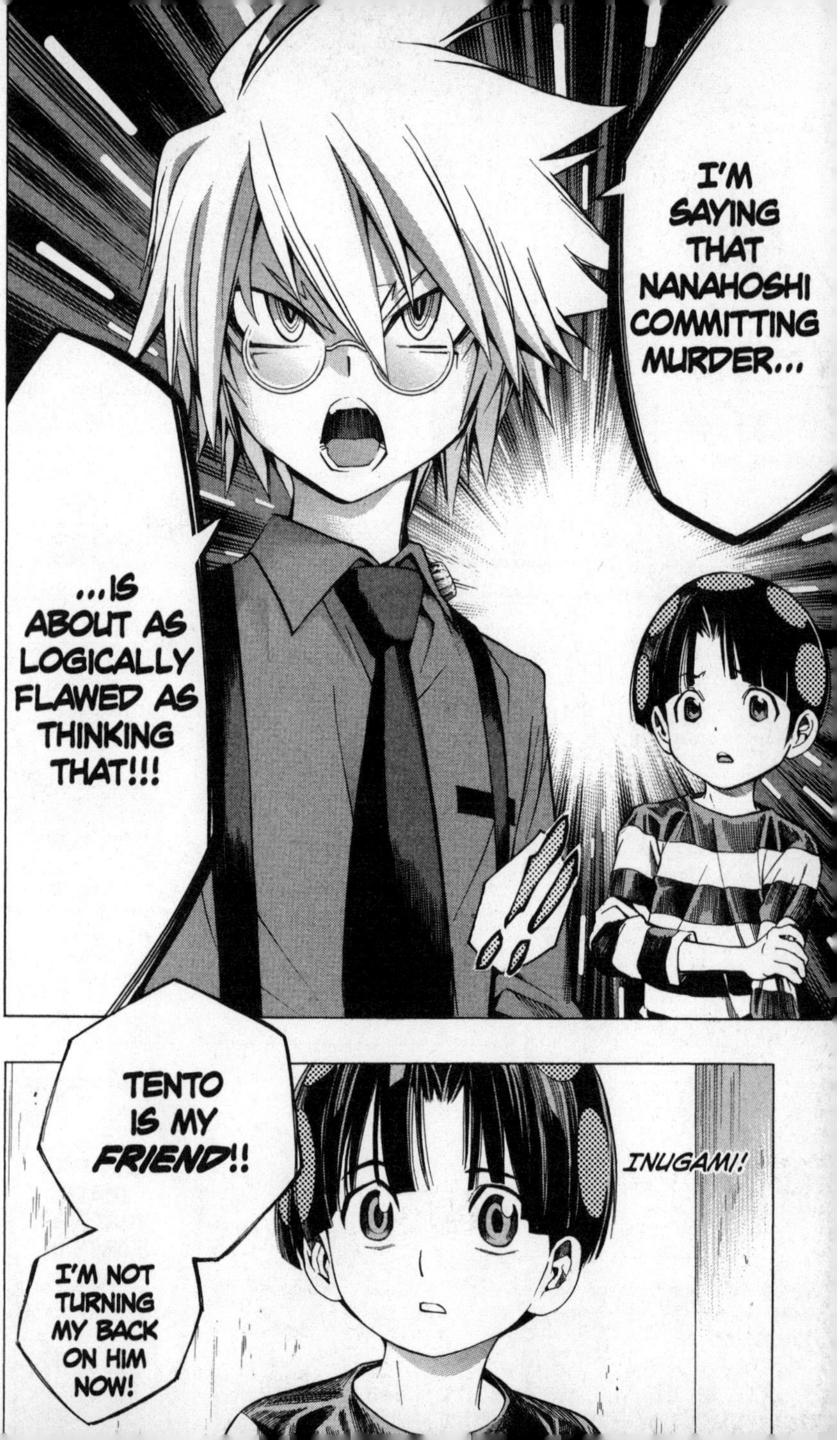
I'M SAYING THAT NANAHOSHI COMMITTING MURDER...
...IS ABOUT AS LOGICALLY FLAWED AS THINKING THAT!!!
INUGAMI!
TENTO IS MY FRIEND!!
I'M NOT TURNING MY BACK ON HIM NOW!

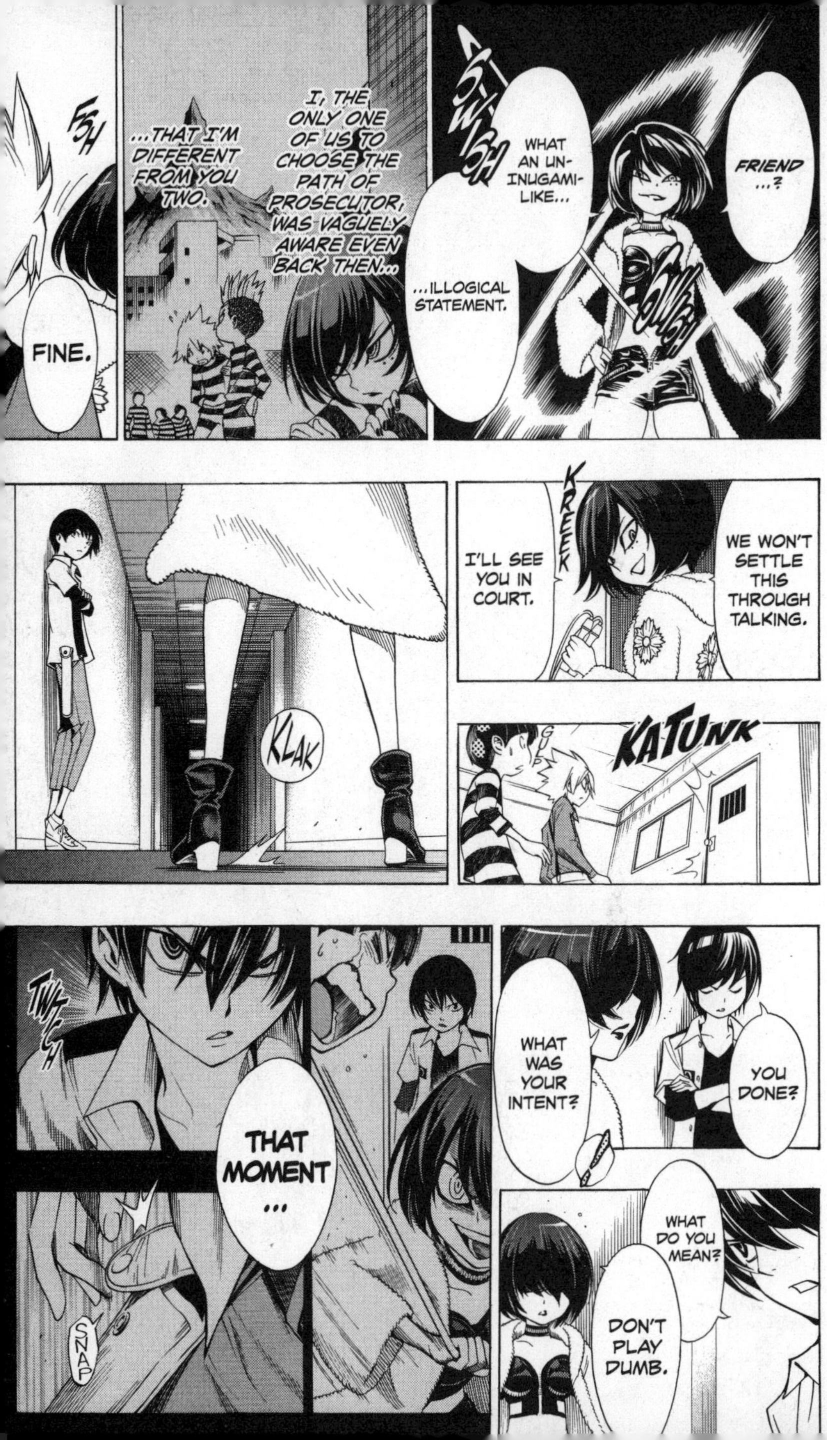
FRIEND ...?
SWISH
WHAT AN UN-INUGAMI-LIKE...
...ILLOGICAL STATEMENT.
I, THE ONLY ONE OF US TO CHOOSE THE PATH OF PROSECUTOR, WAS VAGUELY AWARE EVEN BACK THEN...
...THAT I'M DIFFERENT FROM YOU TWO.
FSH
FINE.
WE WON'T SETTLE THIS THROUGH TALKING.
KREEK
I'LL SEE YOU IN COURT.
KATUNK
KLAK
YOU DONE?
WHAT WAS YOUR INTENT?
WHAT DO YOU MEAN?
DON'T PLAY DUMB.
TWITCH
THAT MOMENT ...
SNAP

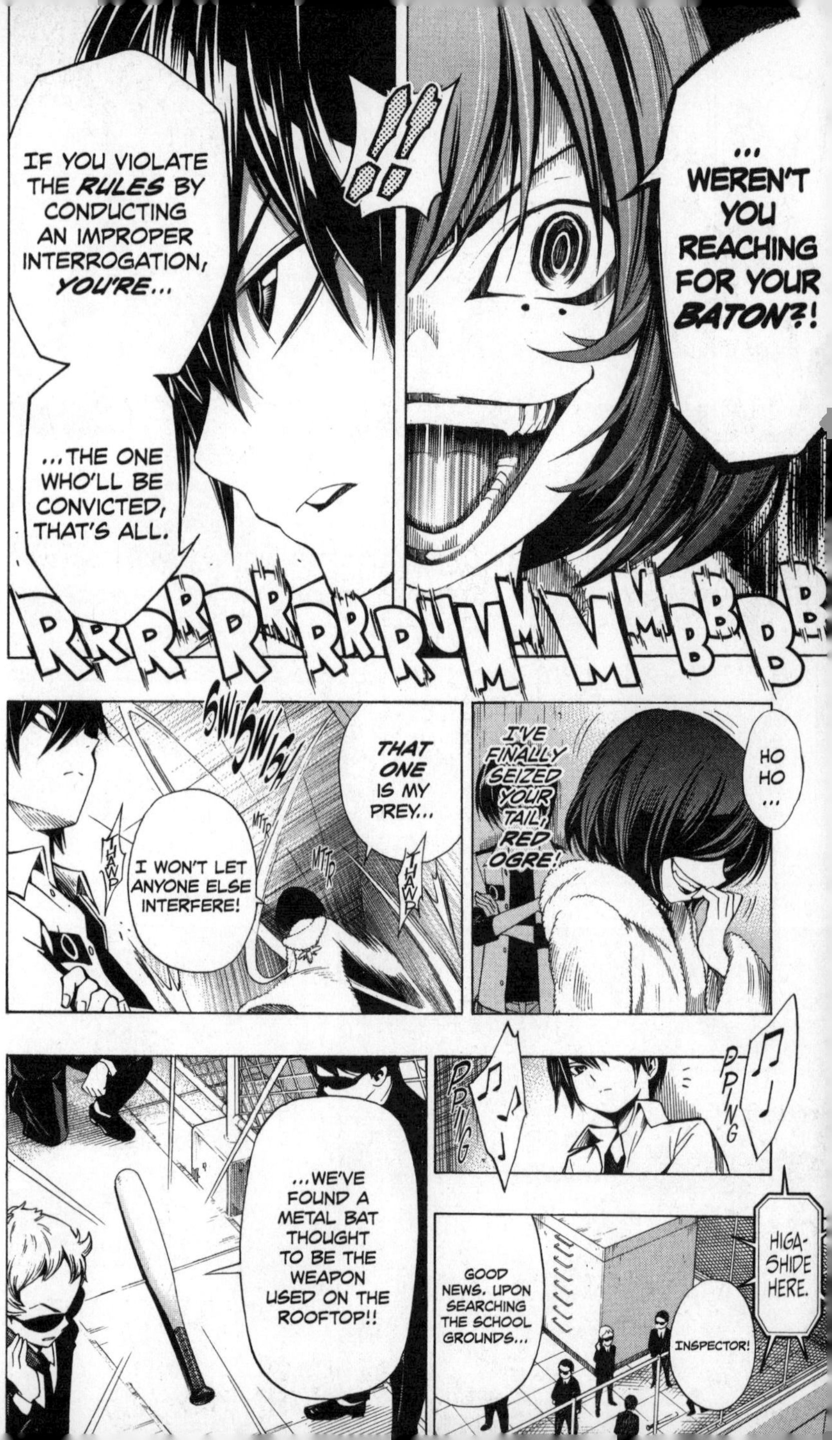
...WEREN'T YOU REACHING FOR YOUR BATON?!
!!
IF YOU VIOLATE THE RULES BY CONDUCTING AN IMPROPER INTERROGATION, YOU'RE...
...THE ONE WHO'LL BE CONVICTED, THAT'S ALL.
RRRRRRRUMMMMBBB
HO HO ...
I'VE FINALLY SEIZED YOUR TAIL, RED OGRE!
THAT ONE IS MY PREY...
SWISWISH
THAWP
MTTR
MTTR
I WON'T LET ANYONE ELSE INTERFERE!
THAWP
PPING
PPING
HIGA-SHIDE HERE.
INSPECTOR!
GOOD NEWS. UPON SEARCHING THE SCHOOL GROUNDS...
...WE'VE FOUND A METAL BAT THOUGHT TO BE THE WEAPON USED ON THE ROOFTOP!!

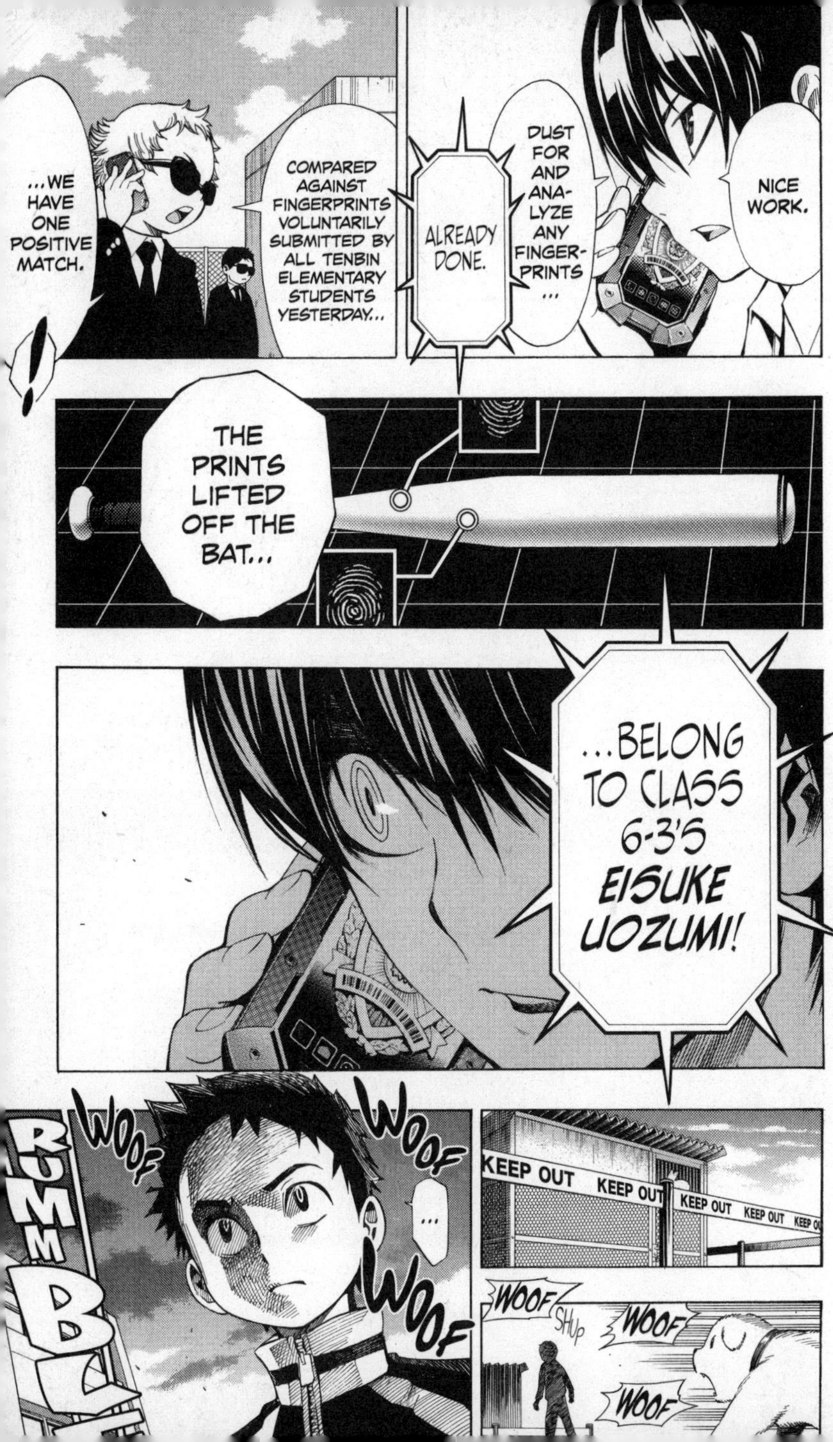
NICE WORK.
DUST FOR AND ANALYZE ANY FINGERPRINTS...
ALREADY DONE.
COMPARED AGAINST FINGERPRINTS VOLUNTARILY SUBMITTED BY ALL TENBIN ELEMENTARY STUDENTS YESTERDAY...
...WE HAVE ONE POSITIVE MATCH.
!
THE PRINTS LIFTED OFF THE BAT...
...BELONG TO CLASS 6-3'S EISUKE UOZUMI!
KEEP OUT
KEEP OUT
KEEP OUT
KEEP OUT
WOOF
SHUP
WOOF
WOOF
WOOF
WOOF
...
WOOF
RUMMBL

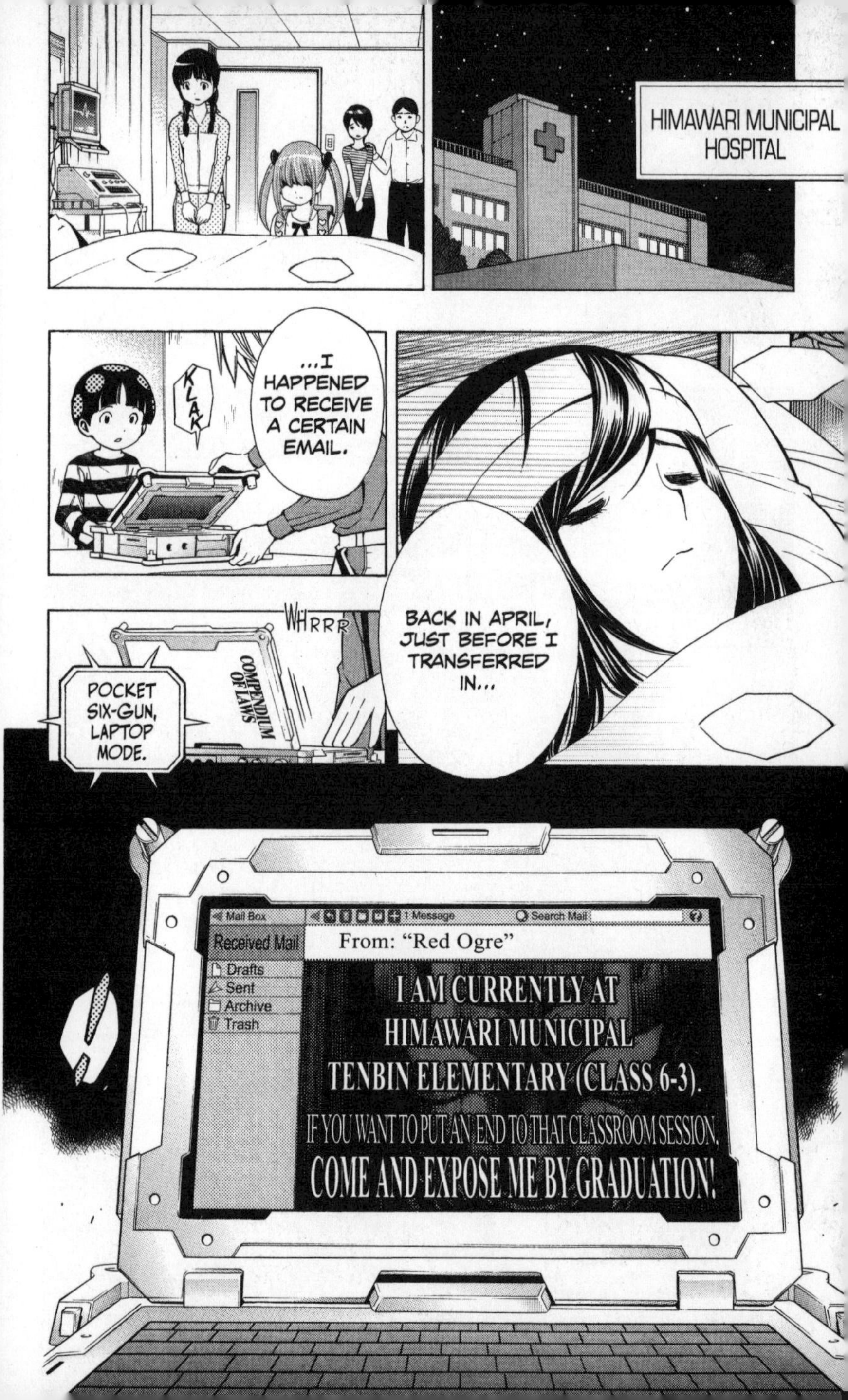

HIMAWARI MUNICIPAL HOSPITAL
BACK IN APRIL, JUST BEFORE I TRANSFERRED IN...
...I HAPPENED TO RECEIVE A CERTAIN EMAIL.
KLAK
WHRRR
COMPENDIUM OF LAWS
POCKET SIX-GUN, LAPTOP MODE.
Mail Box
1 Message
Search Mail
Received Mail
Drafts
Sent
Archive
Trash
From: "Red Ogre"
I AM CURRENTLY AT HIMAWARI MUNICIPAL TENBIN ELEMENTARY (CLASS 6-3).
IF YOU WANT TO PUT AN END TO THAT CLASSROOM SESSION, COME AND EXPOSE ME BY GRADUATION!

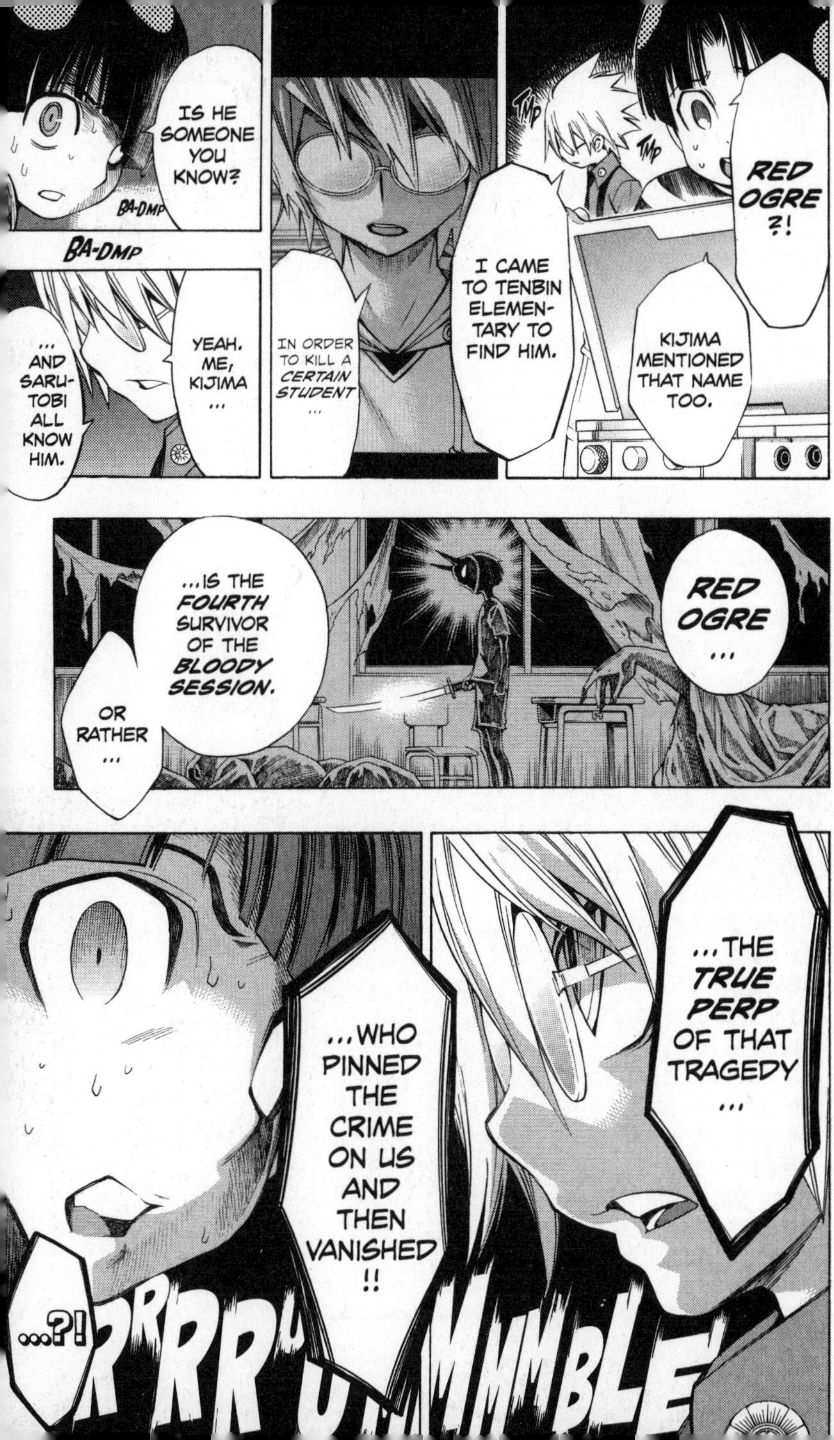
RED OGRE ?!
TMP TMP
KIJIMA MENTIONED THAT NAME TOO.
I CAME TO TENBIN ELEMENTARY TO FIND HIM.
IN ORDER TO KILL A *CERTAIN STUDENT* ...
IS HE SOMEONE YOU KNOW?
BA-DMP
BA-DMP
YEAH. ME, KIJIMA ...
... AND SARUTOBI ALL KNOW HIM.
RED OGRE ...
...IS THE *FOURTH* SURVIVOR OF THE *BLOODY SESSION*.
OR RATHER ...
...THE *TRUE PERP* OF THAT TRAGEDY ...
...WHO PINNED THE CRIME ON US AND THEN VANISHED !!
...?!
RRRRUMMMBLE

② The Plot

Once the meeting is over, I first write a text-only plot.

Here is an example, of the one for chapter 17, "The Beginning of the End." ⟶

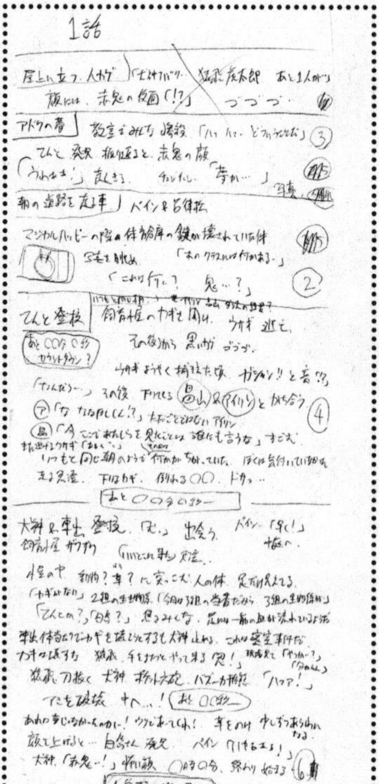

There may be some people who go straight to drawing a storyboard without writing an outline first. But most tend to write an outline.
The numbers written on the right refer to the number of pages that scene will likely take up.
A typical *Jump* series weekly chapter is 19 pages long, so I adjust these numbers so they add up to 19 in the end.
However, if that sum turns out to be, say, 23, I get sad. I forcibly condense the content and get reprimanded for it being really wordy again!
During the serialization, I've often had my editor take a first look while it was still in the outline stage in order to reduce the amount of wasteful revisions later.
For example, in regards to the outline on the right, the first five pages or so were cut and replaced with a different scene...
Once the outline gets a green light, the next step is the storyboard...!

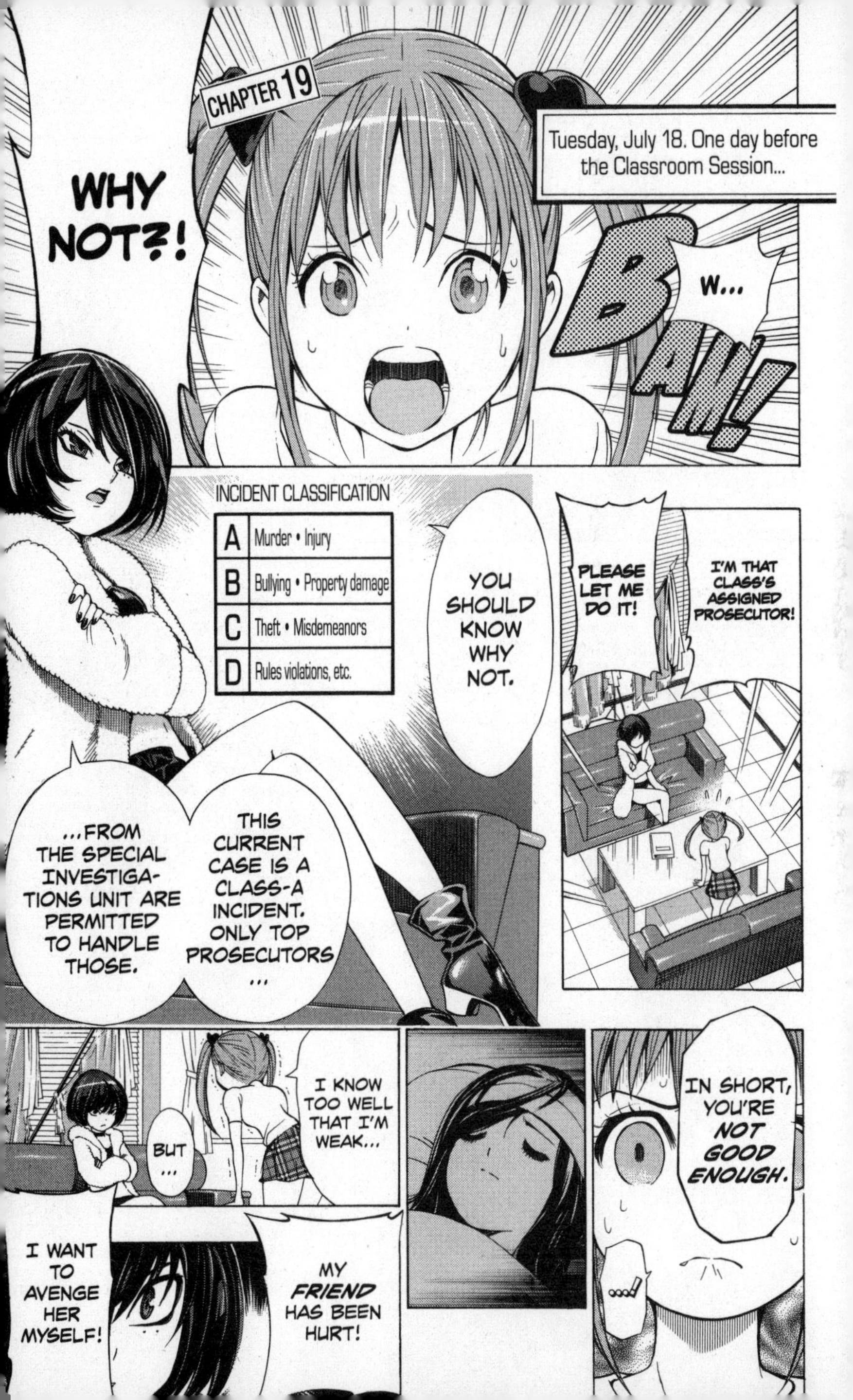
CHAPTER 19
Tuesday, July 18. One day before the Classroom Session...
W...
BAM!!
WHY NOT?!
I'M THAT CLASS'S ASSIGNED PROSECUTOR!
PLEASE LET ME DO IT!
YOU SHOULD KNOW WHY NOT.
INCIDENT CLASSIFICATION
A Murder • Injury
B Bullying • Property damage
C Theft • Misdemeanors
D Rules violations, etc.
THIS CURRENT CASE IS A CLASS-A INCIDENT. ONLY TOP PROSECUTORS...
...FROM THE SPECIAL INVESTIGATIONS UNIT ARE PERMITTED TO HANDLE THOSE.
IN SHORT, YOU'RE *NOT GOOD ENOUGH*.
...!
I KNOW TOO WELL THAT I'M WEAK...
BUT...
MY *FRIEND* HAS BEEN HURT!
I WANT TO AVENGE HER MYSELF!

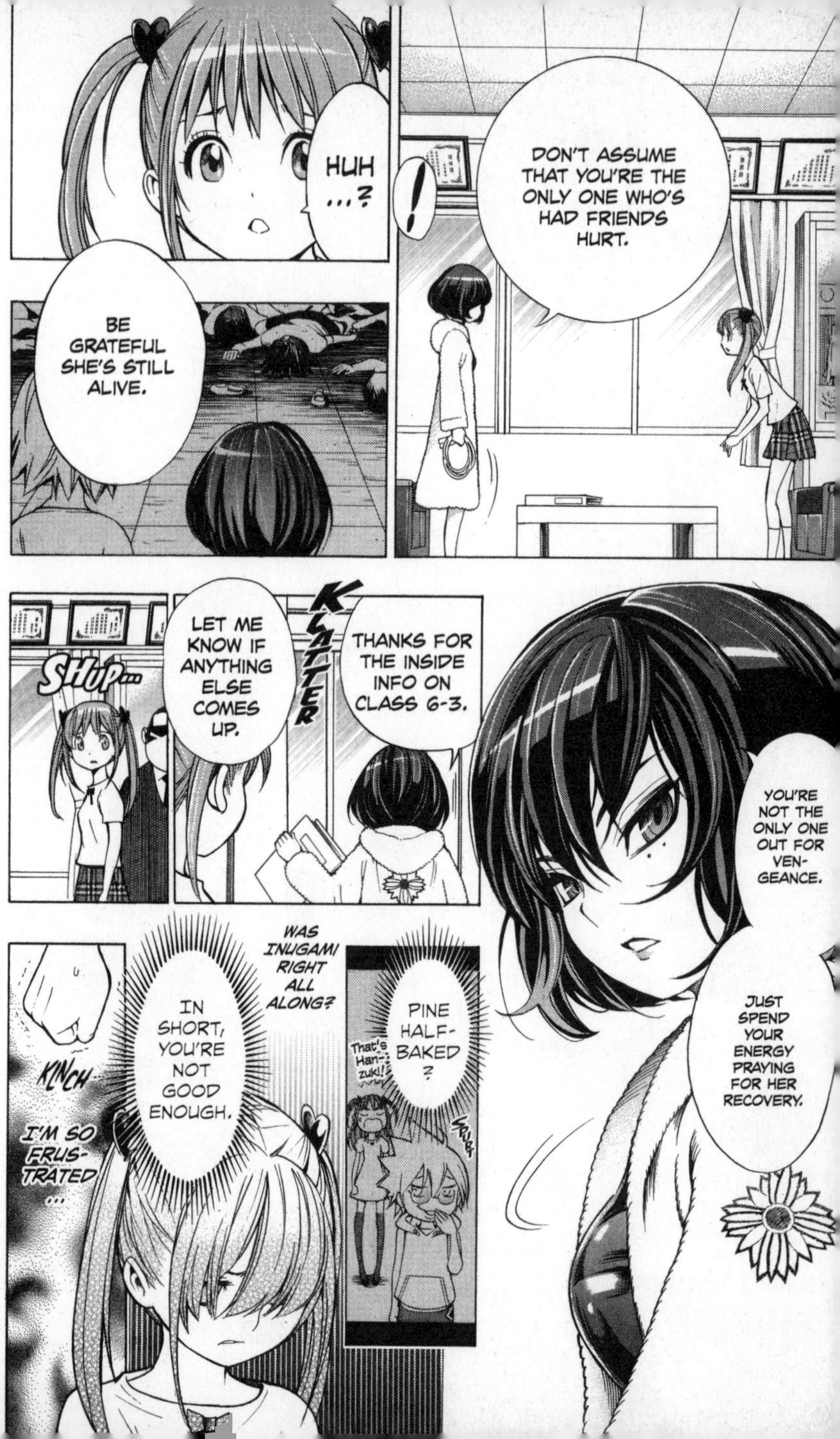
DON'T ASSUME THAT YOU'RE THE ONLY ONE WHO'S HAD FRIENDS HURT.
!
HUH ...?
BE GRATEFUL SHE'S STILL ALIVE.
YOU'RE NOT THE ONLY ONE OUT FOR VEN-GEANCE.
JUST SPEND YOUR ENERGY PRAYING FOR HER RECOVERY.
THANKS FOR THE INSIDE INFO ON CLASS 6-3.
KLATTER
LET ME KNOW IF ANYTHING ELSE COMES UP.
SHUP...
PINE HALF-BAKED?
That's Han-zuki!!
SPURT
WAS INUGAMI RIGHT ALL ALONG?
IN SHORT, YOU'RE NOT GOOD ENOUGH.
KLINCH
I'M SO FRUS-TRATED...

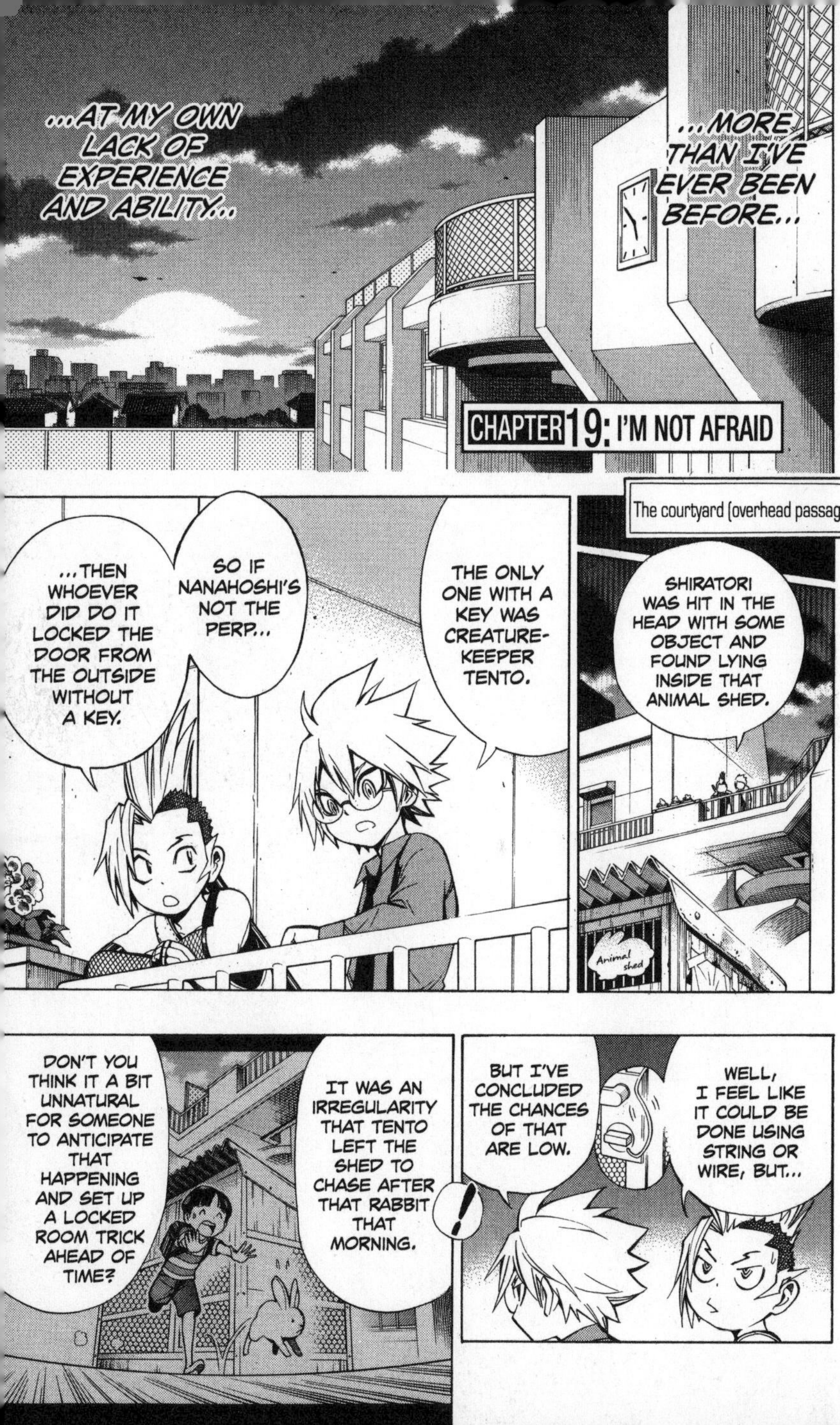
...MORE THAN I'VE EVER BEEN BEFORE...
...AT MY OWN LACK OF EXPERIENCE AND ABILITY...
CHAPTER 19: I'M NOT AFRAID
The courtyard (overhead passage)...
SHIRATORI WAS HIT IN THE HEAD WITH SOME OBJECT AND FOUND LYING INSIDE THAT ANIMAL SHED.
Animal shed
THE ONLY ONE WITH A KEY WAS CREATURE-KEEPER TENTO.
SO IF NANAHOSHI'S NOT THE PERP...
...THEN WHOEVER DID DO IT LOCKED THE DOOR FROM THE OUTSIDE WITHOUT A KEY.
WELL, I FEEL LIKE IT COULD BE DONE USING STRING OR WIRE, BUT...
BUT I'VE CONCLUDED THE CHANCES OF THAT ARE LOW.
!
IT WAS AN IRREGULARITY THAT TENTO LEFT THE SHED TO CHASE AFTER THAT RABBIT THAT MORNING.
DON'T YOU THINK IT A BIT UNNATURAL FOR SOMEONE TO ANTICIPATE THAT HAPPENING AND SET UP A LOCKED ROOM TRICK AHEAD OF TIME?

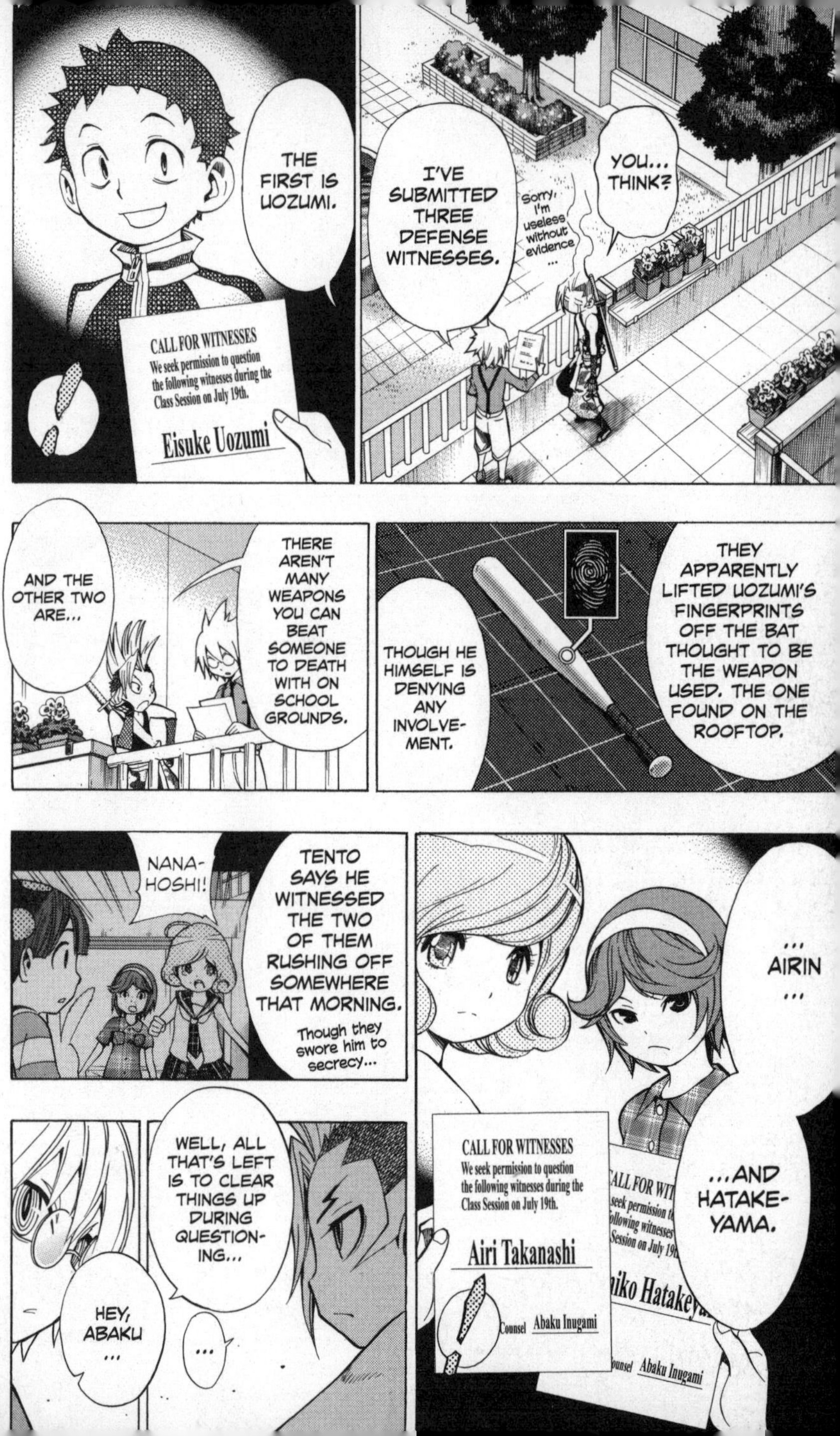
I'VE SUBMITTED THREE DEFENSE WITNESSES.
YOU... THINK?
Sorry, I'm useless without evidence...
THE FIRST IS UOZUMI.
CALL FOR WITNESSES
We seek permission to question the following witnesses during the Class Session on July 19th.
Eisuke Uozumi
THEY APPARENTLY LIFTED UOZUMI'S FINGERPRINTS OFF THE BAT THOUGHT TO BE THE WEAPON USED. THE ONE FOUND ON THE ROOFTOP.
THOUGH HE HIMSELF IS DENYING ANY INVOLVE-MENT.
THERE AREN'T MANY WEAPONS YOU CAN BEAT SOMEONE TO DEATH WITH ON SCHOOL GROUNDS.
AND THE OTHER TWO ARE...
... AIRIN ...
...AND HATAKE-YAMA.
CALL FOR WITNESSES
We seek permission to question the following witnesses during the Class Session on July 19th.
Airi Takanashi
Counsel Abaku Inugami
Counsel Abaku Inugami
TENTO SAYS HE WITNESSED THE TWO OF THEM RUSHING OFF SOMEWHERE THAT MORNING.
Though they swore him to secrecy...
NANA-HOSHI!
WELL, ALL THAT'S LEFT IS TO CLEAR THINGS UP DURING QUESTION-ING...
HEY, ABAKU ...
...

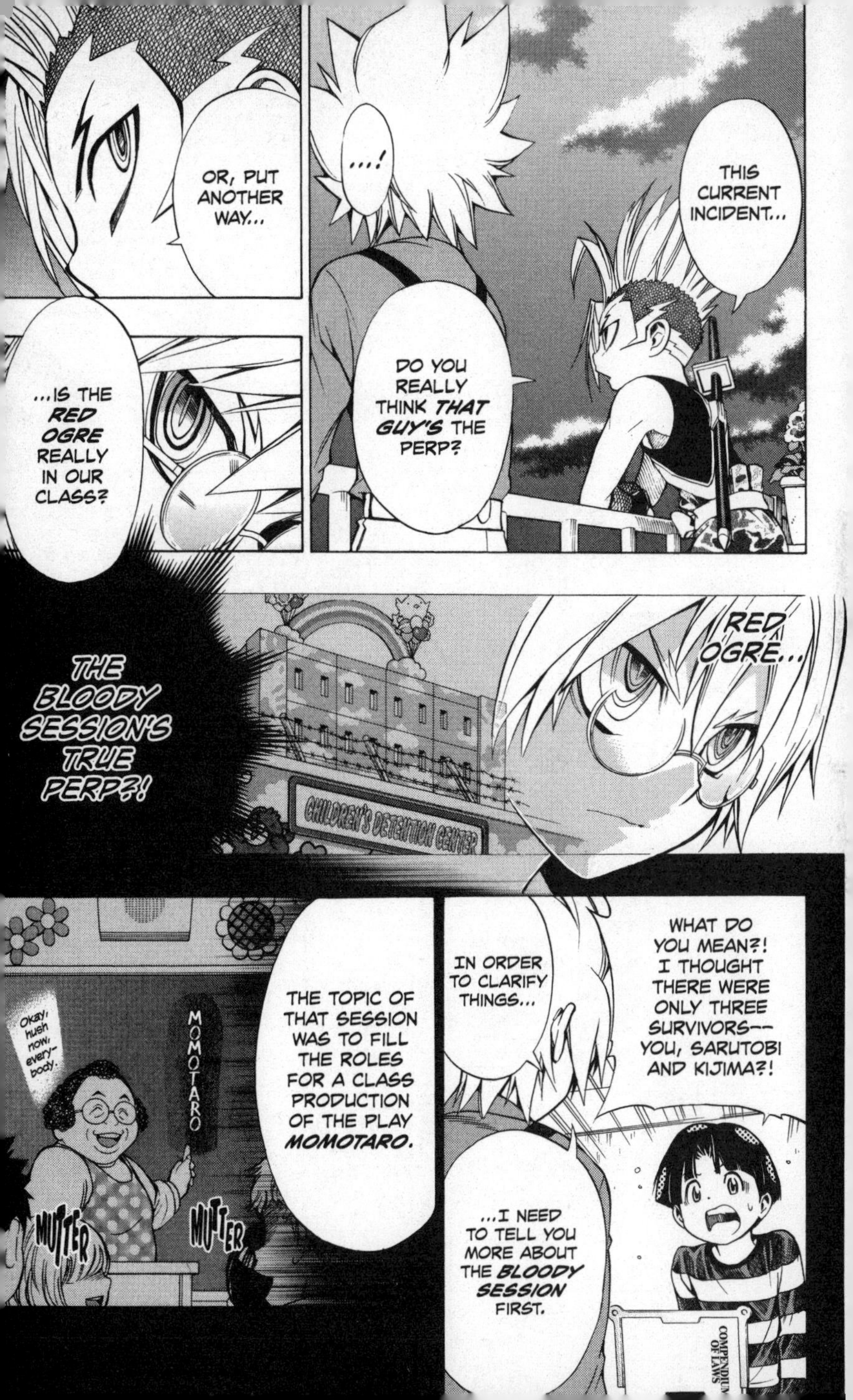
THIS CURRENT INCIDENT...
...!
DO YOU REALLY THINK *THAT GUY'S* THE PERP?
OR, PUT ANOTHER WAY...
...IS THE *RED OGRE* REALLY IN OUR CLASS?
RED OGRE...
CHILDREN'S DETENTION CENTER
THE BLOODY SESSION'S TRUE PERP?!
WHAT DO YOU MEAN?! I THOUGHT THERE WERE ONLY THREE SURVIVORS-- YOU, SARUTOBI AND KIJIMA?!
IN ORDER TO CLARIFY THINGS...
...I NEED TO TELL YOU MORE ABOUT THE *BLOODY SESSION* FIRST.
COMPENDIUM OF LAWS
THE TOPIC OF THAT SESSION WAS TO FILL THE ROLES FOR A CLASS PRODUCTION OF THE PLAY *MOMOTARO*.
MOMOTARO
Okay, hush now, everybody.
MUTTER
MUTTER

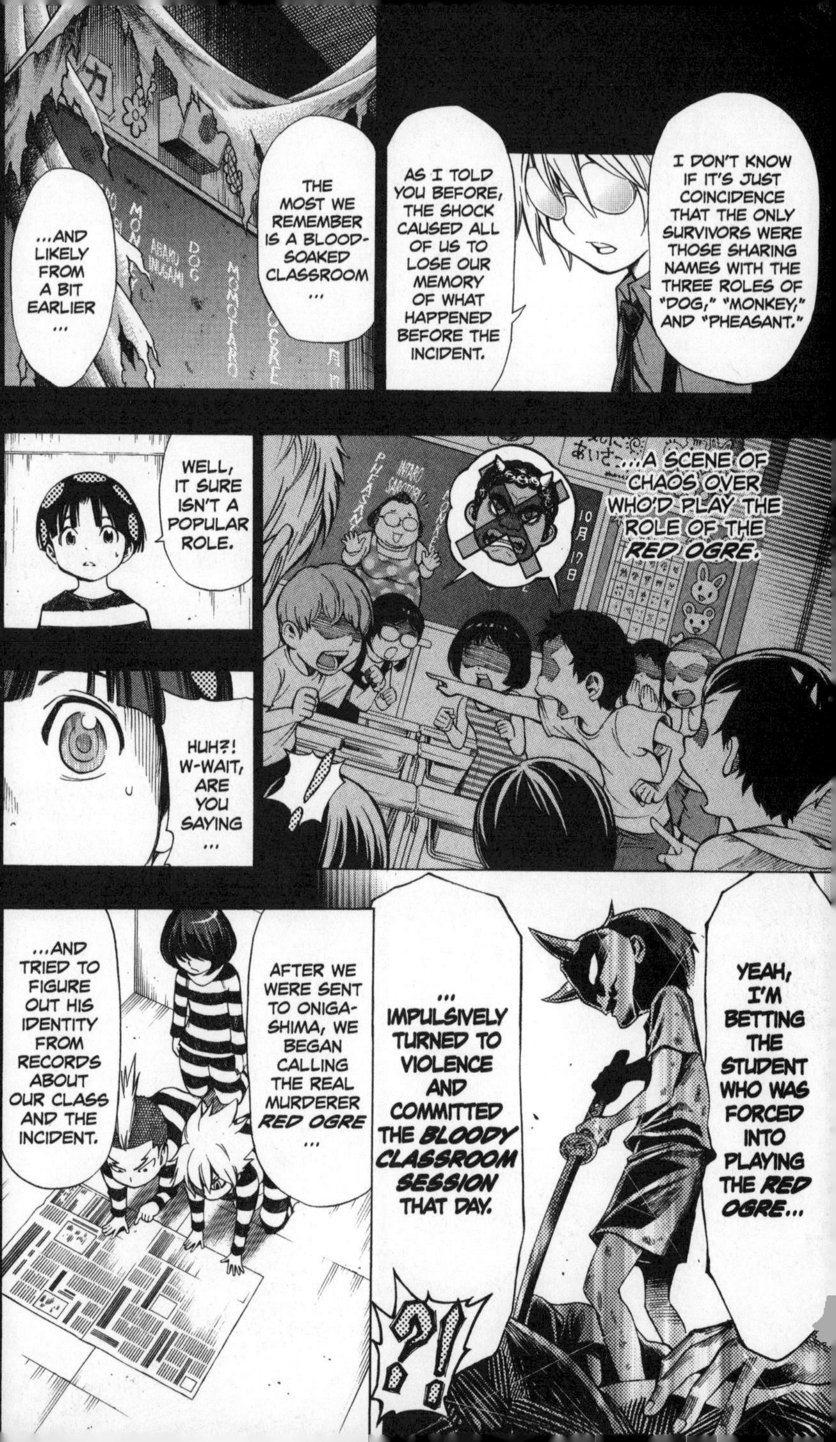
I DON'T KNOW IF IT'S JUST COINCIDENCE THAT THE ONLY SURVIVORS WERE THOSE SHARING NAMES WITH THE THREE ROLES OF "DOG," "MONKEY," AND "PHEASANT."
AS I TOLD YOU BEFORE, THE SHOCK CAUSED ALL OF US TO LOSE OUR MEMORY OF WHAT HAPPENED BEFORE THE INCIDENT.
THE MOST WE REMEMBER IS A BLOOD-SOAKED CLASSROOM ...
...AND LIKELY FROM A BIT EARLIER ...
...A SCENE OF CHAOS OVER WHO'D PLAY THE ROLE OF THE *RED OGRE.*
WELL, IT SURE ISN'T A POPULAR ROLE.
HUH?! W-WAIT, ARE YOU SAYING ...
YEAH, I'M BETTING THE STUDENT WHO WAS FORCED INTO PLAYING THE *RED OGRE*...
... IMPULSIVELY TURNED TO VIOLENCE AND COMMITTED THE *BLOODY CLASSROOM SESSION* THAT DAY.
?!
AFTER WE WERE SENT TO ONIGA-SHIMA, WE BEGAN CALLING THE REAL MURDERER *RED OGRE* ...
...AND TRIED TO FIGURE OUT HIS IDENTITY FROM RECORDS ABOUT OUR CLASS AND THE INCIDENT.

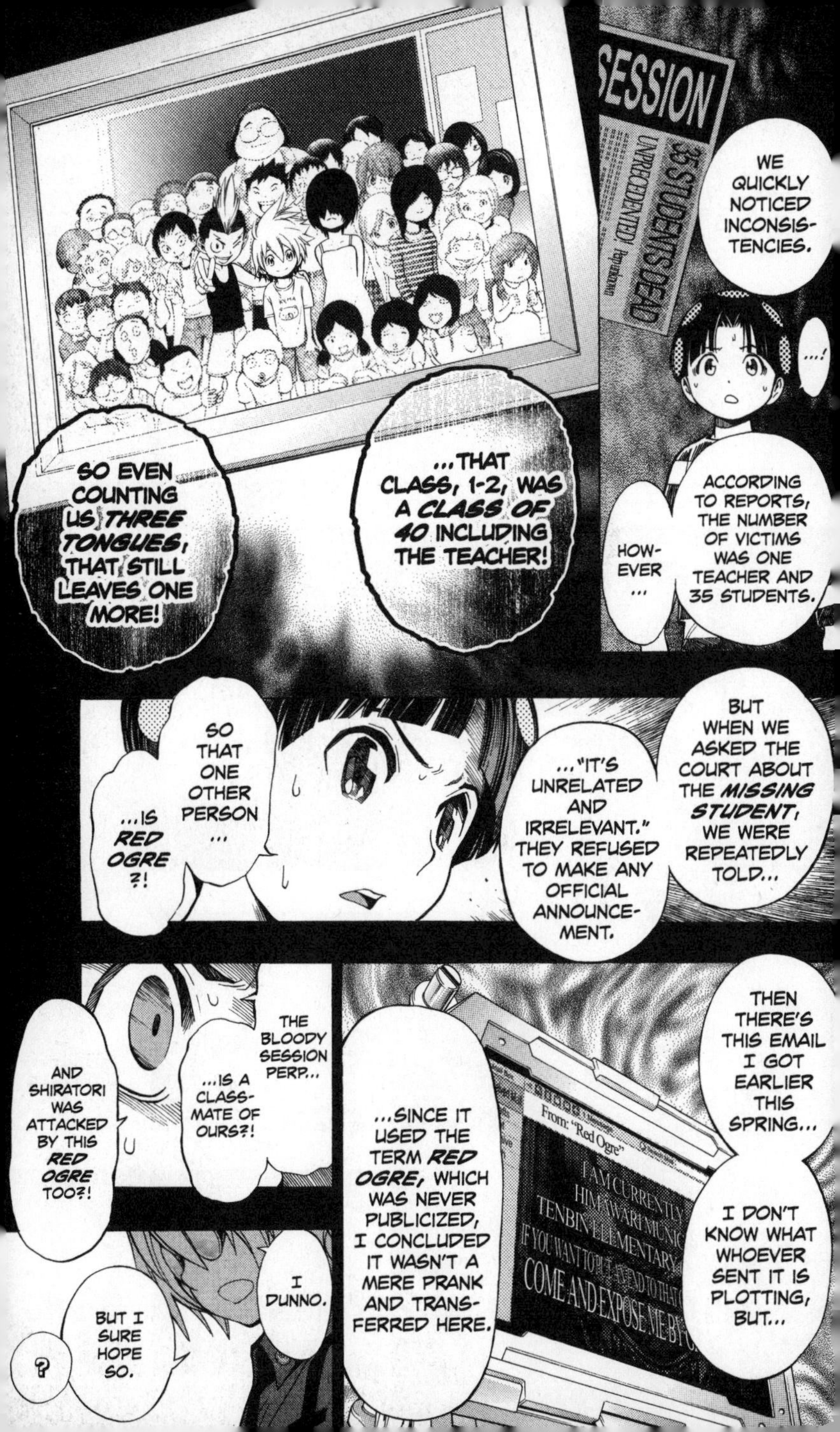
SESSION
35 STUDENTS DEAD
UNPRECEDENTED!
WE QUICKLY NOTICED INCONSISTENCIES.
...!
ACCORDING TO REPORTS, THE NUMBER OF VICTIMS WAS ONE TEACHER AND 35 STUDENTS.
HOWEVER...
...THAT CLASS, 1-2, WAS A *CLASS OF 40* INCLUDING THE TEACHER!
SO EVEN COUNTING US *THREE TONGUES*, THAT STILL LEAVES ONE MORE!
BUT WHEN WE ASKED THE COURT ABOUT THE *MISSING STUDENT*, WE WERE REPEATEDLY TOLD...
..."IT'S UNRELATED AND IRRELEVANT." THEY REFUSED TO MAKE ANY OFFICIAL ANNOUNCEMENT.
SO THAT ONE OTHER PERSON...
...IS *RED OGRE*?!
THEN THERE'S THIS EMAIL I GOT EARLIER THIS SPRING...
I DON'T KNOW WHAT WHOEVER SENT IT IS PLOTTING, BUT...
...SINCE IT USED THE TERM *RED OGRE*, WHICH WAS NEVER PUBLICIZED, I CONCLUDED IT WASN'T A MERE PRANK AND TRANSFERRED HERE.
From: "Red Ogre"
THE BLOODY SESSION PERP...
...IS A CLASSMATE OF OURS?!
AND SHIRATORI WAS ATTACKED BY THIS *RED OGRE* TOO?!
I DUNNO.
BUT I SURE HOPE SO.
?

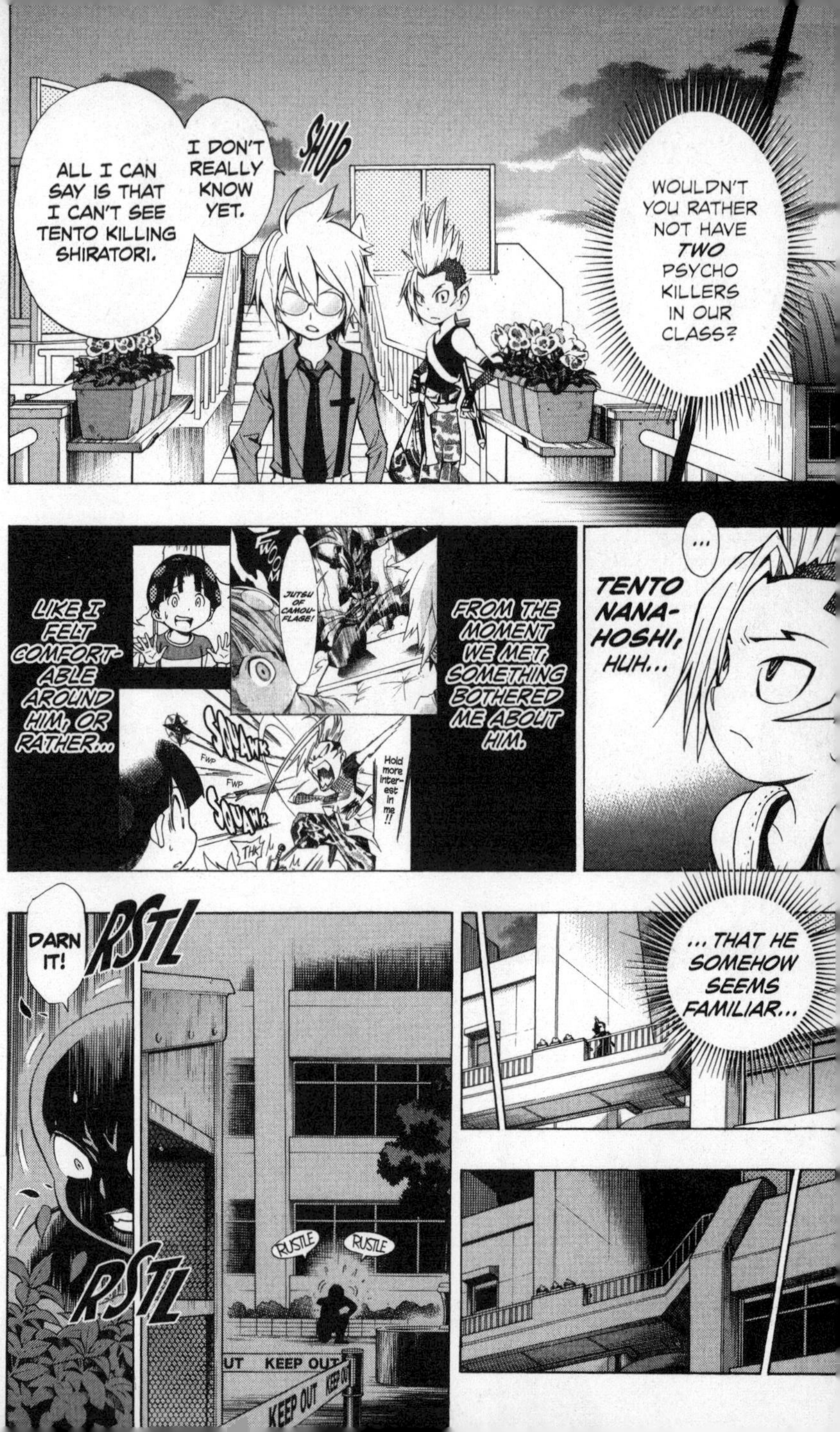
WOULDN'T YOU RATHER NOT HAVE *TWO* PSYCHO KILLERS IN OUR CLASS?
SHUP
I DON'T REALLY KNOW YET.
ALL I CAN SAY IS THAT I CAN'T SEE TENTO KILLING SHIRATORI.
...
TENTO NANA-HOSHI, HUH...
FROM THE MOMENT WE MET, SOMETHING BOTHERED ME ABOUT HIM.
FWOOM
JUTSU OF CAMOU-FLAGE!
SQUAWK
Hold more interest in me!!
FWP
FWP
SQUAWK
THK
LIKE I FELT COMFORTABLE AROUND HIM, OR RATHER...
...THAT HE SOMEHOW SEEMS FAMILIAR...
DARN IT!
RSTL
RUSTLE
RUSTLE
RSTL
UT KEEP OUT
KEEP OUT KEEP OUT

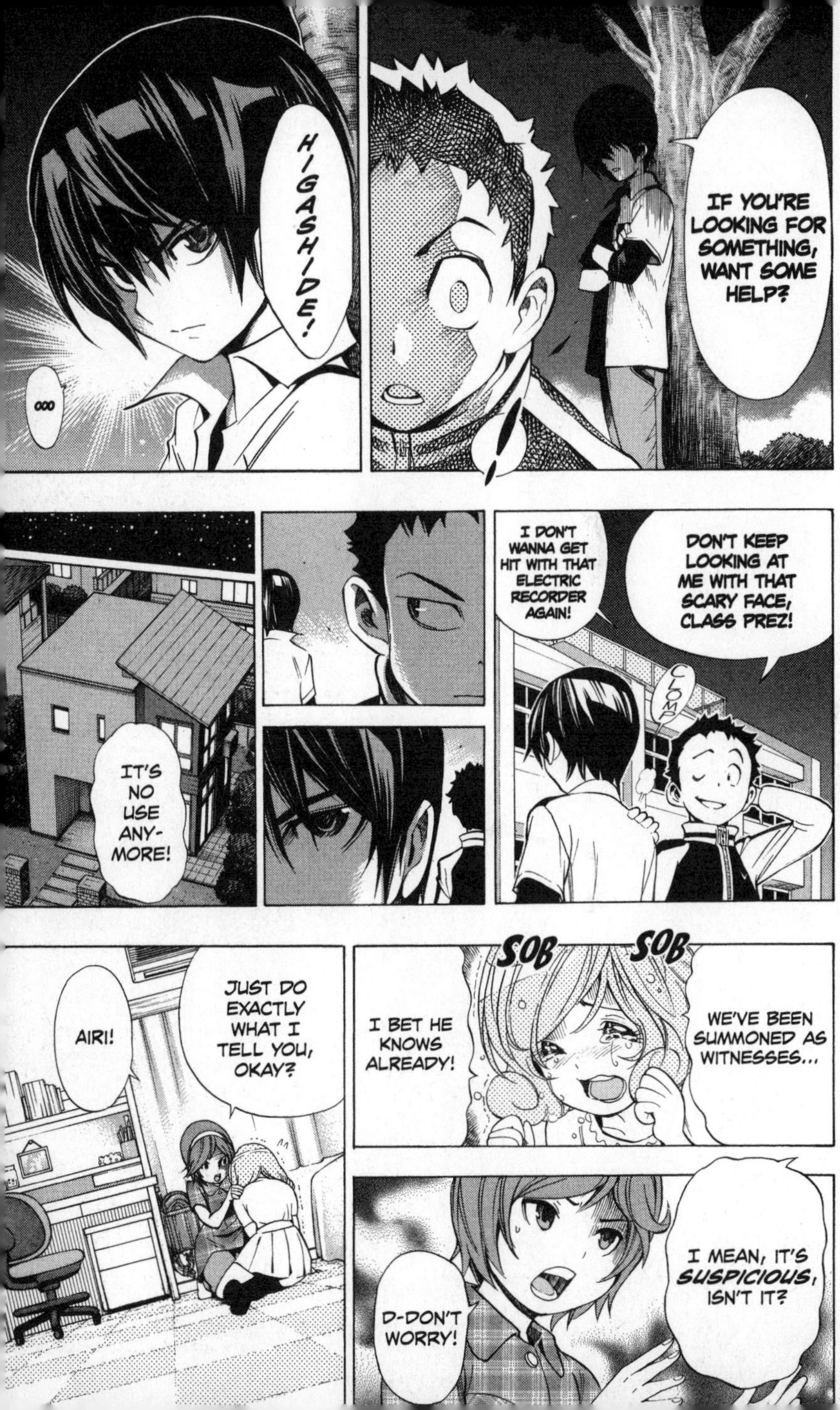
IF YOU'RE LOOKING FOR SOMETHING, WANT SOME HELP?
!
HIGASHIDE!
...
DON'T KEEP LOOKING AT ME WITH THAT SCARY FACE, CLASS PREZ!
I DON'T WANNA GET HIT WITH THAT ELECTRIC RECORDER AGAIN!
CLOMP
IT'S NO USE ANYMORE!
SOB SOB
WE'VE BEEN SUMMONED AS WITNESSES...
I BET HE KNOWS ALREADY!
I MEAN, IT'S *SUSPICIOUS*, ISN'T IT?
D-DON'T WORRY!
JUST DO EXACTLY WHAT I TELL YOU, OKAY?
AIRI!

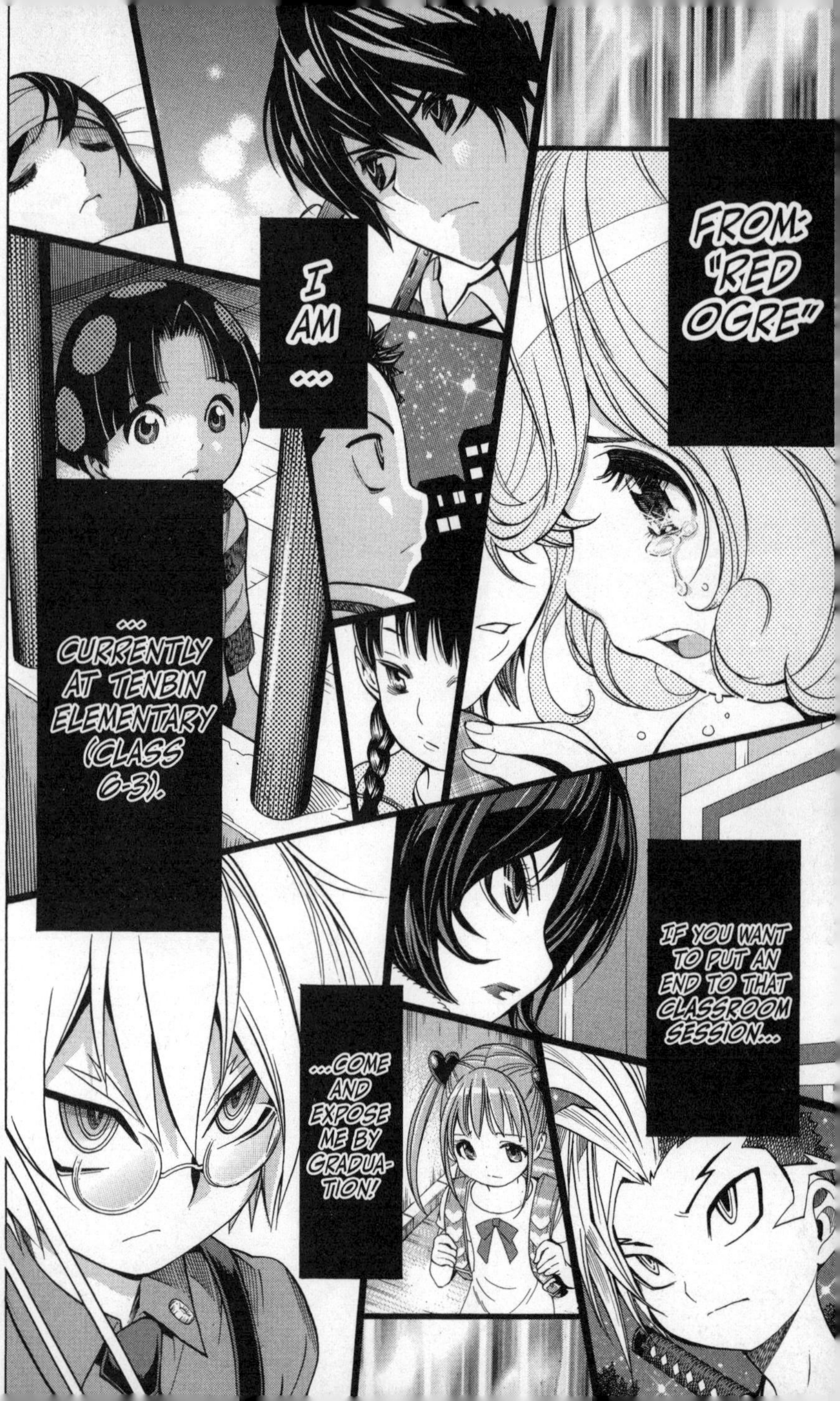
FROM: "RED OGRE"
I AM ...
... CURRENTLY AT TENBIN ELEMENTARY (CLASS 6-3).
IF YOU WANT TO PUT AN END TO THAT CLASSROOM SESSION...
...COME AND EXPOSE ME BY GRADUATION!

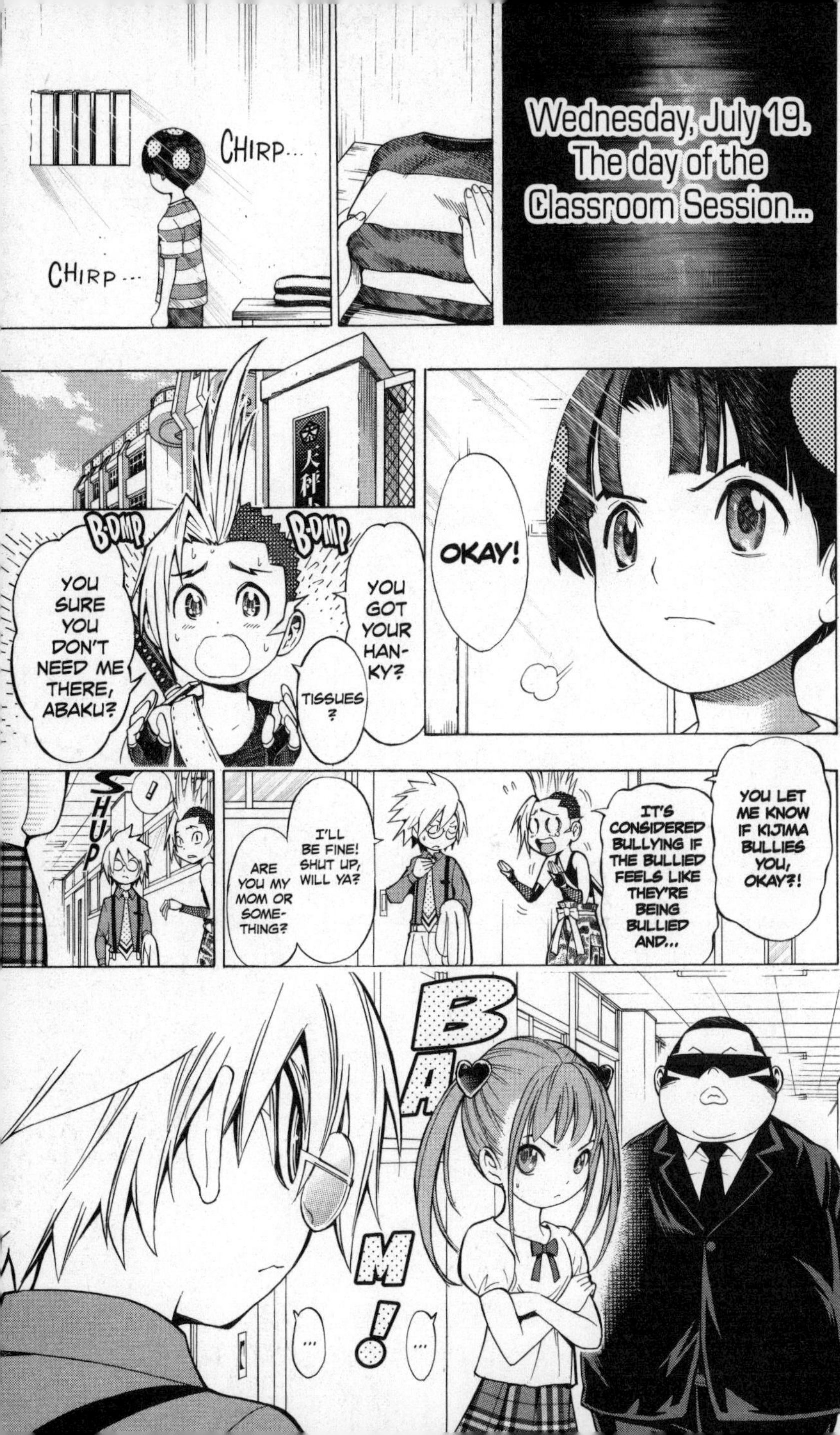
Wednesday, July 19. The day of the Classroom Session...
CHIRP...
CHIRP...
OKAY!
B-DMP
YOU GOT YOUR HAN-KY?
TISSUES?
B-DMP
YOU SURE YOU DON'T NEED ME THERE, ABAKU?
YOU LET ME KNOW IF KIJIMA BULLIES YOU, OKAY?!
IT'S CONSIDERED BULLYING IF THE BULLIED FEELS LIKE THEY'RE BEING BULLIED AND...
I'LL BE FINE! SHUT UP, WILL YA?
ARE YOU MY MOM OR SOME-THING?
!
SHUP
BAM!
...
...

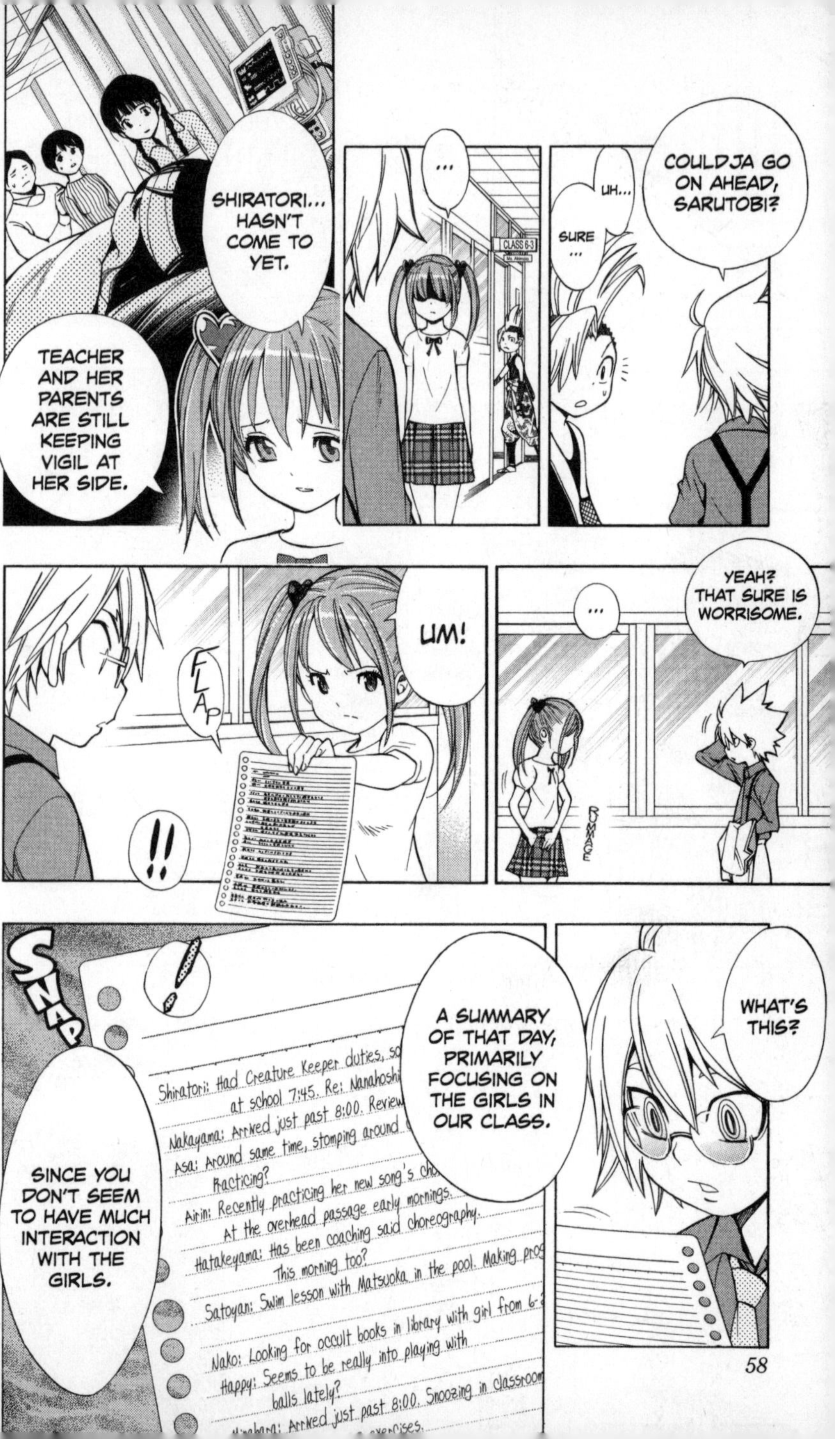
COULDJA GO ON AHEAD, SARUTOBI?
UH...
SURE ...
...
CLASS 6-3
SHIRATORI... HASN'T COME TO YET.
TEACHER AND HER PARENTS ARE STILL KEEPING VIGIL AT HER SIDE.
YEAH? THAT SURE IS WORRISOME.
...
RUMMAGE
UM!
FLAP
!!
WHAT'S THIS?
A SUMMARY OF THAT DAY, PRIMARILY FOCUSING ON THE GIRLS IN OUR CLASS.
SNAP
!
Shiratori: Had Creature Keeper duties, so
at school 7:45. Re: Nanahoshi
Nakayama: Arrived just past 8:00. Review
Asa: Around same time, stomping around
Practicing?
Airin: Recently practicing her new song's
At the overhead passage early mornings.
Hatakeyama: Has been coaching said choreography.
This morning too?
Satoyan: Swim lesson with Matsuoka in the pool. Making prog
Nako: Looking for occult books in library with girl from 6-
Happy: Seems to be really into playing with
balls lately?
Arrived just past 8:00. Snoozing in classroom
exercises.
SINCE YOU DON'T SEEM TO HAVE MUCH INTERACTION WITH THE GIRLS.

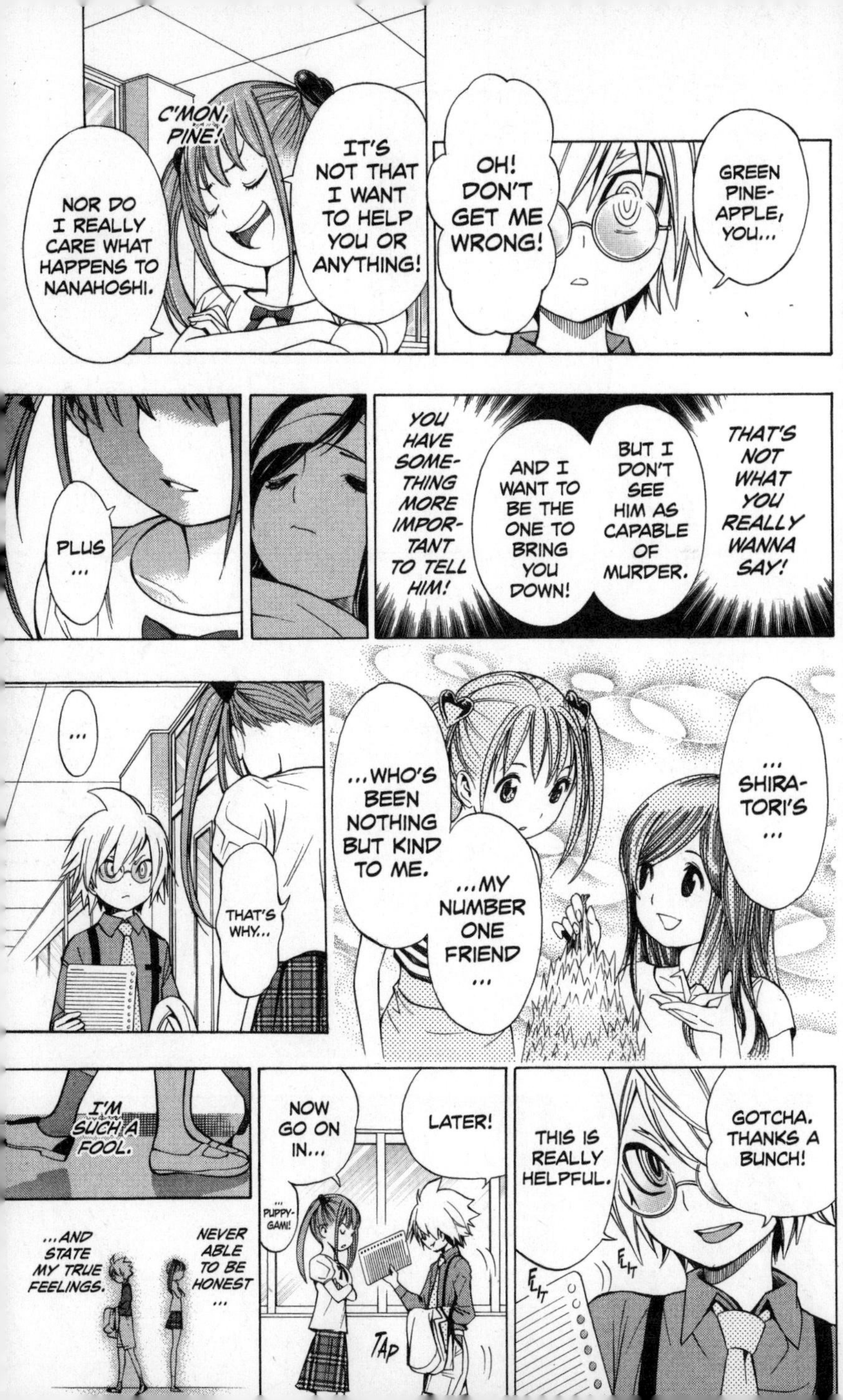
GREEN PINE-APPLE, YOU...
OH! DON'T GET ME WRONG!
IT'S NOT THAT I WANT TO HELP YOU OR ANYTHING!
C'MON, PINE!
NOR DO I REALLY CARE WHAT HAPPENS TO NANAHOSHI.
THAT'S NOT WHAT YOU REALLY WANNA SAY!
BUT I DON'T SEE HIM AS CAPABLE OF MURDER.
AND I WANT TO BE THE ONE TO BRING YOU DOWN!
YOU HAVE SOME-THING MORE IMPOR-TANT TO TELL HIM!
PLUS ...
... SHIRA-TORI'S ...
...MY NUMBER ONE FRIEND ...
...WHO'S BEEN NOTHING BUT KIND TO ME.
THAT'S WHY...
...
GOTCHA. THANKS A BUNCH!
THIS IS REALLY HELPFUL.
FLIT
FLIT
LATER!
NOW GO ON IN...
... PUPPY-GAMI!
TAP
I'M SUCH A FOOL.
NEVER ABLE TO BE HONEST ...
...AND STATE MY TRUE FEELINGS.

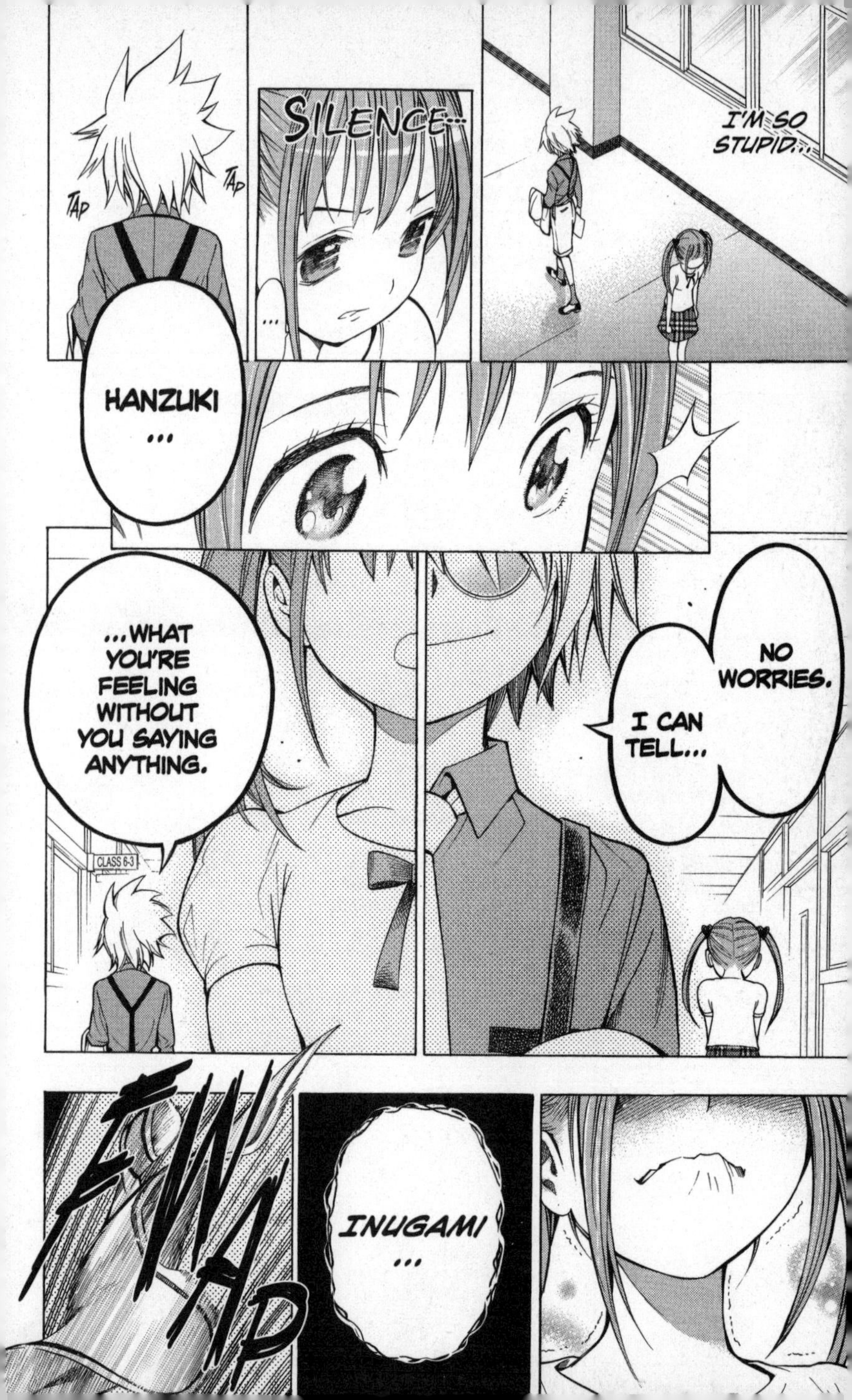
I'M SO STUPID...
SILENCE...
...
TAP
TAP
HANZUKI ...
NO WORRIES. I CAN TELL...
...WHAT YOU'RE FEELING WITHOUT YOU SAYING ANYTHING.
CLASS 6-3
INUGAMI ...
FWAP

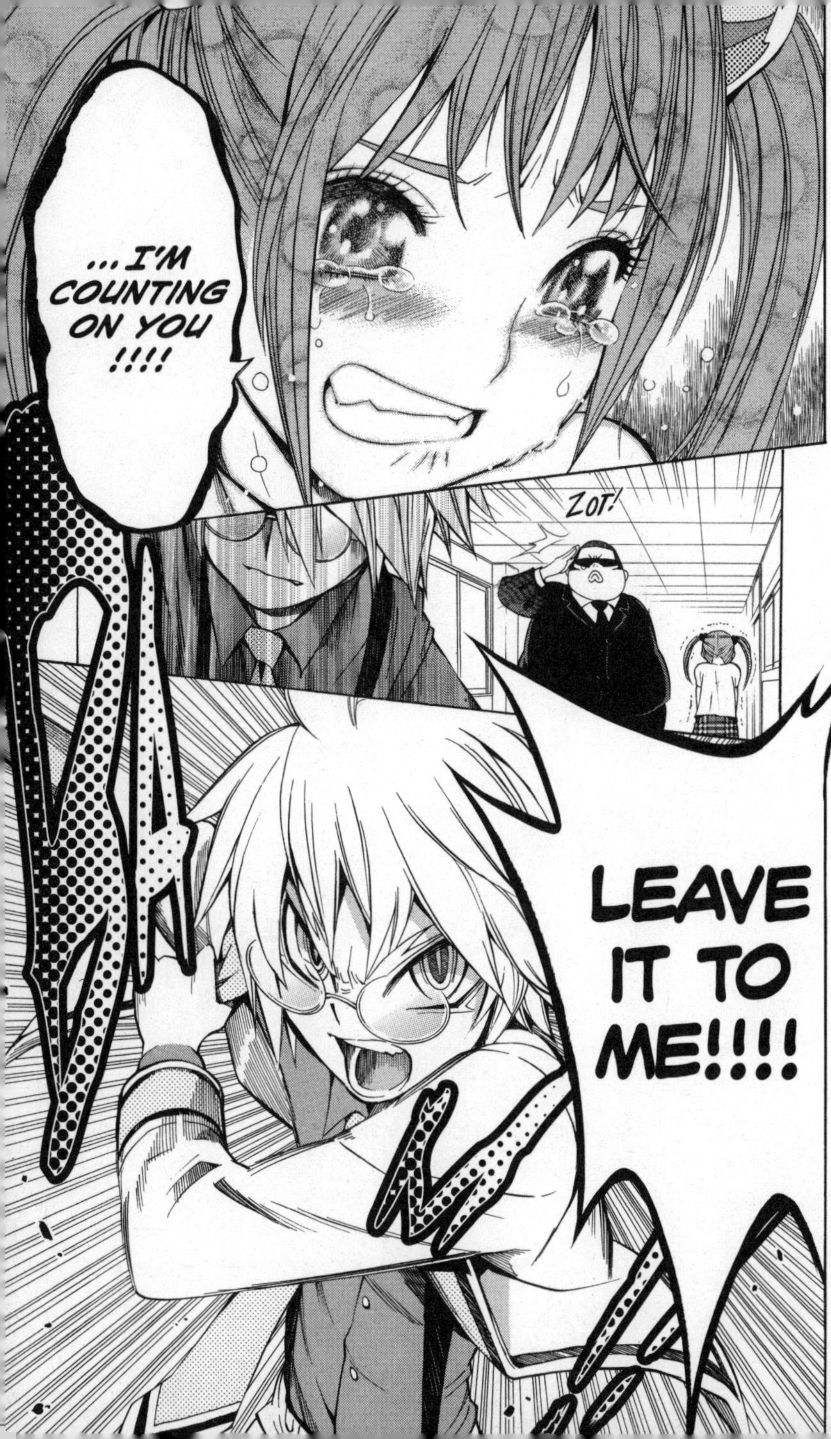
...I'M COUNTING ON YOU !!!!
ZOT!
LEAVE IT TO ME!!!!

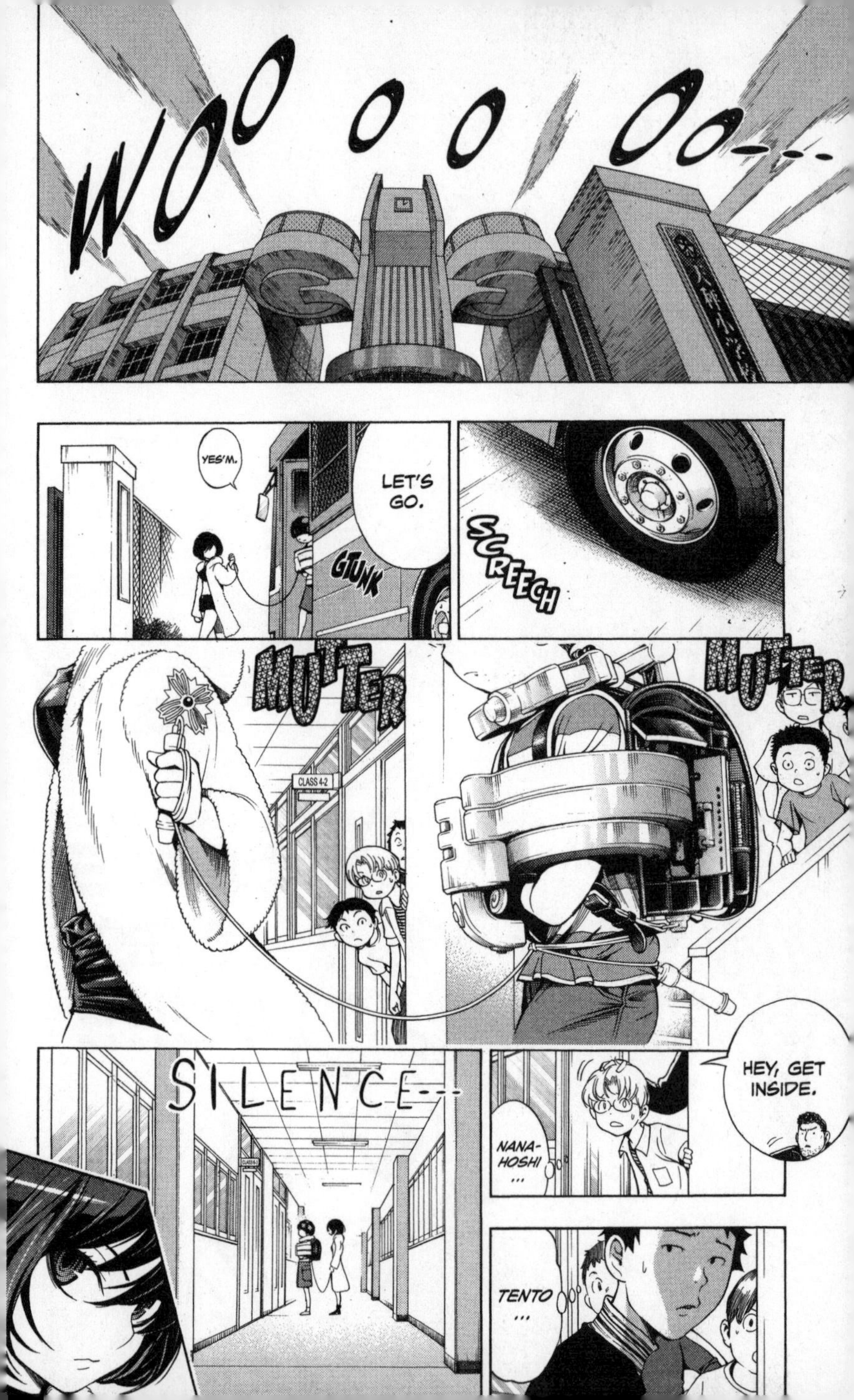
WOOOOOOO...
SCREECH
LET'S GO.
YES'M.
GTUNK
MUTTER
MUTTER
CLASS 4-2
HEY, GET INSIDE.
NANA-HOSHI ...
TENTO ...
SILENCE...

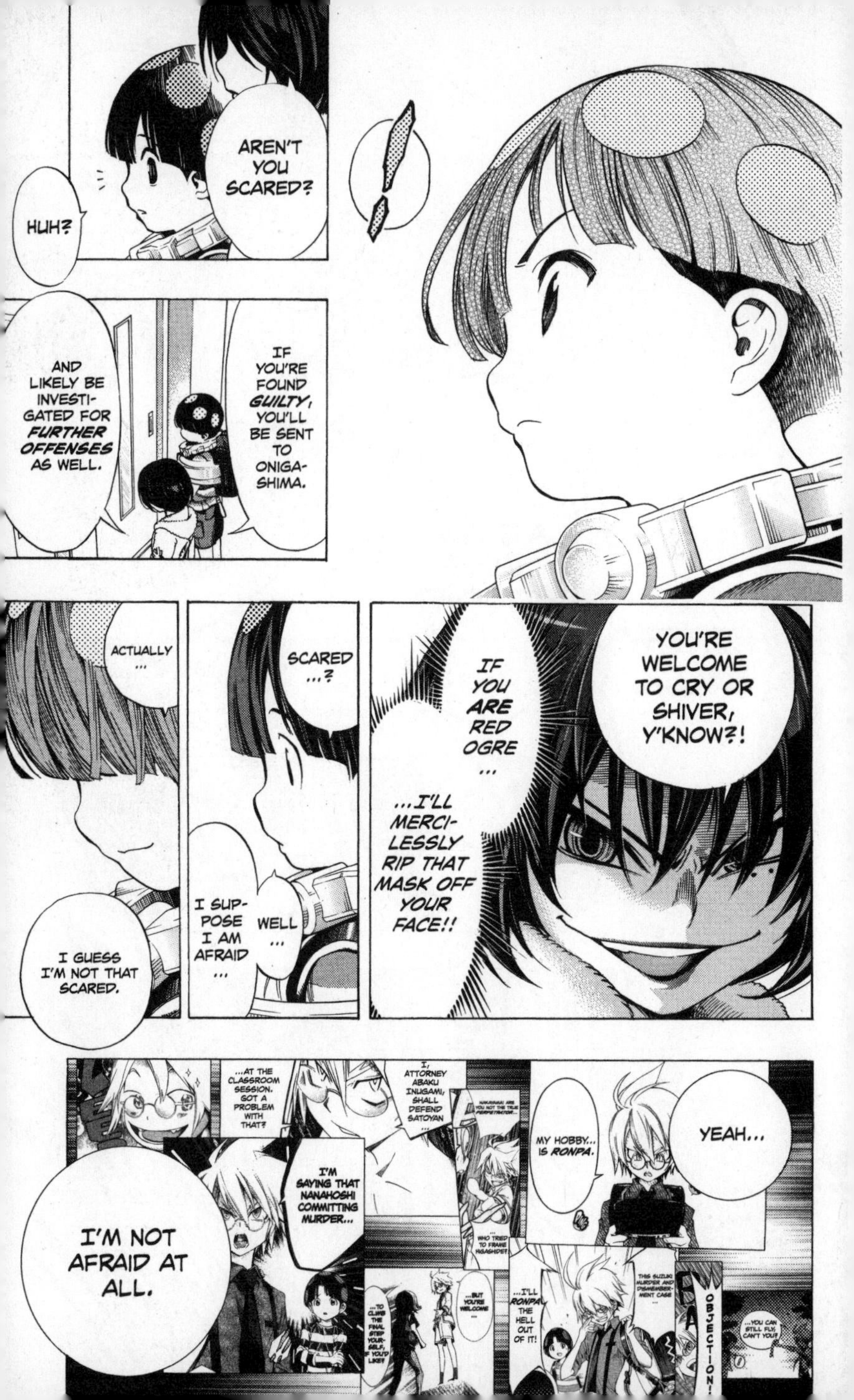
AREN'T YOU SCARED?
HUH?
IF YOU'RE FOUND GUILTY, YOU'LL BE SENT TO ONIGA-SHIMA.
AND LIKELY BE INVESTI-GATED FOR FURTHER OFFENSES AS WELL.
!
YOU'RE WELCOME TO CRY OR SHIVER, Y'KNOW?!
IF YOU ARE RED OGRE...
...I'LL MERCI-LESSLY RIP THAT MASK OFF YOUR FACE!!
SCARED...?
WELL...
I SUP-POSE I AM AFRAID...
ACTUALLY...
I GUESS I'M NOT THAT SCARED.
YEAH...
MY HOBBY... IS RONPA.
...YOU CAN STILL FLY, CAN'T YOU?
OBJECTION!
THIS SUZUKI MURDER AND DISMEMBER-MENT CASE...
...I'LL RONPA THE HELL OUT OF IT!
NAKAYAMA! ARE YOU NOT THE TRUE PERPETRATOR...
...WHO TRIED TO FRAME HIGASHIDE?
I, ATTORNEY ABAKU INUGAMI, SHALL DEFEND SATOYAN...
...AT THE CLASSROOM SESSION. GOT A PROBLEM WITH THAT?
I'M SAYING THAT NANAHOSHI COMMITTING MURDER...
...BUT YOU'RE WELCOME...
...TO CLIMB THE FINAL STEP YOUR-SELF, IF YOU'D LIKE?
I'M NOT AFRAID AT ALL.

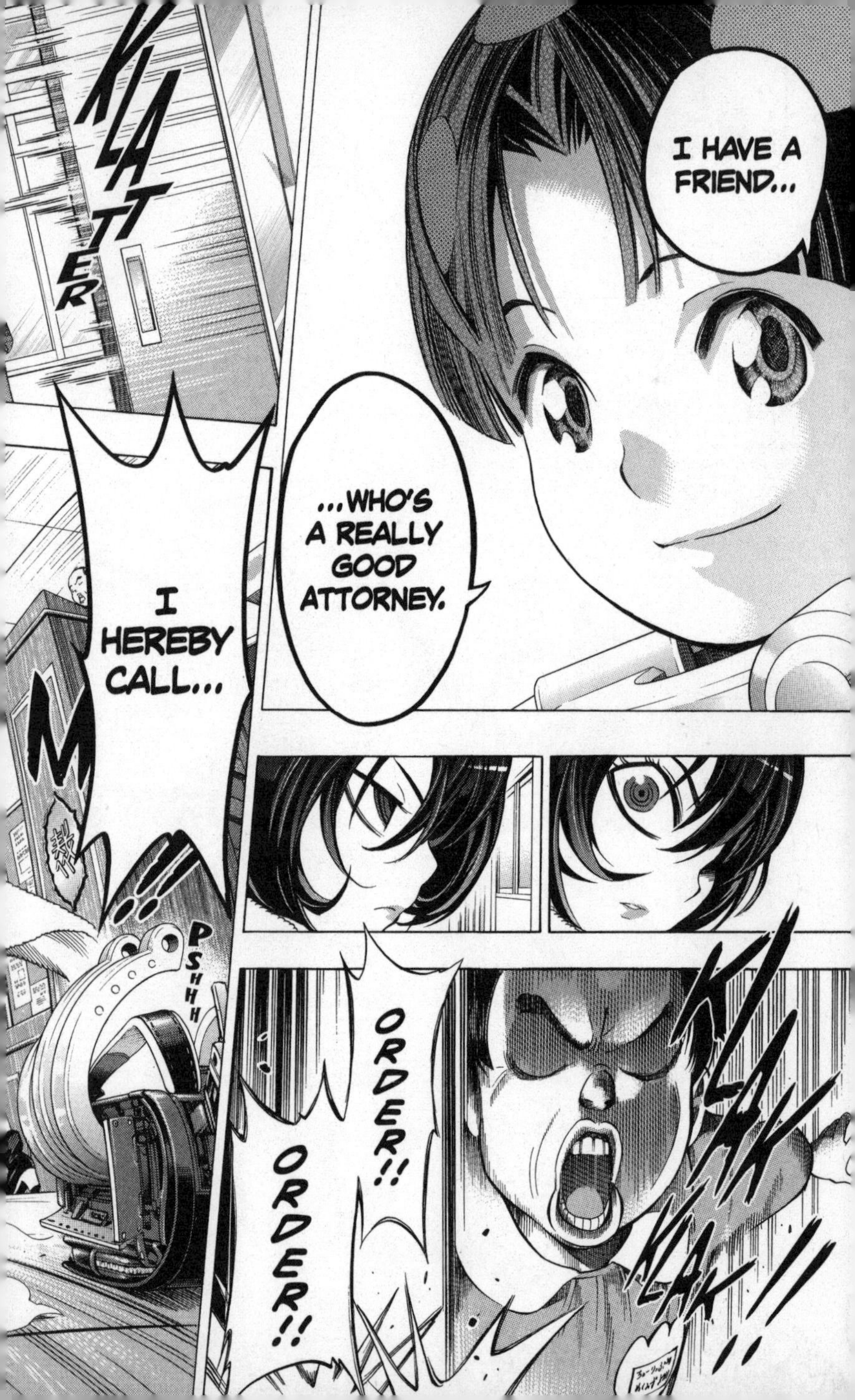
I HAVE A FRIEND...
...WHO'S A REALLY GOOD ATTORNEY.
ORDER!!
ORDER!!
KLAK KLAK!!
KLATTER
I HEREBY CALL...
PSHHH

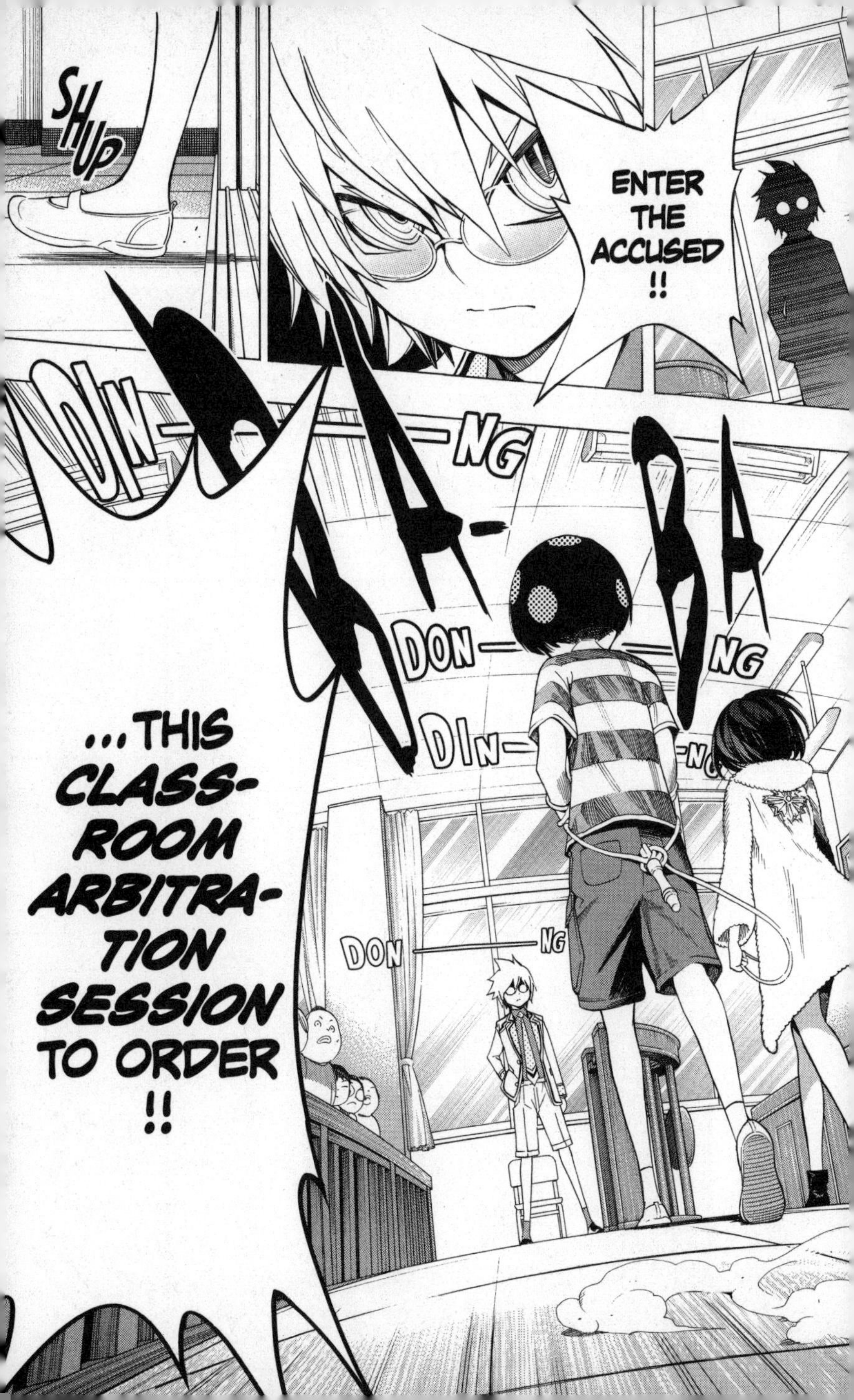
SHUP
ENTER THE ACCUSED !!
DUN-DA-NG
DA-BA
DON—NG
DIN—NG
DON—NG
...THIS CLASS-ROOM ARBITRA-TION SESSION TO ORDER !!

③ The Storyboard

A storyboard is a pencil-drawn rough draft of a manga. A manga artist who draws and writes by him- or herself may not draw a very meticulous storyboard because the final manga is their end product. But for me, my job stops with it, so I try to draw as much detail as possible down to the facial expressions to make things as clear for Obata Sensei as possible. I also want to get better at drawing.

I write notes in the places that still feel a bit vague. I partition a sheet of B4-size paper into quarters and draw four pages of manga per sheet. I used to partition each sheet into halves, but to cut down on the amount of dialogue, I took drastic measures by shrinking the canvas itself.

Perhaps I'll eventually end up splitting the sheet into eighths.

Like cell division...

友人に
いい弁護士を知ってるんで
ただいま
より
学級会を開廷する!!!
静粛に!!

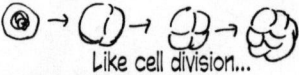

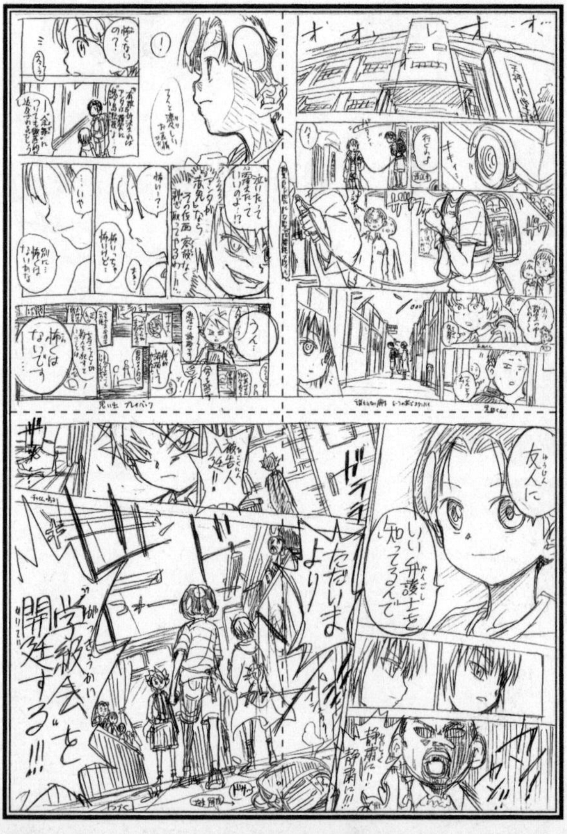

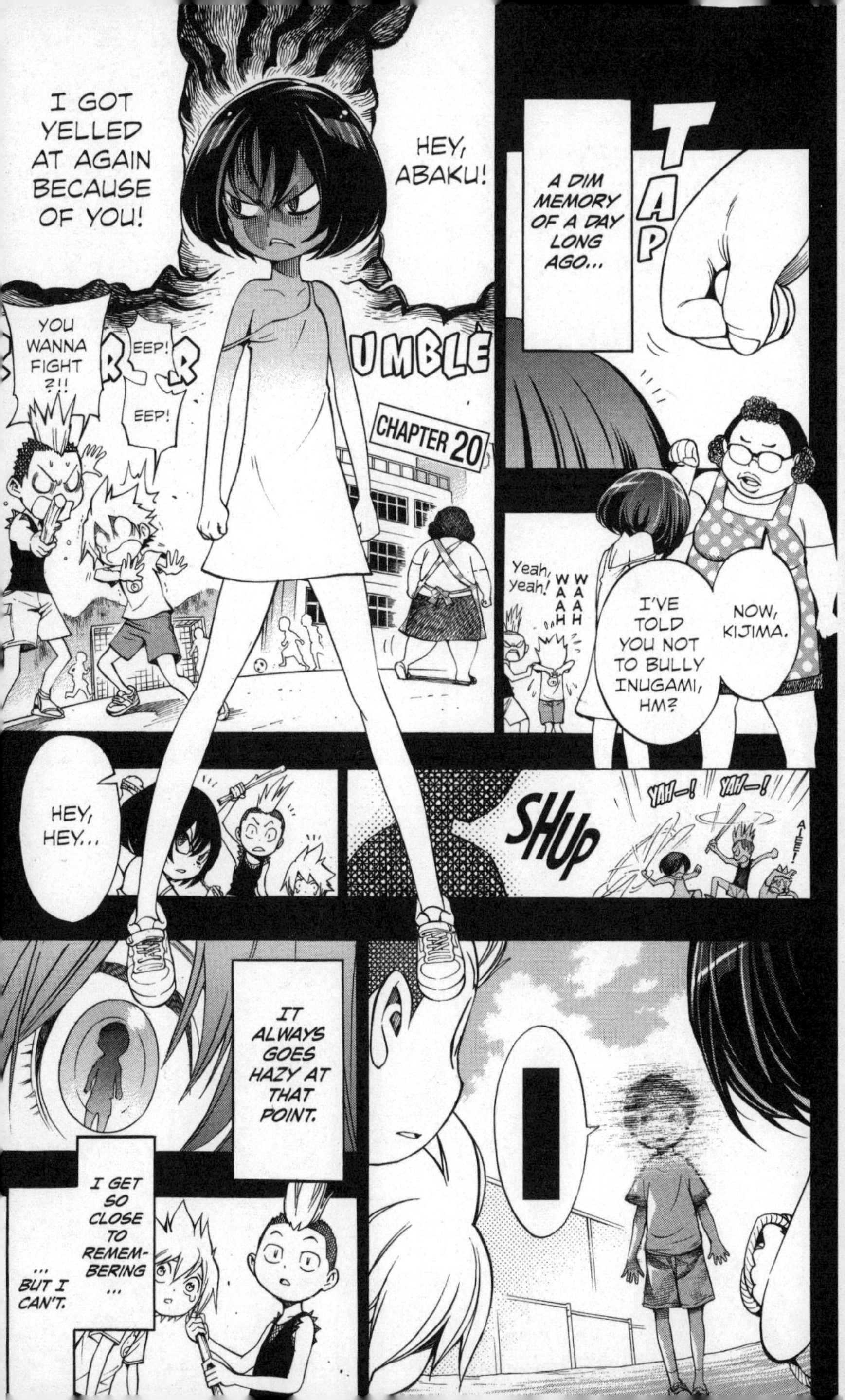

TAP
A DIM MEMORY OF A DAY LONG AGO...
NOW, KIJIMA.
I'VE TOLD YOU NOT TO BULLY INUGAMI, HM?
Yeah, yeah!
WAAH
WAAH
HEY, ABAKU!
I GOT YELLED AT AGAIN BECAUSE OF YOU!
UMBLE
CHAPTER 20
YOU WANNA FIGHT?!!
EEP!
EEP!
YAH—!
YAH—!
SHUP
AIEE!
HEY, HEY...
IT ALWAYS GOES HAZY AT THAT POINT.
I GET SO CLOSE TO REMEMBERING...
...BUT I CAN'T.

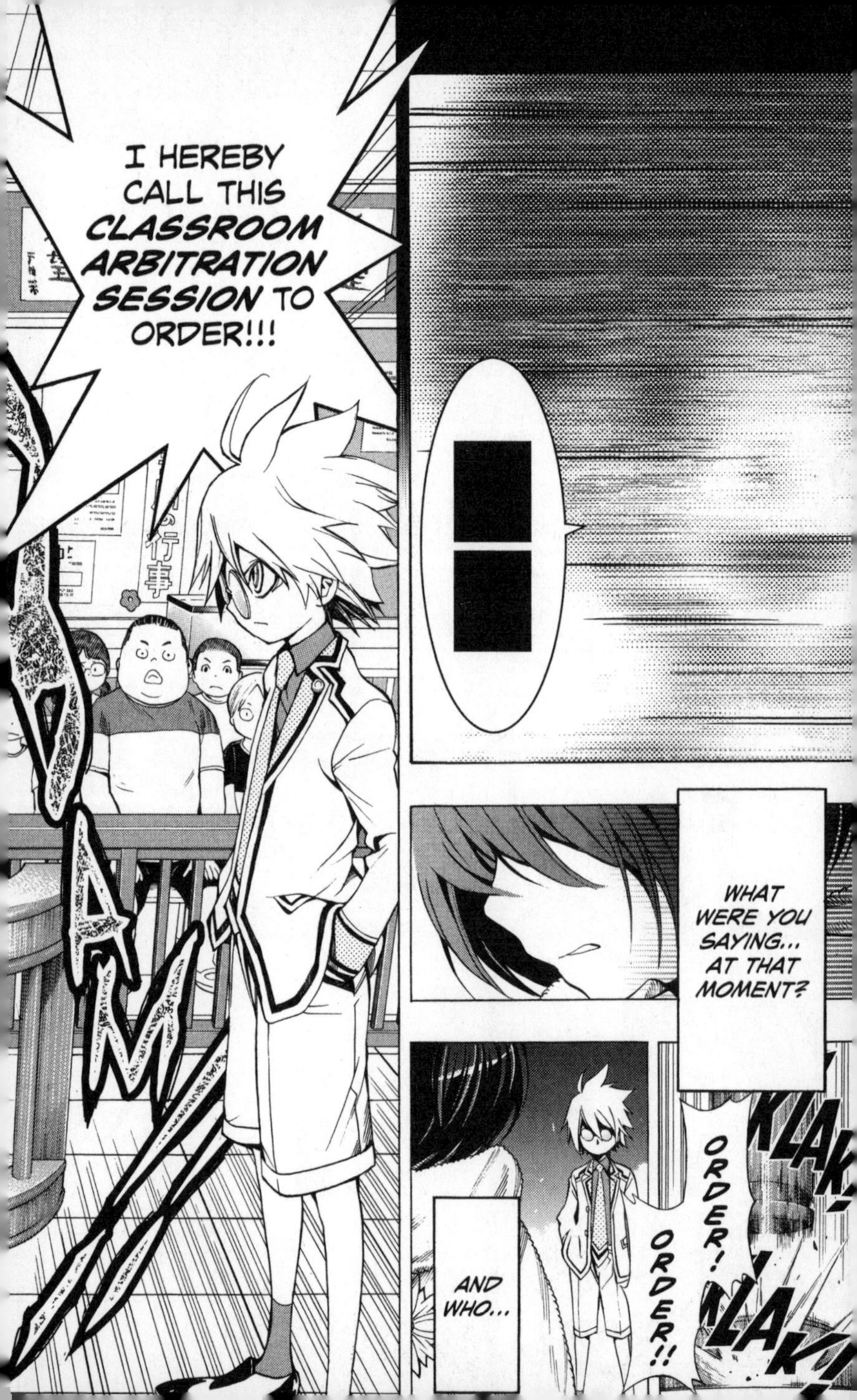
WHAT WERE YOU SAYING... AT THAT MOMENT?
KLAK!
ORDER!
ORDER!
ORDER!!
KLAK!
AND WHO...
I HEREBY CALL THIS CLASSROOM ARBITRATION SESSION TO ORDER!!!
BAM

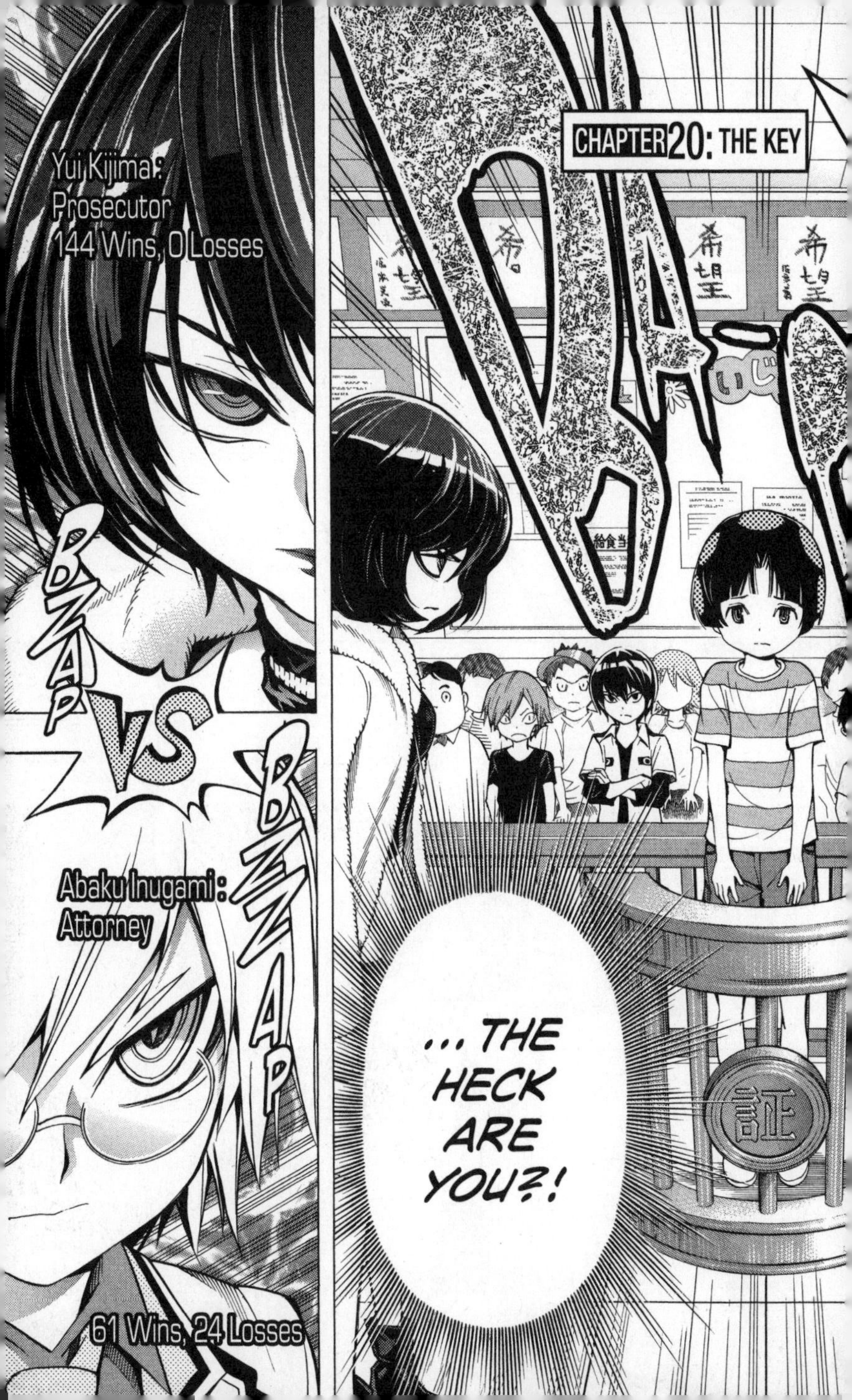
CHAPTER 20: THE KEY
... THE HECK ARE YOU?!
Yui Kijima : Prosecutor
144 Wins, 0 Losses
VS
Abaku Inugami : Attorney
61 Wins, 24 Losses

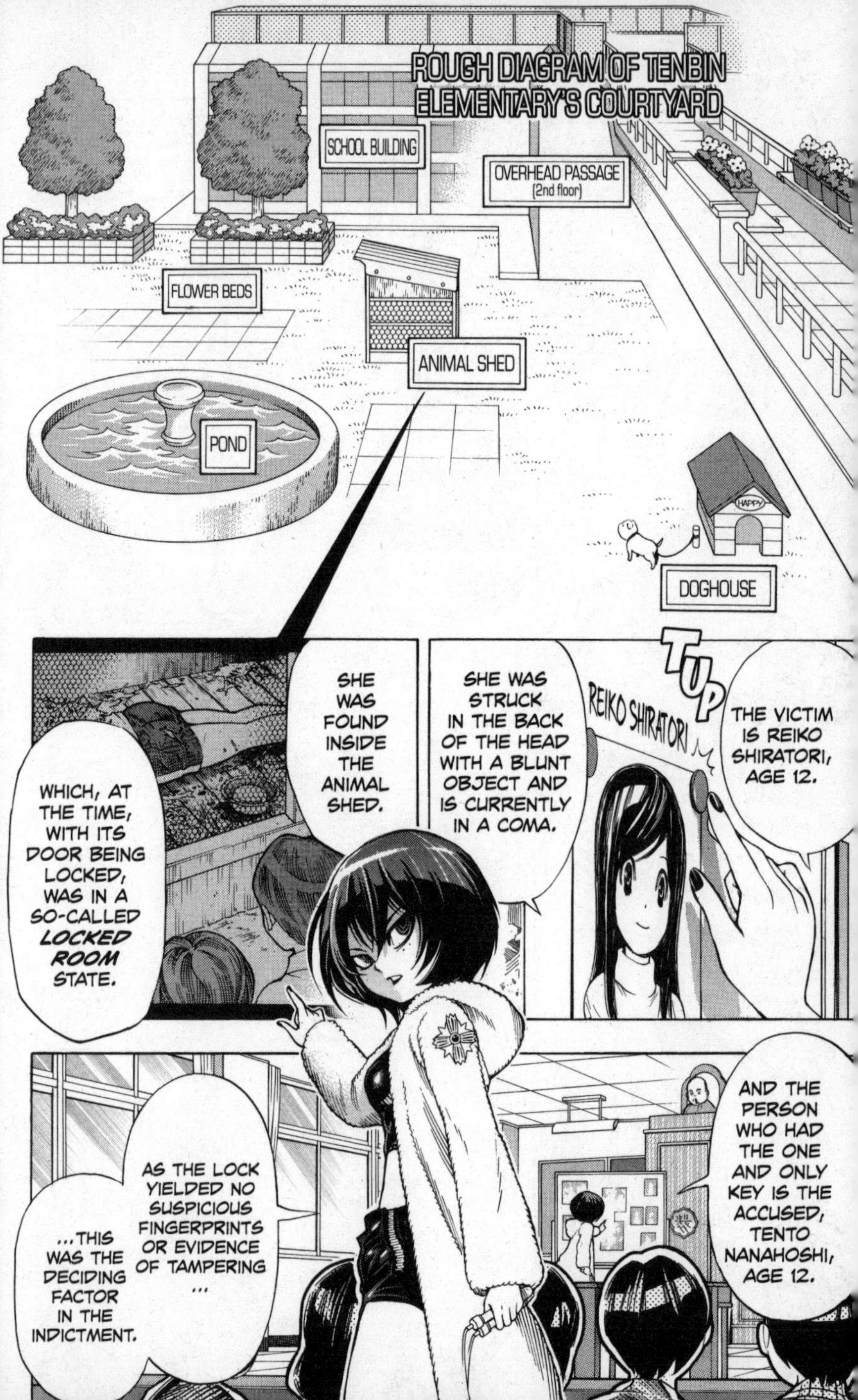
ROUGH DIAGRAM OF TENBIN ELEMENTARY'S COURTYARD
SCHOOL BUILDING
OVERHEAD PASSAGE (2nd floor)
FLOWER BEDS
ANIMAL SHED
POND
HAPPY
DOGHOUSE
TUP
REIKO SHIRATORI
THE VICTIM IS REIKO SHIRATORI, AGE 12.
SHE WAS STRUCK IN THE BACK OF THE HEAD WITH A BLUNT OBJECT AND IS CURRENTLY IN A COMA.
SHE WAS FOUND INSIDE THE ANIMAL SHED.
WHICH, AT THE TIME, WITH ITS DOOR BEING LOCKED, WAS IN A SO-CALLED *LOCKED ROOM* STATE.
AND THE PERSON WHO HAD THE ONE AND ONLY KEY IS THE ACCUSED, TENTO NANAHOSHI, AGE 12.
AS THE LOCK YIELDED NO SUSPICIOUS FINGERPRINTS OR EVIDENCE OF TAMPERING ...
...THIS WAS THE DECIDING FACTOR IN THE INDICTMENT.

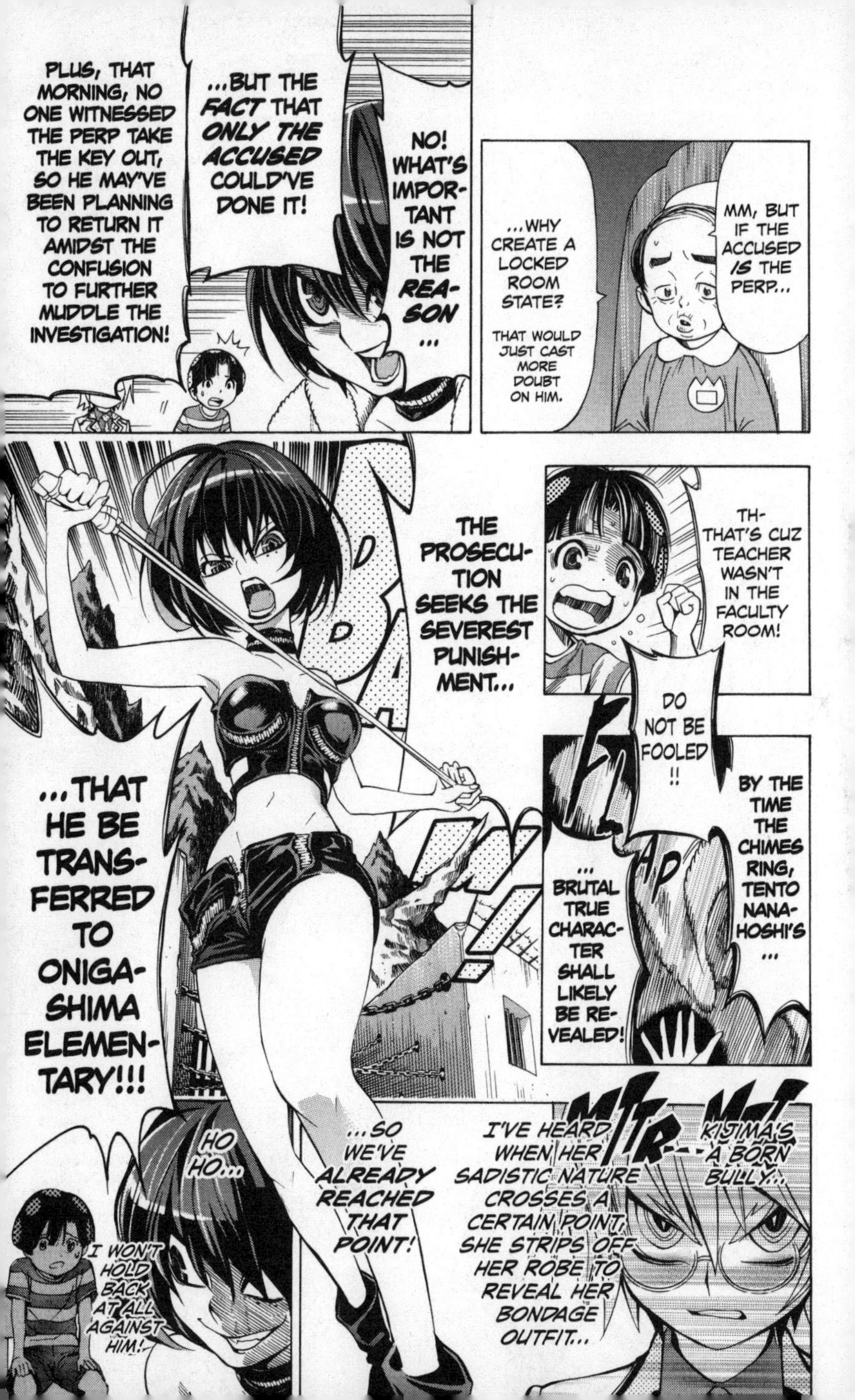
MM, BUT IF THE ACCUSED *IS* THE PERP...
...WHY CREATE A LOCKED ROOM STATE?
THAT WOULD JUST CAST MORE DOUBT ON HIM.
NO! WHAT'S IMPORTANT IS NOT THE *REASON*...
...BUT THE *FACT* THAT *ONLY THE ACCUSED* COULD'VE DONE IT!
PLUS, THAT MORNING, NO ONE WITNESSED THE PERP TAKE THE KEY OUT, SO HE MAY'VE BEEN PLANNING TO RETURN IT AMIDST THE CONFUSION TO FURTHER MUDDLE THE INVESTIGATION!
TH-THAT'S CUZ TEACHER WASN'T IN THE FACULTY ROOM!
DO NOT BE FOOLED!!
BY THE TIME THE CHIMES RING, TENTO NANAHOSHI'S...
...BRUTAL TRUE CHARACTER SHALL LIKELY BE REVEALED!
THE PROSECUTION SEEKS THE SEVEREST PUNISHMENT...
...THAT HE BE TRANSFERRED TO ONIGASHIMA ELEMENTARY!!!
KIJIMA'S A BORN BULLY...
I'VE HEARD WHEN HER SADISTIC NATURE CROSSES A CERTAIN POINT, SHE STRIPS OFF HER ROBE TO REVEAL HER BONDAGE OUTFIT...
...SO WE'VE ALREADY REACHED THAT POINT!
HO HO...
I WON'T HOLD BACK AT ALL AGAINST HIM!

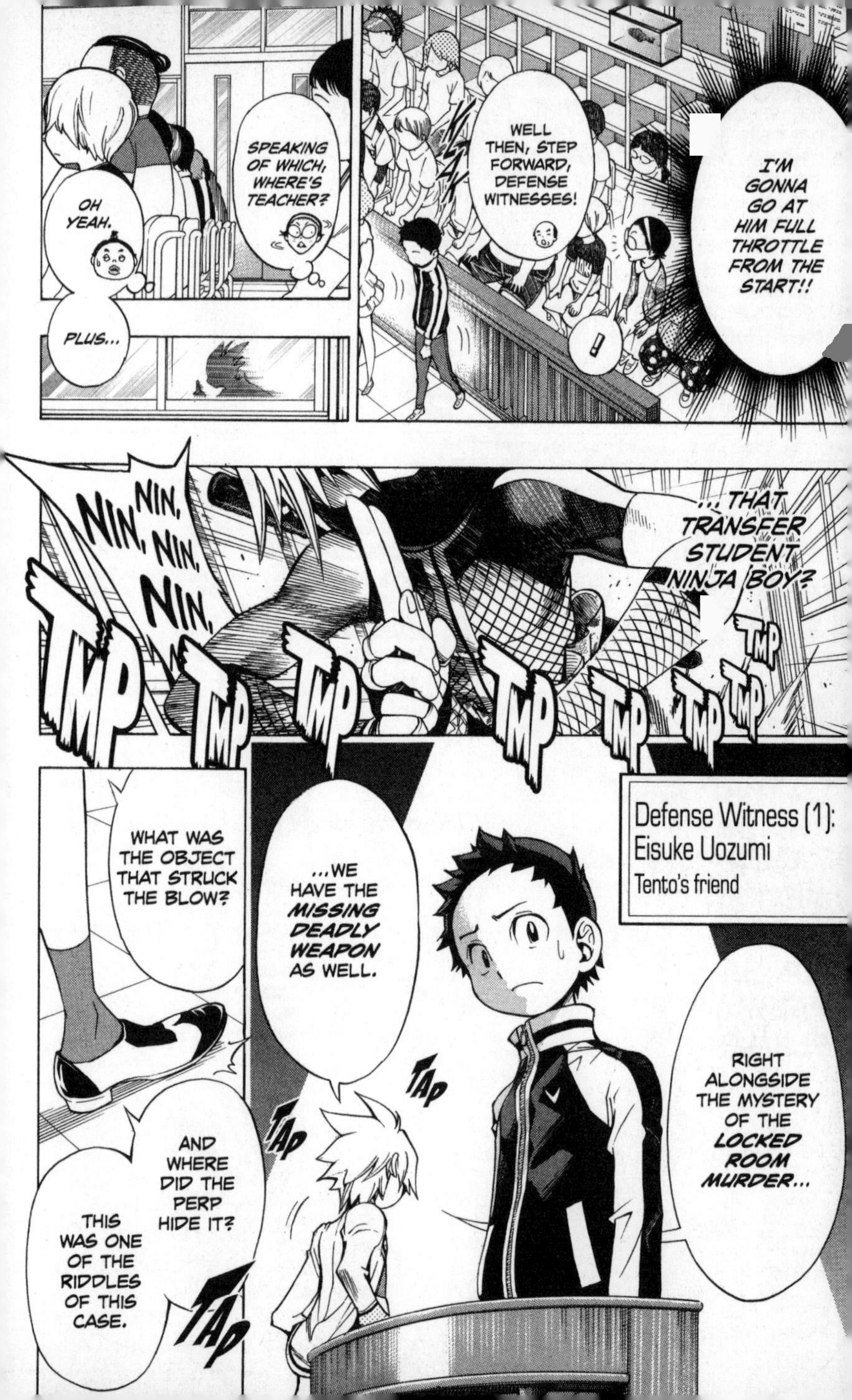
I'M GONNA GO AT HIM FULL THROTTLE FROM THE START!!
WELL THEN, STEP FORWARD, DEFENSE WITNESSES!
!
SPEAKING OF WHICH, WHERE'S TEACHER?
OH YEAH.
PLUS...
...THAT TRANSFER STUDENT NINJA BOY?
NIN, NIN, NIN, NIN,
TMP TMP TMP TMP TMP TMP TMP TMP
Defense Witness (1): Eisuke Uozumi
Tento's friend
RIGHT ALONGSIDE THE MYSTERY OF THE LOCKED ROOM MURDER...
...WE HAVE THE MISSING DEADLY WEAPON AS WELL.
TAP
TAP
TAP
WHAT WAS THE OBJECT THAT STRUCK THE BLOW?
AND WHERE DID THE PERP HIDE IT?
THIS WAS ONE OF THE RIDDLES OF THIS CASE.

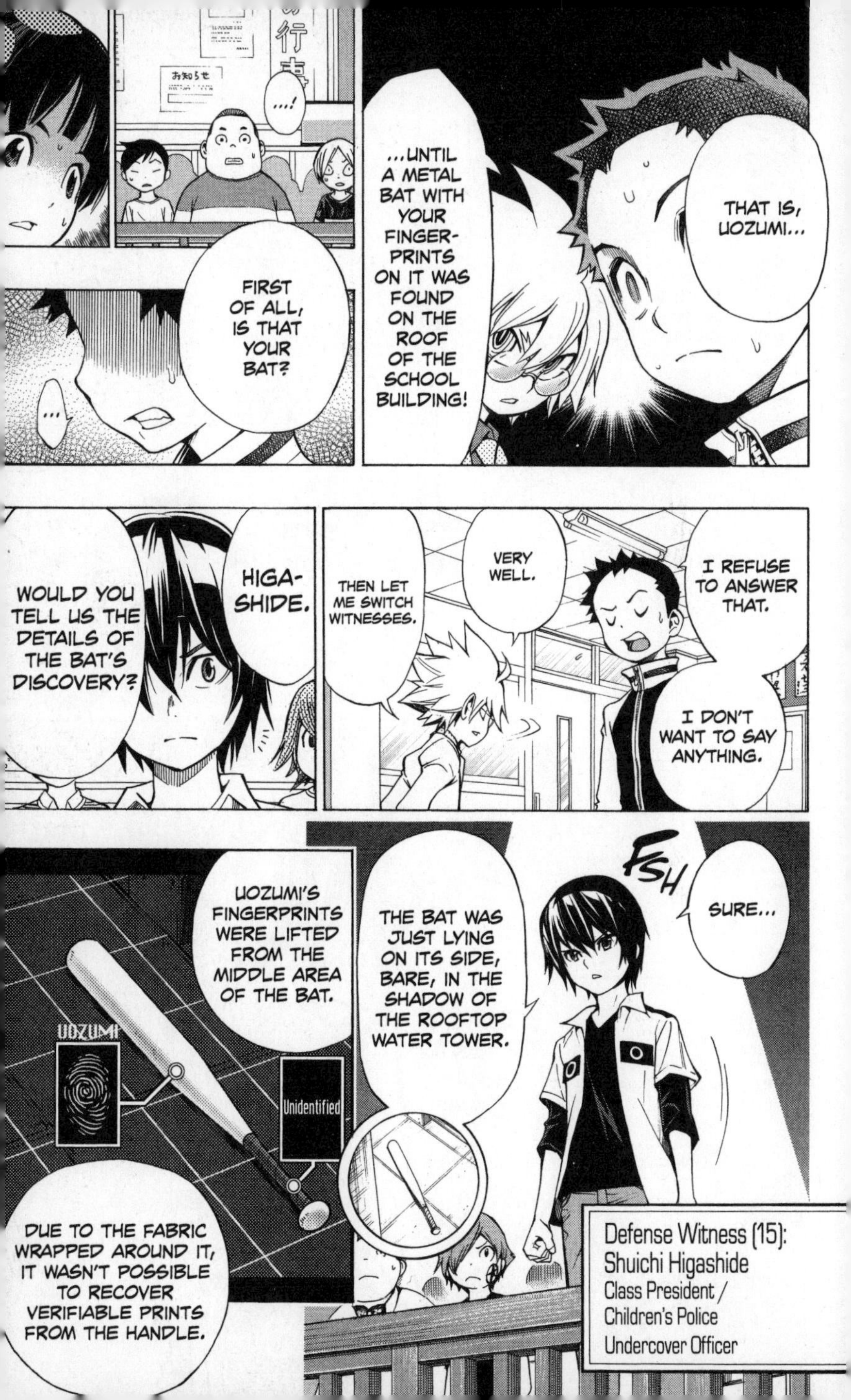
THAT IS, UOZUMI...
...UNTIL A METAL BAT WITH YOUR FINGERPRINTS ON IT WAS FOUND ON THE ROOF OF THE SCHOOL BUILDING!
....!
FIRST OF ALL, IS THAT YOUR BAT?
...
I REFUSE TO ANSWER THAT.
I DON'T WANT TO SAY ANYTHING.
VERY WELL.
THEN LET ME SWITCH WITNESSES.
HIGA-SHIDE.
WOULD YOU TELL US THE DETAILS OF THE BAT'S DISCOVERY?
FSH
SURE...
THE BAT WAS JUST LYING ON ITS SIDE, BARE, IN THE SHADOW OF THE ROOFTOP WATER TOWER.
Defense Witness (15): Shuichi Higashide
Class President / Children's Police Undercover Officer
UOZUMI'S FINGERPRINTS WERE LIFTED FROM THE MIDDLE AREA OF THE BAT.
UOZUMI
Unidentified
DUE TO THE FABRIC WRAPPED AROUND IT, IT WASN'T POSSIBLE TO RECOVER VERIFIABLE PRINTS FROM THE HANDLE.

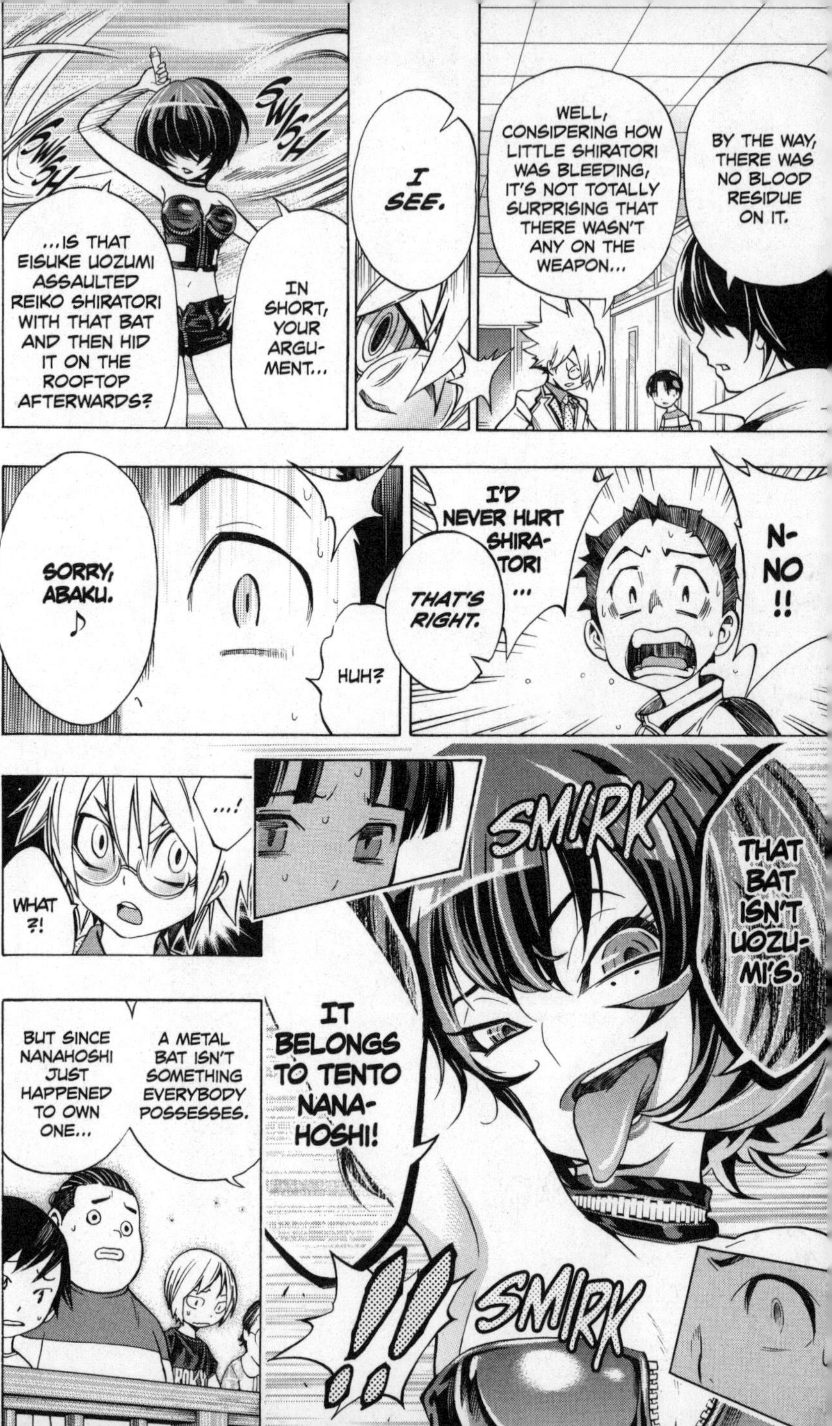
BY THE WAY, THERE WAS NO BLOOD RESIDUE ON IT.
WELL, CONSIDERING HOW LITTLE SHIRATORI WAS BLEEDING, IT'S NOT TOTALLY SURPRISING THAT THERE WASN'T ANY ON THE WEAPON...
I SEE.
SWISH
SWISH
IN SHORT, YOUR ARGUMENT...
...IS THAT EISUKE UOZUMI ASSAULTED REIKO SHIRATORI WITH THAT BAT AND THEN HID IT ON THE ROOFTOP AFTERWARDS?
N-NO!!
I'D NEVER HURT SHIRATORI...
THAT'S RIGHT.
HUH?
SORRY, ABAKU. ♪
SMIRK
THAT BAT ISN'T UOZUMI'S.
IT BELONGS TO TENTO NANAHOSHI!
SMIRK
...!
WHAT?!
A METAL BAT ISN'T SOMETHING EVERYBODY POSSESSES.
BUT SINCE NANAHOSHI JUST HAPPENED TO OWN ONE...

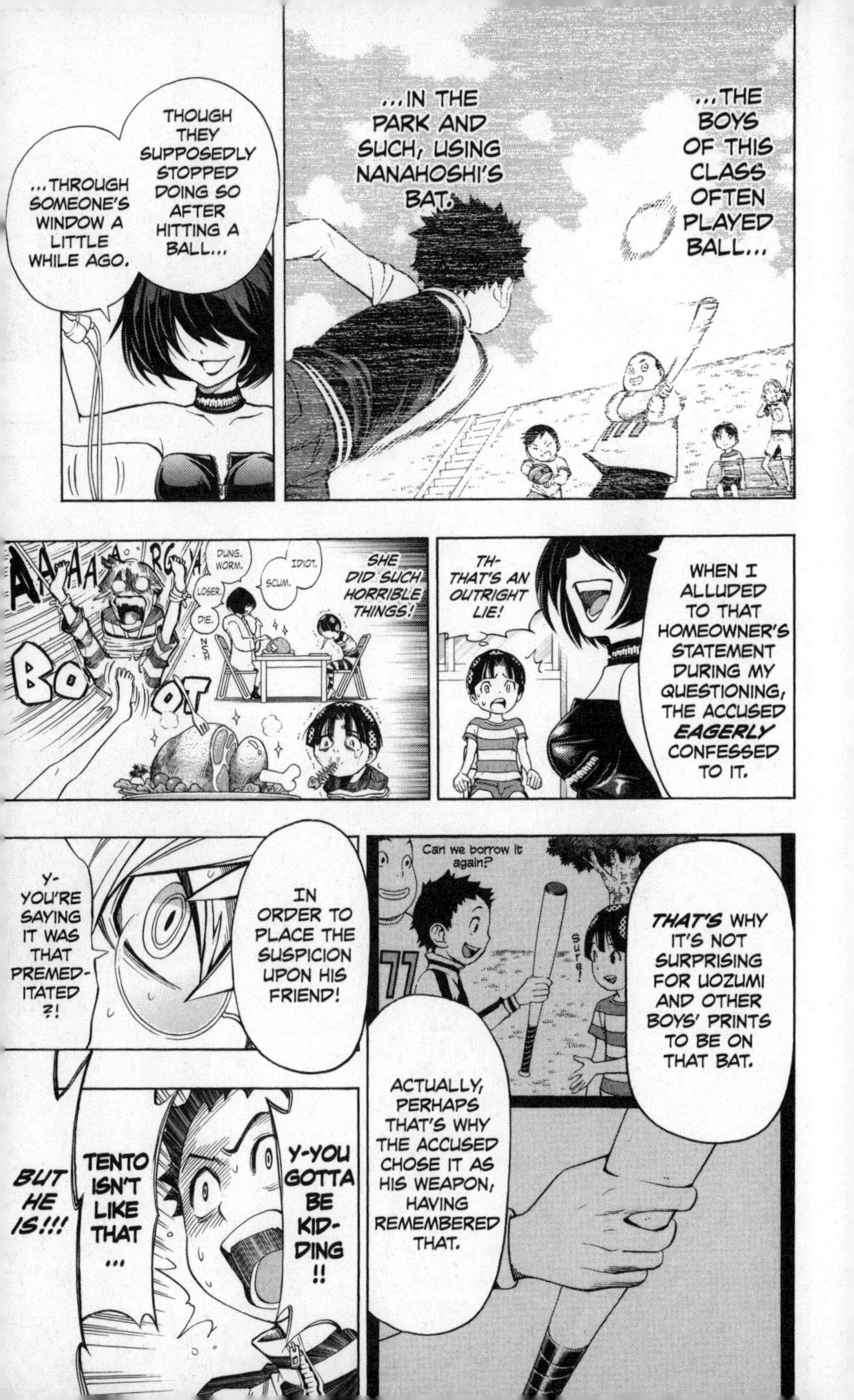
...THE BOYS OF THIS CLASS OFTEN PLAYED BALL...
...IN THE PARK AND SUCH, USING NANAHOSHI'S BAT.
THOUGH THEY SUPPOSEDLY STOPPED DOING SO AFTER HITTING A BALL...
...THROUGH SOMEONE'S WINDOW A LITTLE WHILE AGO.
WHEN I ALLUDED TO THAT HOMEOWNER'S STATEMENT DURING MY QUESTIONING, THE ACCUSED *EAGERLY* CONFESSED TO IT.
TH- THAT'S AN OUTRIGHT LIE!
SHE DID SUCH HORRIBLE THINGS!
IDIOT.
DUNG. WORM.
SCUM.
LOSER.
DIE.
NSH
AAAAARGH
BOOT
Can we borrow it again?
Sure!
THAT'S WHY IT'S NOT SURPRISING FOR UOZUMI AND OTHER BOYS' PRINTS TO BE ON THAT BAT.
ACTUALLY, PERHAPS THAT'S WHY THE ACCUSED CHOSE IT AS HIS WEAPON, HAVING REMEMBERED THAT.
IN ORDER TO PLACE THE SUSPICION UPON HIS FRIEND!
Y- YOU'RE SAYING IT WAS THAT PREMED-ITATED?!
Y-YOU GOTTA BE KID-DING!!
TENTO ISN'T LIKE THAT...
BUT HE IS!!!

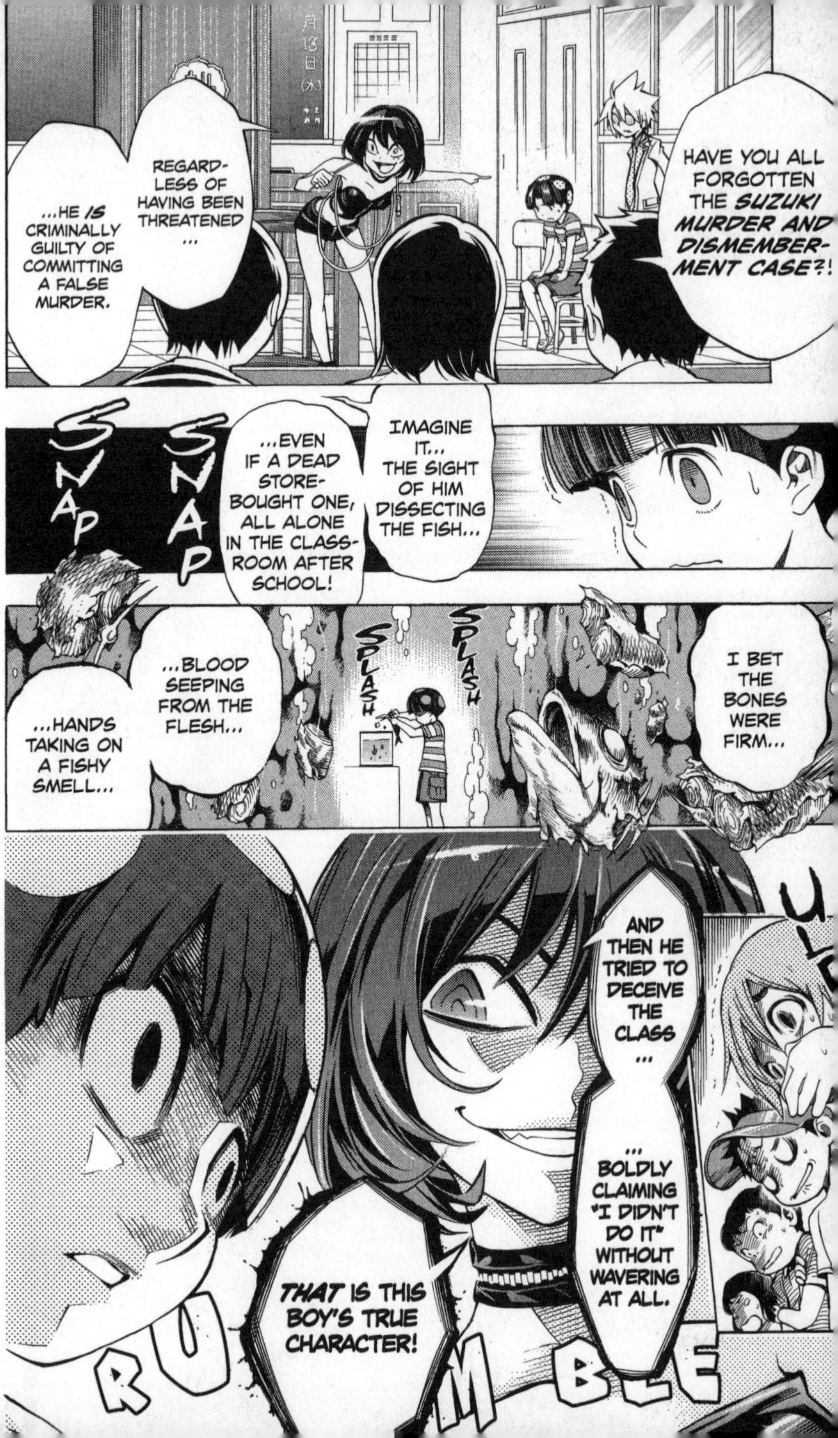
HAVE YOU ALL FORGOTTEN THE *SUZUKI MURDER AND DISMEMBERMENT CASE*?!
REGARDLESS OF HAVING BEEN THREATENED...
...HE *IS* CRIMINALLY GUILTY OF COMMITTING A FALSE MURDER.
IMAGINE IT... THE SIGHT OF HIM DISSECTING THE FISH...
...EVEN IF A DEAD STORE-BOUGHT ONE, ALL ALONE IN THE CLASSROOM AFTER SCHOOL!
SNAP
SNAP
I BET THE BONES WERE FIRM...
SPLASH
SPLASH
...BLOOD SEEPING FROM THE FLESH...
...HANDS TAKING ON A FISHY SMELL...
AND THEN HE TRIED TO DECEIVE THE CLASS...
...BOLDLY CLAIMING "I DIDN'T DO IT" WITHOUT WAVERING AT ALL.
THAT IS THIS BOY'S TRUE CHARACTER!
RUMBLE

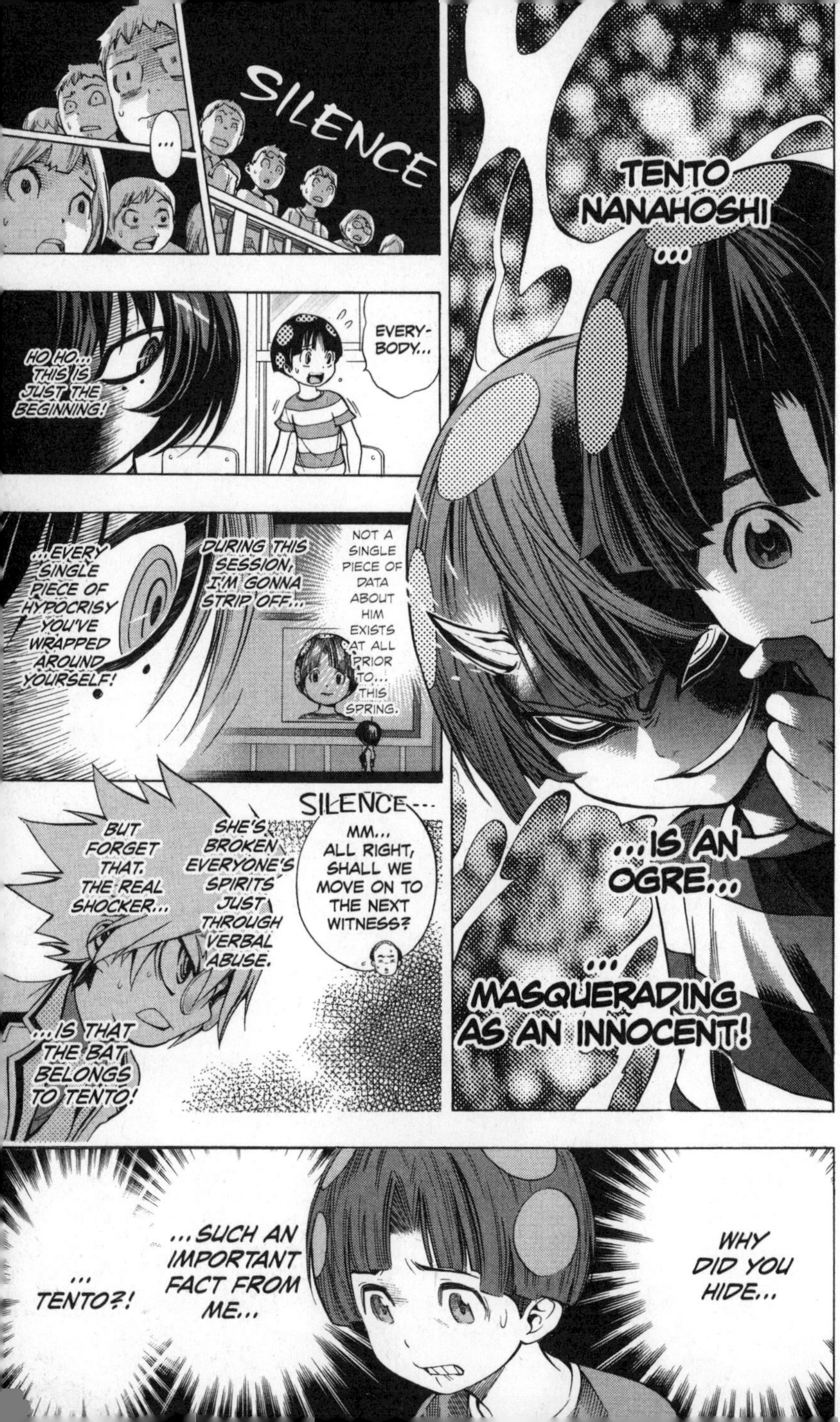
TENTO NANAHOSHI ...
...IS AN OGRE...
... MASQUERADING AS AN INNOCENT!
SILENCE
...
EVERY-BODY...
HO HO... THIS IS JUST THE BEGINNING!
NOT A SINGLE PIECE OF DATA ABOUT HIM EXISTS AT ALL PRIOR TO... THIS SPRING.
DURING THIS SESSION, I'M GONNA STRIP OFF...
...EVERY SINGLE PIECE OF HYPOCRISY YOU'VE WRAPPED AROUND YOURSELF!
SILENCE---
MM... ALL RIGHT, SHALL WE MOVE ON TO THE NEXT WITNESS?
SHE'S BROKEN EVERYONE'S SPIRITS JUST THROUGH VERBAL ABUSE.
BUT FORGET THAT. THE REAL SHOCKER...
...IS THAT THE BAT BELONGS TO TENTO!
WHY DID YOU HIDE...
...SUCH AN IMPORTANT FACT FROM ME...
... TENTO?!

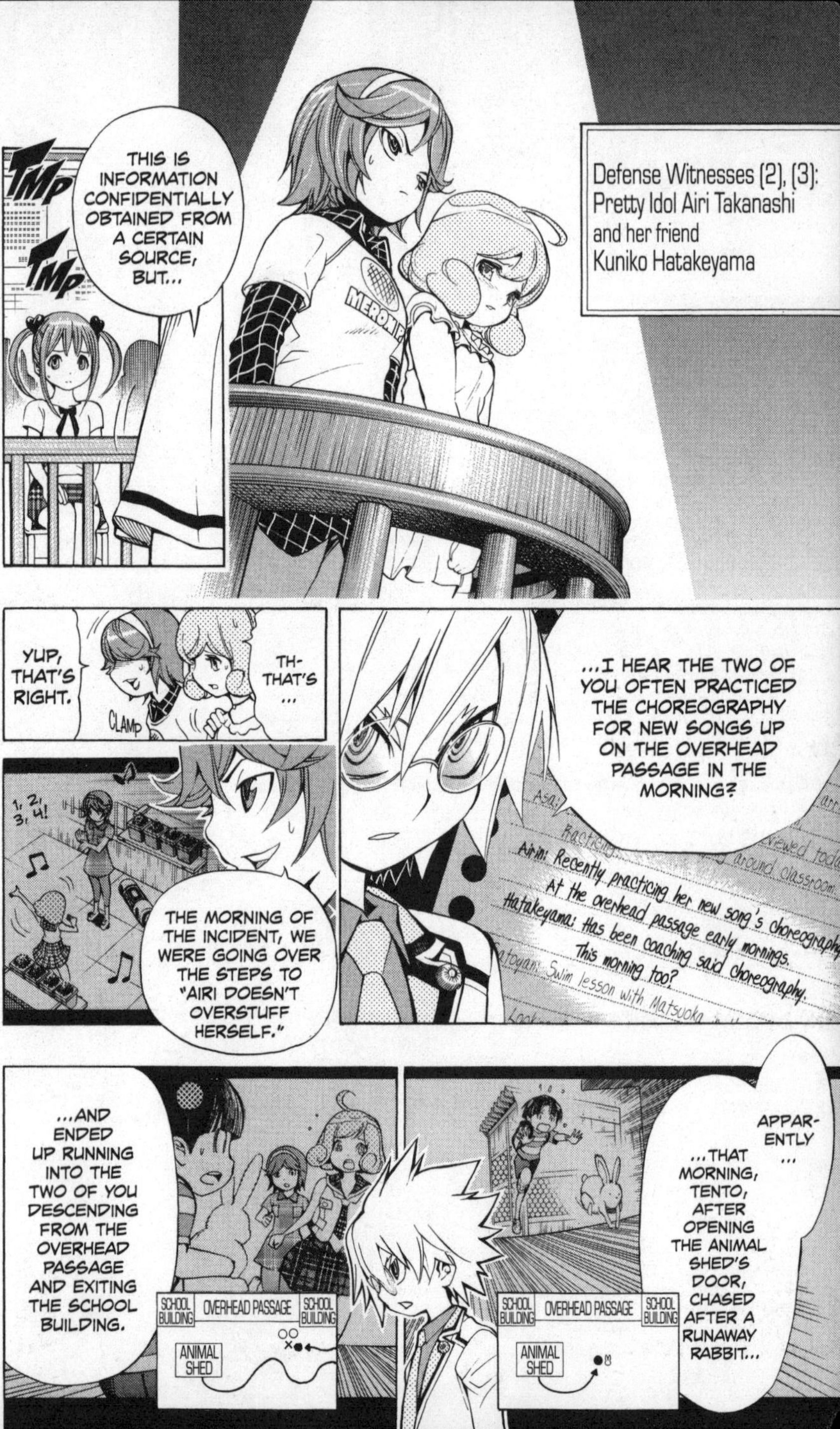
Defense Witnesses (2), (3): Pretty Idol Airi Takanashi and her friend Kuniko Hatakeyama
THIS IS INFORMATION CONFIDENTIALLY OBTAINED FROM A CERTAIN SOURCE, BUT...
TMP
TMP
...I HEAR THE TWO OF YOU OFTEN PRACTICED THE CHOREOGRAPHY FOR NEW SONGS UP ON THE OVERHEAD PASSAGE IN THE MORNING?
Airi: Recently practicing her new song's choreography
At the overhead passage early mornings.
Hatakeyama: Has been coaching said choreography.
This morning too?
Swim lesson with Matsuoka
TH-THAT'S ...
YUP, THAT'S RIGHT.
CLAMP
1, 2, 3, 4!
THE MORNING OF THE INCIDENT, WE WERE GOING OVER THE STEPS TO "AIRI DOESN'T OVERSTUFF HERSELF."
APPARENTLY ...
...THAT MORNING, TENTO, AFTER OPENING THE ANIMAL SHED'S DOOR, CHASED AFTER A RUNAWAY RABBIT...
SCHOOL BUILDING
OVERHEAD PASSAGE
SCHOOL BUILDING
ANIMAL SHED
...AND ENDED UP RUNNING INTO THE TWO OF YOU DESCENDING FROM THE OVERHEAD PASSAGE AND EXITING THE SCHOOL BUILDING.
SCHOOL BUILDING
OVERHEAD PASSAGE
SCHOOL BUILDING
ANIMAL SHED

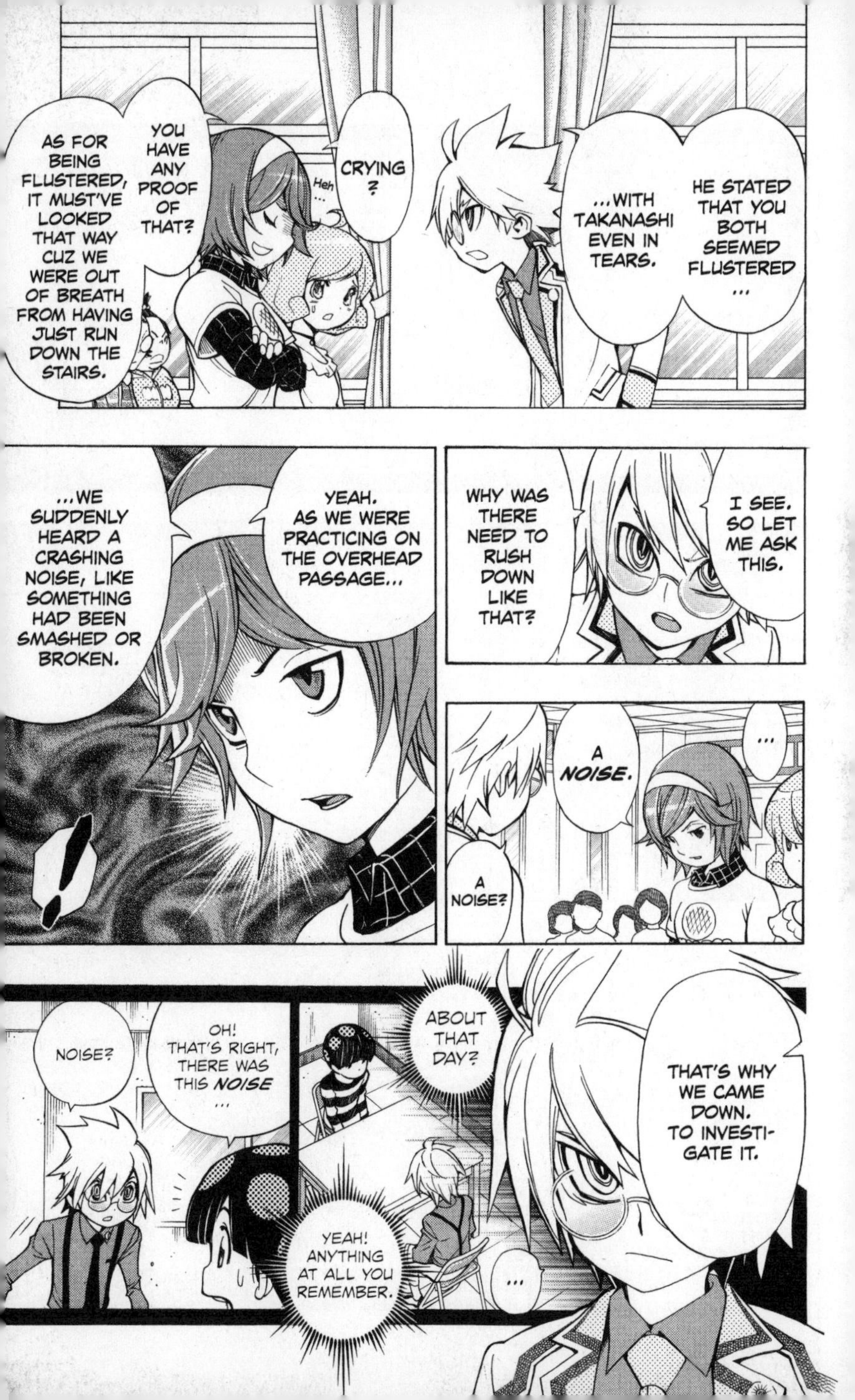
HE STATED THAT YOU BOTH SEEMED FLUSTERED ...
...WITH TAKANASHI EVEN IN TEARS.
CRYING?
Heh ...
YOU HAVE ANY PROOF OF THAT?
AS FOR BEING FLUSTERED, IT MUST'VE LOOKED THAT WAY CUZ WE WERE OUT OF BREATH FROM HAVING JUST RUN DOWN THE STAIRS.
I SEE. SO LET ME ASK THIS.
WHY WAS THERE NEED TO RUSH DOWN LIKE THAT?
...
A *NOISE*.
A NOISE?
YEAH. AS WE WERE PRACTICING ON THE OVERHEAD PASSAGE...
...WE SUDDENLY HEARD A CRASHING NOISE, LIKE SOMETHING HAD BEEN SMASHED OR BROKEN.
!
THAT'S WHY WE CAME DOWN. TO INVESTIGATE IT.
...
ABOUT THAT DAY?
YEAH! ANYTHING AT ALL YOU REMEMBER.
OH! THAT'S RIGHT, THERE WAS THIS *NOISE* ...
NOISE?

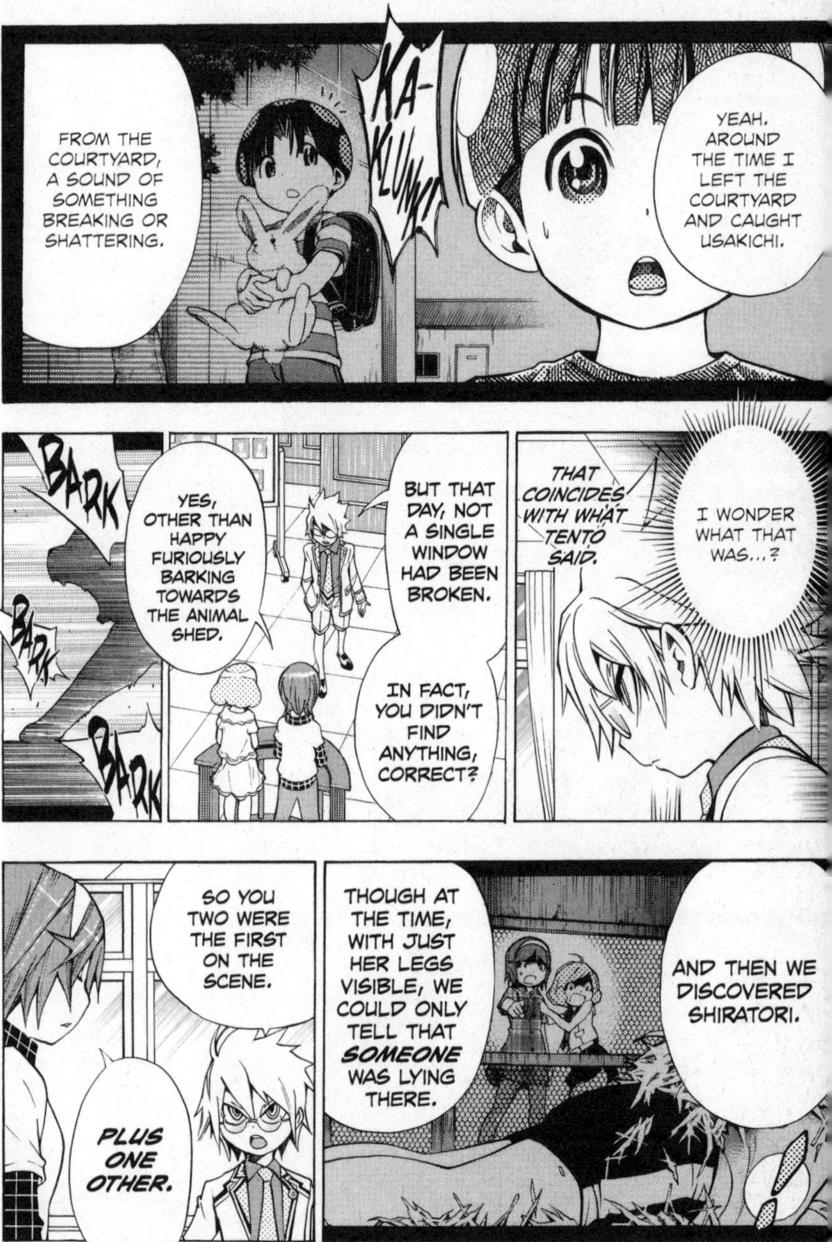
YEAH. AROUND THE TIME I LEFT THE COURTYARD AND CAUGHT USAKICHI.
KA-KLUNK!
FROM THE COURTYARD, A SOUND OF SOMETHING BREAKING OR SHATTERING.
I WONDER WHAT THAT WAS...?
THAT COINCIDES WITH WHAT TENTO SAID.
BUT THAT DAY, NOT A SINGLE WINDOW HAD BEEN BROKEN.
YES, OTHER THAN HAPPY FURIOUSLY BARKING TOWARDS THE ANIMAL SHED.
IN FACT, YOU DIDN'T FIND ANYTHING, CORRECT?
BARK
BARK
BARK
AND THEN WE DISCOVERED SHIRATORI.
THOUGH AT THE TIME, WITH JUST HER LEGS VISIBLE, WE COULD ONLY TELL THAT ***SOMEONE*** WAS LYING THERE.
SO YOU TWO WERE THE FIRST ON THE SCENE.
PLUS ONE OTHER.

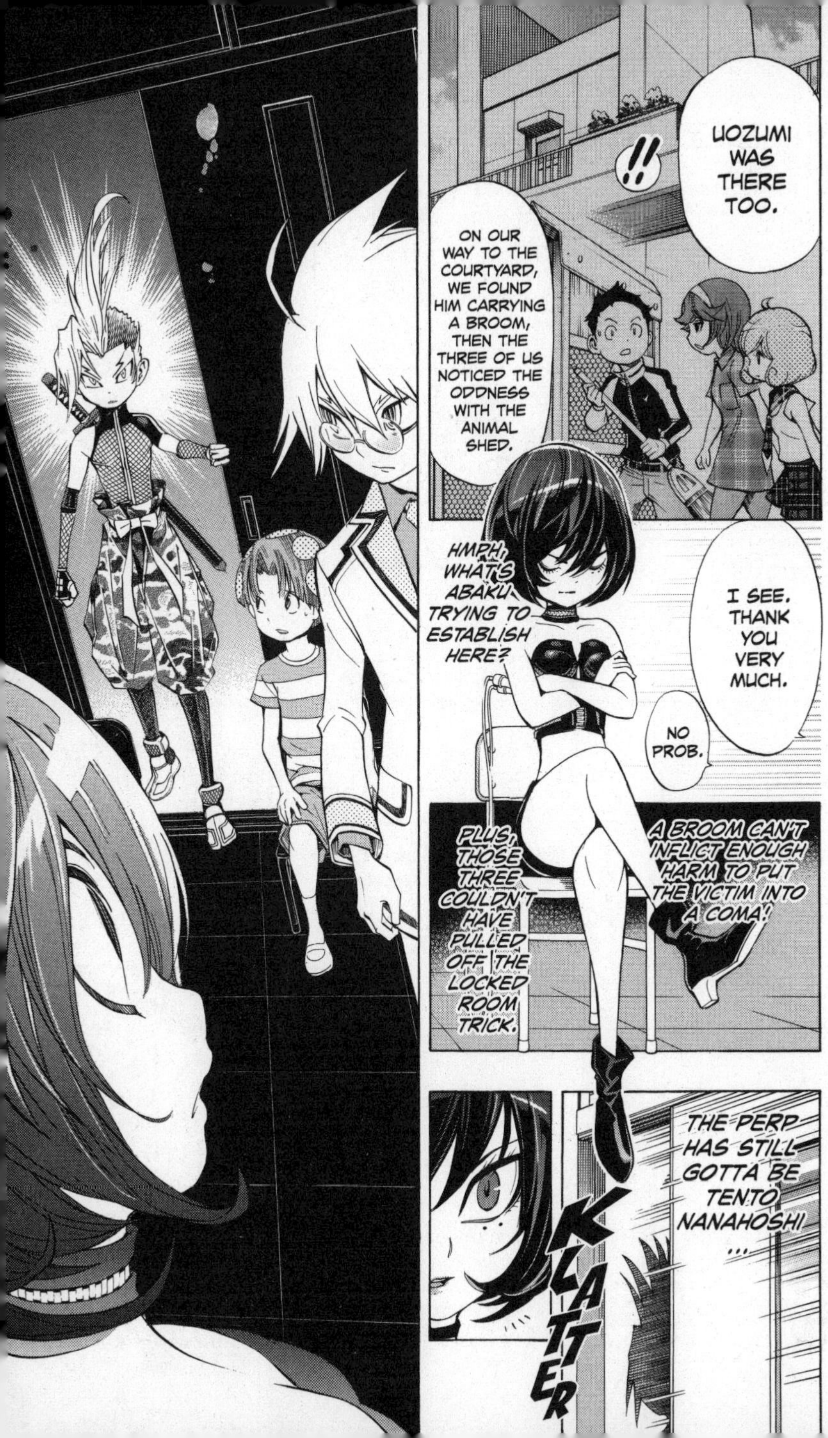
UOZUMI WAS THERE TOO.
!!
ON OUR WAY TO THE COURTYARD, WE FOUND HIM CARRYING A BROOM, THEN THE THREE OF US NOTICED THE ODDNESS WITH THE ANIMAL SHED.
I SEE. THANK YOU VERY MUCH.
NO PROB.
HMPH, WHAT'S ABAKU TRYING TO ESTABLISH HERE?
A BROOM CAN'T INFLICT ENOUGH HARM TO PUT THE VICTIM INTO A COMA!
PLUS, THOSE THREE COULDN'T HAVE PULLED OFF THE LOCKED ROOM TRICK.
THE PERP HAS STILL GOTTA BE TENTO NANAHOSHI...
KLATTER

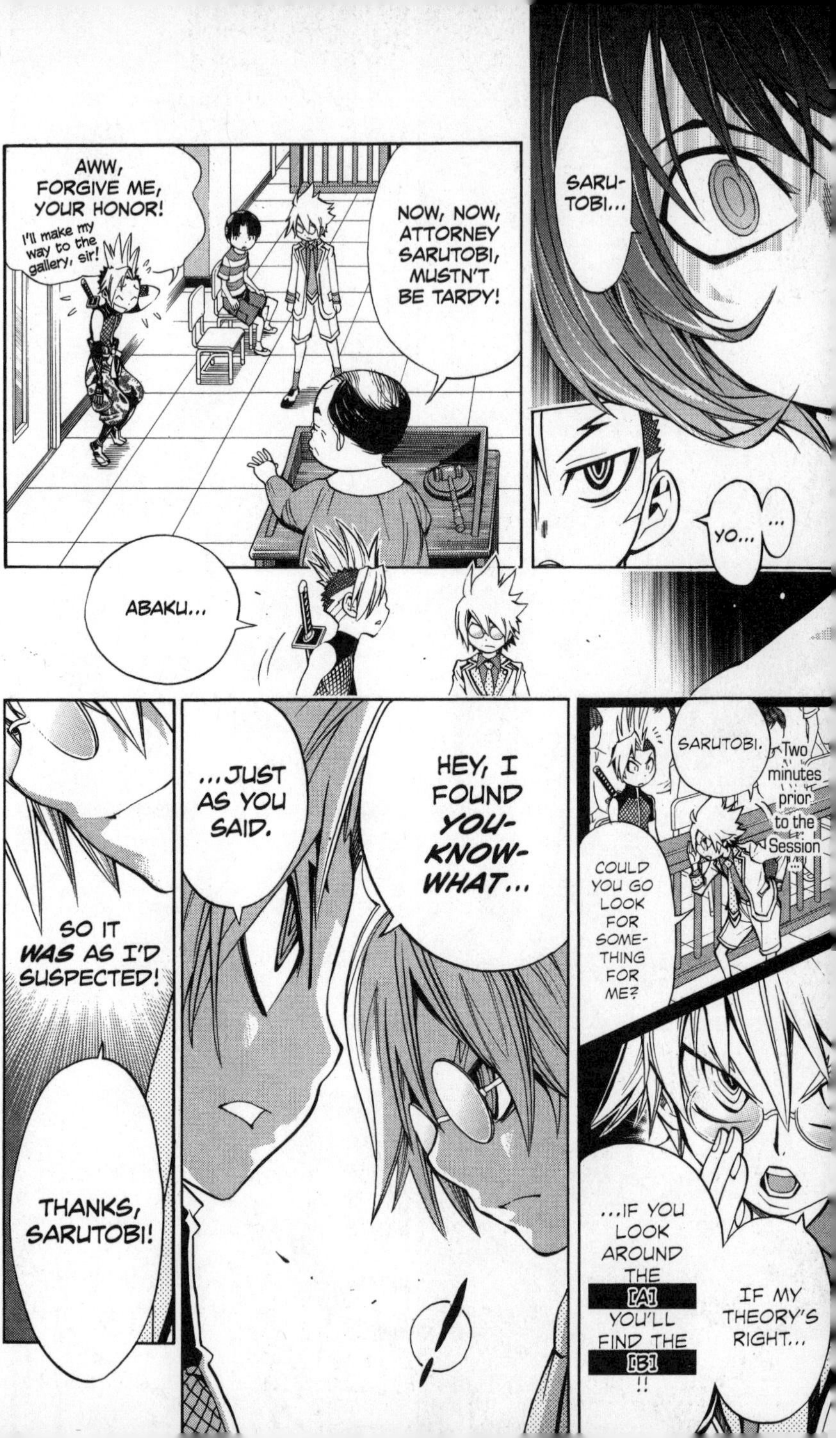
SARU-TOBI...
YO...
...
NOW, NOW, ATTORNEY SARUTOBI, MUSTN'T BE TARDY!
AWW, FORGIVE ME, YOUR HONOR!
I'll make my way to the gallery, sir!
ABAKU...
Two minutes prior to the Session...
SARUTOBI.
COULD YOU GO LOOK FOR SOME-THING FOR ME?
IF MY THEORY'S RIGHT...
...IF YOU LOOK AROUND THE [A] YOU'LL FIND THE [B]!!
HEY, I FOUND *YOU-KNOW-WHAT*...
...JUST AS YOU SAID.
!
SO IT *WAS* AS I'D SUSPECTED!
THANKS, SARUTOBI!

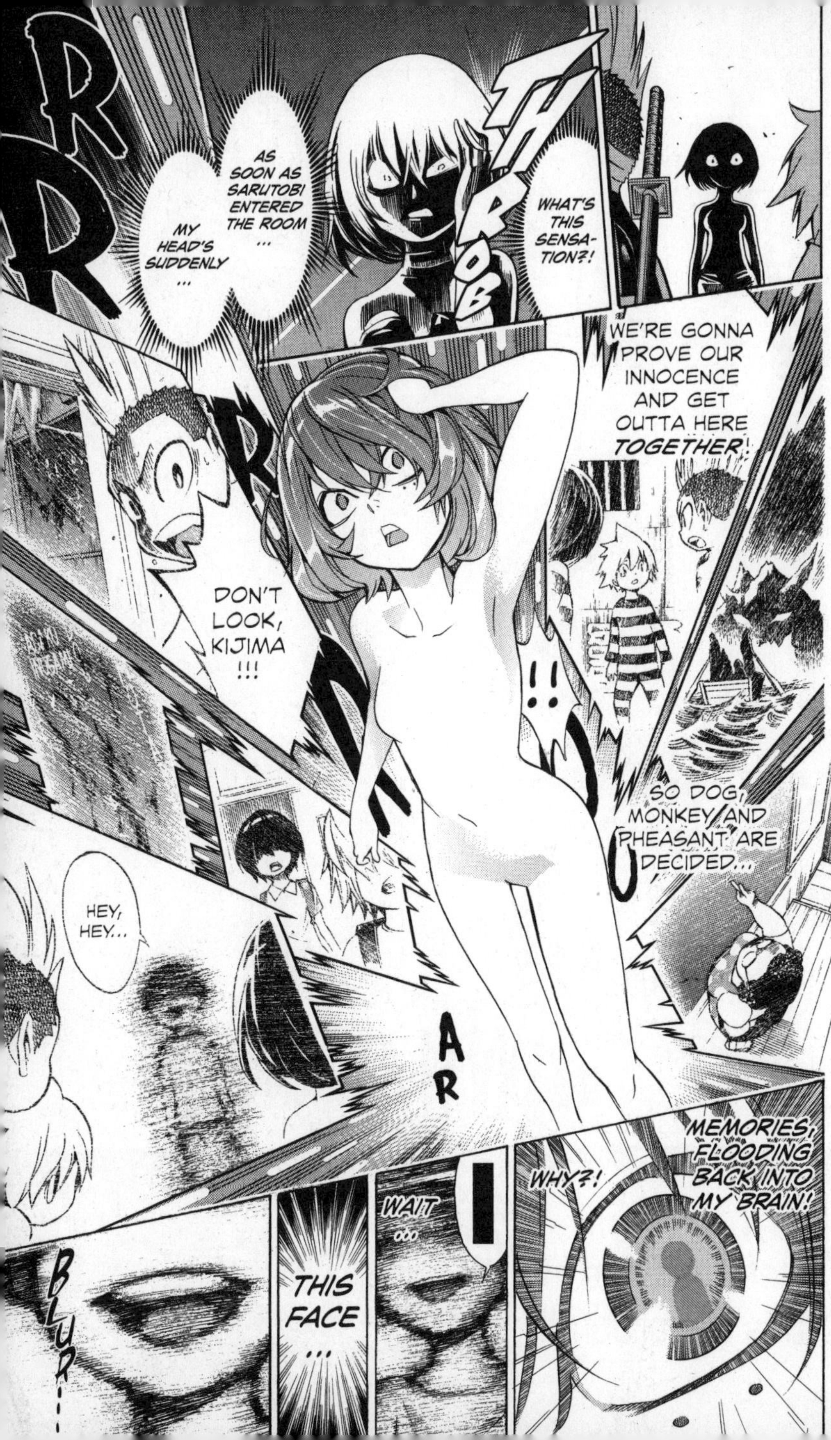
WHAT'S THIS SENSATION?!
THROB
AS SOON AS SARUTOBI ENTERED THE ROOM ...
MY HEAD'S SUDDENLY ...
WE'RE GONNA PROVE OUR INNOCENCE AND GET OUTTA HERE TOGETHER!
!!
DON'T LOOK, KIJIMA!!!
SO DOG, MONKEY AND PHEASANT ARE DECIDED...
HEY, HEY...
MEMORIES, FLOODING BACK INTO MY BRAIN!
WHY?!
WAIT ...
THIS FACE ...
BLUR...

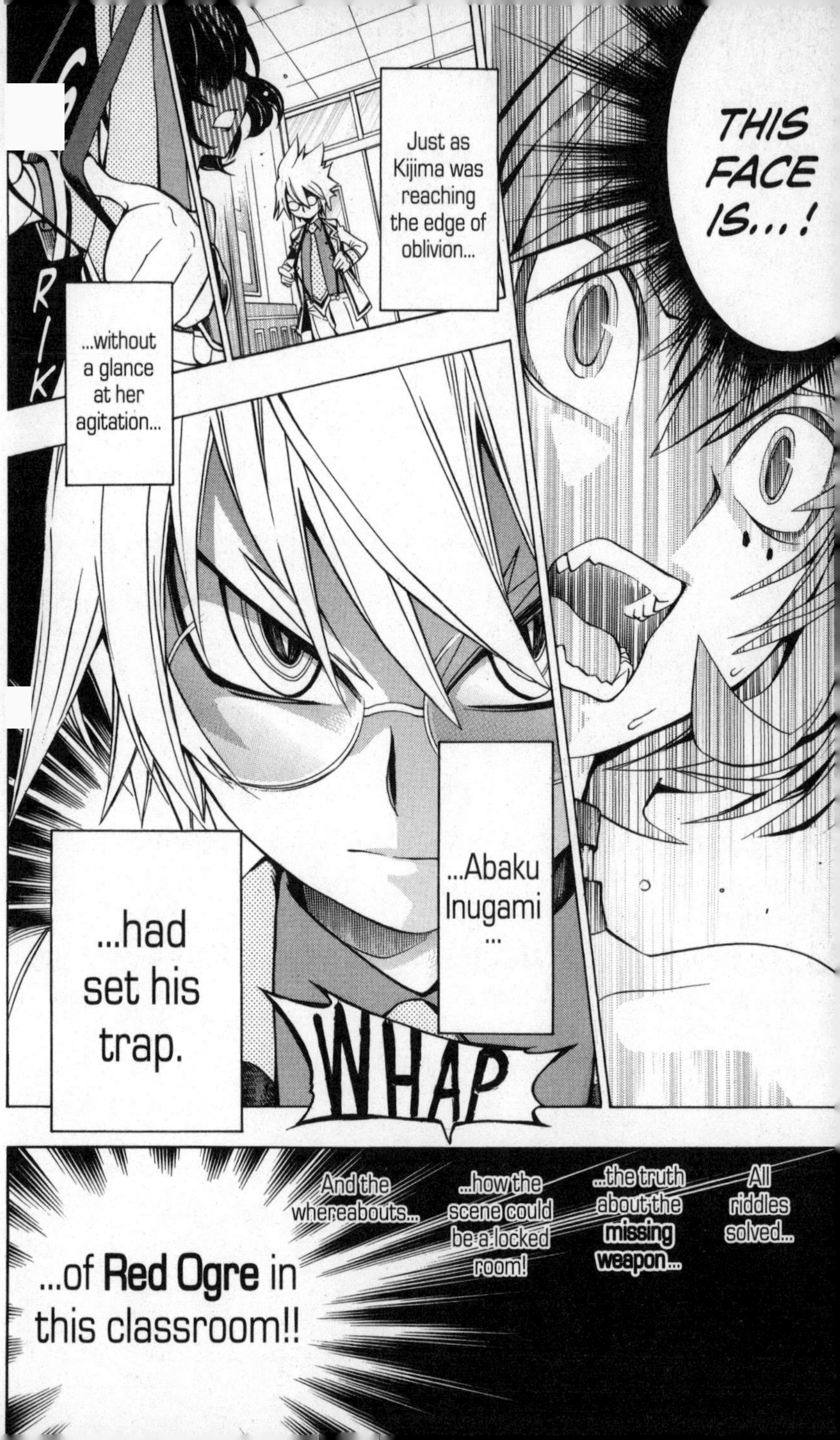
THIS FACE IS...!
Just as Kijima was reaching the edge of oblivion...
...without a glance at her agitation...
...Abaku Inugami...
...had set his trap.
WHAP
All riddles solved...
...the truth about the **missing weapon**...
...how the scene could be a locked room!
And the whereabouts...
...of **Red Ogre** in this classroom!!

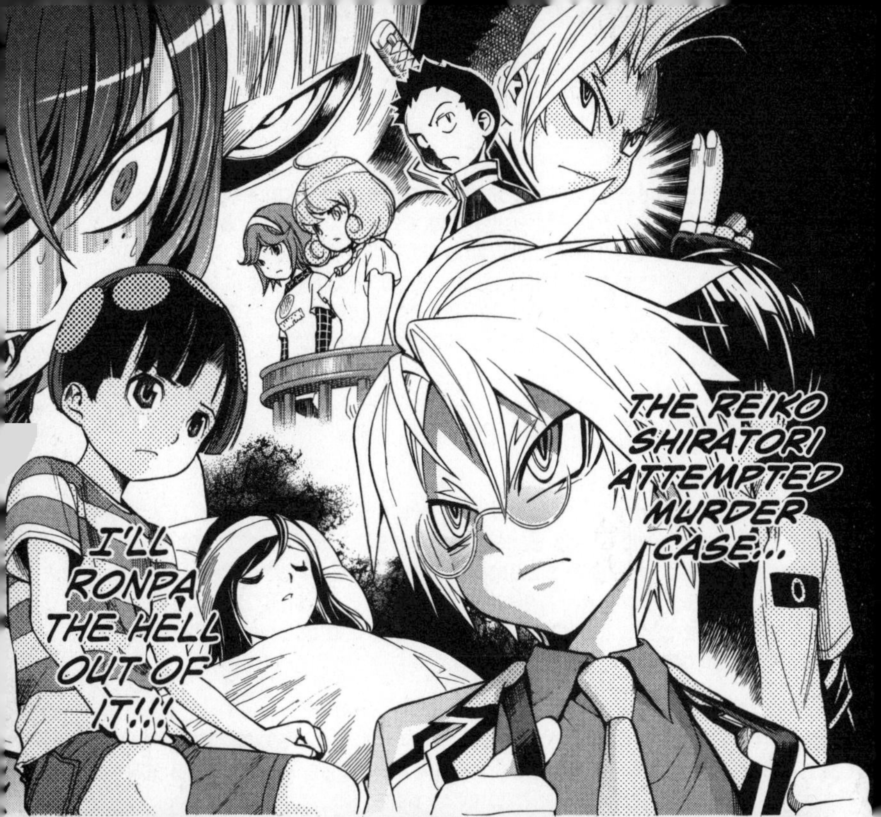
THE REIKO SHIRATORI ATTEMPTED MURDER CASE...
I'LL RONPA THE HELL OUT OF IT!!!

Abaku Inugami would later state that "the identity of the perp in this case was the saddest one yet."

Homework from Abaku Inugami

<Q> Please fill in the following blanks.

Abaku's line on page 82, panel 5, "If my theory's right, if you look around the **A** you'll find the **B**!"

<A>

A		B	

④ Revision

The most intense work begins after the storyboard is done. I have my editor look at the storyboard either directly or by fax and have him mark the problems, and then I fix them. It is extremely rare that the storyboard goes through without any revisions. If I end up redoing about ten pages, the storyboard that I've worked so hard on is pretty much gone. However, I trust that it'll end up even more fun to read, so I hunker down and fix it.

⑤~ Completion

Once the storyboard is done, I add on a single page of supplementary written notes of things I want Obata Sensei to pay particular attention to while drawing that case and hand the storyboard over to Obata Sensei.
(By the way, I don't give him a storyboard chapter by chapter, but rather by case so that he can understand the plot twists and be able to draw the entire case at once.)

After that, I actually don't know what happens (LOL). Through the dizzyingly detailed work and transcendent skills of Obata Sensei and all of his staff, brilliant manga chapters are finished every week.

And once it's available for all of you readers to enjoy, a manga is complete!

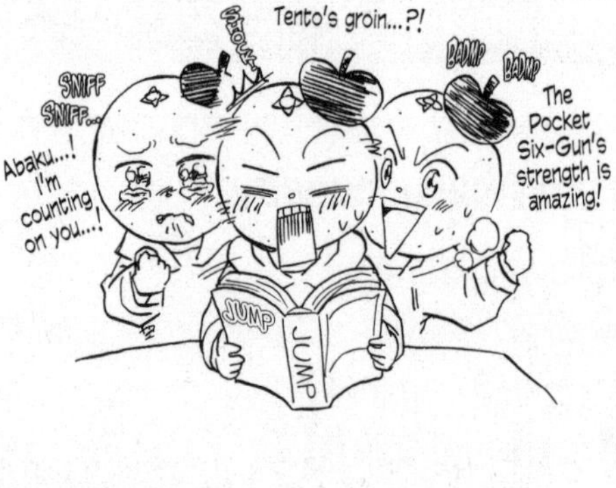
Tento's groin...?!
SHOCK
SNIFF SNIFF...
Abaku...! I'm counting on you...!
BADMP BADMP
The Pocket Six-Gun's strength is amazing!
JUMP
JUMP

Though the one who most looks forward to reading *School Judgment* every week is, without a doubt, me.
That's all.
Thank you so much for listening quietly!!

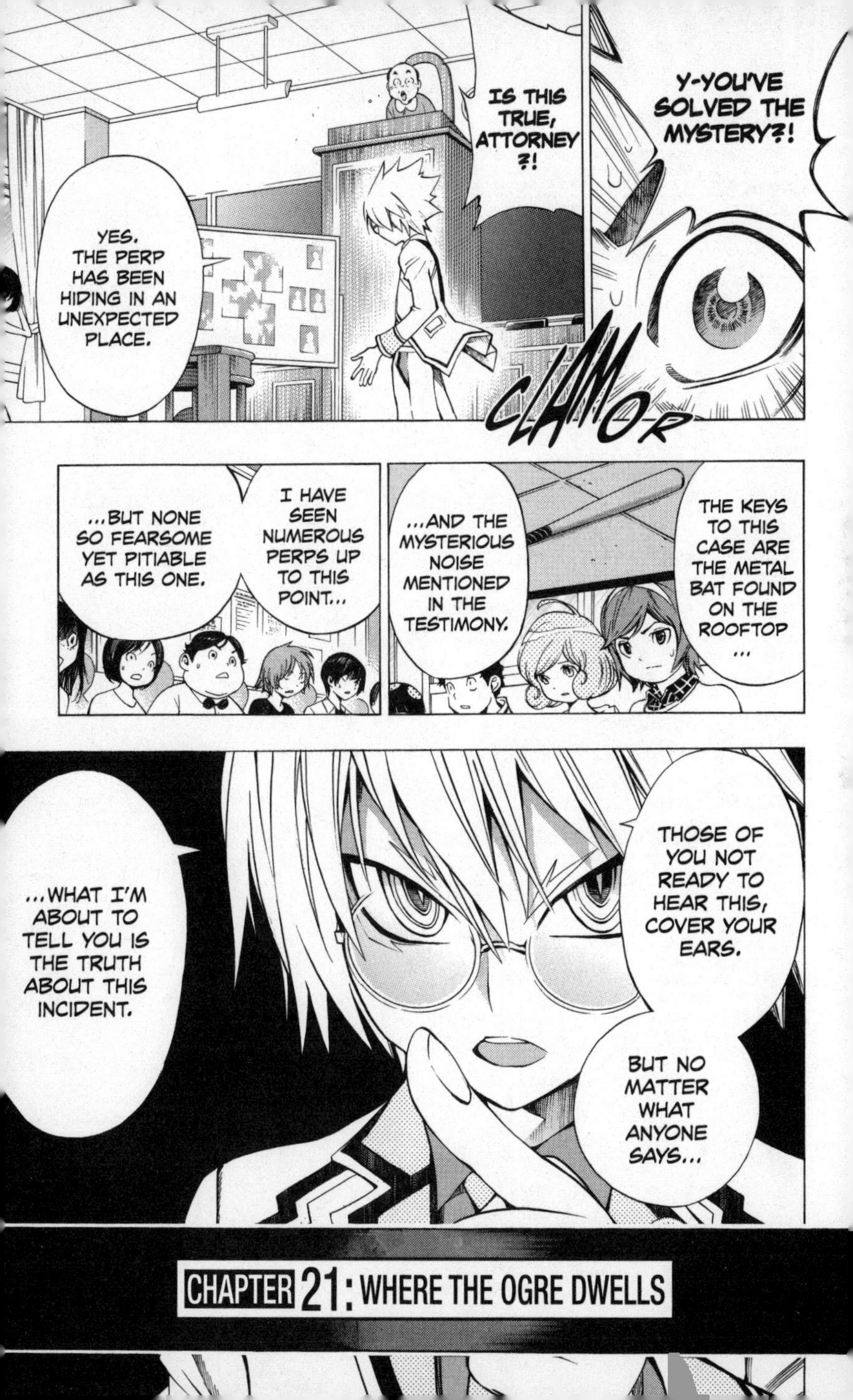
Y-YOU'VE SOLVED THE MYSTERY?!
CLAMOR
IS THIS TRUE, ATTORNEY?!
YES. THE PERP HAS BEEN HIDING IN AN UNEXPECTED PLACE.
THE KEYS TO THIS CASE ARE THE METAL BAT FOUND ON THE ROOFTOP ...
...AND THE MYSTERIOUS NOISE MENTIONED IN THE TESTIMONY.
I HAVE SEEN NUMEROUS PERPS UP TO THIS POINT...
...BUT NONE SO FEARSOME YET PITIABLE AS THIS ONE.
THOSE OF YOU NOT READY TO HEAR THIS, COVER YOUR EARS.
BUT NO MATTER WHAT ANYONE SAYS...
...WHAT I'M ABOUT TO TELL YOU IS THE TRUTH ABOUT THIS INCIDENT.
CHAPTER 21: WHERE THE OGRE DWELLS

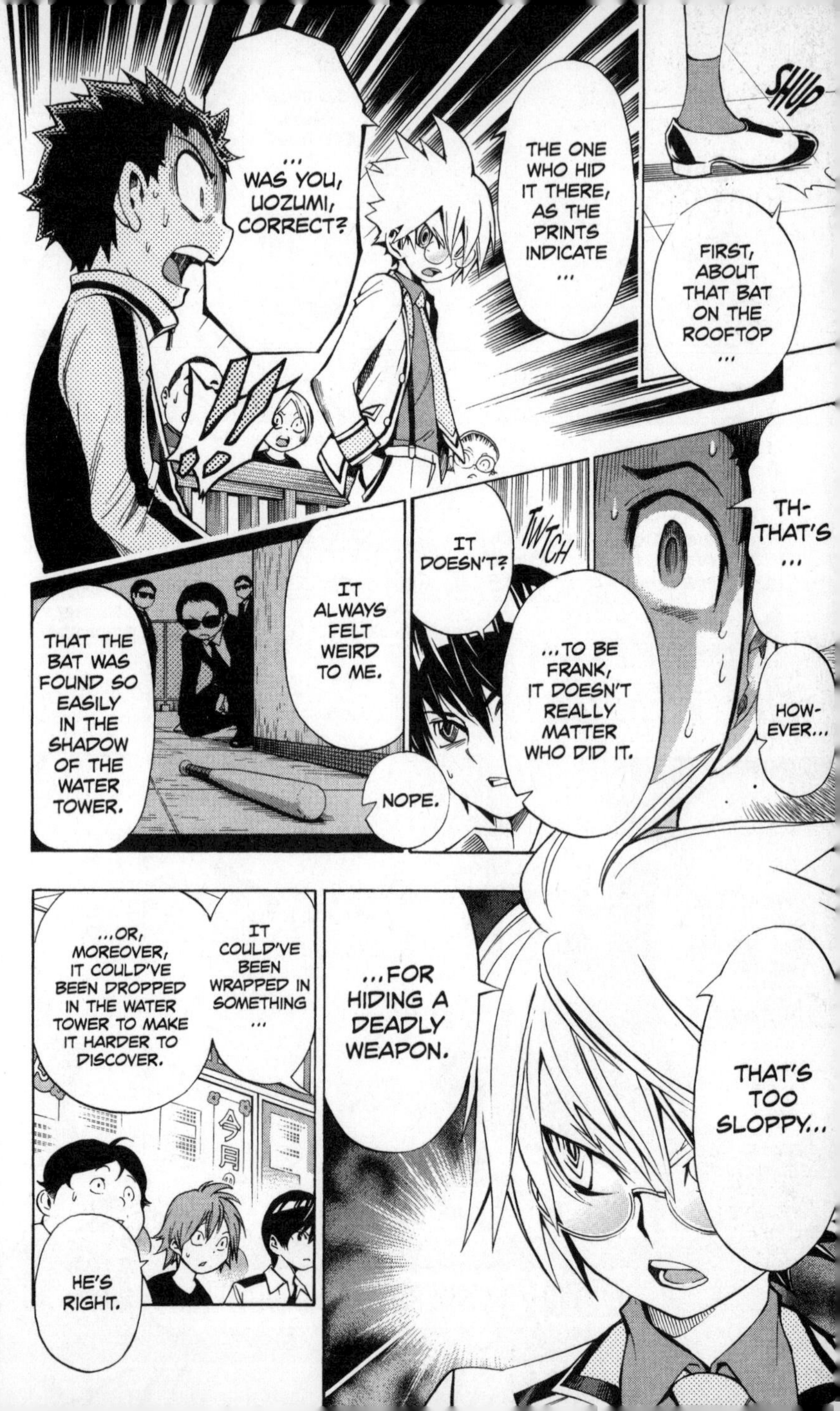
SHUP
FIRST, ABOUT THAT BAT ON THE ROOFTOP...
THE ONE WHO HID IT THERE, AS THE PRINTS INDICATE...
...WAS YOU, UOZUMI, CORRECT?
TH-THAT'S...
HOW-EVER...
...TO BE FRANK, IT DOESN'T REALLY MATTER WHO DID IT.
TWITCH
IT DOESN'T?
NOPE.
IT ALWAYS FELT WEIRD TO ME.
THAT THE BAT WAS FOUND SO EASILY IN THE SHADOW OF THE WATER TOWER.
THAT'S TOO SLOPPY...
...FOR HIDING A DEADLY WEAPON.
IT COULD'VE BEEN WRAPPED IN SOMETHING...
...OR, MOREOVER, IT COULD'VE BEEN DROPPED IN THE WATER TOWER TO MAKE IT HARDER TO DISCOVER.
HE'S RIGHT.

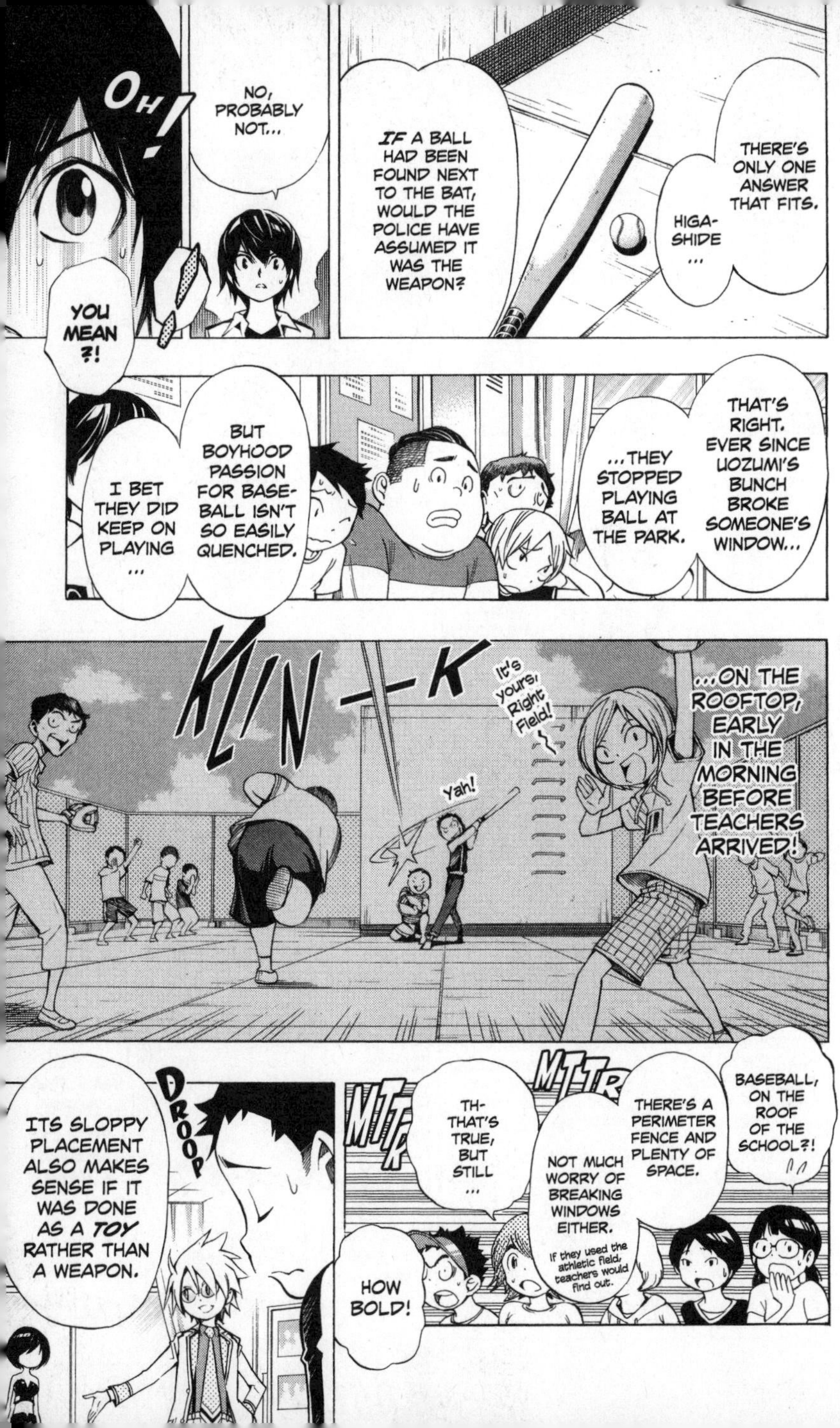
THERE'S ONLY ONE ANSWER THAT FITS.
HIGA-SHIDE...
IF A BALL HAD BEEN FOUND NEXT TO THE BAT, WOULD THE POLICE HAVE ASSUMED IT WAS THE WEAPON?
NO, PROBABLY NOT...
OH!
YOU MEAN ?!
THAT'S RIGHT. EVER SINCE UOZUMI'S BUNCH BROKE SOMEONE'S WINDOW...
...THEY STOPPED PLAYING BALL AT THE PARK.
BUT BOYHOOD PASSION FOR BASE-BALL ISN'T SO EASILY QUENCHED.
I BET THEY DID KEEP ON PLAYING...
...ON THE ROOFTOP, EARLY IN THE MORNING BEFORE TEACHERS ARRIVED!
It's yours, Right Field!
Yah!
KLIN—K
BASEBALL, ON THE ROOF OF THE SCHOOL?!
THERE'S A PERIMETER FENCE AND PLENTY OF SPACE.
MTTR
TH-THAT'S TRUE, BUT STILL...
NOT MUCH WORRY OF BREAKING WINDOWS EITHER.
If they used the athletic field, teachers would find out.
MTTR
HOW BOLD!
DROOP
ITS SLOPPY PLACEMENT ALSO MAKES SENSE IF IT WAS DONE AS A *TOY* RATHER THAN A WEAPON.

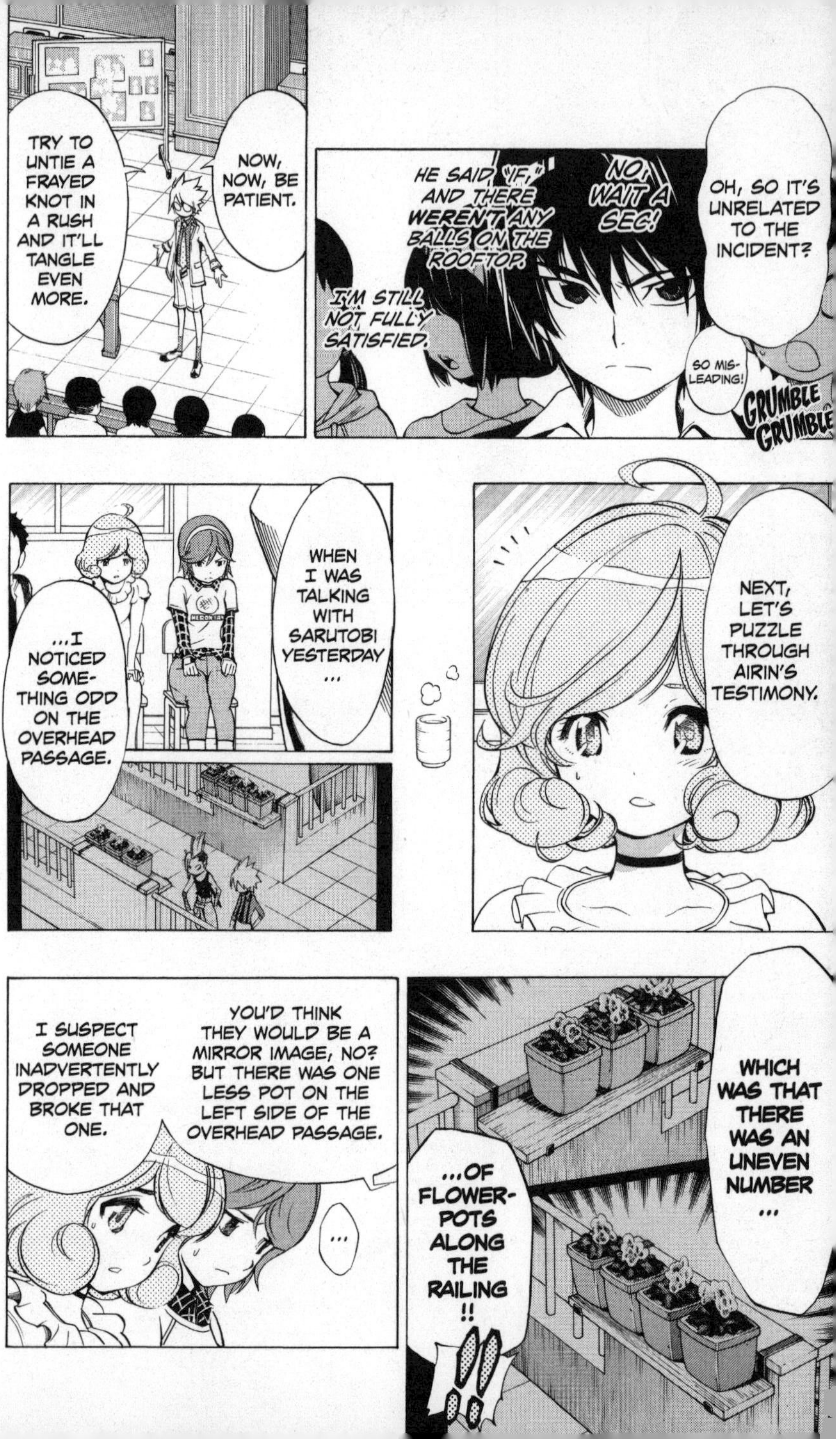
OH, SO IT'S UNRELATED TO THE INCIDENT?
NO, WAIT A SEC!
HE SAID "IF," AND THERE WEREN'T ANY BALLS ON THE ROOFTOP.
I'M STILL NOT FULLY SATISFIED.
SO MIS-LEADING!
GRUMBLE GRUMBLE
NOW, NOW, BE PATIENT.
TRY TO UNTIE A FRAYED KNOT IN A RUSH AND IT'LL TANGLE EVEN MORE.
NEXT, LET'S PUZZLE THROUGH AIRIN'S TESTIMONY.
WHEN I WAS TALKING WITH SARUTOBI YESTERDAY...
...I NOTICED SOME-THING ODD ON THE OVERHEAD PASSAGE.
WHICH WAS THAT THERE WAS AN UNEVEN NUMBER...
...OF FLOWER-POTS ALONG THE RAILING!!
YOU'D THINK THEY WOULD BE A MIRROR IMAGE, NO? BUT THERE WAS ONE LESS POT ON THE LEFT SIDE OF THE OVERHEAD PASSAGE.
I SUSPECT SOMEONE INADVERTENTLY DROPPED AND BROKE THAT ONE.
...

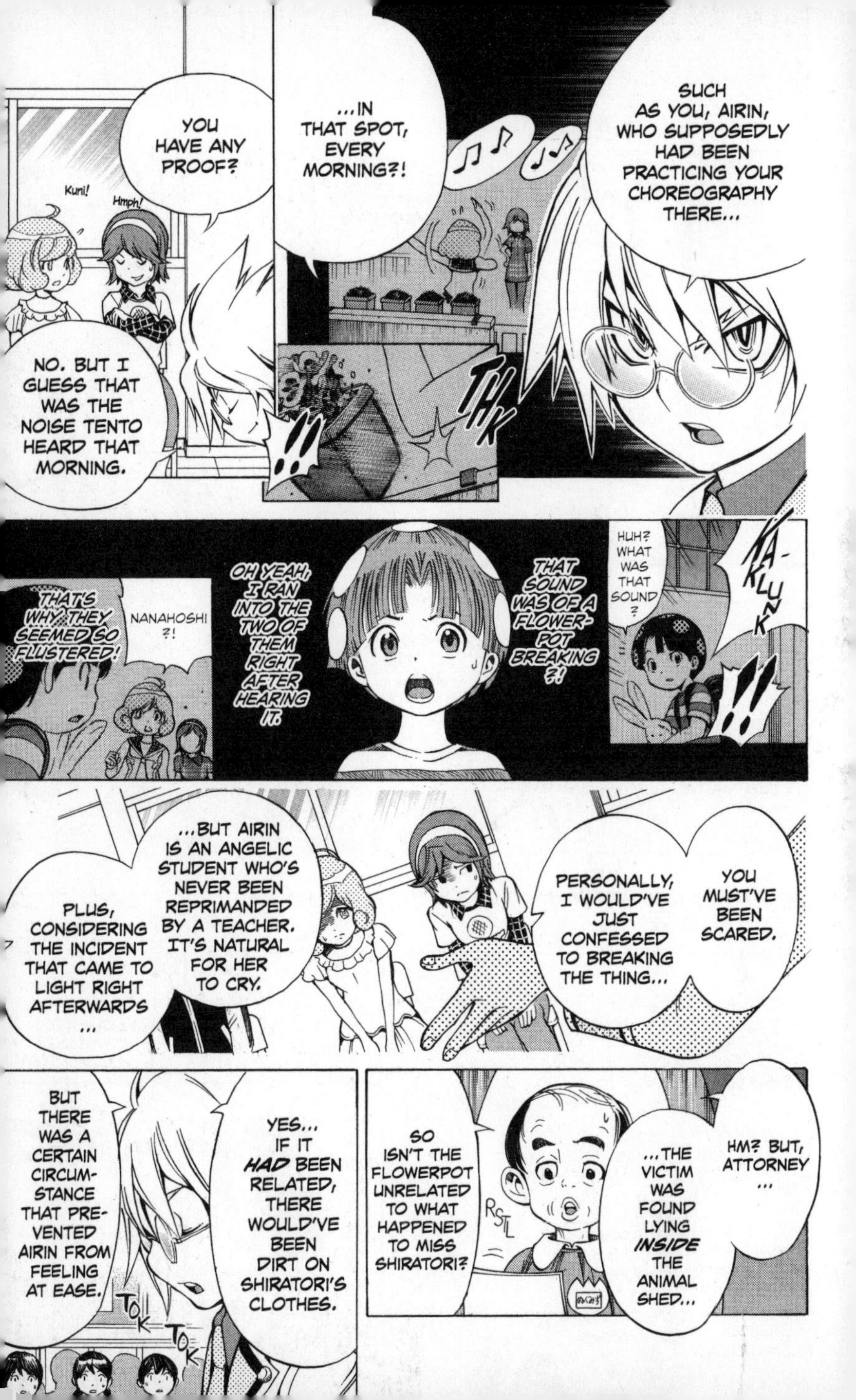
SUCH AS YOU, AIRIN, WHO SUPPOSEDLY HAD BEEN PRACTICING YOUR CHOREOGRAPHY THERE...
...IN THAT SPOT, EVERY MORNING?!
THK
YOU HAVE ANY PROOF?
Kuni!
Hmph!
NO. BUT I GUESS THAT WAS THE NOISE TENTO HEARD THAT MORNING.
KA-KLUNK!!
HUH? WHAT WAS THAT SOUND?
THAT SOUND WAS OF A FLOWER-POT BREAKING?!
OH YEAH, I RAN INTO THE TWO OF THEM RIGHT AFTER HEARING IT.
NANAHOSHI?!
THAT'S WHY THEY SEEMED SO FLUSTERED!
YOU MUST'VE BEEN SCARED.
PERSONALLY, I WOULD'VE JUST CONFESSED TO BREAKING THE THING...
...BUT AIRIN IS AN ANGELIC STUDENT WHO'S NEVER BEEN REPRIMANDED BY A TEACHER. IT'S NATURAL FOR HER TO CRY.
PLUS, CONSIDERING THE INCIDENT THAT CAME TO LIGHT RIGHT AFTERWARDS...
HM? BUT, ATTORNEY...
...THE VICTIM WAS FOUND LYING *INSIDE* THE ANIMAL SHED...
RSTL
SO ISN'T THE FLOWERPOT UNRELATED TO WHAT HAPPENED TO MISS SHIRATORI?
YES... IF IT *HAD* BEEN RELATED, THERE WOULD'VE BEEN DIRT ON SHIRATORI'S CLOTHES.
BUT THERE WAS A CERTAIN CIRCUM-STANCE THAT PRE-VENTED AIRIN FROM FEELING AT EASE.
TOK TOK

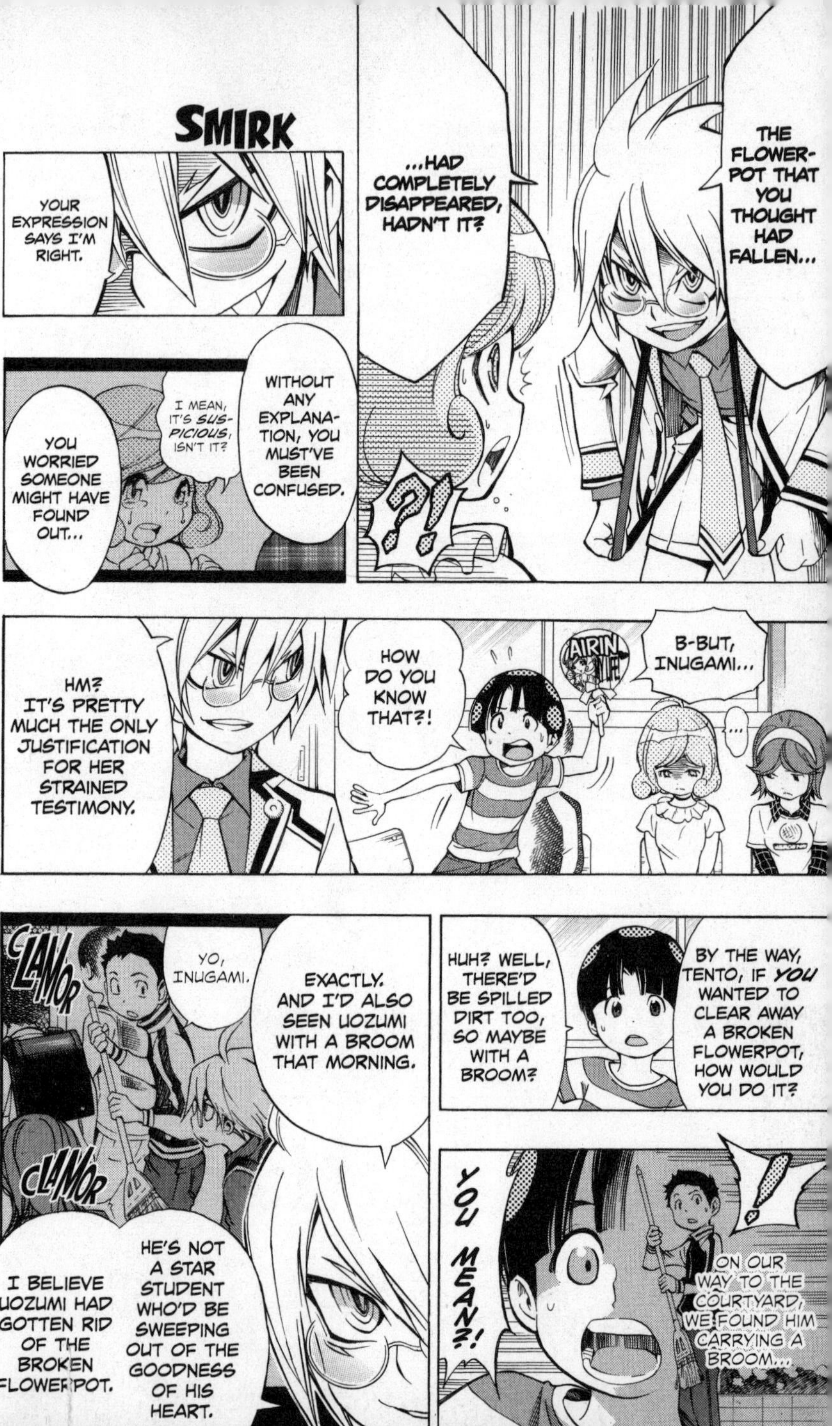
THE FLOWER-POT THAT YOU THOUGHT HAD FALLEN...
...HAD COMPLETELY DISAPPEARED, HADN'T IT?
?!
SMIRK
YOUR EXPRESSION SAYS I'M RIGHT.
WITHOUT ANY EXPLANATION, YOU MUST'VE BEEN CONFUSED.
I MEAN, IT'S *SUSPICIOUS*, ISN'T IT?
YOU WORRIED SOMEONE MIGHT HAVE FOUND OUT...
B-BUT, INUGAMI...
...
AIRIN
HOW DO YOU KNOW THAT?!
HM? IT'S PRETTY MUCH THE ONLY JUSTIFICATION FOR HER STRAINED TESTIMONY.
BY THE WAY, TENTO, IF *YOU* WANTED TO CLEAR AWAY A BROKEN FLOWERPOT, HOW WOULD YOU DO IT?
HUH? WELL, THERE'D BE SPILLED DIRT TOO, SO MAYBE WITH A BROOM?
!
YOU MEAN?!
ON OUR WAY TO THE COURTYARD, WE FOUND HIM CARRYING A BROOM...
EXACTLY. AND I'D ALSO SEEN UOZUMI WITH A BROOM THAT MORNING.
YO, INUGAMI.
CLAMOR
CLAMOR
HE'S NOT A STAR STUDENT WHO'D BE SWEEPING OUT OF THE GOODNESS OF HIS HEART.
I BELIEVE UOZUMI HAD GOTTEN RID OF THE BROKEN FLOWERPOT.

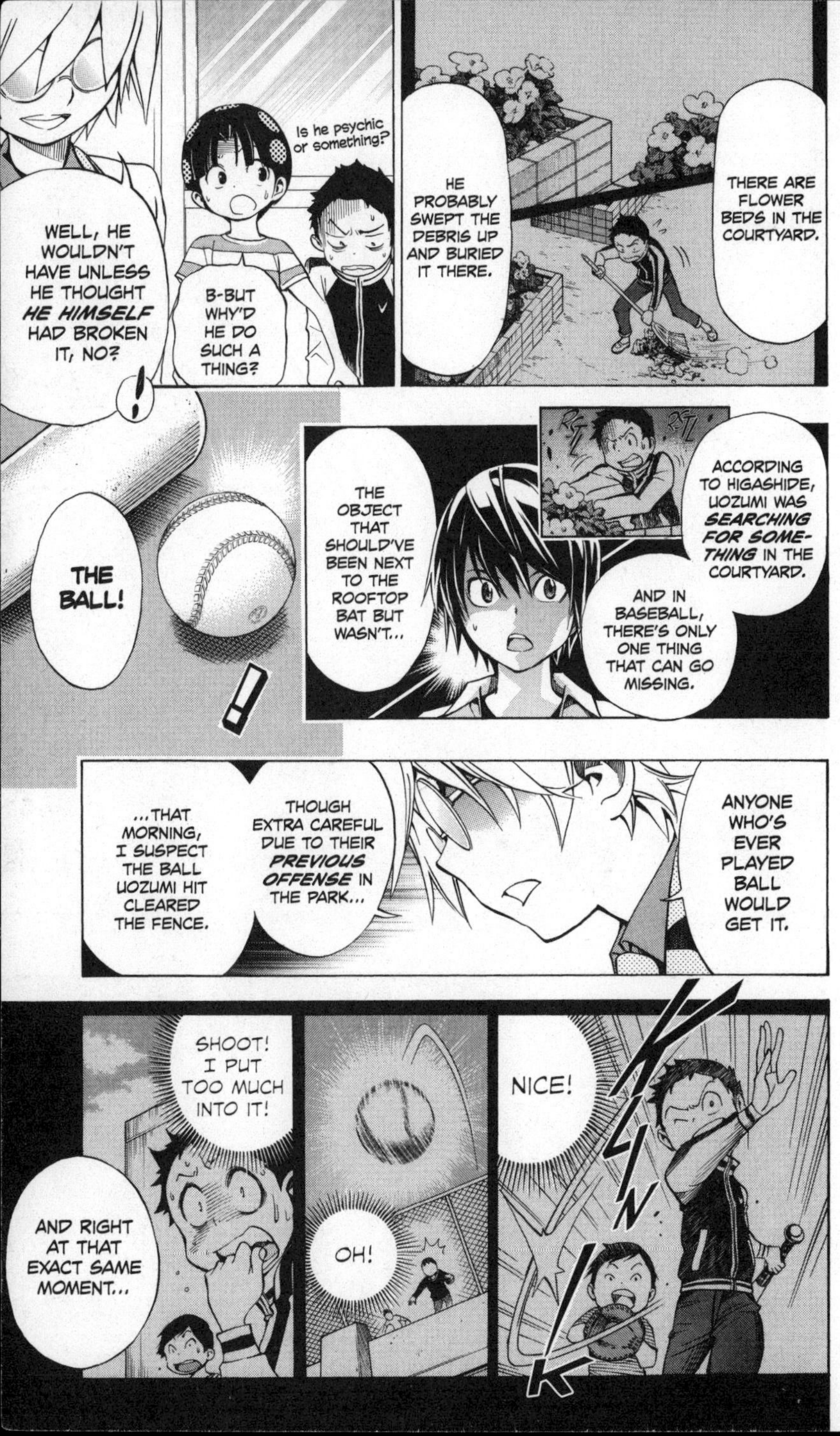

THERE ARE FLOWER BEDS IN THE COURTYARD.
HE PROBABLY SWEPT THE DEBRIS UP AND BURIED IT THERE.
Is he psychic or something?
B-BUT WHY'D HE DO SUCH A THING?
WELL, HE WOULDN'T HAVE UNLESS HE THOUGHT *HE HIMSELF* HAD BROKEN IT, NO?
!
RSTL
RSTL
ACCORDING TO HIGASHIDE, UOZUMI WAS *SEARCHING FOR SOMETHING* IN THE COURTYARD.
AND IN BASEBALL, THERE'S ONLY ONE THING THAT CAN GO MISSING.
THE OBJECT THAT SHOULD'VE BEEN NEXT TO THE ROOFTOP BAT BUT WASN'T...
THE BALL!
!
ANYONE WHO'S EVER PLAYED BALL WOULD GET IT.
THOUGH EXTRA CAREFUL DUE TO THEIR *PREVIOUS OFFENSE* IN THE PARK...
...THAT MORNING, I SUSPECT THE BALL UOZUMI HIT CLEARED THE FENCE.
NICE!
OH!
SHOOT! I PUT TOO MUCH INTO IT!
AND RIGHT AT THAT EXACT SAME MOMENT...

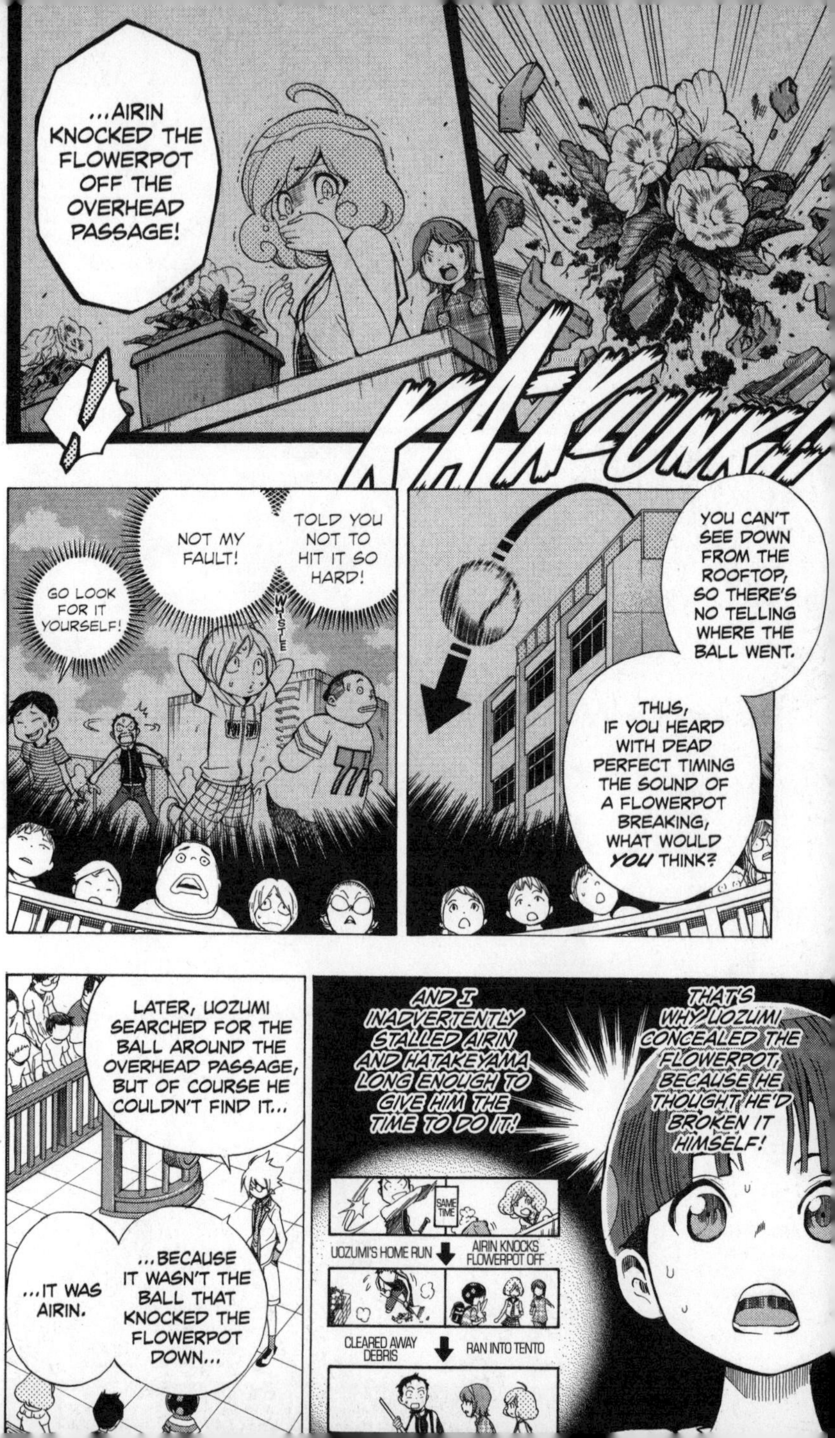
KAKUNK
...AIRIN KNOCKED THE FLOWERPOT OFF THE OVERHEAD PASSAGE!
!
YOU CAN'T SEE DOWN FROM THE ROOFTOP, SO THERE'S NO TELLING WHERE THE BALL WENT.
THUS, IF YOU HEARD WITH DEAD PERFECT TIMING THE SOUND OF A FLOWERPOT BREAKING, WHAT WOULD *YOU* THINK?
TOLD YOU NOT TO HIT IT SO HARD!
NOT MY FAULT!
GO LOOK FOR IT YOURSELF!
WHISTLE
THAT'S WHY UOZUMI CONCEALED THE FLOWERPOT, BECAUSE HE THOUGHT HE'D BROKEN IT HIMSELF!
AND I INADVERTENTLY STALLED AIRIN AND HATAKEYAMA LONG ENOUGH TO GIVE HIM THE TIME TO DO IT!
SAME TIME
UOZUMI'S HOME RUN
AIRIN KNOCKS FLOWERPOT OFF
CLEARED AWAY DEBRIS
RAN INTO TENTO
LATER, UOZUMI SEARCHED FOR THE BALL AROUND THE OVERHEAD PASSAGE, BUT OF COURSE HE COULDN'T FIND IT...
...BECAUSE IT WASN'T THE BALL THAT KNOCKED THE FLOWERPOT DOWN...
...IT WAS AIRIN.

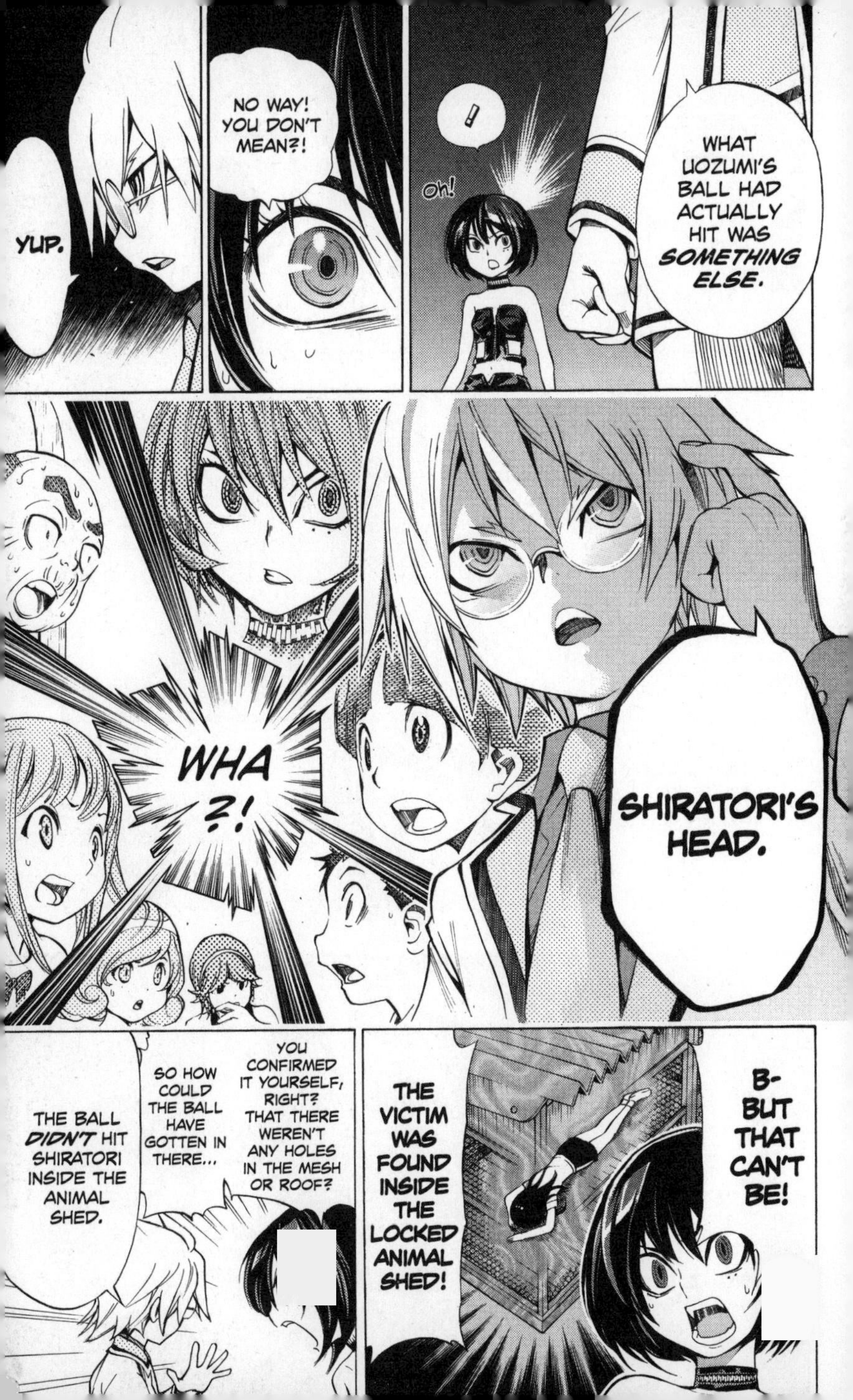
WHAT UOZUMI'S BALL HAD ACTUALLY HIT WAS *SOMETHING ELSE.*
!
Oh!
NO WAY! YOU DON'T MEAN?!
YUP.
SHIRATORI'S HEAD.
WHA ?!
B- BUT THAT CAN'T BE!
THE VICTIM WAS FOUND INSIDE THE LOCKED ANIMAL SHED!
YOU CONFIRMED IT YOURSELF, RIGHT? THAT THERE WEREN'T ANY HOLES IN THE MESH OR ROOF?
SO HOW COULD THE BALL HAVE GOTTEN IN THERE...
THE BALL *DIDN'T* HIT SHIRATORI INSIDE THE ANIMAL SHED.

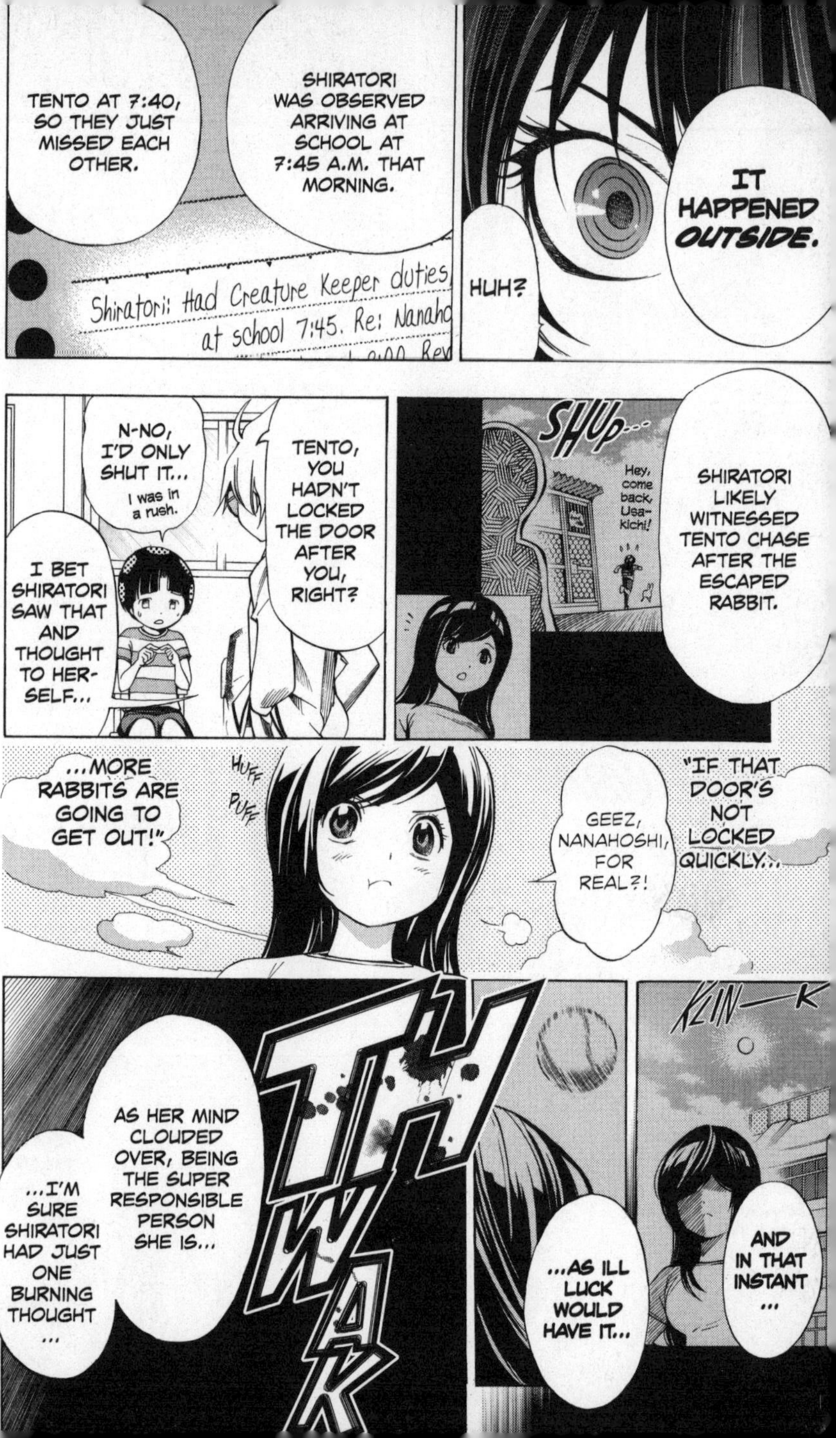
IT HAPPENED OUTSIDE.
HUH?
SHIRATORI WAS OBSERVED ARRIVING AT SCHOOL AT 7:45 A.M. THAT MORNING.
TENTO AT 7:40, SO THEY JUST MISSED EACH OTHER.
Shiratori: Had Creature Keeper duties, at school 7:45.
SHIRATORI LIKELY WITNESSED TENTO CHASE AFTER THE ESCAPED RABBIT.
SHUP...
Hey, come back, Usa-kichi!
TENTO, YOU HADN'T LOCKED THE DOOR AFTER YOU, RIGHT?
N-NO, I'D ONLY SHUT IT...
I was in a rush.
I BET SHIRATORI SAW THAT AND THOUGHT TO HER-SELF...
"IF THAT DOOR'S NOT LOCKED QUICKLY...
GEEZ, NANAHOSHI, FOR REAL?!
HUFF
PUFF
...MORE RABBITS ARE GOING TO GET OUT!"
KLIN—K
AND IN THAT INSTANT...
...AS ILL LUCK WOULD HAVE IT...
THWAK
AS HER MIND CLOUDED OVER, BEING THE SUPER RESPONSIBLE PERSON SHE IS...
...I'M SURE SHIRATORI HAD JUST ONE BURNING THOUGHT...

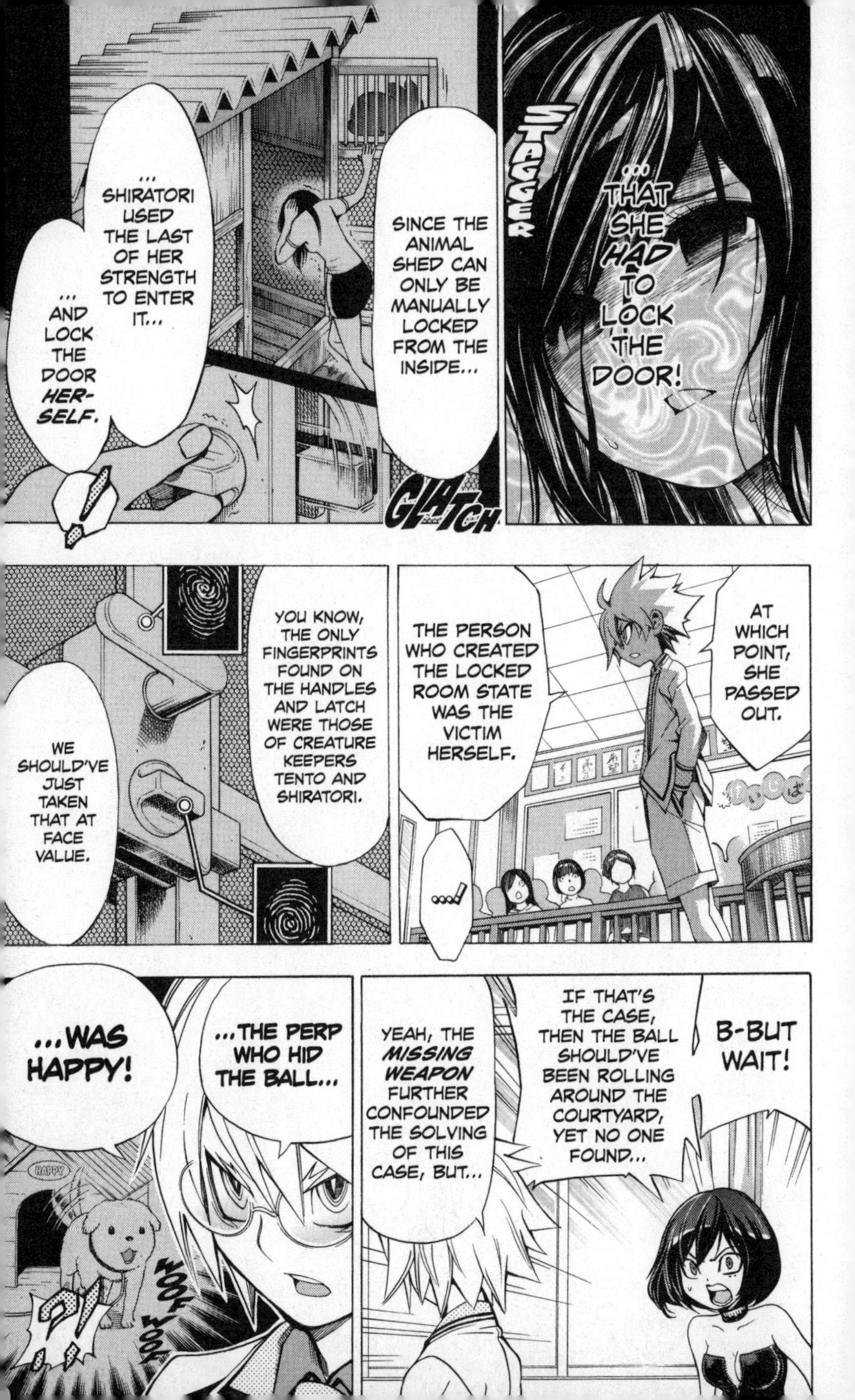
STAGGER
...THAT SHE HAD TO LOCK THE DOOR!
SINCE THE ANIMAL SHED CAN ONLY BE MANUALLY LOCKED FROM THE INSIDE...
...SHIRATORI USED THE LAST OF HER STRENGTH TO ENTER IT...
...AND LOCK THE DOOR HERSELF.
GLATCH
AT WHICH POINT, SHE PASSED OUT.
THE PERSON WHO CREATED THE LOCKED ROOM STATE WAS THE VICTIM HERSELF.
...!
YOU KNOW, THE ONLY FINGERPRINTS FOUND ON THE HANDLES AND LATCH WERE THOSE OF CREATURE KEEPERS TENTO AND SHIRATORI.
WE SHOULD'VE JUST TAKEN THAT AT FACE VALUE.
B-BUT WAIT!
IF THAT'S THE CASE, THEN THE BALL SHOULD'VE BEEN ROLLING AROUND THE COURTYARD, YET NO ONE FOUND...
YEAH, THE MISSING WEAPON FURTHER CONFOUNDED THE SOLVING OF THIS CASE, BUT...
...THE PERP WHO HID THE BALL...
...WAS HAPPY!
HAPPY
WOOF WOOF
?!

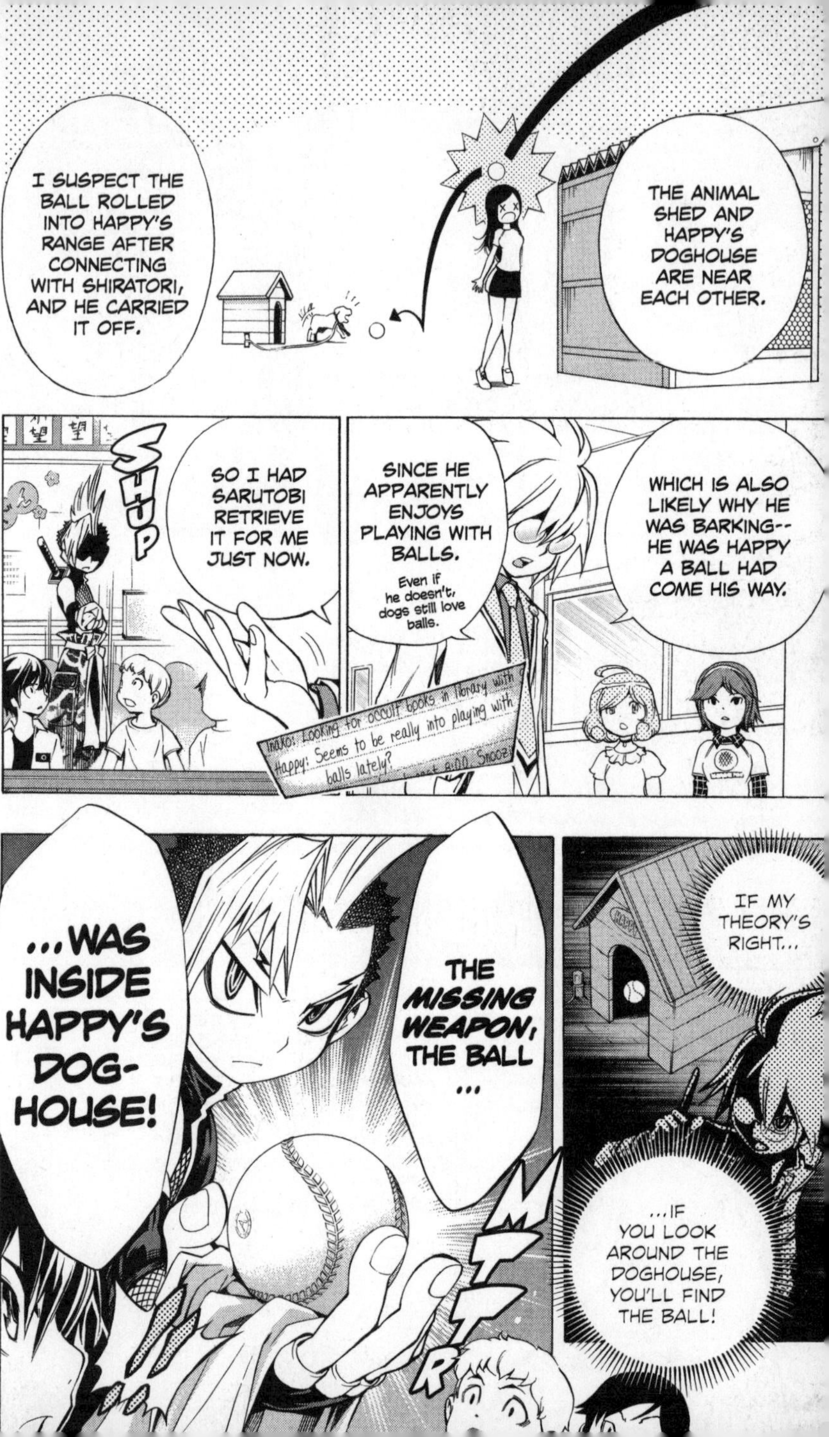
THE ANIMAL SHED AND HAPPY'S DOGHOUSE ARE NEAR EACH OTHER.
I SUSPECT THE BALL ROLLED INTO HAPPY'S RANGE AFTER CONNECTING WITH SHIRATORI, AND HE CARRIED IT OFF.
WHICH IS ALSO LIKELY WHY HE WAS BARKING-- HE WAS HAPPY A BALL HAD COME HIS WAY.
SINCE HE APPARENTLY ENJOYS PLAYING WITH BALLS.
Even if he doesn't, dogs still love balls.
Inako: Looking for occult books in library with
Happy: Seems to be really into playing with balls lately?
SO I HAD SARUTOBI RETRIEVE IT FOR ME JUST NOW.
SHUP
IF MY THEORY'S RIGHT...
...IF YOU LOOK AROUND THE DOGHOUSE, YOU'LL FIND THE BALL!
THE *MISSING WEAPON*, THE BALL...
...WAS INSIDE HAPPY'S DOG-HOUSE!

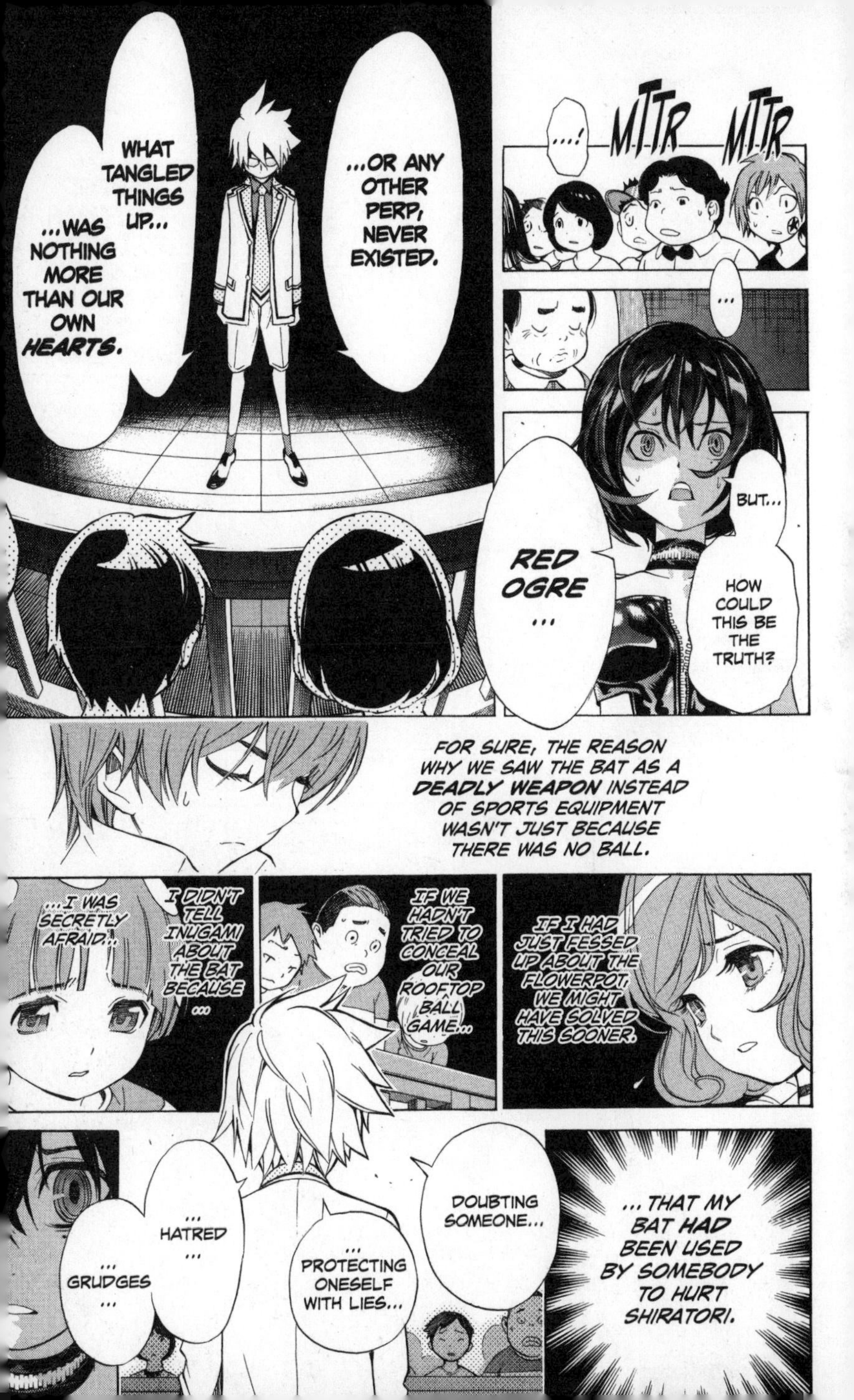
...!
MTTR
MTTR
...
BUT...
HOW COULD THIS BE THE TRUTH?
RED OGRE ...
...OR ANY OTHER PERP, NEVER EXISTED.
WHAT TANGLED THINGS UP...
...WAS NOTHING MORE THAN OUR OWN HEARTS.
FOR SURE, THE REASON WHY WE SAW THE BAT AS A DEADLY WEAPON INSTEAD OF SPORTS EQUIPMENT WASN'T JUST BECAUSE THERE WAS NO BALL.
IF I HAD JUST FESSED UP ABOUT THE FLOWERPOT, WE MIGHT HAVE SOLVED THIS SOONER.
IF WE HADN'T TRIED TO CONCEAL OUR ROOFTOP BALL GAME...
I DIDN'T TELL INUGAMI ABOUT THE BAT BECAUSE ...
...I WAS SECRETLY AFRAID...
... THAT MY BAT HAD BEEN USED BY SOMEBODY TO HURT SHIRATORI.
DOUBTING SOMEONE...
... PROTECTING ONESELF WITH LIES...
... HATRED ...
... GRUDGES ...

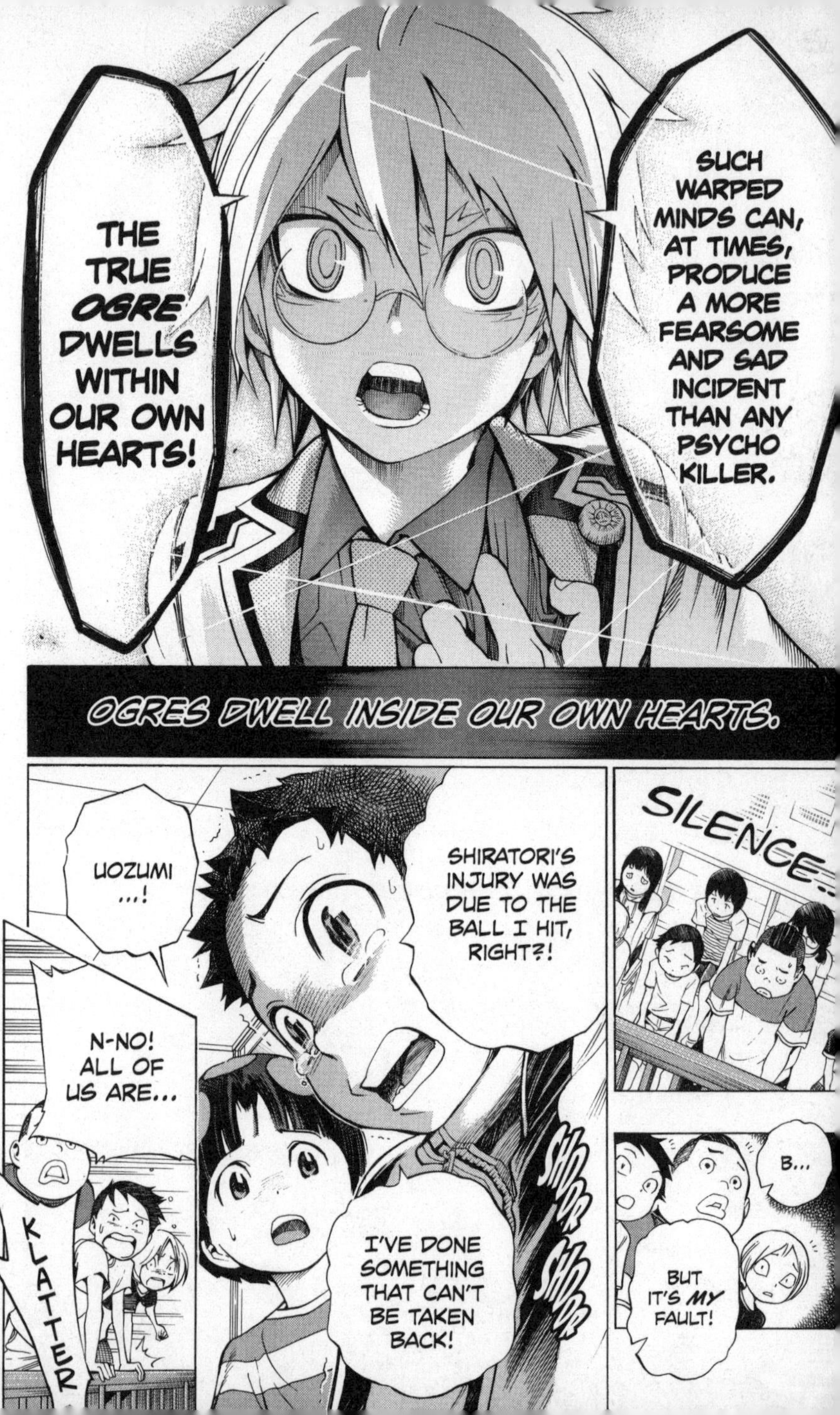
SUCH WARPED MINDS CAN, AT TIMES, PRODUCE A MORE FEARSOME AND SAD INCIDENT THAN ANY PSYCHO KILLER.
THE TRUE *OGRE* DWELLS WITHIN OUR OWN HEARTS!
OGRES DWELL INSIDE OUR OWN HEARTS.
UOZUMI ...!
SHIRATORI'S INJURY WAS DUE TO THE BALL I HIT, RIGHT?!
I'VE DONE SOMETHING THAT CAN'T BE TAKEN BACK!
SHOR SHOR
N-NO! ALL OF US ARE...
KLATTER
SILENCE...
B...
BUT IT'S *MY* FAULT!

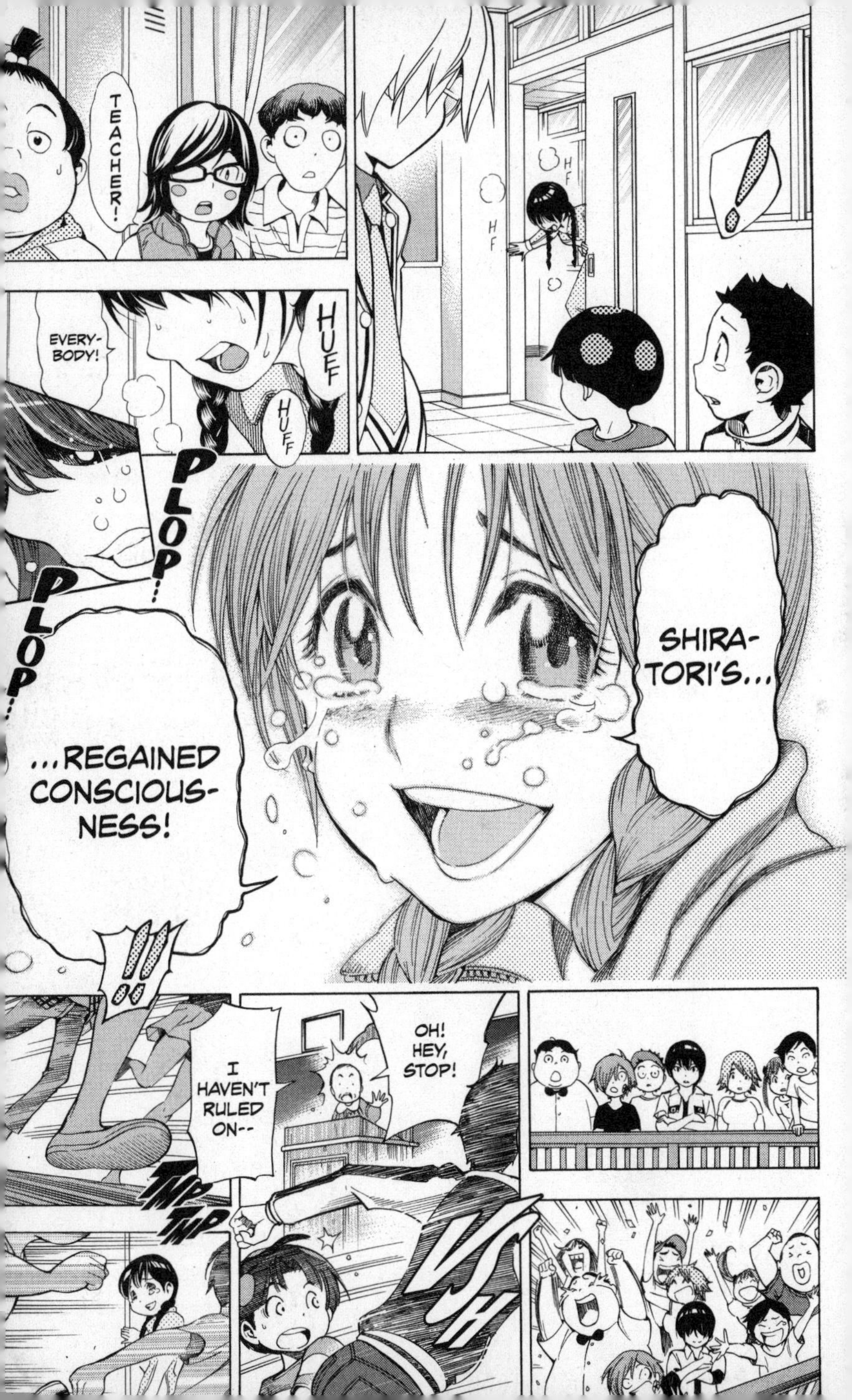
HF
HF
!
TEACHER!
EVERY-BODY!
HUFF
HUFF
PLOP...
PLOP...
SHIRA-TORI'S...
...REGAINED CONSCIOUSNESS!
!!!!
OH! HEY, STOP!
I HAVEN'T RULED ON--
THMP
THMP

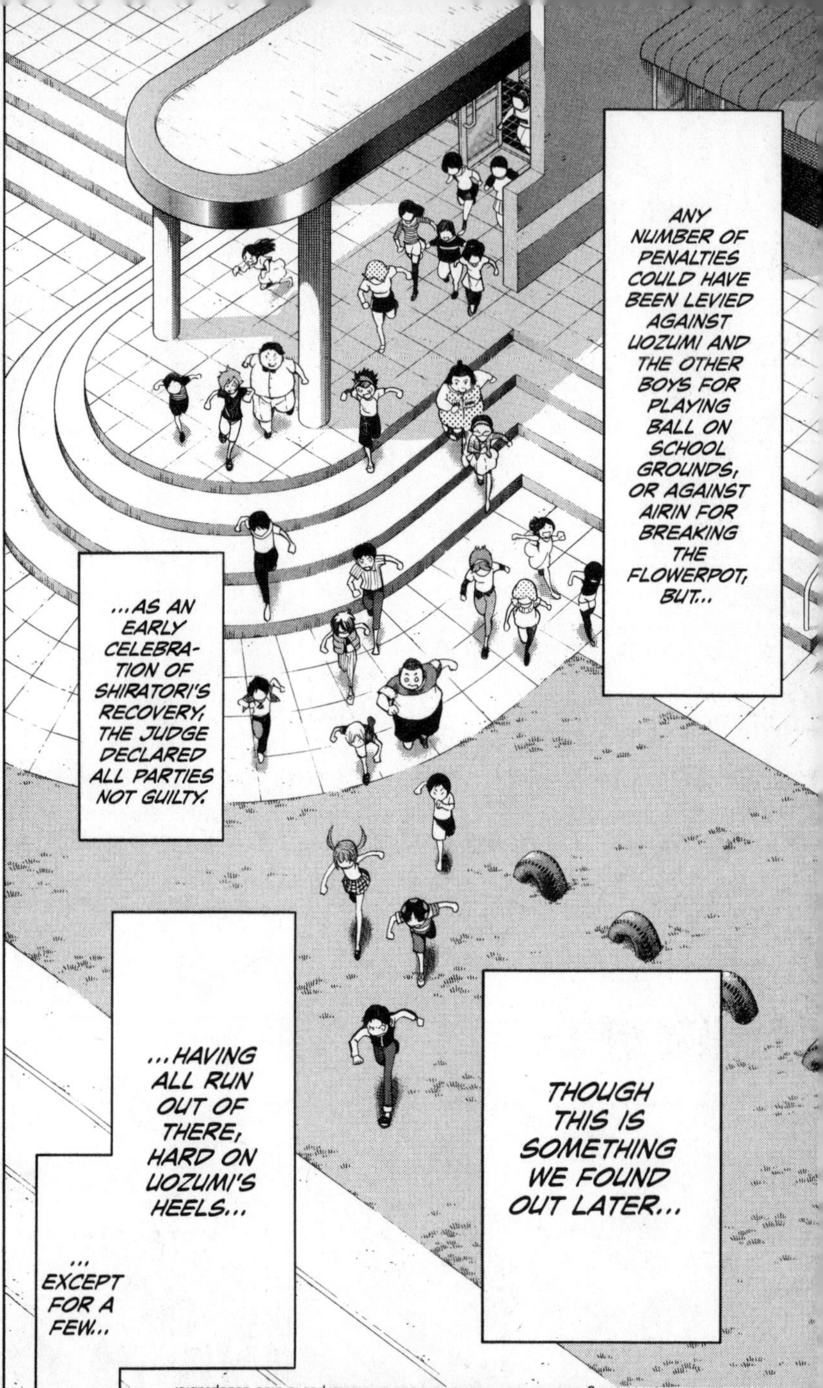
ANY NUMBER OF PENALTIES COULD HAVE BEEN LEVIED AGAINST UOZUMI AND THE OTHER BOYS FOR PLAYING BALL ON SCHOOL GROUNDS, OR AGAINST AIRIN FOR BREAKING THE FLOWERPOT, BUT...
...AS AN EARLY CELEBRATION OF SHIRATORI'S RECOVERY, THE JUDGE DECLARED ALL PARTIES NOT GUILTY.
THOUGH THIS IS SOMETHING WE FOUND OUT LATER...
...HAVING ALL RUN OUT OF THERE, HARD ON UOZUMI'S HEELS...
...EXCEPT FOR A FEW...

Homework answer: A. Doghouse B. Ball (A. Flowerbeds B. Flowerpot is also acceptable)

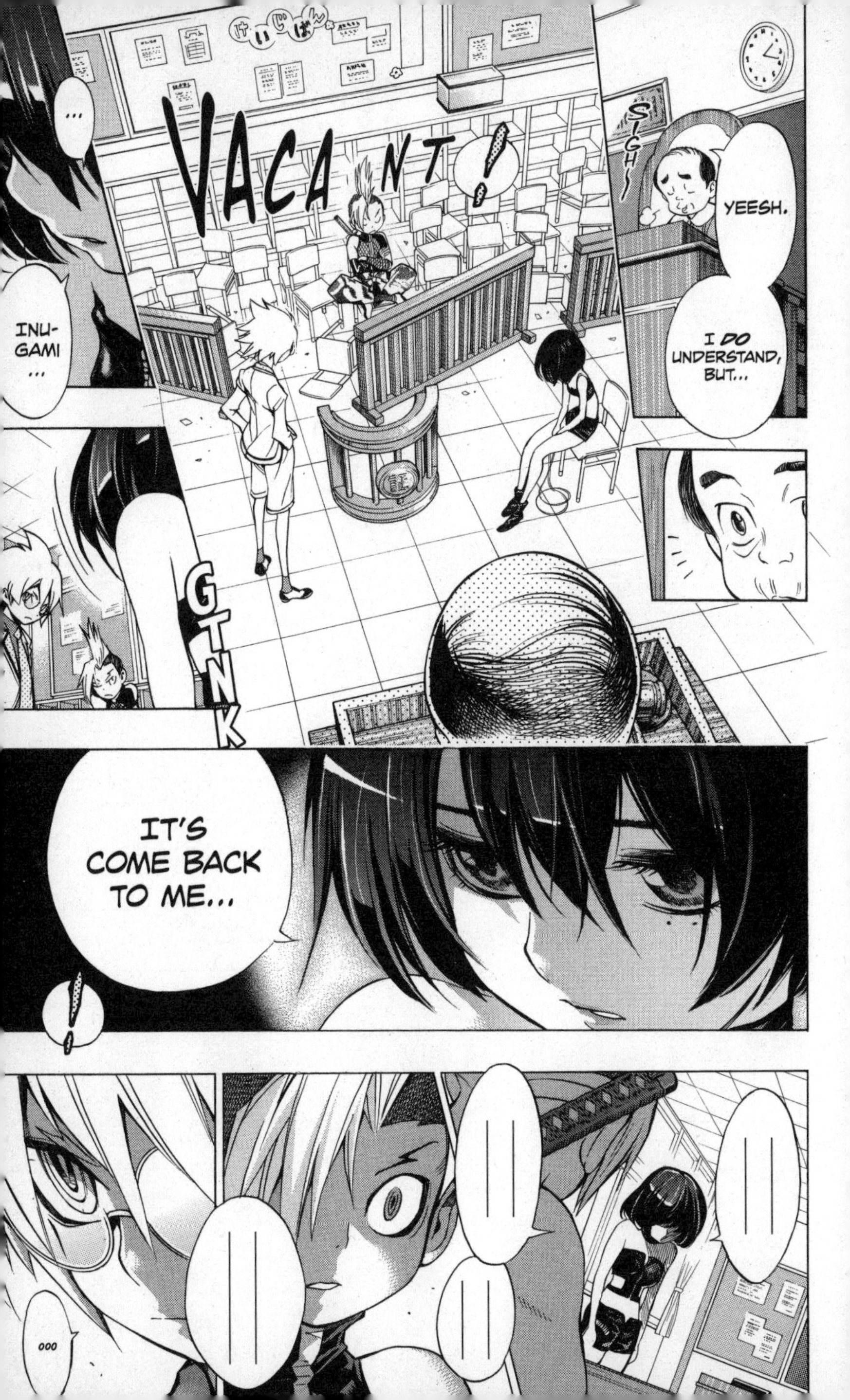
SIGH~
YEESH.
I DO UNDERSTAND, BUT...
けいじばん
VACANT!
!
...
INU-GAMI ...
GTNK
IT'S COME BACK TO ME...
!
ooo

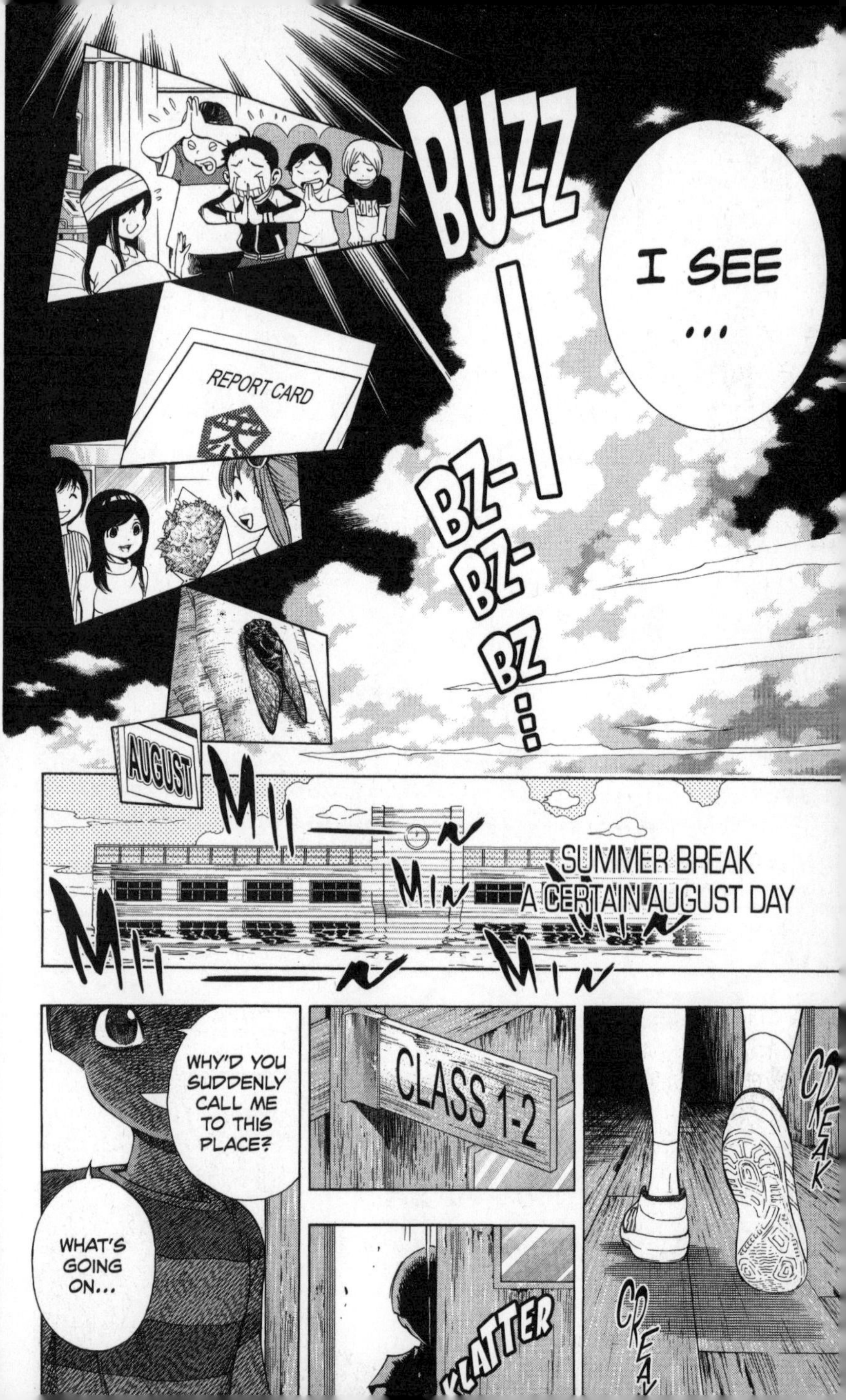
I SEE ...
BUZZ
BZ-BZ-BZ...
REPORT CARD
AUGUST
MIIN MIN
SUMMER BREAK
A CERTAIN AUGUST DAY
MIIN MIN
CREAK
CREAK
CLASS 1-2
KLATTER
WHY'D YOU SUDDENLY CALL ME TO THIS PLACE?
WHAT'S GOING ON...

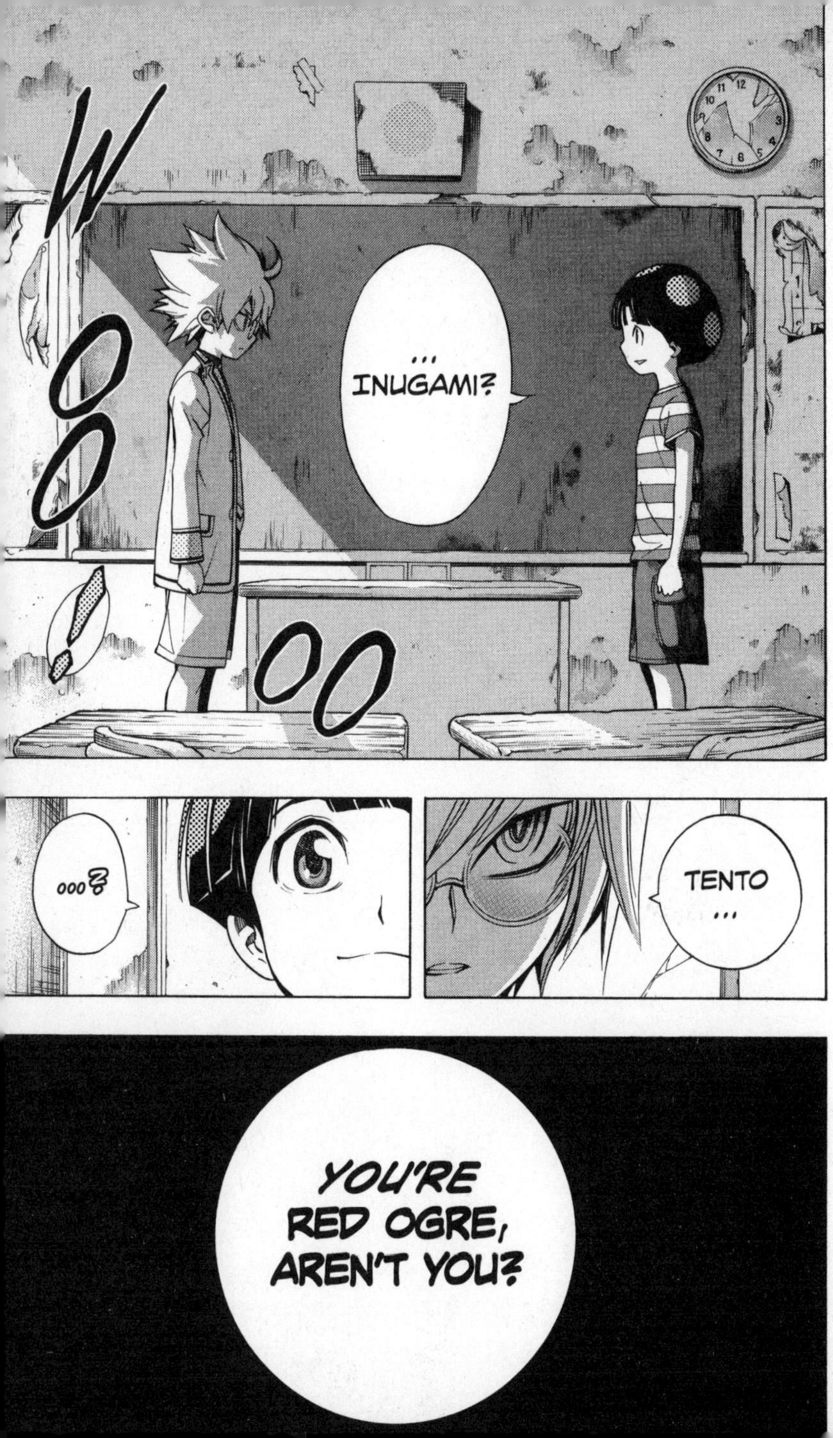
WOOOOO
!
... INUGAMI?
TENTO ...
...?
YOU'RE RED OGRE, AREN'T YOU?

This is the final chapter that ran in *Jump+*.

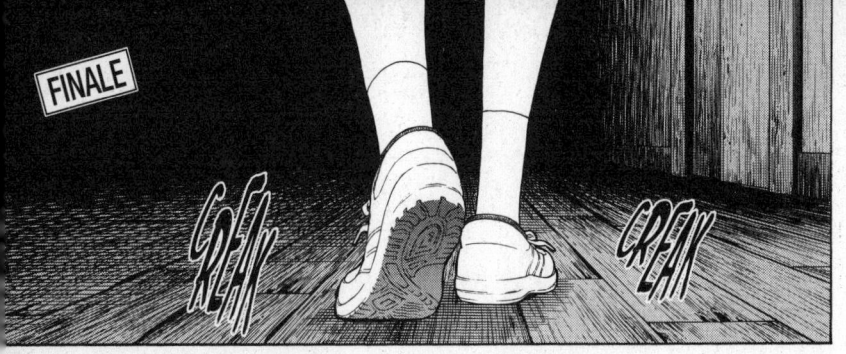

FINALE
CREAK
CREAK
TAP
NOW, KIJIMA.
I'VE TOLD YOU NOT TO BULLY INUGAMI, HMM?
HRUMF
WAAH
WAAH
YEAH!
YEAH!
S MUNICIPAL ELEMENTARY
IT WAS AT THE LOCATION OF THE BLOODY SESSION...
CREAK
CREAK
...IN THE CLASSROOM WHICH HAS STOOD EMPTY SINCE THE INCIDENT...
CLASS 1-2
...THAT I WAS SUMMONED ONE SUMMER-BREAK DAY.
KLATTER
WHY'D YOU SUDDENLY CALL ME TO THIS PLACE?
WHAT'S GOING ON...

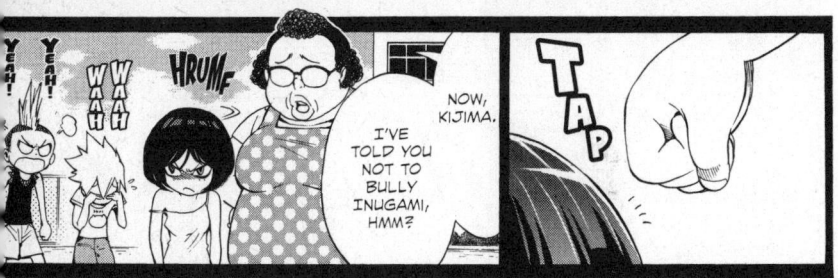

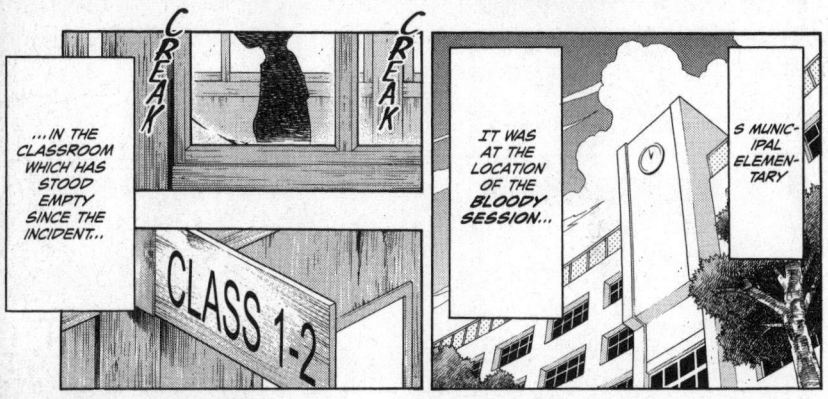

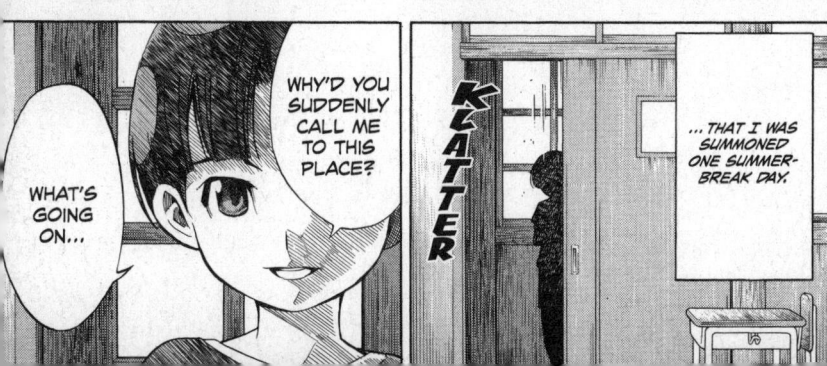

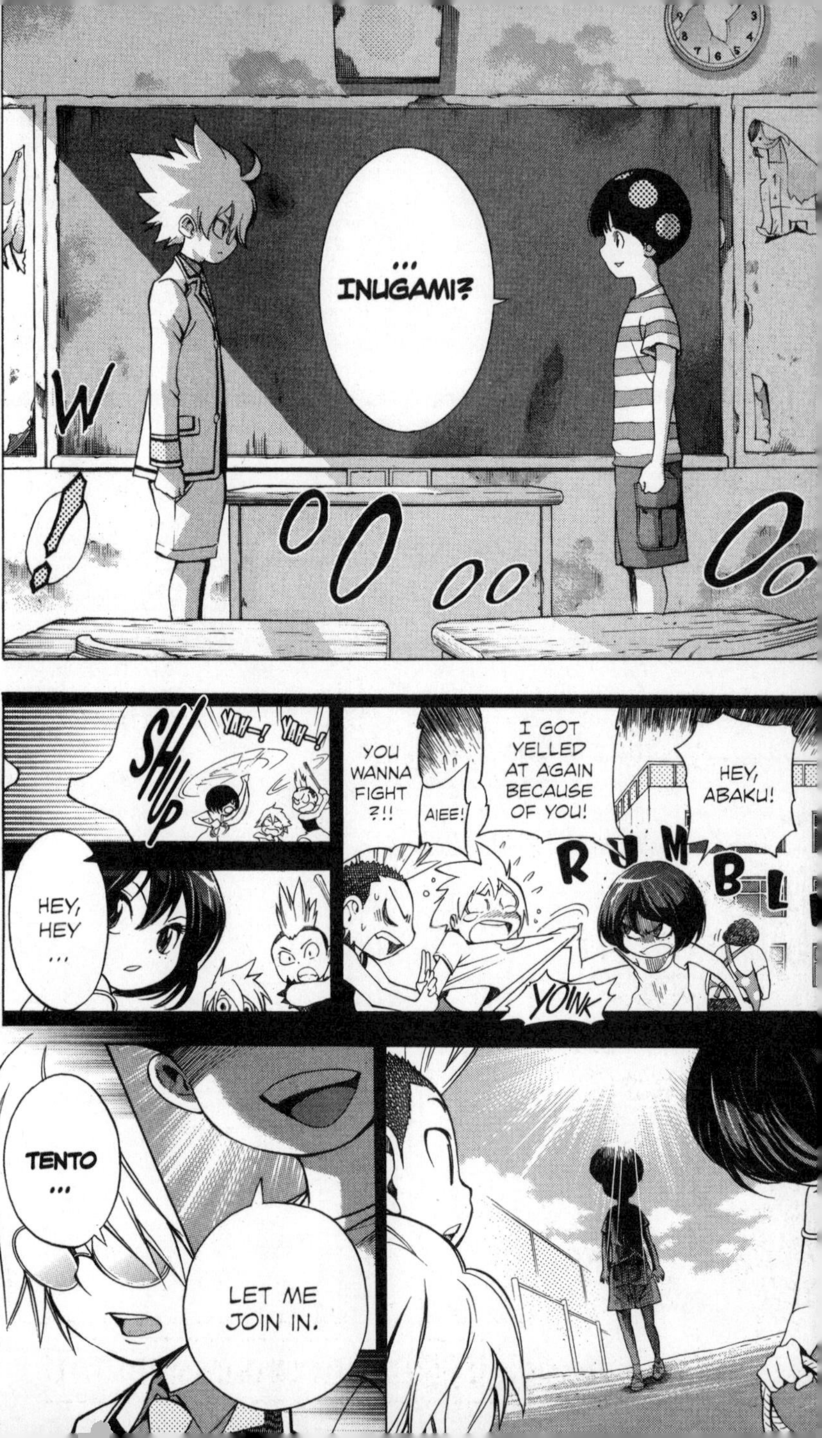
... INUGAMI?
W
!
OOOO
HEY, ABAKU!
RUMBL
I GOT YELLED AT AGAIN BECAUSE OF YOU!
AIEE!
YOU WANNA FIGHT ?!!
YOINK
YAH-! YAH-!
SHUP
HEY, HEY ...
TENTO ...
LET ME JOIN IN.

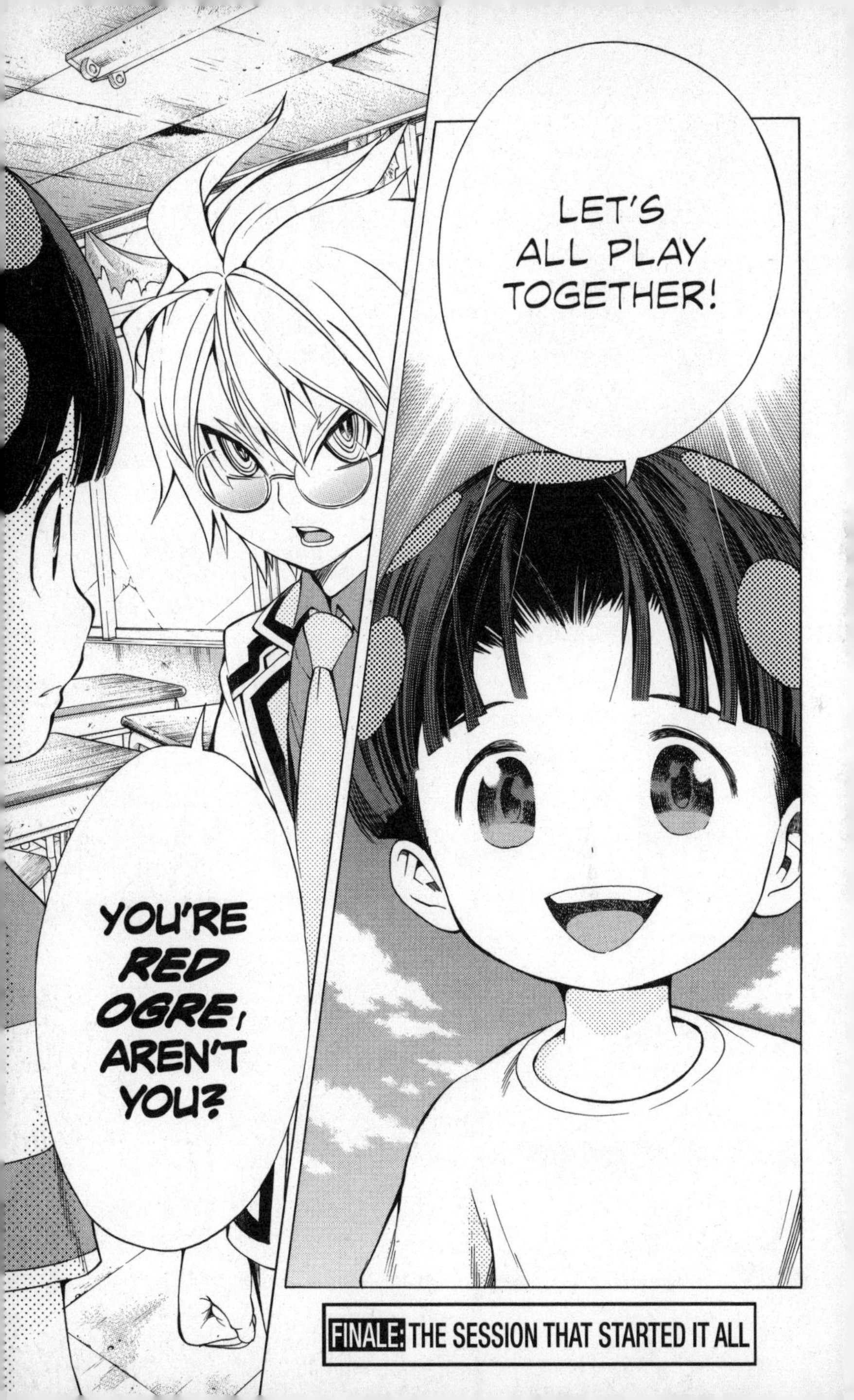
LET'S ALL PLAY TOGETHER!
YOU'RE RED OGRE, AREN'T YOU?
FINALE: THE SESSION THAT STARTED IT ALL

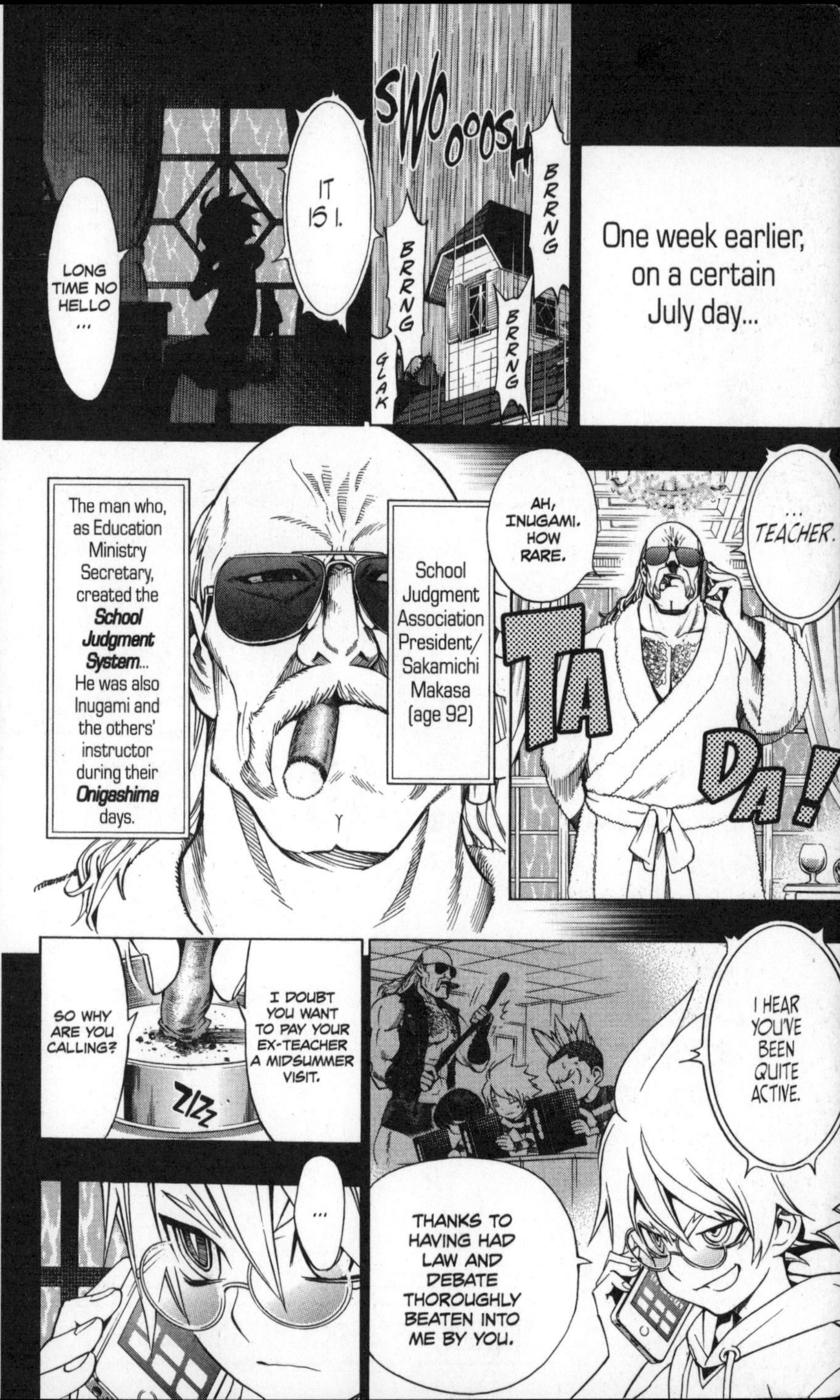
One week earlier, on a certain July day...
SWOOOSH
BRRNG
BRRNG
BRRNG
GLAK
IT IS I.
LONG TIME NO HELLO...
...TEACHER.
AH, INUGAMI. HOW RARE.
TA DA!
School Judgment Association President/ Sakamichi Makasa (age 92)
The man who, as Education Ministry Secretary, created the ***School Judgment System***... He was also Inugami and the others' instructor during their ***Onigashima*** days.
I HEAR YOU'VE BEEN QUITE ACTIVE.
I DOUBT YOU WANT TO PAY YOUR EX-TEACHER A MIDSUMMER VISIT.
SO WHY ARE YOU CALLING?
ZIZZ
THANKS TO HAVING HAD LAW AND DEBATE THOROUGHLY BEATEN INTO ME BY YOU.
...

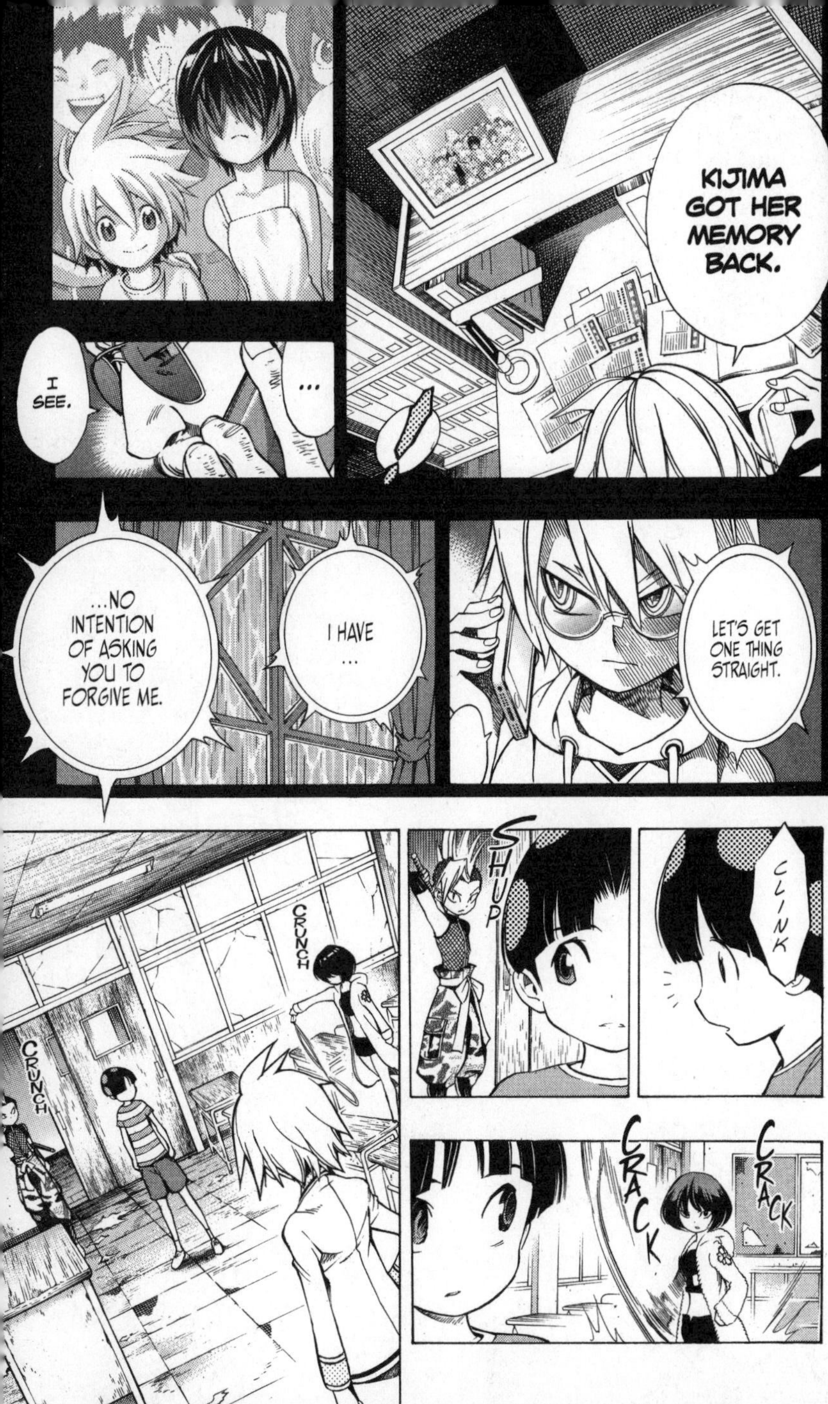
KIJIMA GOT HER MEMORY BACK.
...
I SEE.
LET'S GET ONE THING STRAIGHT.
I HAVE ...
...NO INTENTION OF ASKING YOU TO FORGIVE ME.
CLINK
SHUP
CRACK
CRACK
CRUNCH
CRUNCH

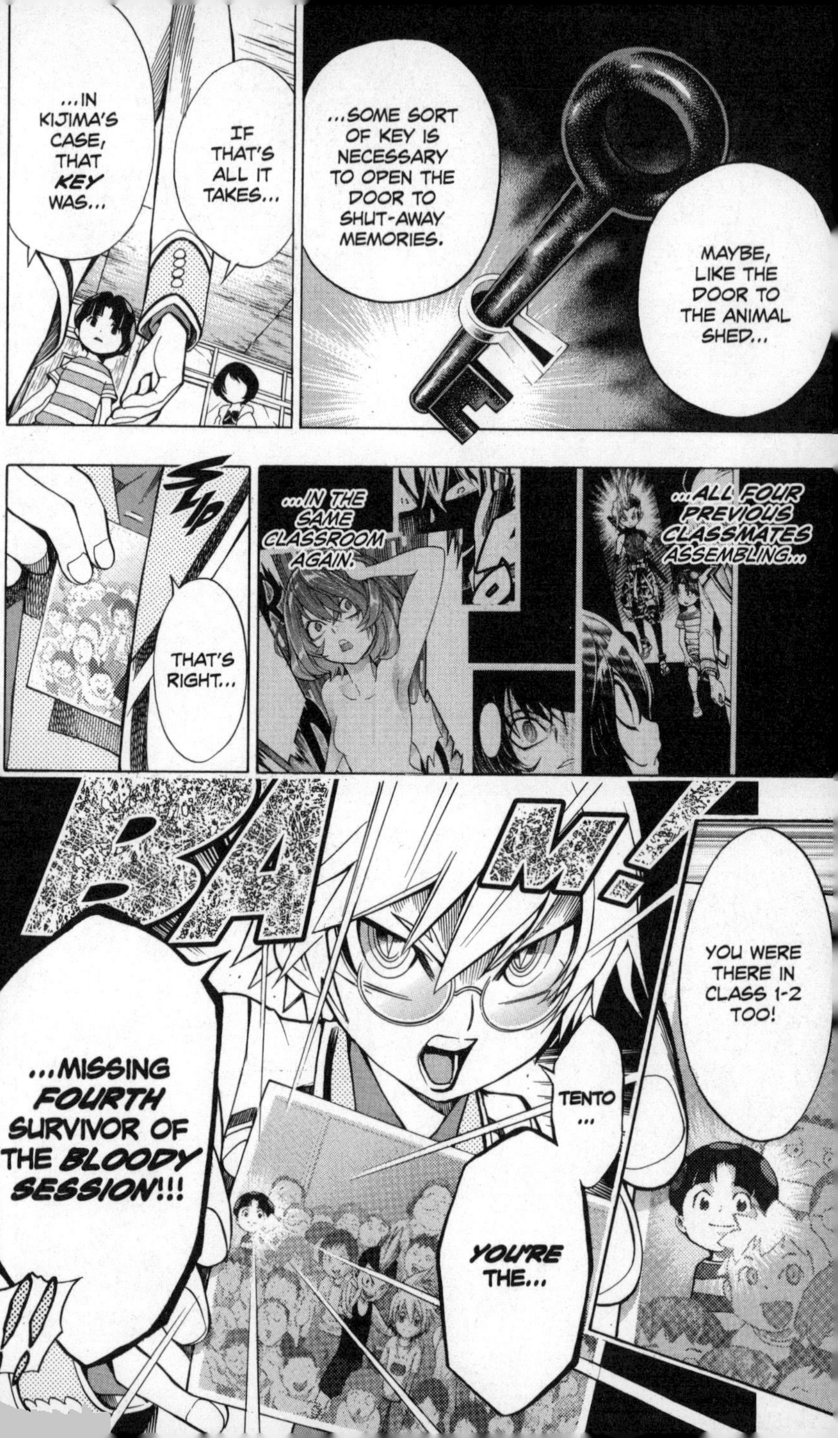
MAYBE, LIKE THE DOOR TO THE ANIMAL SHED...
...SOME SORT OF KEY IS NECESSARY TO OPEN THE DOOR TO SHUT-AWAY MEMORIES.
IF THAT'S ALL IT TAKES...
...IN KIJIMA'S CASE, THAT KEY WAS...
...ALL FOUR PREVIOUS CLASSMATES ASSEMBLING...
...IN THE SAME CLASSROOM AGAIN.
SLIP
THAT'S RIGHT...
BAM!
YOU WERE THERE IN CLASS 1-2 TOO!
TENTO...
YOU'RE THE...
...MISSING FOURTH SURVIVOR OF THE BLOODY SESSION!!!
!!

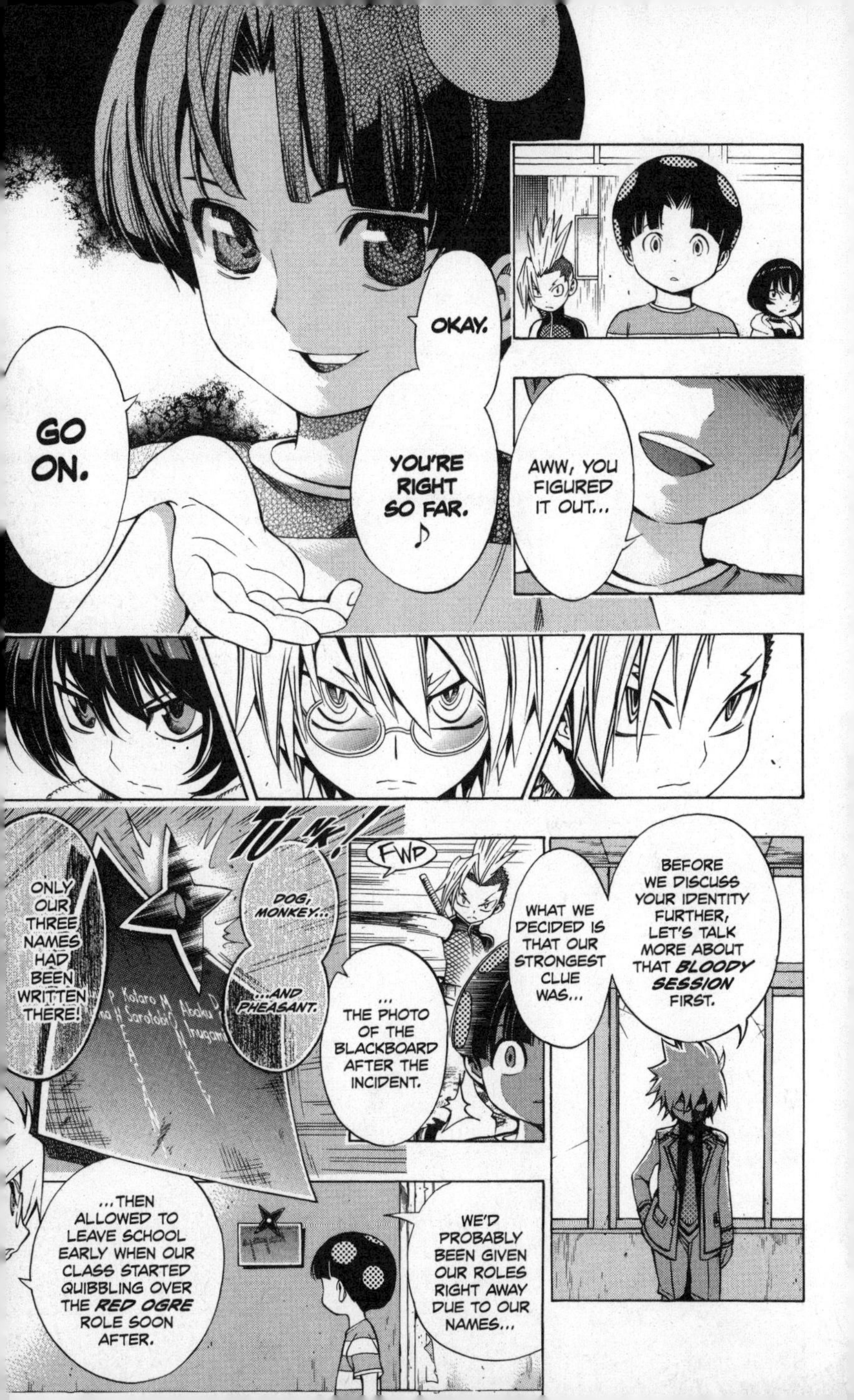
AWW, YOU FIGURED IT OUT...
OKAY.
YOU'RE RIGHT SO FAR. ♪
GO ON.
BEFORE WE DISCUSS YOUR IDENTITY FURTHER, LET'S TALK MORE ABOUT THAT *BLOODY SESSION* FIRST.
WHAT WE DECIDED IS THAT OUR STRONGEST CLUE WAS...
FWP
...THE PHOTO OF THE BLACKBOARD AFTER THE INCIDENT.
TUNK!
DOG, MONKEY...
...AND PHEASANT.
ONLY OUR THREE NAMES HAD BEEN WRITTEN THERE!
WE'D PROBABLY BEEN GIVEN OUR ROLES RIGHT AWAY DUE TO OUR NAMES...
...THEN ALLOWED TO LEAVE SCHOOL EARLY WHEN OUR CLASS STARTED QUIBBLING OVER THE *RED OGRE* ROLE SOON AFTER.

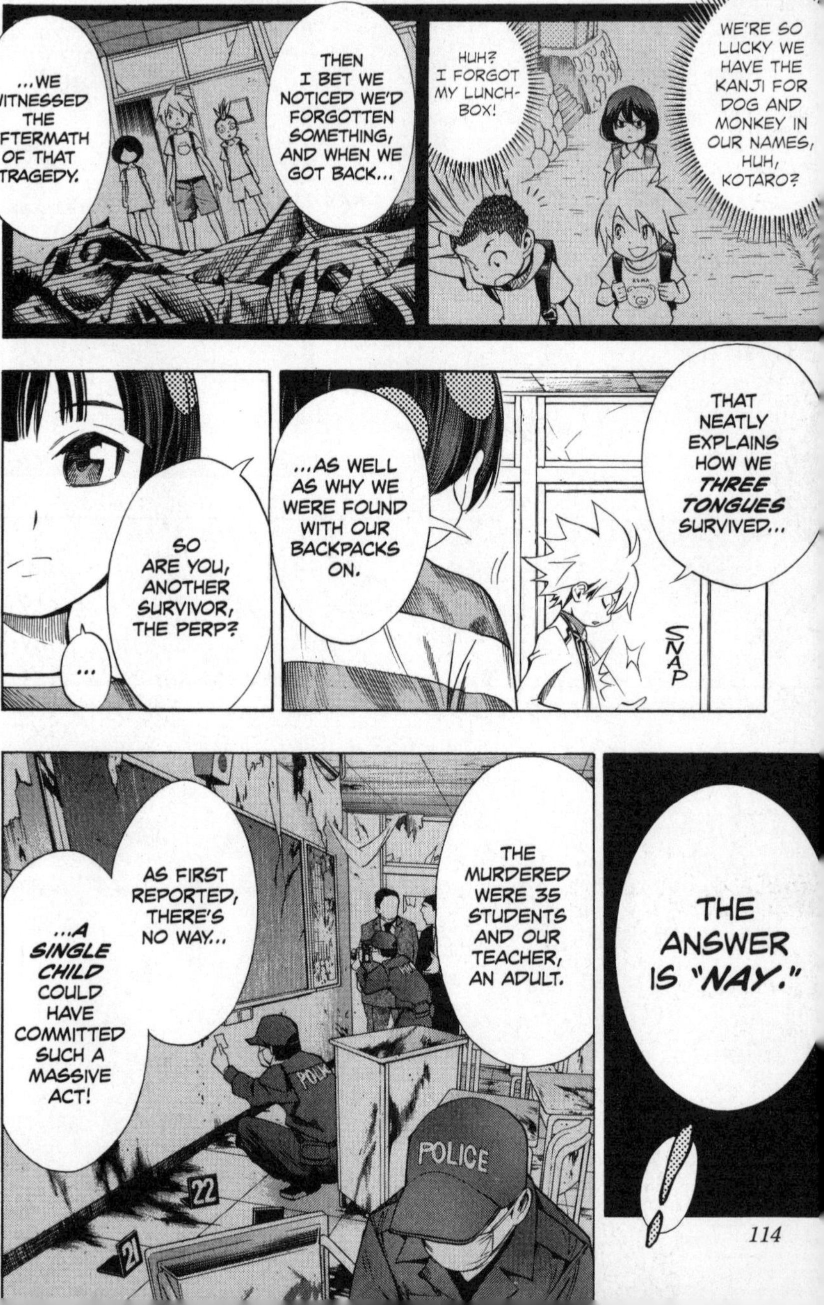
WE'RE SO LUCKY WE HAVE THE KANJI FOR DOG AND MONKEY IN OUR NAMES, HUH, KOTARO?
HUH? I FORGOT MY LUNCH-BOX!
THEN I BET WE NOTICED WE'D FORGOTTEN SOMETHING, AND WHEN WE GOT BACK...
...WE WITNESSED THE AFTERMATH OF THAT TRAGEDY.
THAT NEATLY EXPLAINS HOW WE *THREE TONGUES* SURVIVED...
SNAP
...AS WELL AS WHY WE WERE FOUND WITH OUR BACKPACKS ON.
SO ARE YOU, ANOTHER SURVIVOR, THE PERP?
...
THE ANSWER IS "*NAY.*"
THE MURDERED WERE 35 STUDENTS AND OUR TEACHER, AN ADULT.
AS FIRST REPORTED, THERE'S NO WAY...
...A *SINGLE CHILD* COULD HAVE COMMITTED SUCH A MASSIVE ACT!
POLICE

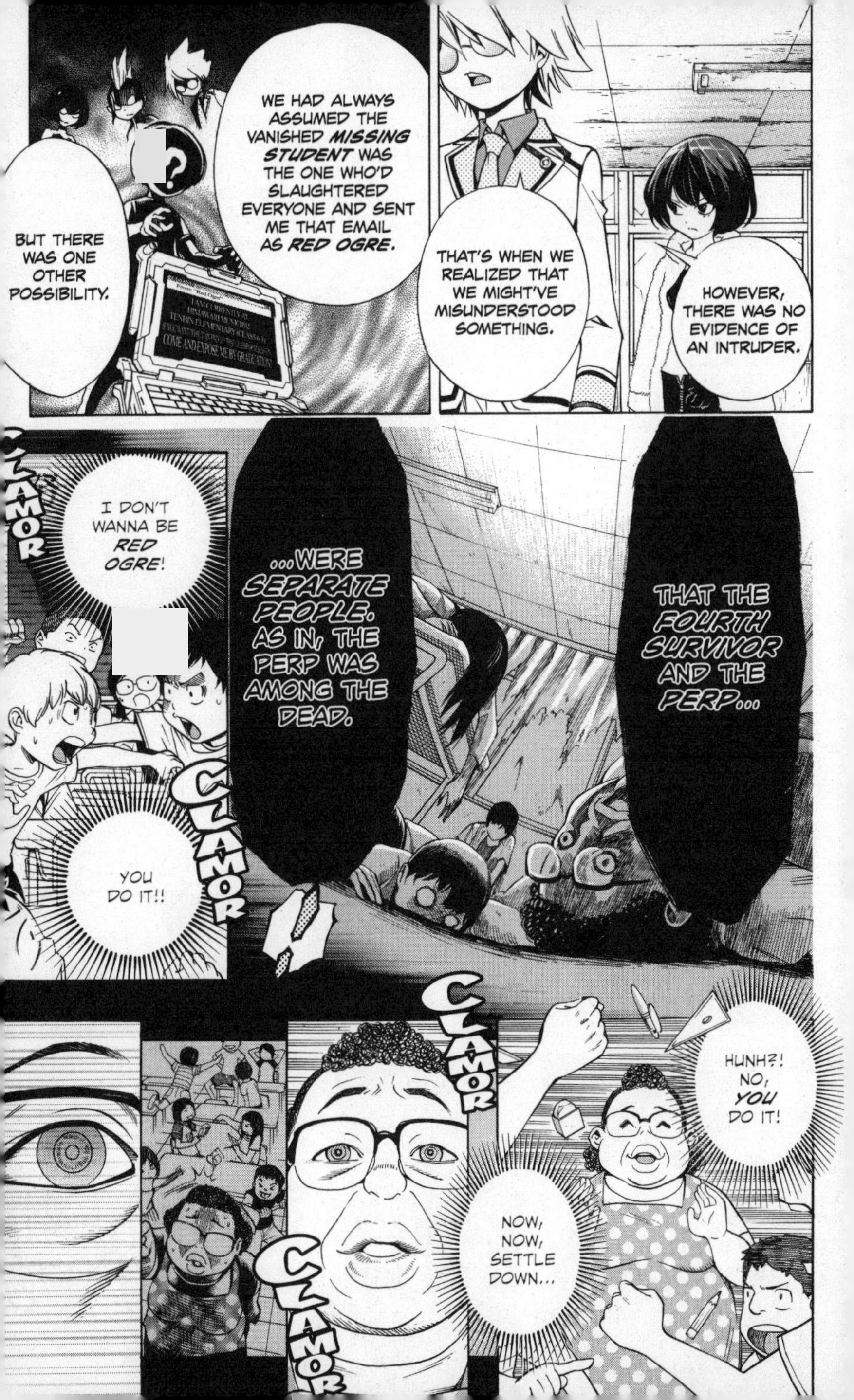
HOWEVER, THERE WAS NO EVIDENCE OF AN INTRUDER.
THAT'S WHEN WE REALIZED THAT WE MIGHT'VE MISUNDERSTOOD SOMETHING.
WE HAD ALWAYS ASSUMED THE VANISHED MISSING STUDENT WAS THE ONE WHO'D SLAUGHTERED EVERYONE AND SENT ME THAT EMAIL AS RED OGRE.
COME AND EXPOSE ME BY GRADUATION
BUT THERE WAS ONE OTHER POSSIBILITY.
THAT THE FOURTH SURVIVOR AND THE PERP...
...WERE SEPARATE PEOPLE. AS IN, THE PERP WAS AMONG THE DEAD.
CLAMOR
I DON'T WANNA BE RED OGRE!
CLAMOR
YOU DO IT!!
CLAMOR
HUNH?! NO, YOU DO IT!
NOW, NOW, SETTLE DOWN...
CLAMOR

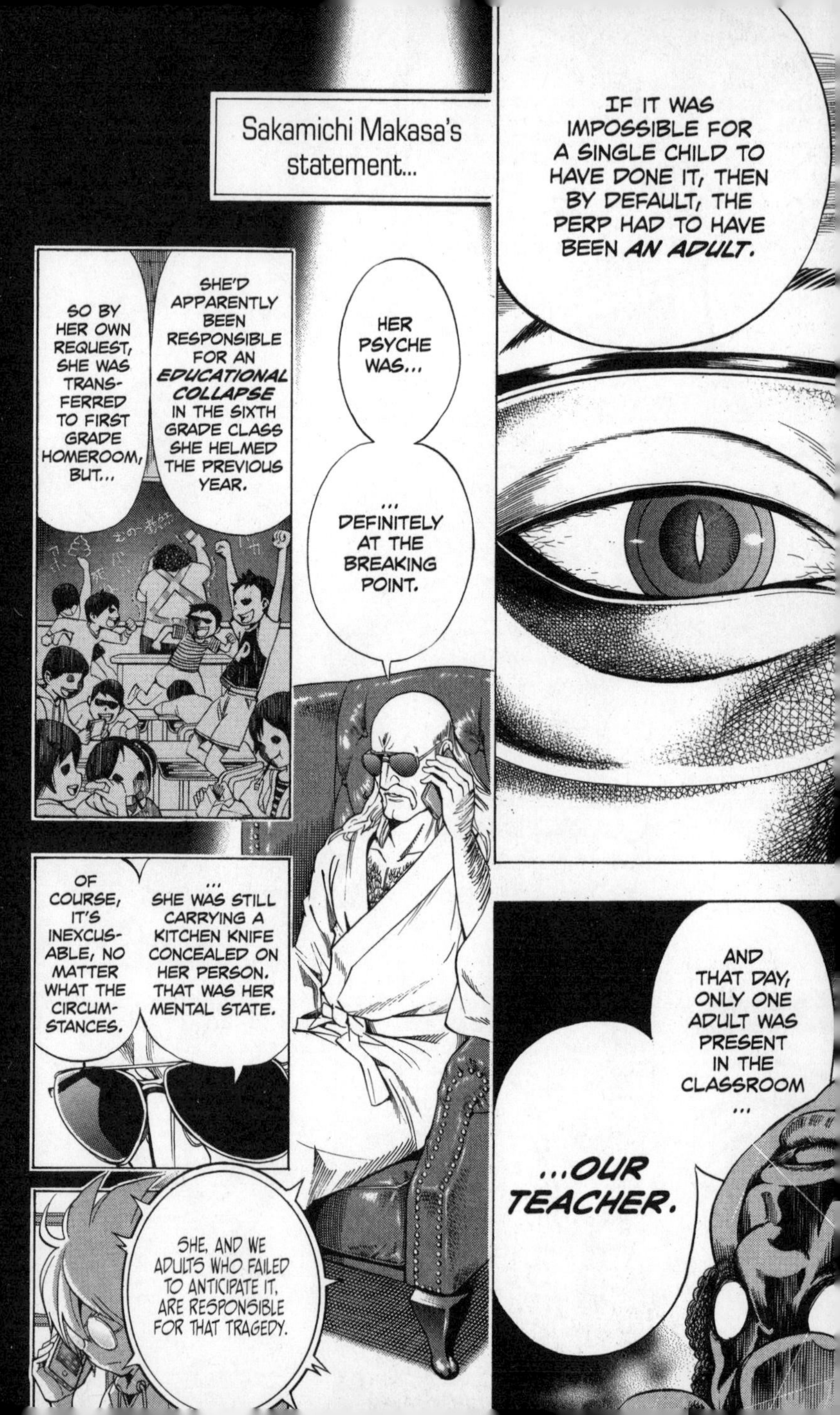
IF IT WAS IMPOSSIBLE FOR A SINGLE CHILD TO HAVE DONE IT, THEN BY DEFAULT, THE PERP HAD TO HAVE BEEN *AN ADULT*.
AND THAT DAY, ONLY ONE ADULT WAS PRESENT IN THE CLASSROOM ...
...*OUR TEACHER*.
Sakamichi Makasa's statement...
HER PSYCHE WAS...
... DEFINITELY AT THE BREAKING POINT.
SHE'D APPARENTLY BEEN RESPONSIBLE FOR AN *EDUCATIONAL COLLAPSE* IN THE SIXTH GRADE CLASS SHE HELMED THE PREVIOUS YEAR.
SO BY HER OWN REQUEST, SHE WAS TRANS-FERRED TO FIRST GRADE HOMEROOM, BUT...
... SHE WAS STILL CARRYING A KITCHEN KNIFE CONCEALED ON HER PERSON. THAT WAS HER MENTAL STATE.
OF COURSE, IT'S INEXCUS-ABLE, NO MATTER WHAT THE CIRCUM-STANCES.
SHE, AND WE ADULTS WHO FAILED TO ANTICIPATE IT, ARE RESPONSIBLE FOR THAT TRAGEDY.

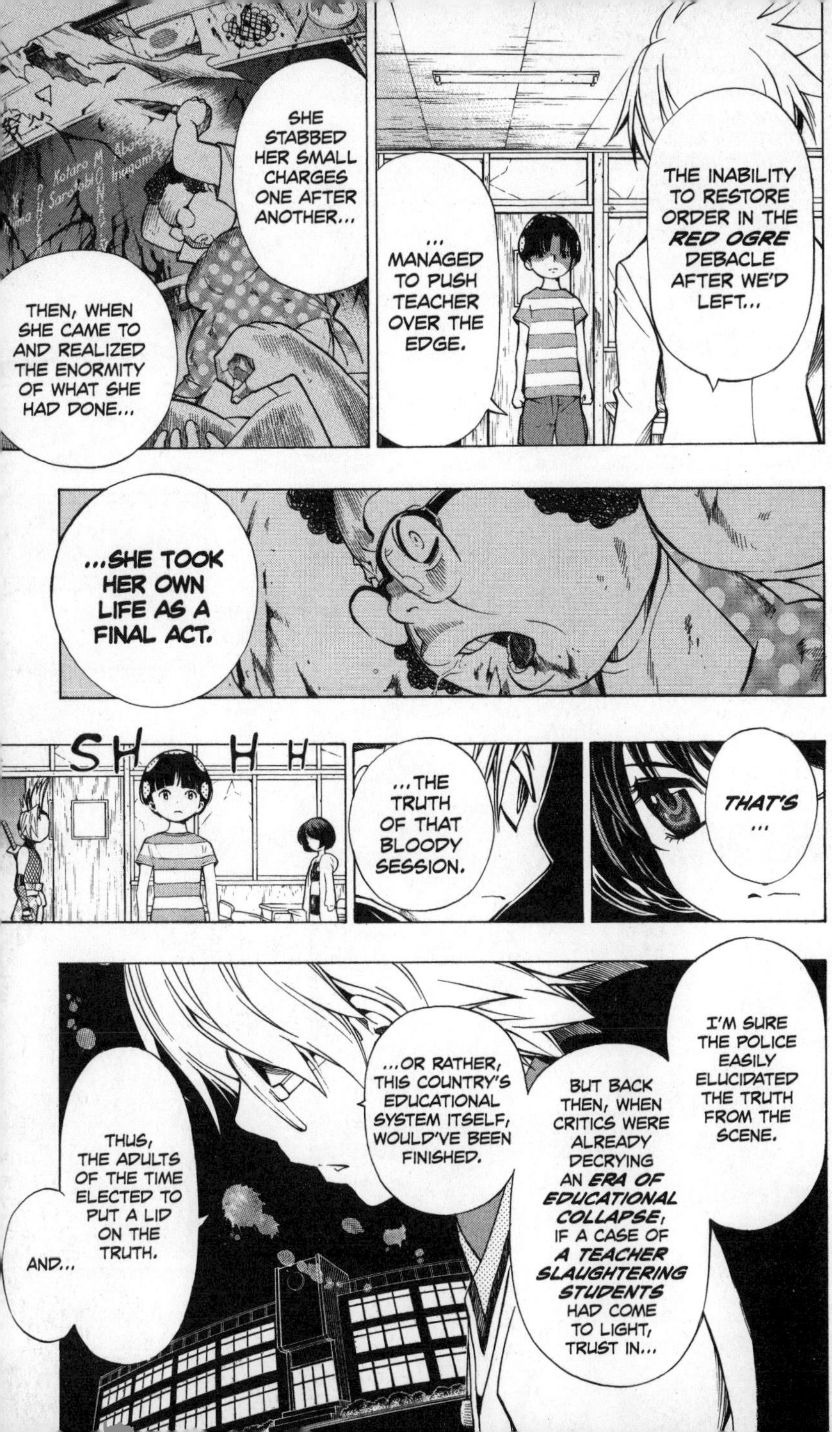
THE INABILITY TO RESTORE ORDER IN THE *RED OGRE* DEBACLE AFTER WE'D LEFT...
...MANAGED TO PUSH TEACHER OVER THE EDGE.
SHE STABBED HER SMALL CHARGES ONE AFTER ANOTHER...
THEN, WHEN SHE CAME TO AND REALIZED THE ENORMITY OF WHAT SHE HAD DONE...
...SHE TOOK HER OWN LIFE AS A FINAL ACT.
THAT'S ...
...THE TRUTH OF THAT BLOODY SESSION.
SH H H
I'M SURE THE POLICE EASILY ELUCIDATED THE TRUTH FROM THE SCENE.
BUT BACK THEN, WHEN CRITICS WERE ALREADY DECRYING AN *ERA OF EDUCATIONAL COLLAPSE*, IF A CASE OF *A TEACHER SLAUGHTERING STUDENTS* HAD COME TO LIGHT, TRUST IN...
...OR RATHER, THIS COUNTRY'S EDUCATIONAL SYSTEM ITSELF, WOULD'VE BEEN FINISHED.
THUS, THE ADULTS OF THE TIME ELECTED TO PUT A LID ON THE TRUTH.
AND...

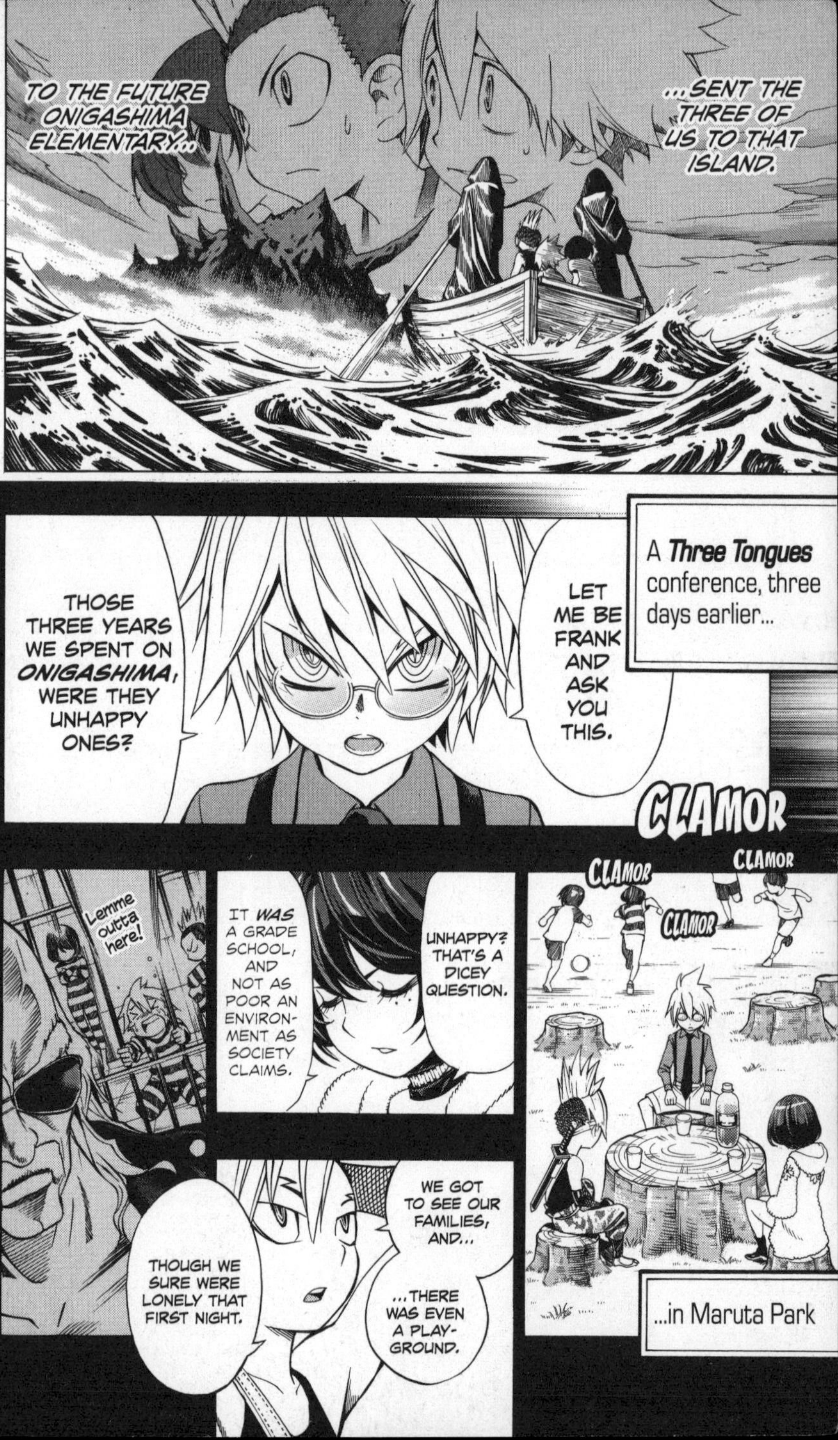
...SENT THE THREE OF US TO THAT ISLAND.
TO THE FUTURE ONIGASHIMA ELEMENTARY...
A **Three Tongues** conference, three days earlier...
LET ME BE FRANK AND ASK YOU THIS.
THOSE THREE YEARS WE SPENT ON ***ONIGASHIMA***, WERE THEY UNHAPPY ONES?
CLAMOR
CLAMOR
CLAMOR
CLAMOR
...in Maruta Park
UNHAPPY? THAT'S A DICEY QUESTION.
IT ***WAS*** A GRADE SCHOOL, AND NOT AS POOR AN ENVIRONMENT AS SOCIETY CLAIMS.
WE GOT TO SEE OUR FAMILIES, AND...
...THERE WAS EVEN A PLAYGROUND.
THOUGH WE SURE WERE LONELY THAT FIRST NIGHT.
Lemme outta here!

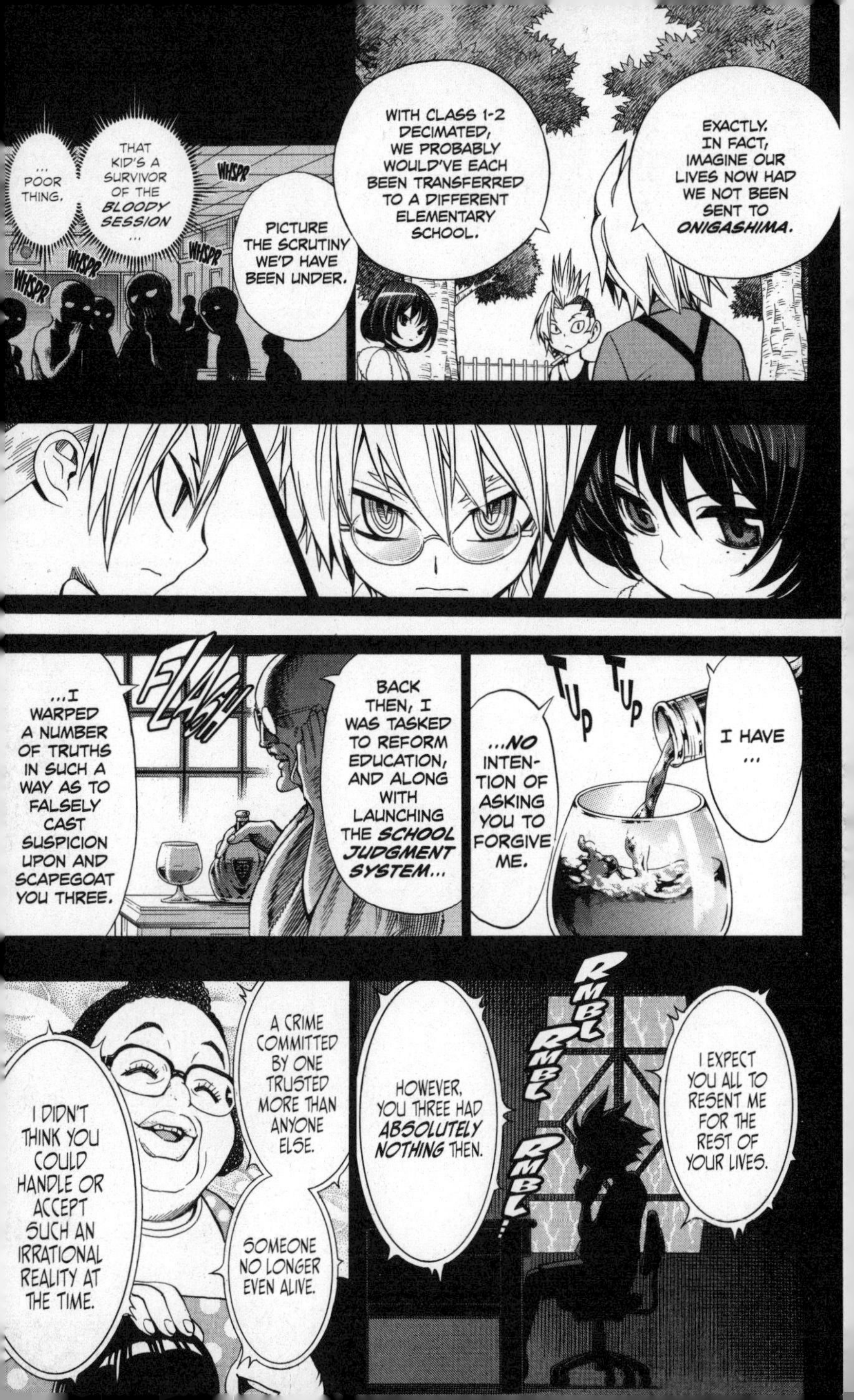
EXACTLY. IN FACT, IMAGINE OUR LIVES NOW HAD WE NOT BEEN SENT TO ONIGASHIMA.
WITH CLASS 1-2 DECIMATED, WE PROBABLY WOULD'VE EACH BEEN TRANSFERRED TO A DIFFERENT ELEMENTARY SCHOOL.
PICTURE THE SCRUTINY WE'D HAVE BEEN UNDER.
WHSPR
THAT KID'S A SURVIVOR OF THE BLOODY SESSION...
...POOR THING.
WHSPR
WHSPR
WHSPR
TUP TUP
I HAVE...
...NO INTENTION OF ASKING YOU TO FORGIVE ME.
BACK THEN, I WAS TASKED TO REFORM EDUCATION, AND ALONG WITH LAUNCHING THE SCHOOL JUDGMENT SYSTEM...
...I WARPED A NUMBER OF TRUTHS IN SUCH A WAY AS TO FALSELY CAST SUSPICION UPON AND SCAPEGOAT YOU THREE.
RMBL RMBL RMBL
I EXPECT YOU ALL TO RESENT ME FOR THE REST OF YOUR LIVES.
HOWEVER, YOU THREE HAD ABSOLUTELY NOTHING THEN.
A CRIME COMMITTED BY ONE TRUSTED MORE THAN ANYONE ELSE.
SOMEONE NO LONGER EVEN ALIVE.
I DIDN'T THINK YOU COULD HANDLE OR ACCEPT SUCH AN IRRATIONAL REALITY AT THE TIME.

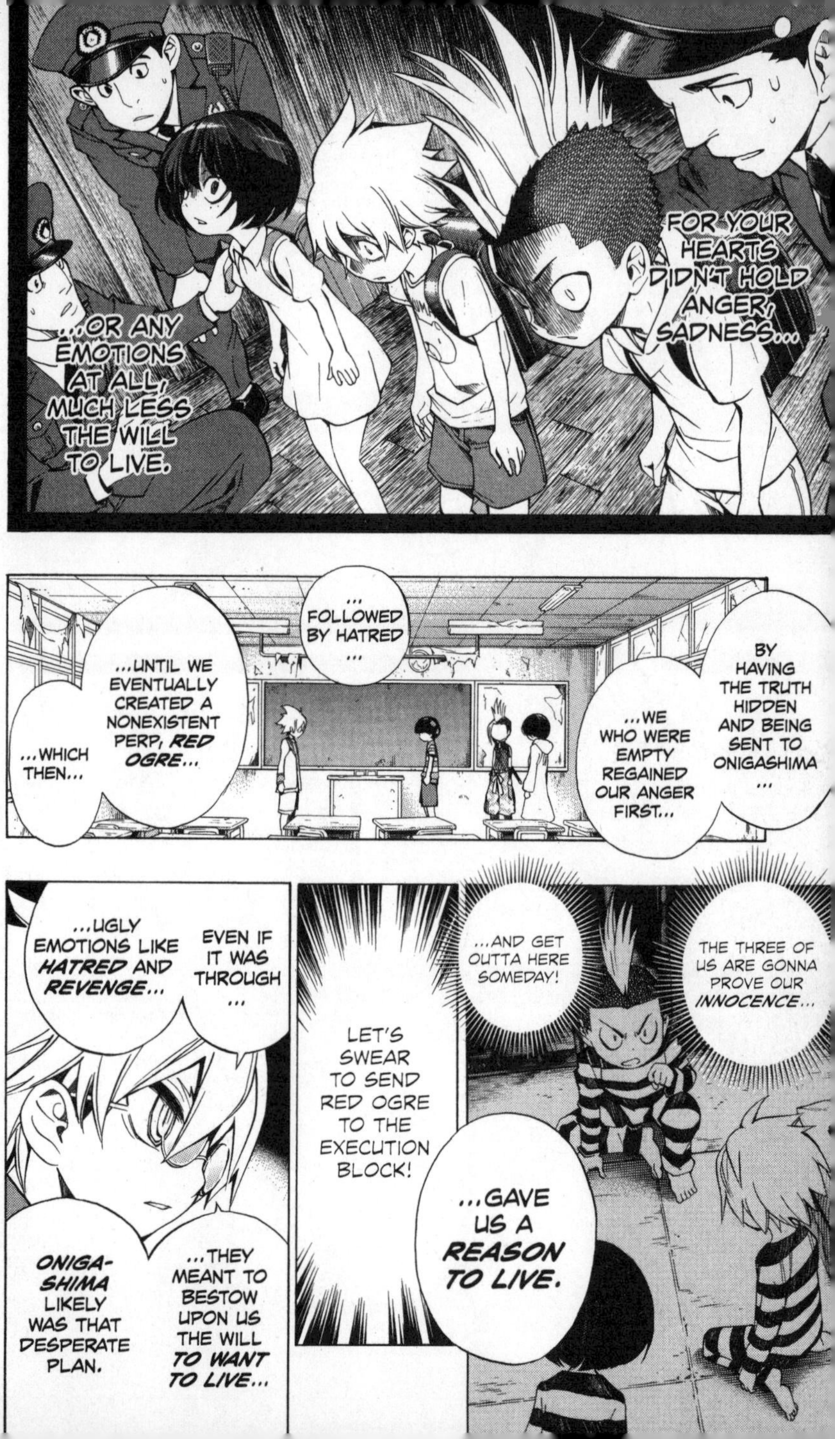
FOR YOUR HEARTS DIDN'T HOLD ANGER, SADNESS...
...OR ANY EMOTIONS AT ALL, MUCH LESS THE WILL TO LIVE.
BY HAVING THE TRUTH HIDDEN AND BEING SENT TO ONIGASHIMA...
...WE WHO WERE EMPTY REGAINED OUR ANGER FIRST...
...FOLLOWED BY HATRED...
...UNTIL WE EVENTUALLY CREATED A NONEXISTENT PERP, RED OGRE...
...WHICH THEN...
THE THREE OF US ARE GONNA PROVE OUR INNOCENCE...
...AND GET OUTTA HERE SOMEDAY!
LET'S SWEAR TO SEND RED OGRE TO THE EXECUTION BLOCK!
...GAVE US A REASON TO LIVE.
EVEN IF IT WAS THROUGH...
...UGLY EMOTIONS LIKE HATRED AND REVENGE...
...THEY MEANT TO BESTOW UPON US THE WILL TO WANT TO LIVE...
ONIGASHIMA LIKELY WAS THAT DESPERATE PLAN.

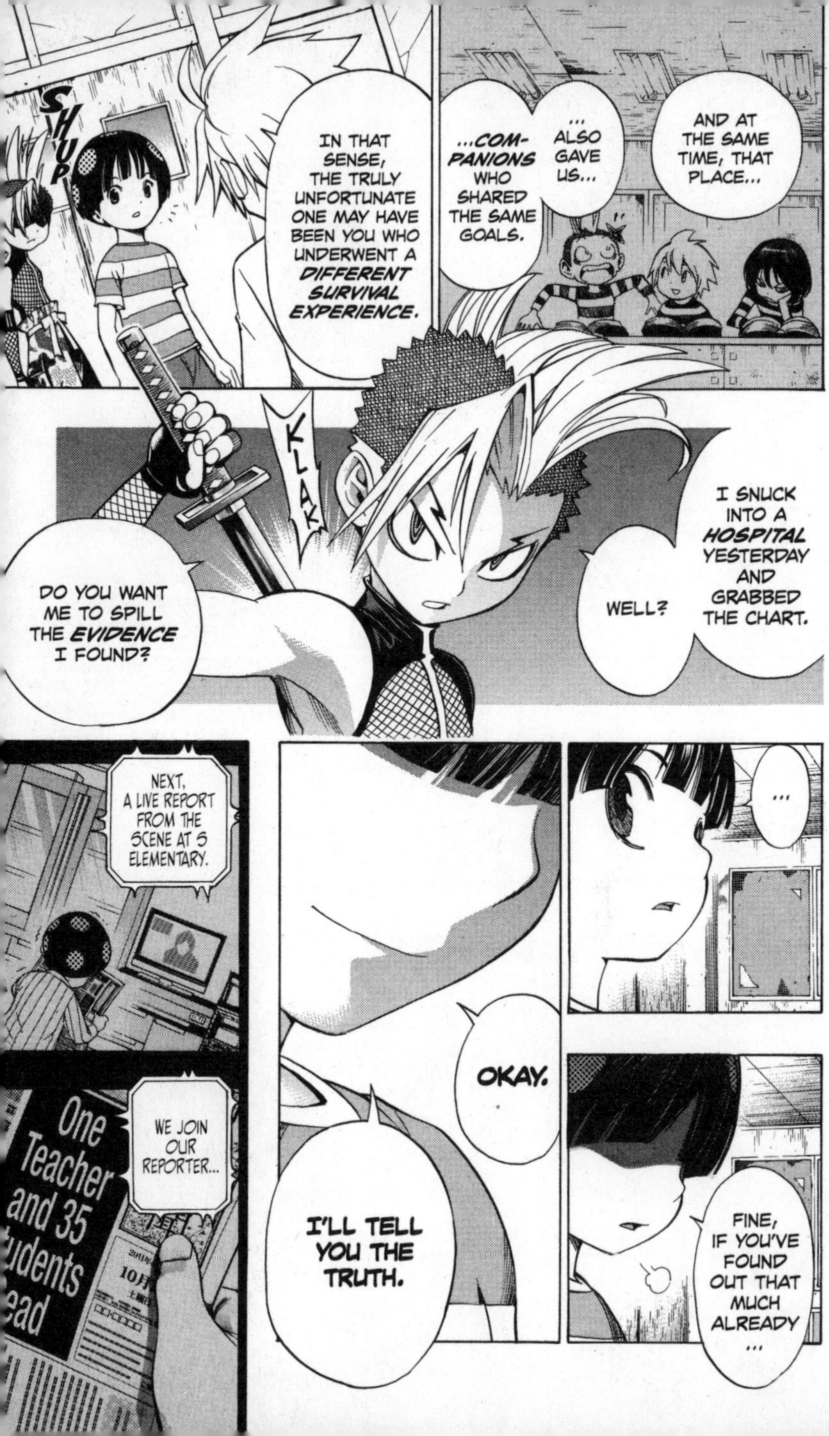
AND AT THE SAME TIME, THAT PLACE...
...ALSO GAVE US...
...COMPANIONS WHO SHARED THE SAME GOALS.
IN THAT SENSE, THE TRULY UNFORTUNATE ONE MAY HAVE BEEN YOU WHO UNDERWENT A DIFFERENT SURVIVAL EXPERIENCE.
SHUP
KLAK
I SNUCK INTO A HOSPITAL YESTERDAY AND GRABBED THE CHART.
WELL?
DO YOU WANT ME TO SPILL THE EVIDENCE I FOUND?
...
FINE, IF YOU'VE FOUND OUT THAT MUCH ALREADY...
OKAY.
I'LL TELL YOU THE TRUTH.
NEXT, A LIVE REPORT FROM THE SCENE AT S ELEMENTARY.
WE JOIN OUR REPORTER...
One Teacher and 35

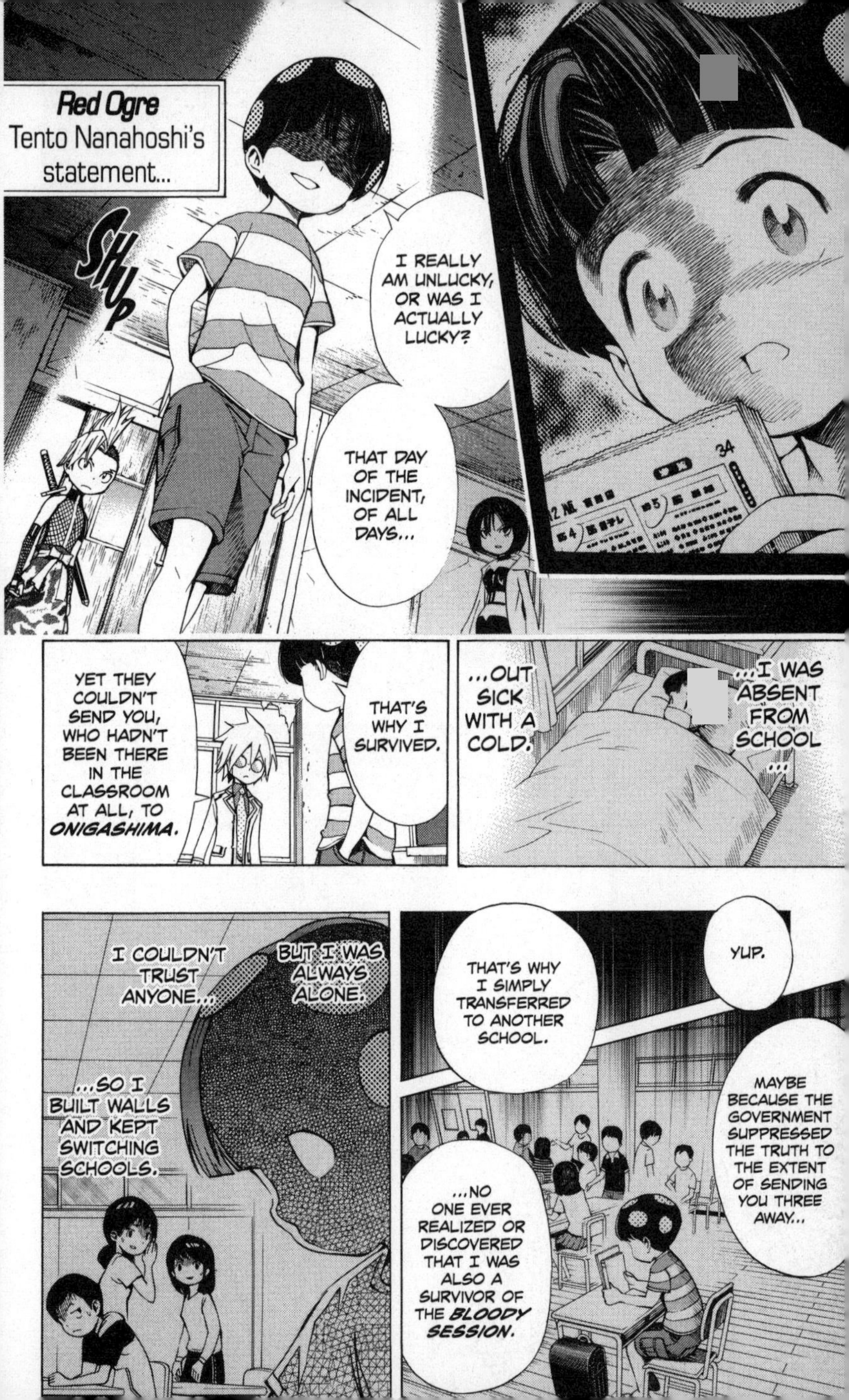
Red Ogre
Tento Nanahoshi's statement...
SHUP
I REALLY AM UNLUCKY, OR WAS I ACTUALLY LUCKY?
THAT DAY OF THE INCIDENT, OF ALL DAYS...
...I WAS ABSENT FROM SCHOOL...
...OUT SICK WITH A COLD.
THAT'S WHY I SURVIVED.
YET THEY COULDN'T SEND YOU, WHO HADN'T BEEN THERE IN THE CLASSROOM AT ALL, TO ONIGASHIMA.
YUP.
THAT'S WHY I SIMPLY TRANSFERRED TO ANOTHER SCHOOL.
MAYBE BECAUSE THE GOVERNMENT SUPPRESSED THE TRUTH TO THE EXTENT OF SENDING YOU THREE AWAY...
...NO ONE EVER REALIZED OR DISCOVERED THAT I WAS ALSO A SURVIVOR OF THE BLOODY SESSION.
BUT I WAS ALWAYS ALONE.
I COULDN'T TRUST ANYONE...
...SO I BUILT WALLS AND KEPT SWITCHING SCHOOLS.

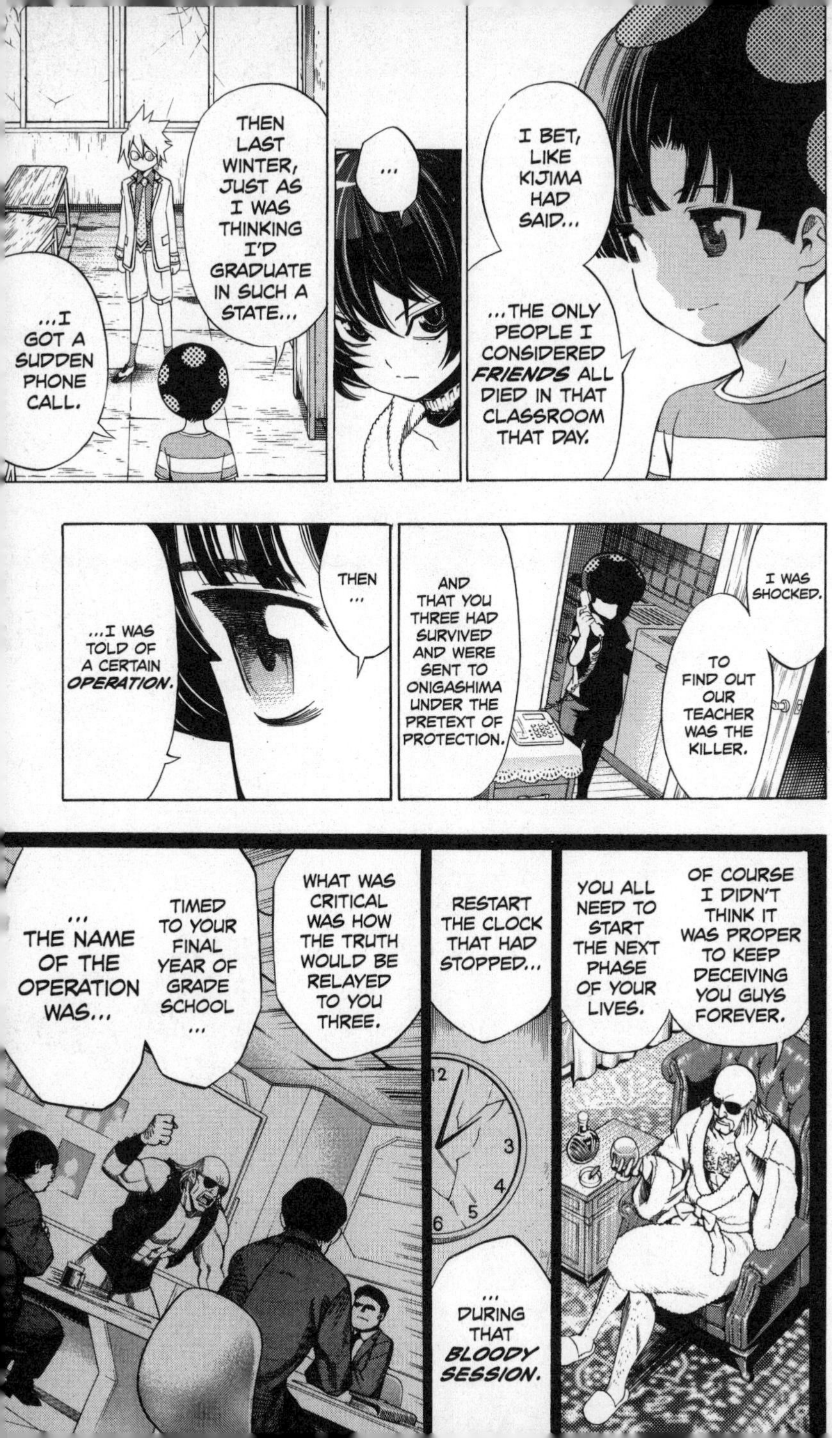
I BET, LIKE KIJIMA HAD SAID...
...THE ONLY PEOPLE I CONSIDERED FRIENDS ALL DIED IN THAT CLASSROOM THAT DAY.
...
THEN LAST WINTER, JUST AS I WAS THINKING I'D GRADUATE IN SUCH A STATE...
...I GOT A SUDDEN PHONE CALL.
I WAS SHOCKED.
TO FIND OUT OUR TEACHER WAS THE KILLER.
AND THAT YOU THREE HAD SURVIVED AND WERE SENT TO ONIGASHIMA UNDER THE PRETEXT OF PROTECTION.
THEN ...
...I WAS TOLD OF A CERTAIN OPERATION.
OF COURSE I DIDN'T THINK IT WAS PROPER TO KEEP DECEIVING YOU GUYS FOREVER.
YOU ALL NEED TO START THE NEXT PHASE OF YOUR LIVES.
RESTART THE CLOCK THAT HAD STOPPED...
... DURING THAT BLOODY SESSION.
WHAT WAS CRITICAL WAS HOW THE TRUTH WOULD BE RELAYED TO YOU THREE.
TIMED TO YOUR FINAL YEAR OF GRADE SCHOOL ...
... THE NAME OF THE OPERATION WAS...

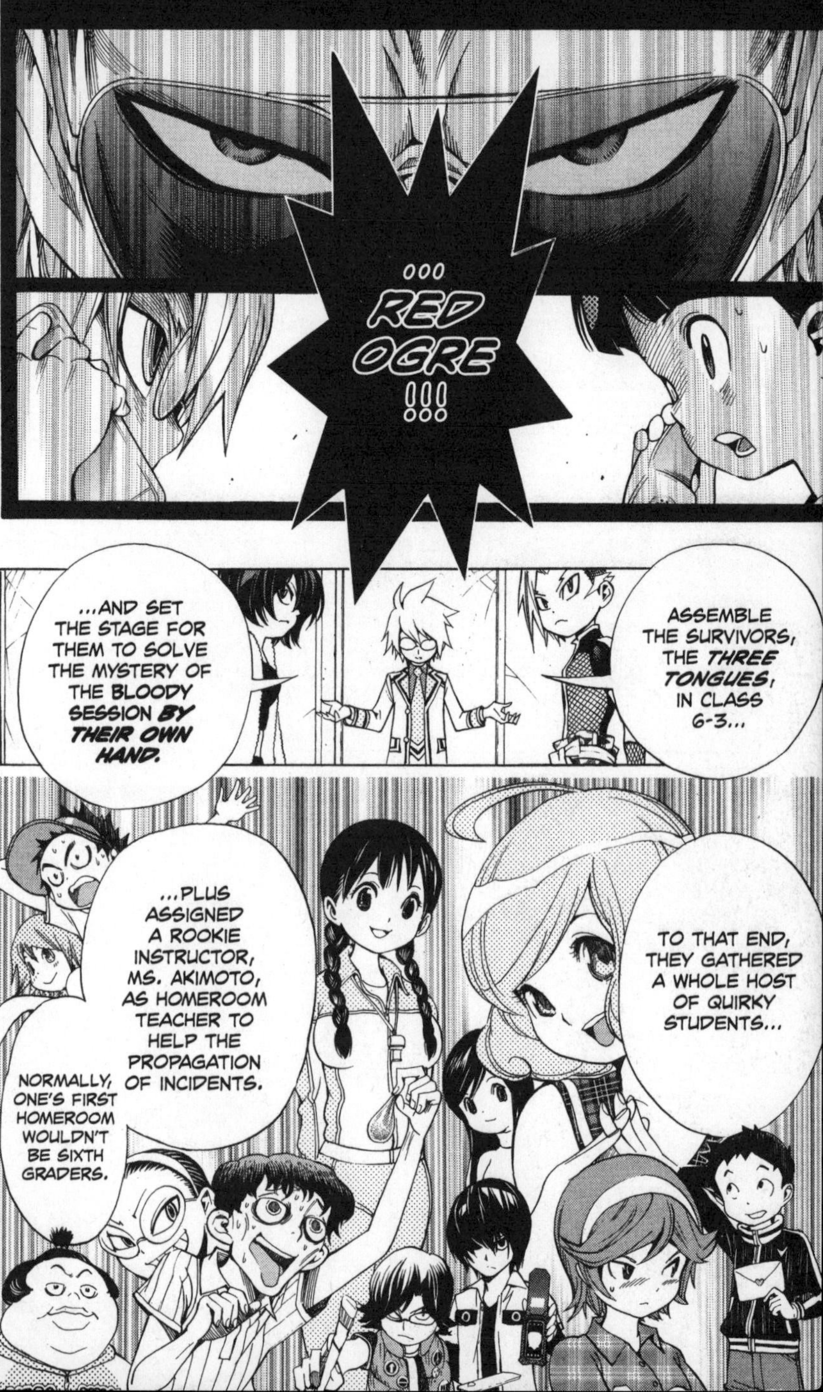
ooo RED OGRE !!!
ASSEMBLE THE SURVIVORS, THE *THREE TONGUES*, IN CLASS 6-3...
...AND SET THE STAGE FOR THEM TO SOLVE THE MYSTERY OF THE BLOODY SESSION *BY THEIR OWN HAND.*
TO THAT END, THEY GATHERED A WHOLE HOST OF QUIRKY STUDENTS...
...PLUS ASSIGNED A ROOKIE INSTRUCTOR, MS. AKIMOTO, AS HOMEROOM TEACHER TO HELP THE PROPAGATION OF INCIDENTS.
NORMALLY, ONE'S FIRST HOMEROOM WOULDN'T BE SIXTH GRADERS.

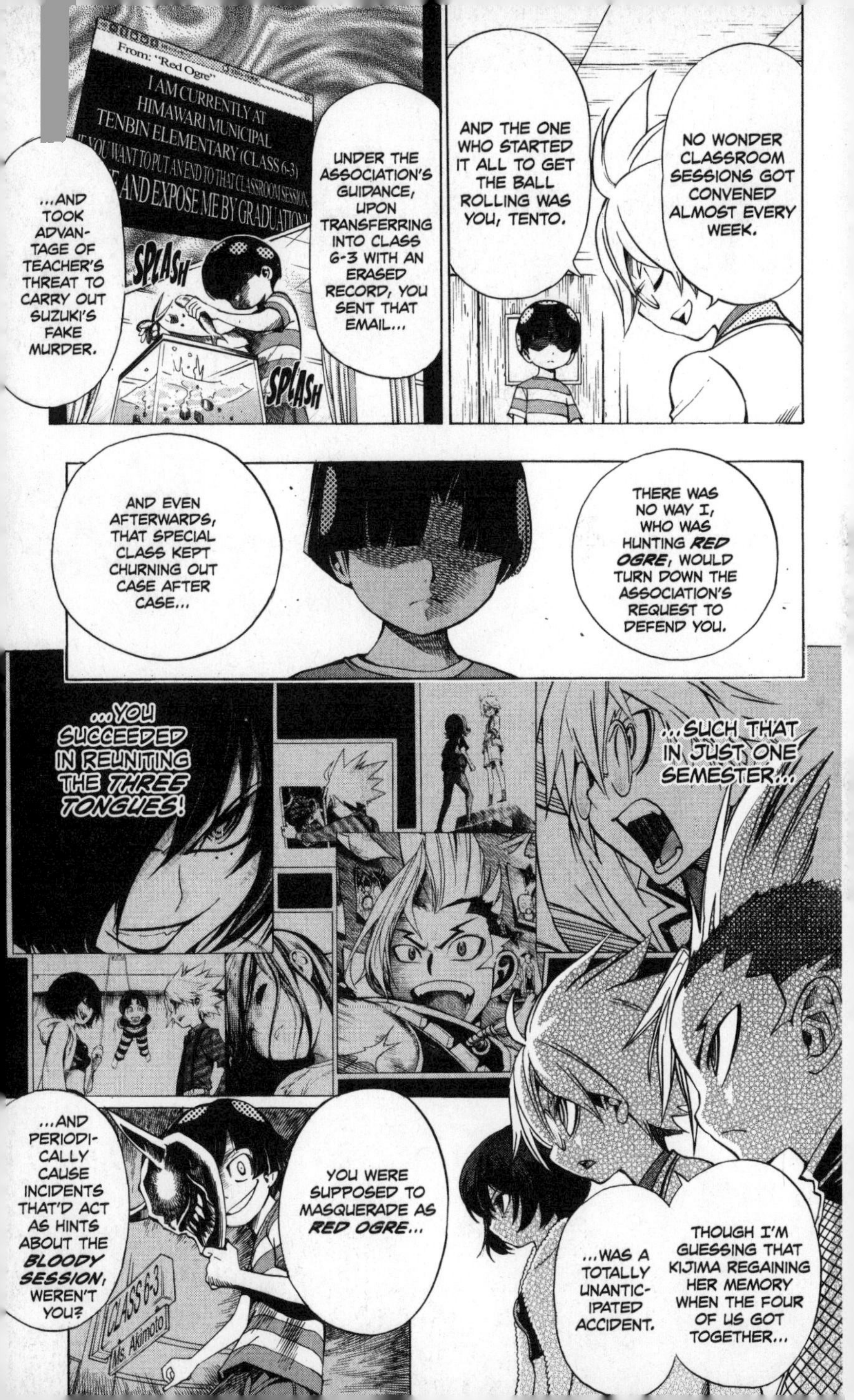
NO WONDER CLASSROOM SESSIONS GOT CONVENED ALMOST EVERY WEEK.
AND THE ONE WHO STARTED IT ALL TO GET THE BALL ROLLING WAS YOU, TENTO.
UNDER THE ASSOCIATION'S GUIDANCE, UPON TRANSFERRING INTO CLASS 6-3 WITH AN ERASED RECORD, YOU SENT THAT EMAIL...
From: "Red Ogre"
I AM CURRENTLY AT HIMAWARI MUNICIPAL TENBIN ELEMENTARY (CLASS 6-3)
IF YOU WANT TO PUT AN END TO THAT CLASSROOM SESSION,
AND EXPOSE ME BY GRADUATION!
SPLASH
SPLASH
...AND TOOK ADVANTAGE OF TEACHER'S THREAT TO CARRY OUT SUZUKI'S FAKE MURDER.
THERE WAS NO WAY I, WHO WAS HUNTING RED OGRE, WOULD TURN DOWN THE ASSOCIATION'S REQUEST TO DEFEND YOU.
AND EVEN AFTERWARDS, THAT SPECIAL CLASS KEPT CHURNING OUT CASE AFTER CASE...
...SUCH THAT IN JUST ONE SEMESTER...
...YOU SUCCEEDED IN REUNITING THE THREE TONGUES!
THOUGH I'M GUESSING THAT KIJIMA REGAINING HER MEMORY WHEN THE FOUR OF US GOT TOGETHER...
...WAS A TOTALLY UNANTICIPATED ACCIDENT.
YOU WERE SUPPOSED TO MASQUERADE AS RED OGRE...
...AND PERIODICALLY CAUSE INCIDENTS THAT'D ACT AS HINTS ABOUT THE BLOODY SESSION, WEREN'T YOU?
CLASS 6-3
Ms. Akimoto

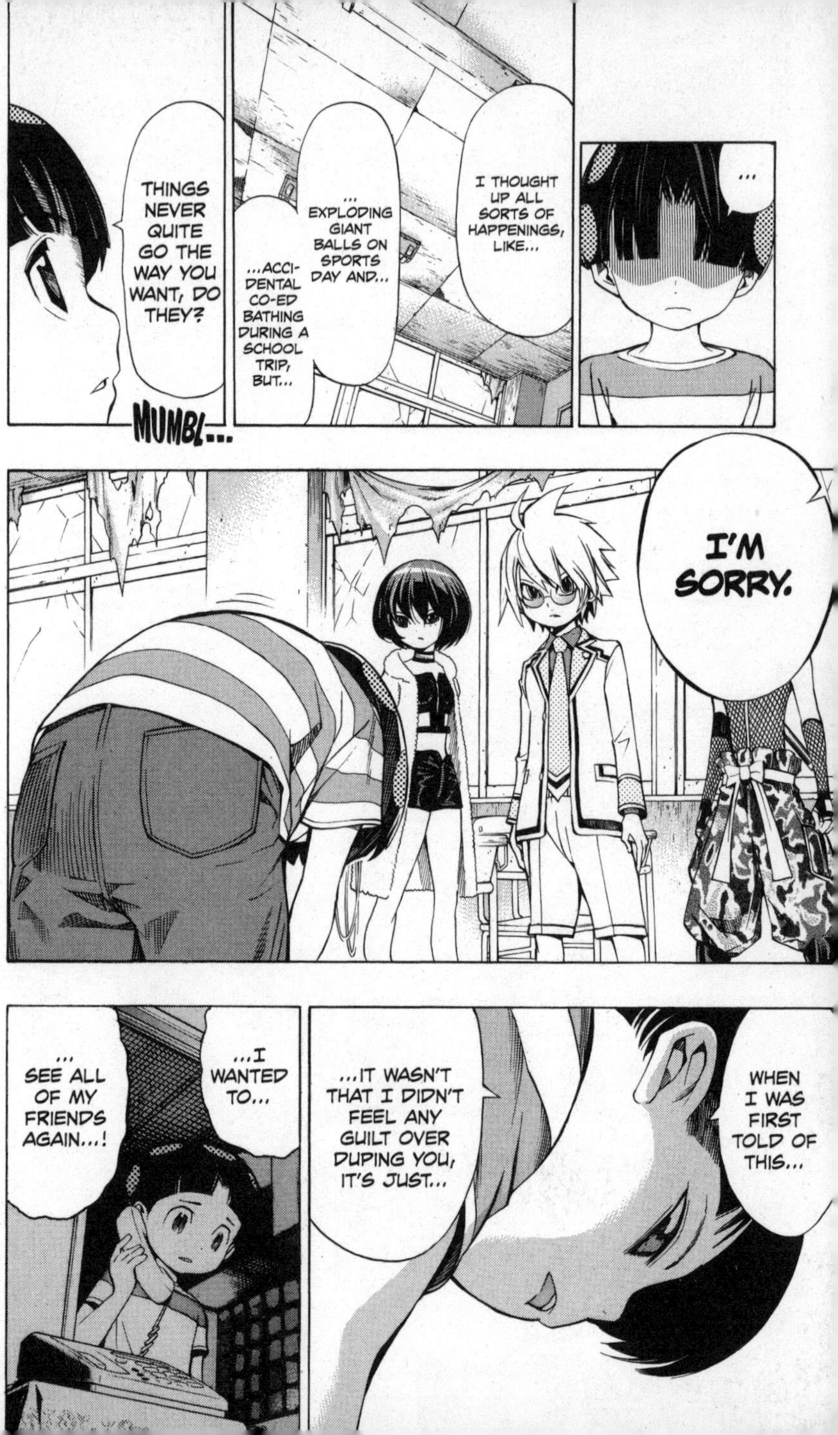
...
I THOUGHT UP ALL SORTS OF HAPPENINGS, LIKE...
...EXPLODING GIANT BALLS ON SPORTS DAY AND...
...ACCI-DENTAL CO-ED BATHING DURING A SCHOOL TRIP, BUT...
THINGS NEVER QUITE GO THE WAY YOU WANT, DO THEY?
MUMBL...
I'M SORRY.
WHEN I WAS FIRST TOLD OF THIS...
...IT WASN'T THAT I DIDN'T FEEL ANY GUILT OVER DUPING YOU, IT'S JUST...
...I WANTED TO...
... SEE ALL OF MY FRIENDS AGAIN...!

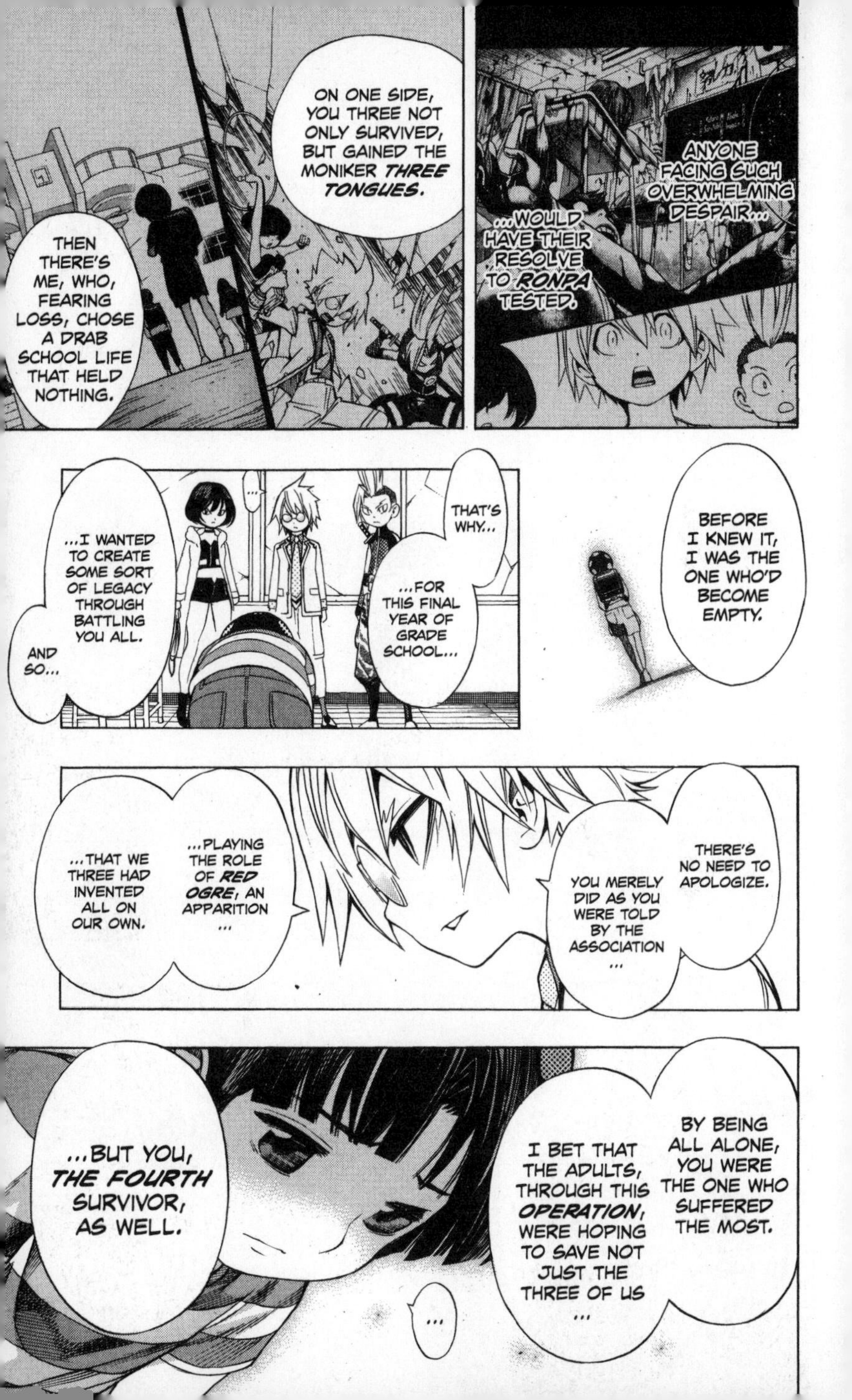
ANYONE FACING SUCH OVERWHELMING DESPAIR...
...WOULD HAVE THEIR RESOLVE TO RONPA TESTED.
ON ONE SIDE, YOU THREE NOT ONLY SURVIVED, BUT GAINED THE MONIKER THREE TONGUES.
THEN THERE'S ME, WHO, FEARING LOSS, CHOSE A DRAB SCHOOL LIFE THAT HELD NOTHING.
BEFORE I KNEW IT, I WAS THE ONE WHO'D BECOME EMPTY.
THAT'S WHY...
...
...FOR THIS FINAL YEAR OF GRADE SCHOOL...
...I WANTED TO CREATE SOME SORT OF LEGACY THROUGH BATTLING YOU ALL.
AND SO...
THERE'S NO NEED TO APOLOGIZE.
YOU MERELY DID AS YOU WERE TOLD BY THE ASSOCIATION...
...PLAYING THE ROLE OF RED OGRE, AN APPARITION...
...THAT WE THREE HAD INVENTED ALL ON OUR OWN.
BY BEING ALL ALONE, YOU WERE THE ONE WHO SUFFERED THE MOST.
I BET THAT THE ADULTS, THROUGH THIS OPERATION, WERE HOPING TO SAVE NOT JUST THE THREE OF US...
...
...BUT YOU, THE FOURTH SURVIVOR, AS WELL.

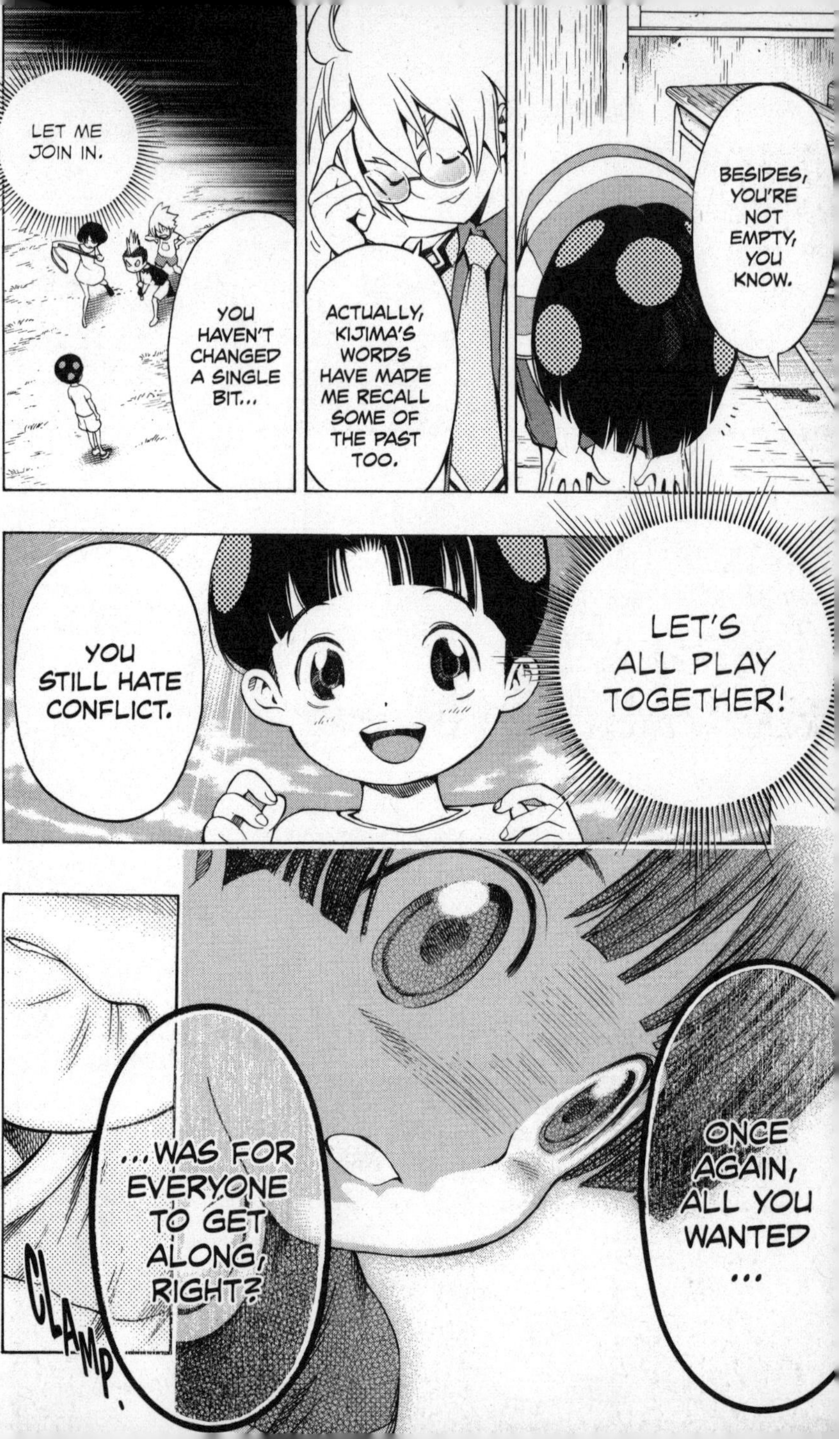
BESIDES, YOU'RE NOT EMPTY, YOU KNOW.
ACTUALLY, KIJIMA'S WORDS HAVE MADE ME RECALL SOME OF THE PAST TOO.
YOU HAVEN'T CHANGED A SINGLE BIT...
LET ME JOIN IN.
LET'S ALL PLAY TOGETHER!
YOU STILL HATE CONFLICT.
ONCE AGAIN, ALL YOU WANTED...
...WAS FOR EVERYONE TO GET ALONG, RIGHT?
CLAMP.

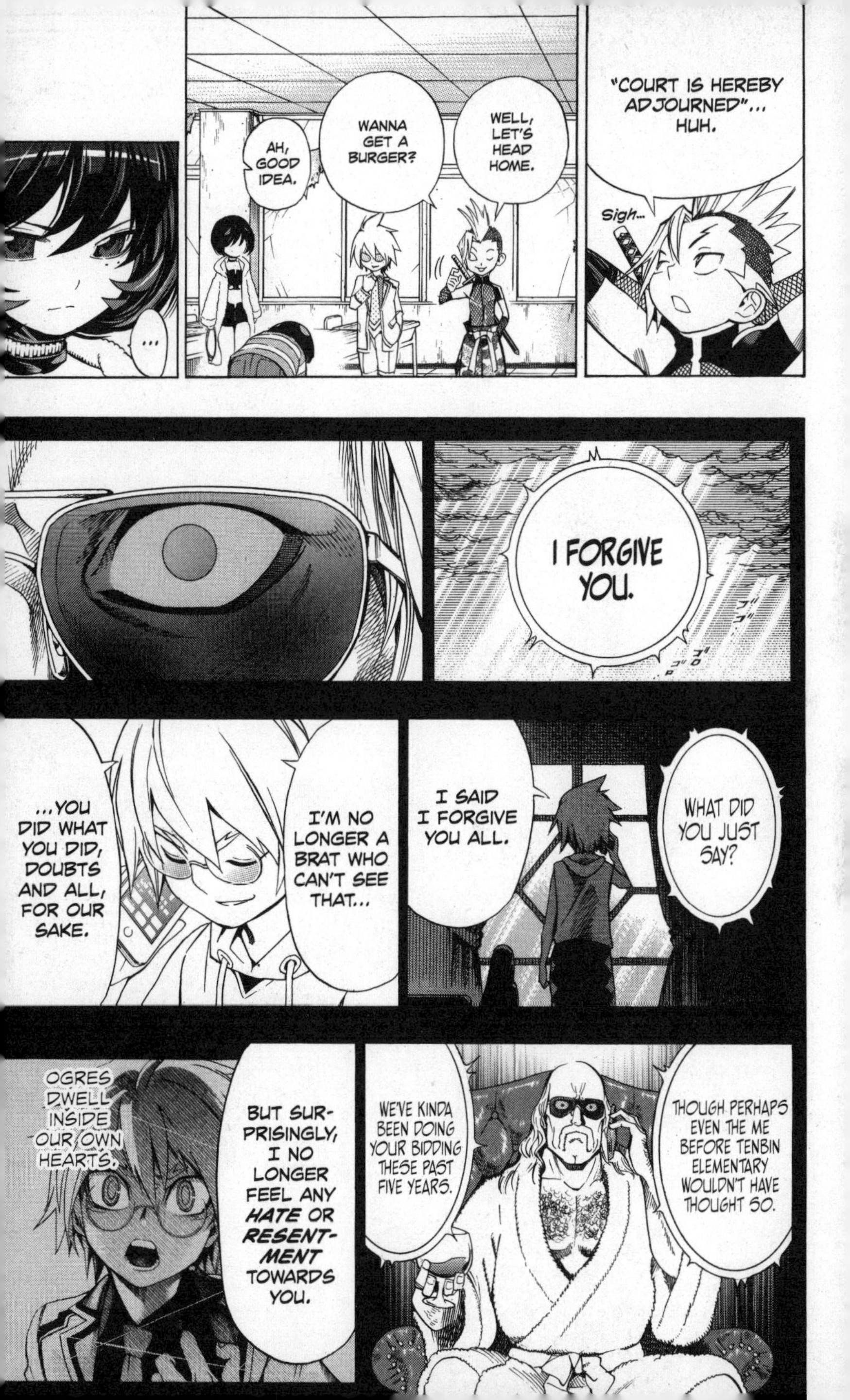
"COURT IS HEREBY ADJOURNED"... HUH.
Sigh...
WELL, LET'S HEAD HOME.
WANNA GET A BURGER?
AH, GOOD IDEA.
...
I FORGIVE YOU.
WHAT DID YOU JUST SAY?
I SAID I FORGIVE YOU ALL.
I'M NO LONGER A BRAT WHO CAN'T SEE THAT...
...YOU DID WHAT YOU DID, DOUBTS AND ALL, FOR OUR SAKE.
THOUGH PERHAPS EVEN THE ME BEFORE TENBIN ELEMENTARY WOULDN'T HAVE THOUGHT SO.
WE'VE KINDA BEEN DOING YOUR BIDDING THESE PAST FIVE YEARS.
BUT SURPRISINGLY, I NO LONGER FEEL ANY *HATE* OR *RESENTMENT* TOWARDS YOU.
OGRES DWELL INSIDE OUR OWN HEARTS.

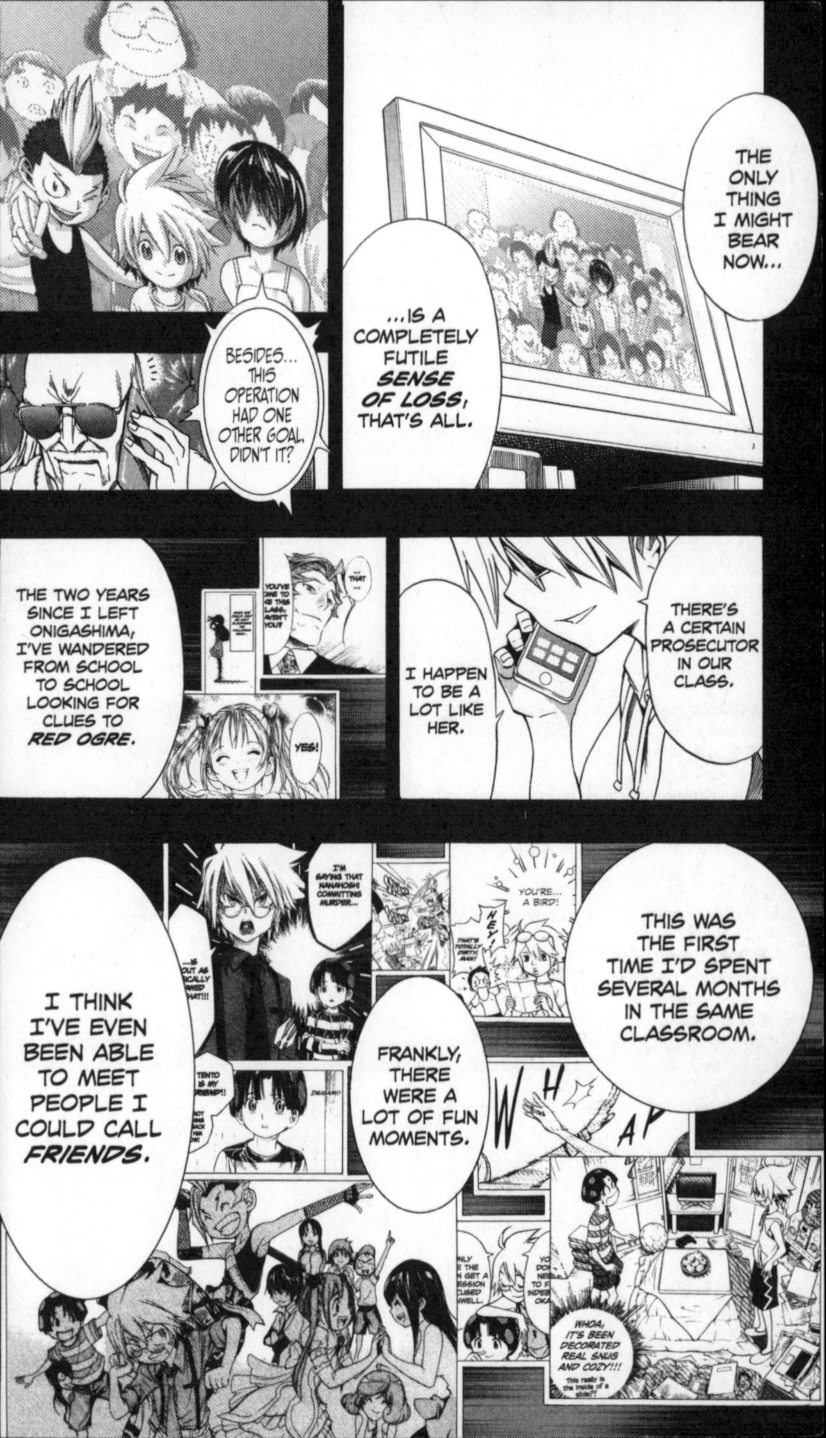
THE ONLY THING I MIGHT BEAR NOW...
...IS A COMPLETELY FUTILE SENSE OF LOSS, THAT'S ALL.
BESIDES... THIS OPERATION HAD ONE OTHER GOAL, DIDN'T IT?
THERE'S A CERTAIN PROSECUTOR IN OUR CLASS.
I HAPPEN TO BE A LOT LIKE HER.
...THAT...
YES!
THE TWO YEARS SINCE I LEFT ONIGASHIMA, I'VE WANDERED FROM SCHOOL TO SCHOOL LOOKING FOR CLUES TO RED OGRE.
THIS WAS THE FIRST TIME I'D SPENT SEVERAL MONTHS IN THE SAME CLASSROOM.
YOU'RE... A BIRD!
HEY!
THAT'S TOTALLY DIRTY, MAN!
I'M SAYING THAT NANAHOSHI COMMITTING MURDER...
FRANKLY, THERE WERE A LOT OF FUN MOMENTS.
TENTO IS MY FRIEND!!
WHOA, IT'S BEEN DECORATED REAL SNUG AND COZY!!!
This really is the inside of a slide?!
I THINK I'VE EVEN BEEN ABLE TO MEET PEOPLE I COULD CALL FRIENDS.

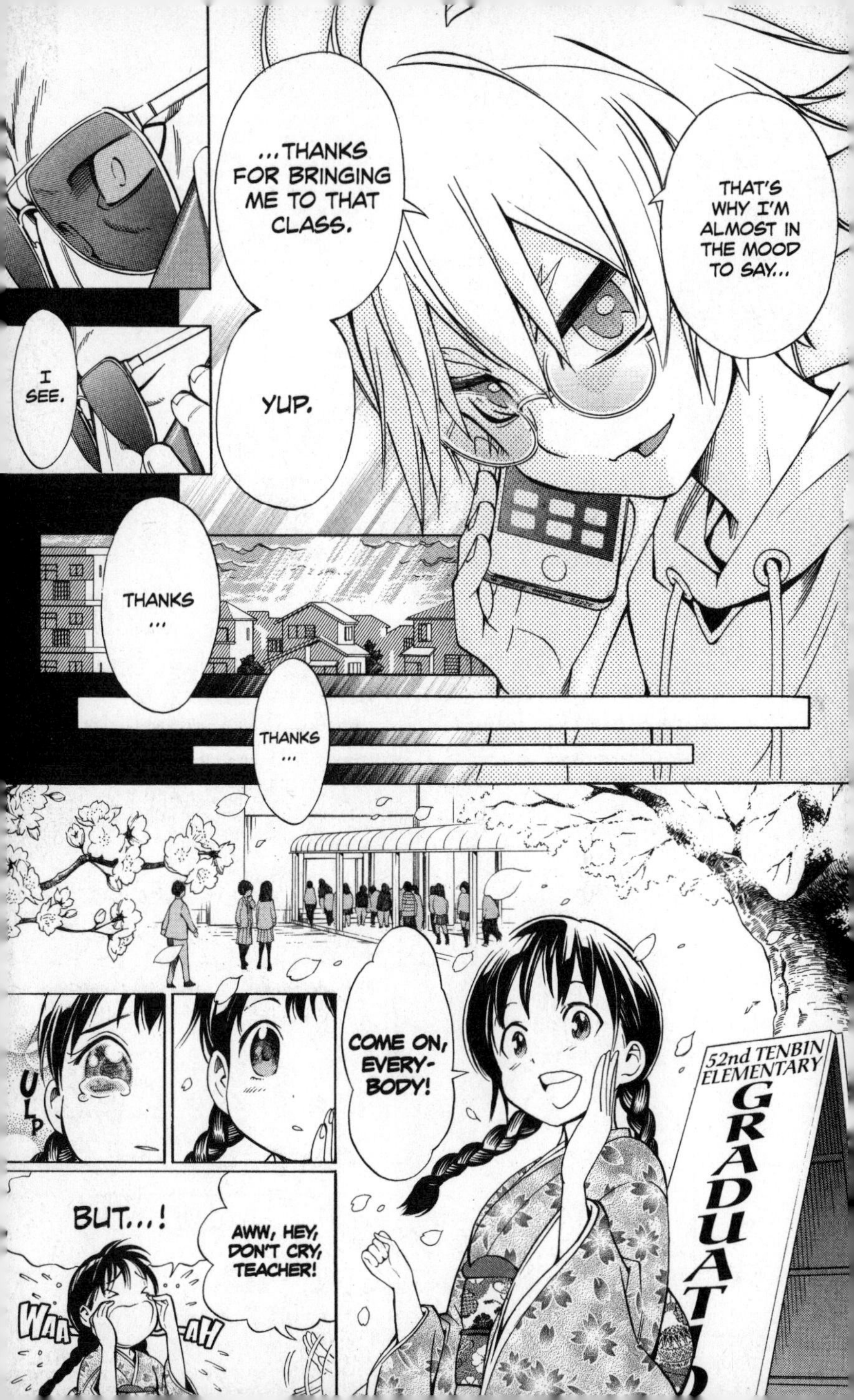
THAT'S WHY I'M ALMOST IN THE MOOD TO SAY...
...THANKS FOR BRINGING ME TO THAT CLASS.
YUP.
I SEE.
THANKS ...
THANKS ...
52nd TENBIN ELEMENTARY
GRADUATI
COME ON, EVERY-BODY!
ULP
AWW, HEY, DON'T CRY, TEACHER!
BUT...!
WAA-AH

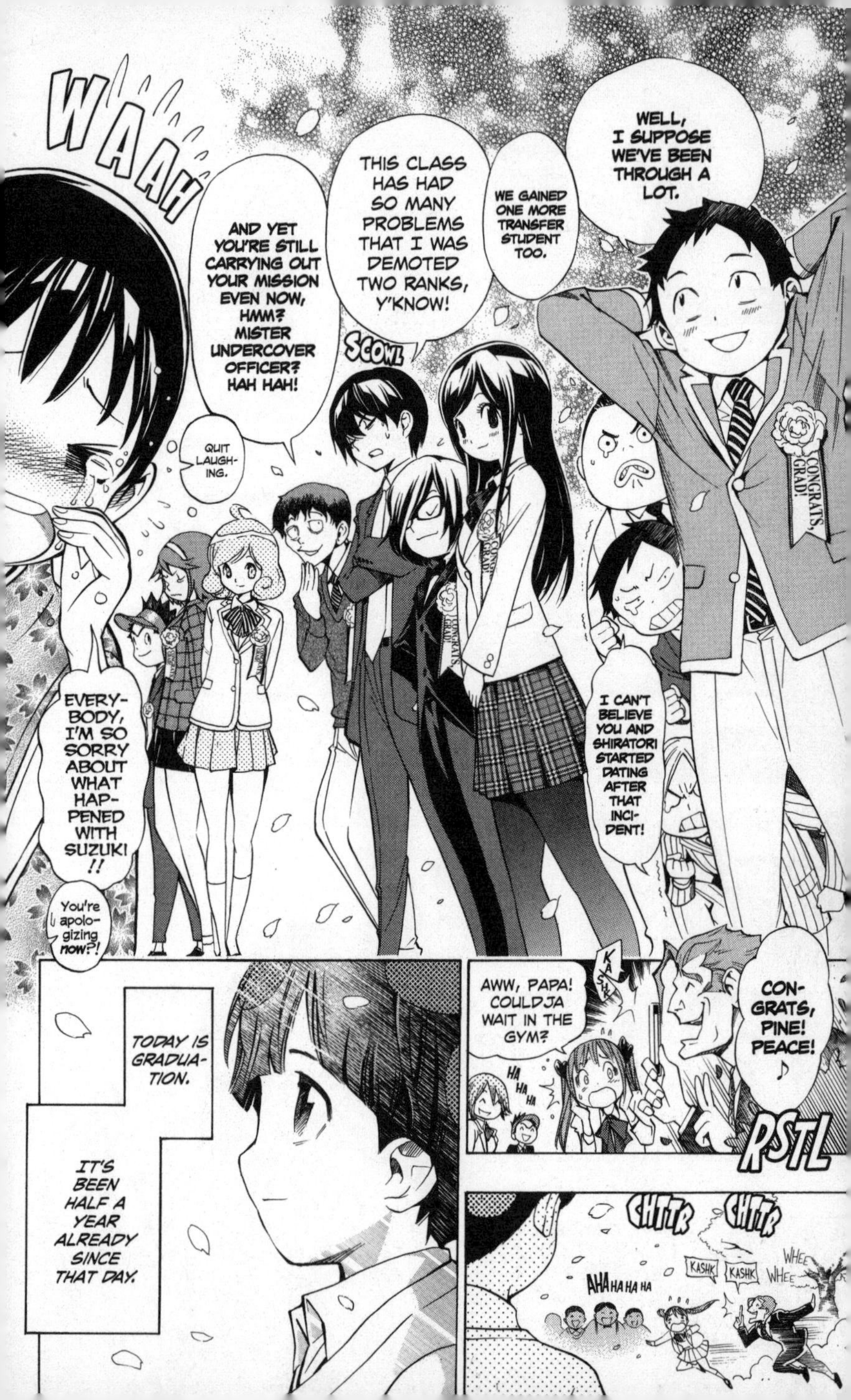
WELL, I SUPPOSE WE'VE BEEN THROUGH A LOT.
CONGRATS, GRAD!
WE GAINED ONE MORE TRANSFER STUDENT TOO.
THIS CLASS HAS HAD SO MANY PROBLEMS THAT I WAS DEMOTED TWO RANKS, Y'KNOW!
SCOWL
AND YET YOU'RE STILL CARRYING OUT YOUR MISSION EVEN NOW, HMM? MISTER UNDERCOVER OFFICER? HAH HAH!
QUIT LAUGH-ING.
WAAAH
I CAN'T BELIEVE YOU AND SHIRATORI STARTED DATING AFTER THAT INCI-DENT!
EVERY-BODY, I'M SO SORRY ABOUT WHAT HAP-PENED WITH SUZUKI !!
You're apolo-gizing now?!
CON-GRATS, PINE! PEACE! ♪
KASHK
AWW, PAPA! COULDJA WAIT IN THE GYM?
HA HA HA
RSTL
CHTTR CHTTR
WHEE WHEE
KASHK KASHK
AHA HA HA HA
TODAY IS GRADUA-TION.
IT'S BEEN HALF A YEAR ALREADY SINCE THAT DAY.

READ THIS WAY

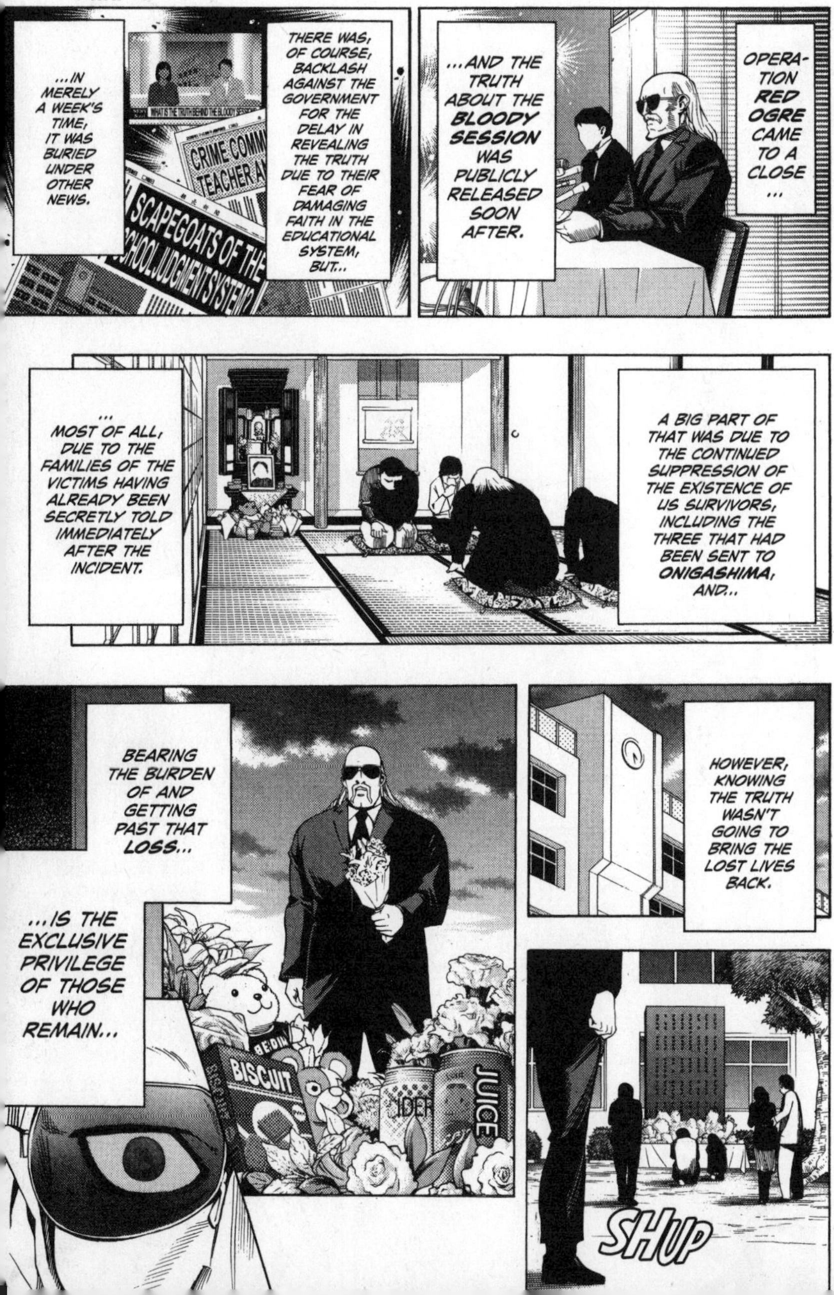
OPERATION RED OGRE CAME TO A CLOSE...
...AND THE TRUTH ABOUT THE BLOODY SESSION WAS PUBLICLY RELEASED SOON AFTER.
THERE WAS, OF COURSE, BACKLASH AGAINST THE GOVERNMENT FOR THE DELAY IN REVEALING THE TRUTH DUE TO THEIR FEAR OF DAMAGING FAITH IN THE EDUCATIONAL SYSTEM, BUT...
WHAT IS THE TRUTH BEHIND THE BLOODY SESSION
SCAPEGOATS OF THE SCHOOLJUDGMENTSYSTEM?
...IN MERELY A WEEK'S TIME, IT WAS BURIED UNDER OTHER NEWS.
A BIG PART OF THAT WAS DUE TO THE CONTINUED SUPPRESSION OF THE EXISTENCE OF US SURVIVORS, INCLUDING THE THREE THAT HAD BEEN SENT TO ONIGASHIMA, AND...
...MOST OF ALL, DUE TO THE FAMILIES OF THE VICTIMS HAVING ALREADY BEEN SECRETLY TOLD IMMEDIATELY AFTER THE INCIDENT.
HOWEVER, KNOWING THE TRUTH WASN'T GOING TO BRING THE LOST LIVES BACK.
SHUP
BEARING THE BURDEN OF AND GETTING PAST THAT LOSS...
...IS THE EXCLUSIVE PRIVILEGE OF THOSE WHO REMAIN...
BISCUIT
JUICE

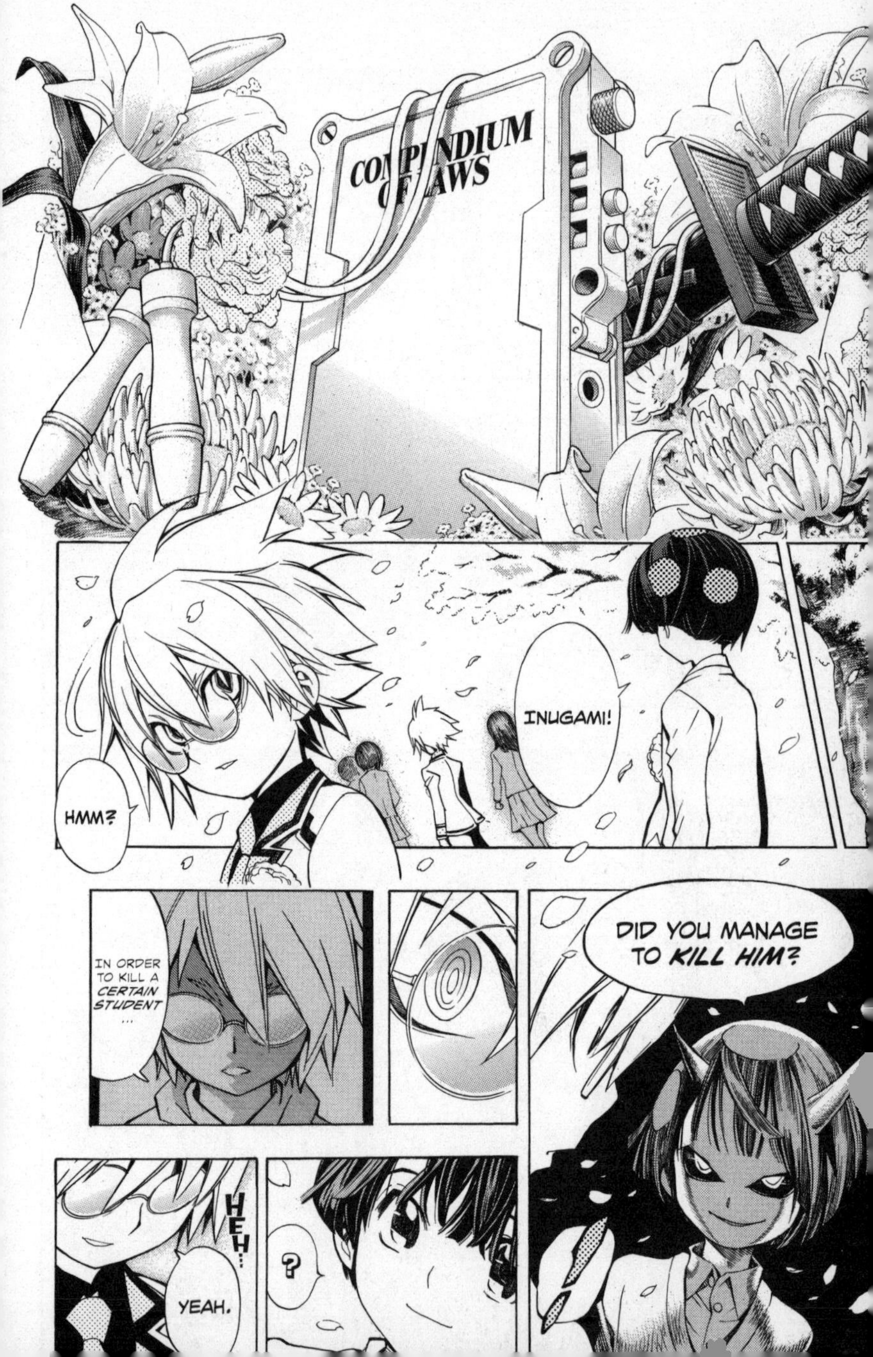
COMPENDIUM OF LAWS
INUGAMI!
HMM?
DID YOU MANAGE TO *KILL HIM?*
IN ORDER TO KILL A *CERTAIN STUDENT* ...
?
HEH!!
YEAH.

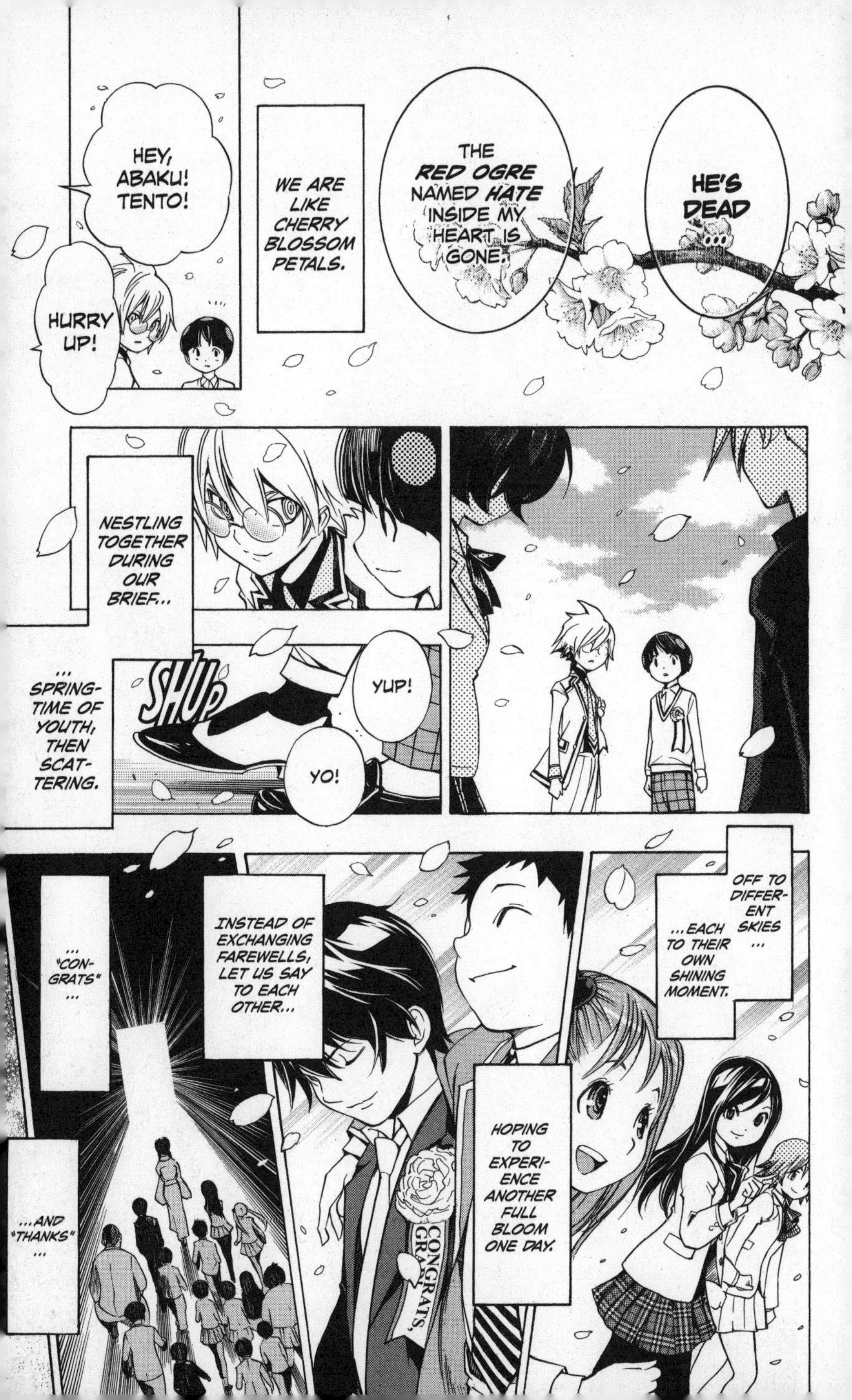
HE'S DEAD...
THE RED OGRE NAMED HATE INSIDE MY HEART IS GONE.
WE ARE LIKE CHERRY BLOSSOM PETALS.
HEY, ABAKU! TENTO!
HURRY UP!
NESTLING TOGETHER DURING OUR BRIEF...
YUP!
YO!
SHUP
...SPRING-TIME OF YOUTH, THEN SCAT-TERING.
OFF TO DIFFER-ENT SKIES...
...EACH TO THEIR OWN SHINING MOMENT.
HOPING TO EXPERI-ENCE ANOTHER FULL BLOOM ONE DAY.
INSTEAD OF EXCHANGING FAREWELLS, LET US SAY TO EACH OTHER...
CONGRATS, GRAD
..."CON-GRATS"...
...AND "THANKS"...

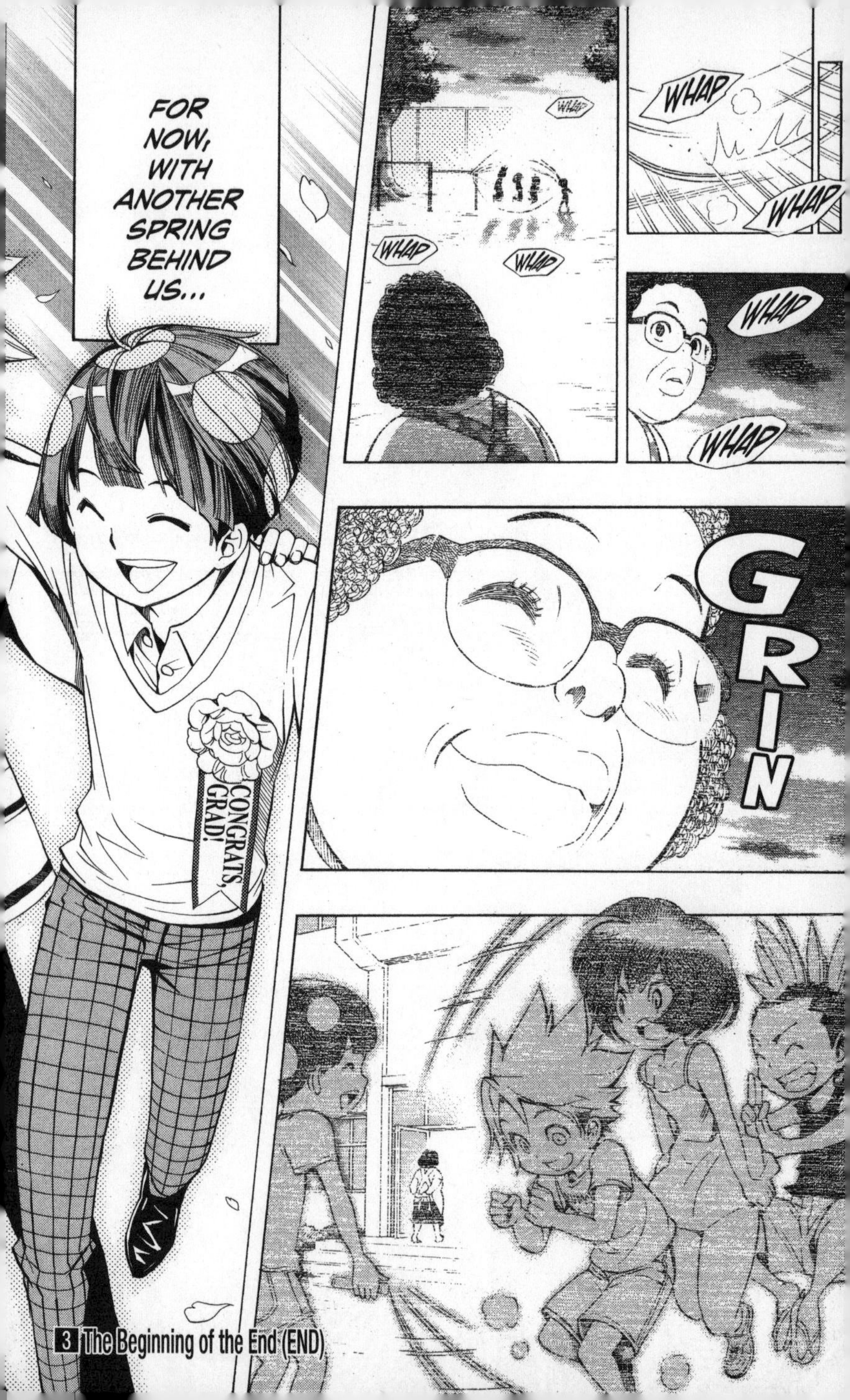
WHAP
WHAP
WHAP
WHAP
WHAP
WHAP
WHAP
GRIN
FOR NOW, WITH ANOTHER SPRING BEHIND US...
CONGRATS, GRAD!

3 The Beginning of the End (END)

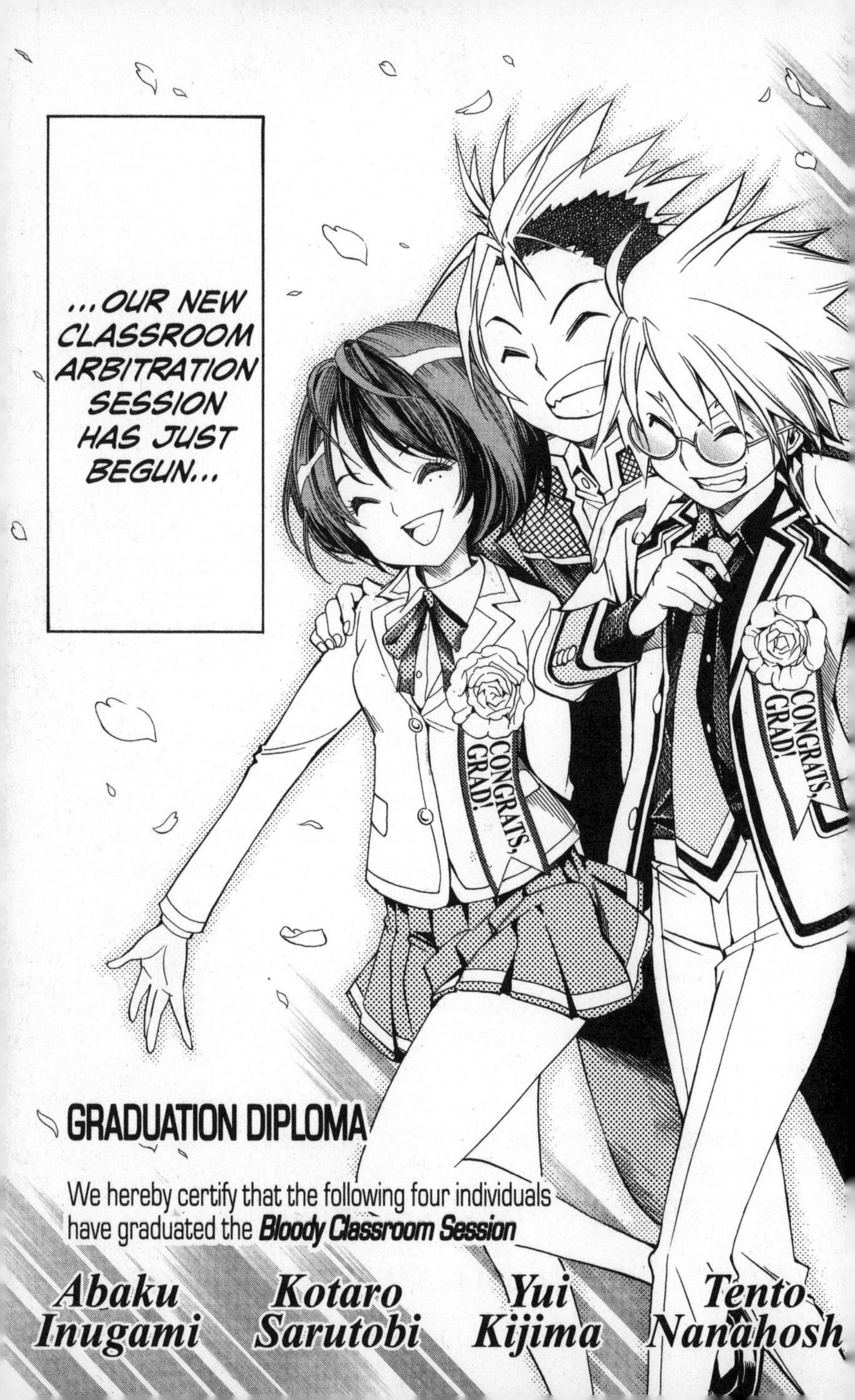
...OUR NEW CLASSROOM ARBITRATION SESSION HAS JUST BEGUN...
CONGRATS, GRAD!
CONGRATS, GRAD!
GRADUATION DIPLOMA
We hereby certify that the following four individuals have graduated the Bloody Classroom Session
Abaku Inugami
Kotaro Sarutobi
Yui Kijima
Tento Nanahosh

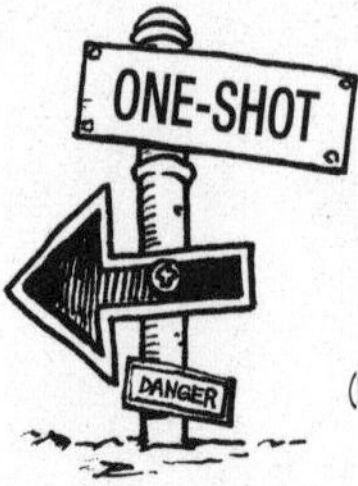
ONE-SHOT
DANGER

Starting on the next page is the one-shot version of *School Judgment* that I drew all by myself two years ago!

(Both Abaku and Tento appear, but it's otherwise completely different.)

After I drew the one-shot spy story *006* 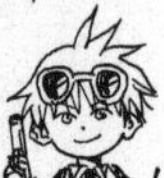, I was working on the storyboard for the serialization, but it wasn't going well, and I strayed off course.
And so, I totally gave up on *006*, and I decided to work on a mystery instead! This one-shot's storyboard happened to win a competition for the newly launched digital manga magazine *Jump LIVE* (now *Jump+*). Both parts A and B were published, and it led to the subsequent series.
In a way, this one-shot is the prototype for *School Judgment* and is very special to me as the work that started it all.
However, there's something that has made me very uneasy after hearing that this one-shot would be included in volume 3. To give an analogy, you know how while flying in an airplane, one's ears or head can ache when there's a change in pressure due to a sudden drop in altitude...?
I wonder if that happens with drawing ability as well...? Yup...
Warning: The art quality takes a nosedive from this point on...!!
Readers may become nauseated, unable to bear the precipitous decline in art quality...but I cannot take responsibility for that...
Well, I am also the type of person whose ears clog when flying, but I hear that one can get some amount of relief by periodically swallowing, so it may be prudent to consciously swallow your saliva every two pages as you read beyond this point.

Now then... Have A Nice Flight!!

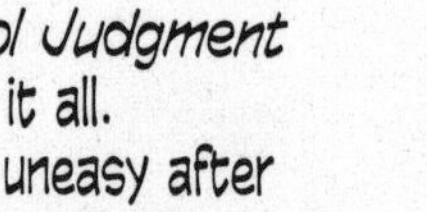

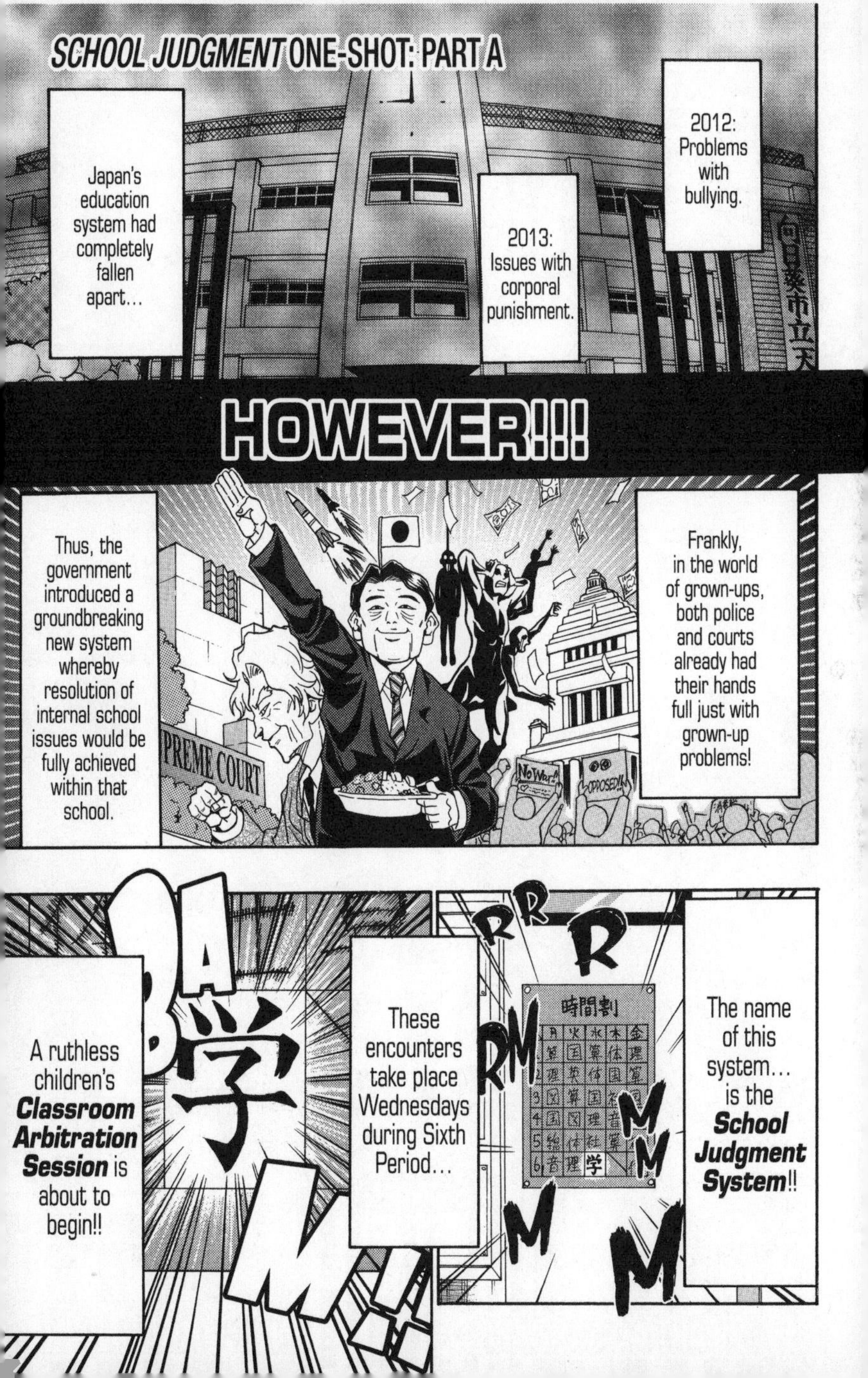
SCHOOL JUDGMENT ONE-SHOT: PART A
2012: Problems with bullying.
2013: Issues with corporal punishment.
Japan's education system had completely fallen apart…
向日葵市立天
HOWEVER!!!
Frankly, in the world of grown-ups, both police and courts already had their hands full just with grown-up problems!
No War!!
OPPOSED!!
PREME COURT
Thus, the government introduced a groundbreaking new system whereby resolution of internal school issues would be fully achieved within that school.
The name of this system… is the ***School Judgment System***!!
RRRRMMMMM
時間割
These encounters take place Wednesdays during Sixth Period…
A ruthless children's ***Classroom Arbitration Session*** is about to begin!!

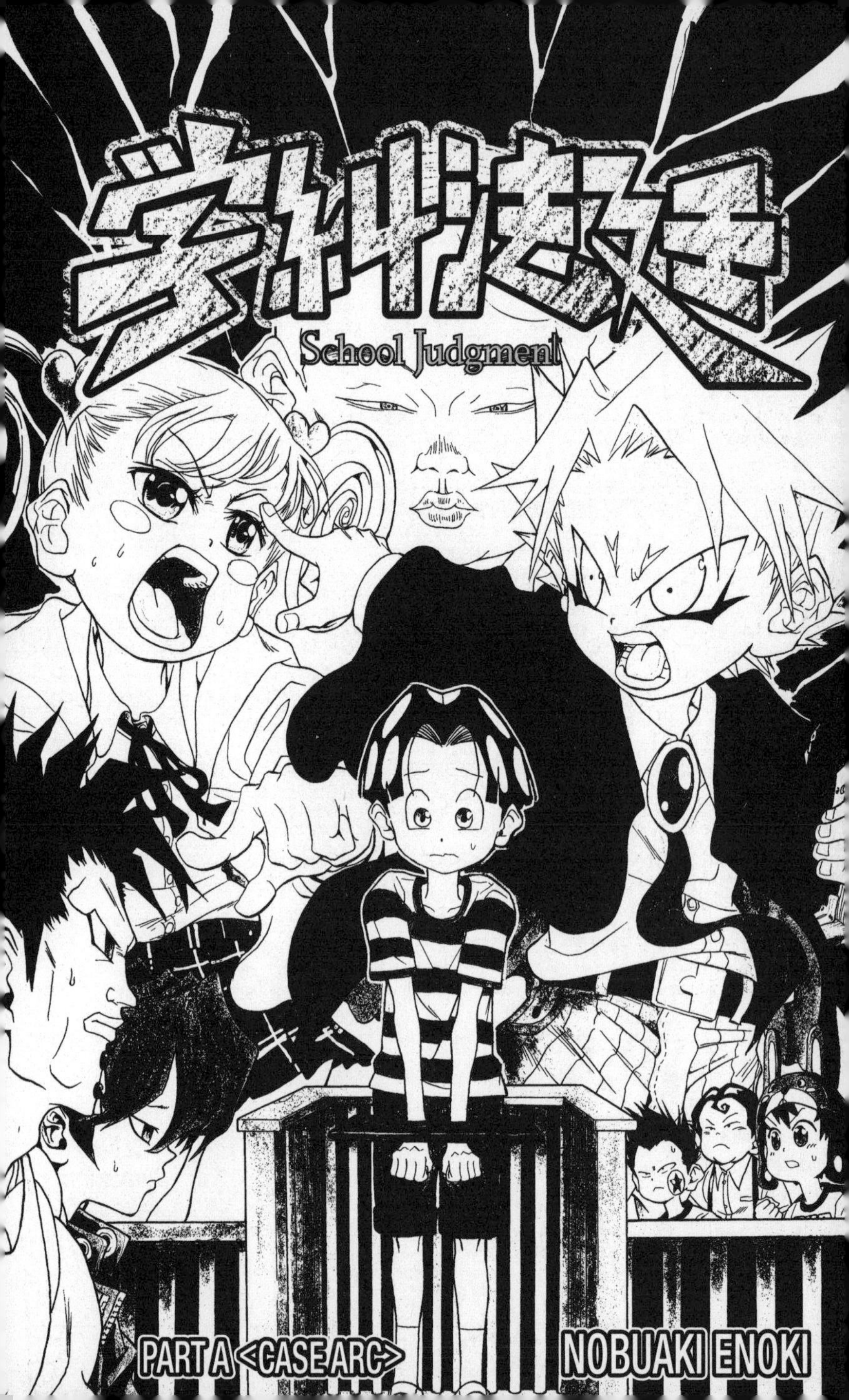
School Judgment
PART A <CASE ARC>
NOBUAKI ENOKI

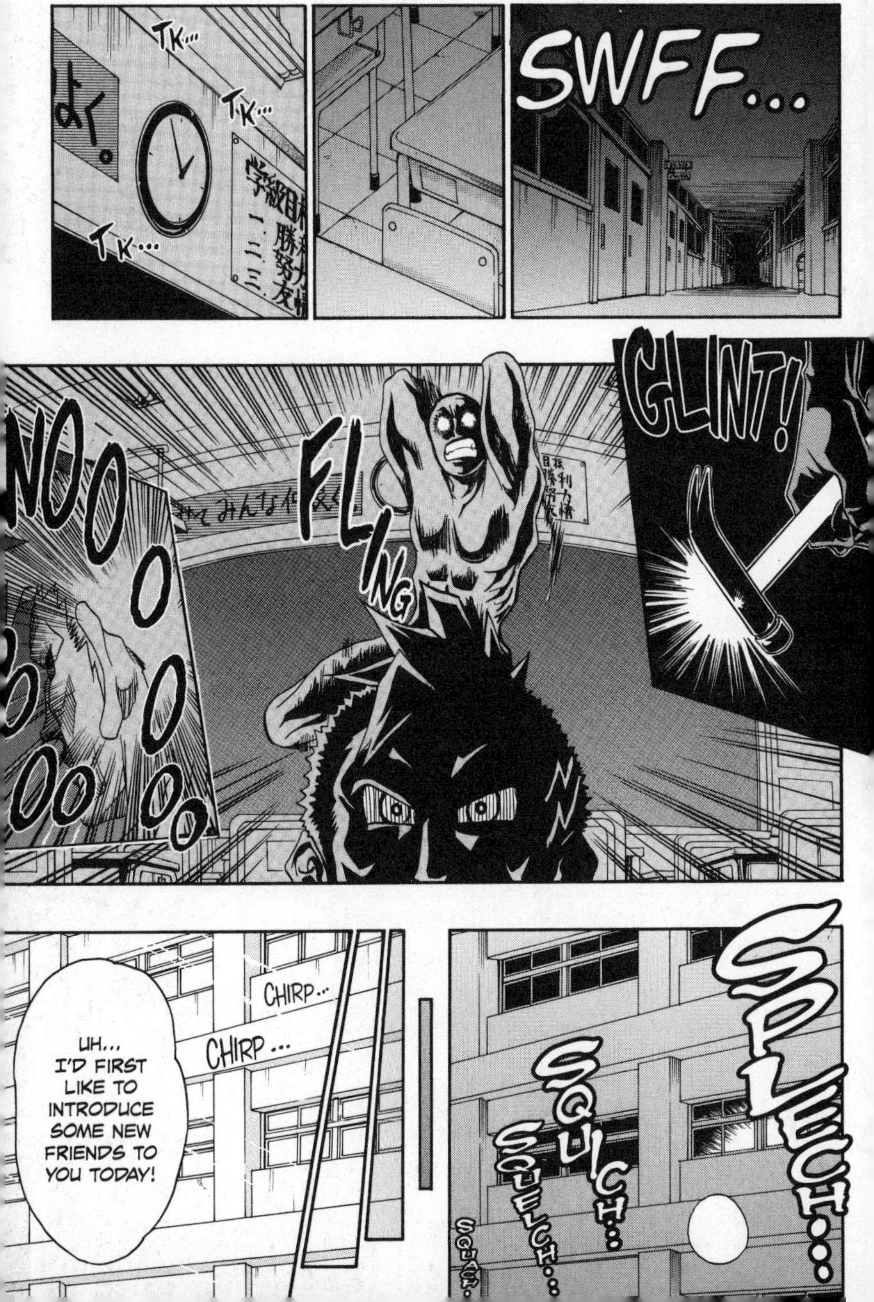
SWFF...
TK...
TK...
TK...
GLINT!
FLING
NOOOOOOOOOOOO
SPLECH...
SQUICH...
SQUELCH...
SQUACI...
CHIRP...
CHIRP...
UH... I'D FIRST LIKE TO INTRODUCE SOME NEW FRIENDS TO YOU TODAY!

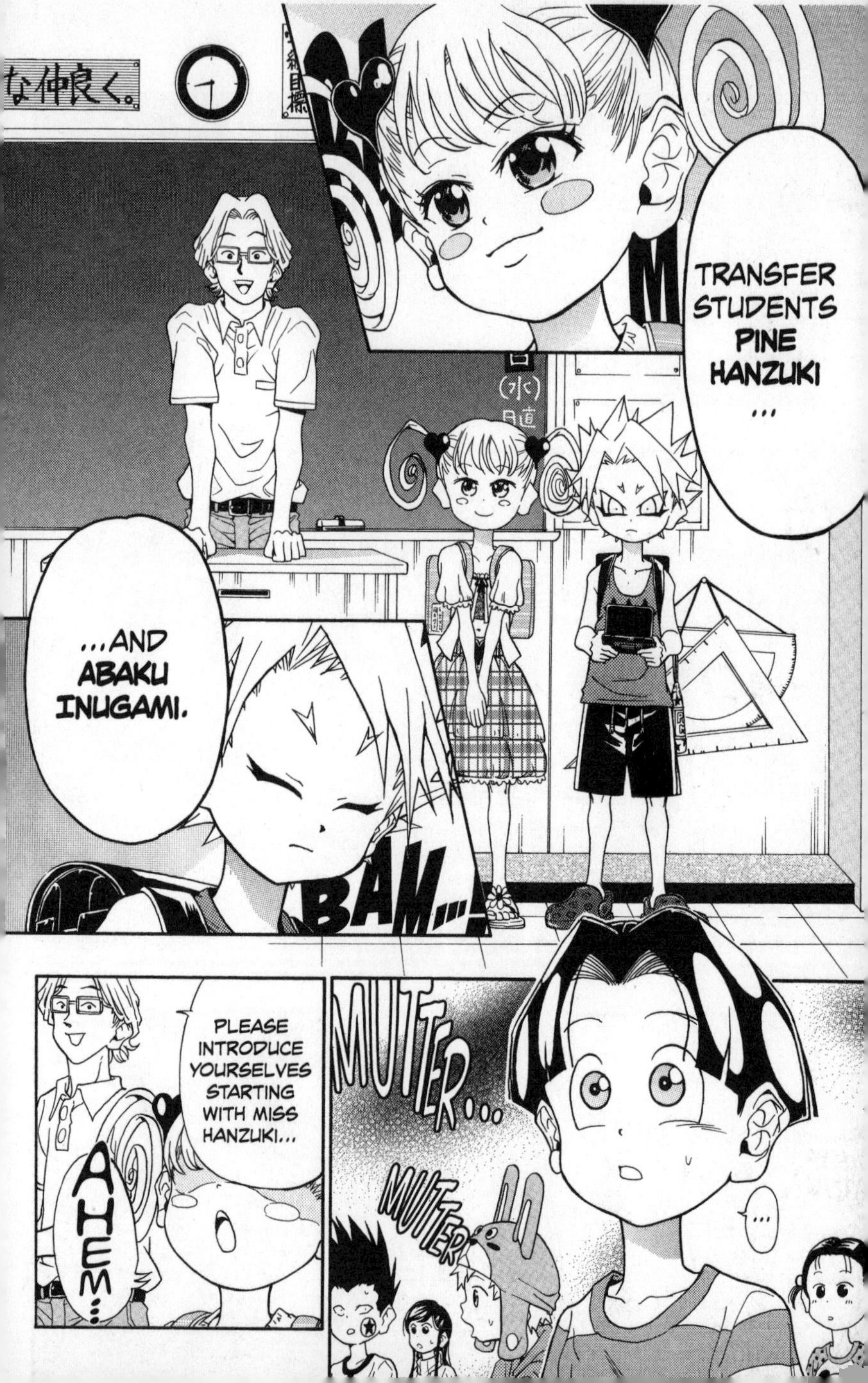
な仲良く。
TRANSFER STUDENTS PINE HANZUKI ...
...AND ABAKU INUGAMI.
BAM...!
MUTTER...
MUTTER
...
PLEASE INTRODUCE YOURSELVES STARTING WITH MISS HANZUKI...
AHEM...

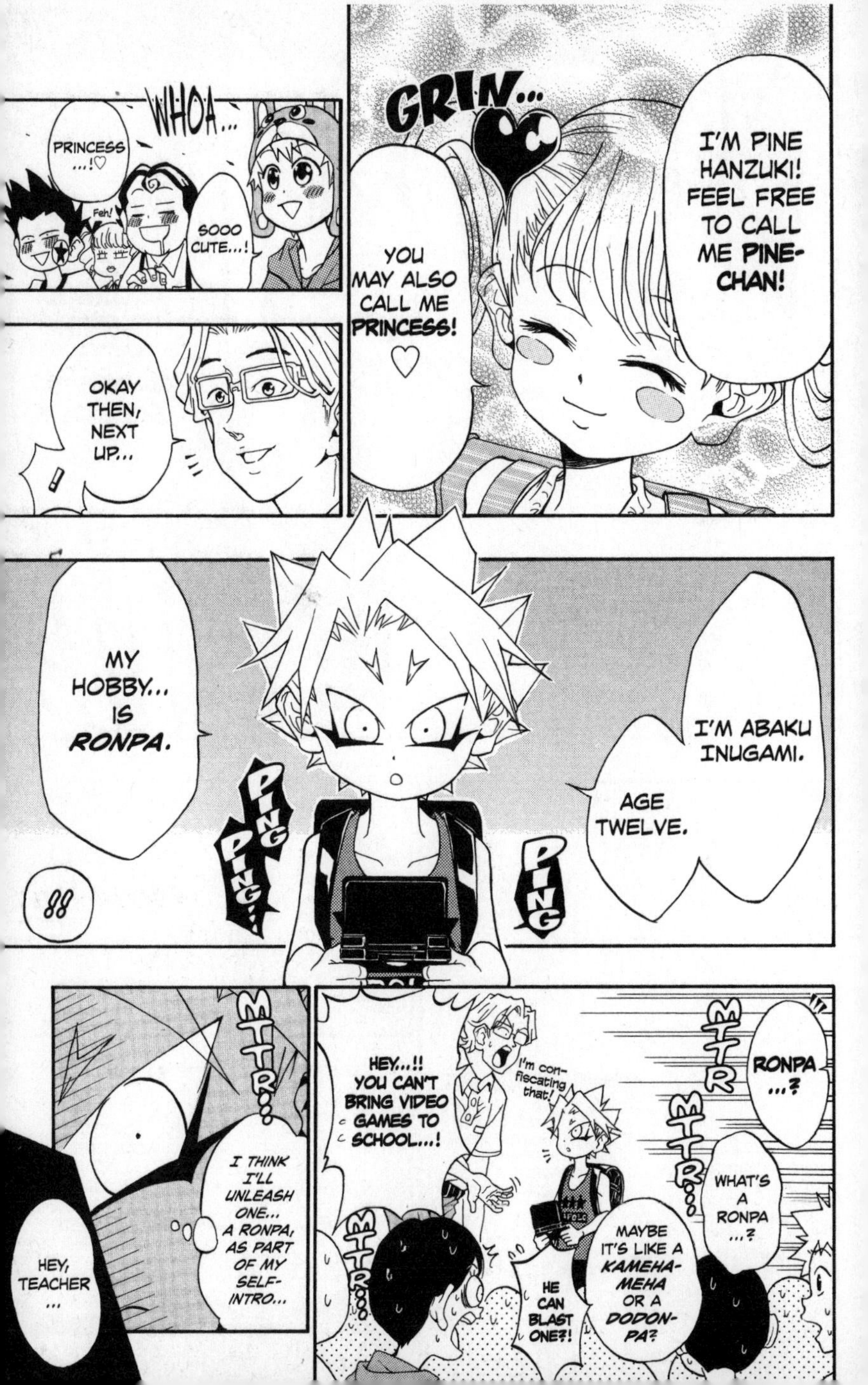
GRIN...
I'M PINE HANZUKI! FEEL FREE TO CALL ME PINE-CHAN!
YOU MAY ALSO CALL ME PRINCESS! ♡
WHOA...
SOOO CUTE...!
PRINCESS ...!♡
Feh!
OKAY THEN, NEXT UP...
!
I'M ABAKU INUGAMI.
AGE TWELVE.
MY HOBBY... IS RONPA.
PING
PING PING...
PING
RONPA ...?
MTTR
MTTR
WHAT'S A RONPA ...?
MAYBE IT'S LIKE A KAMEHA-MEHA OR A DODONPA?
HE CAN BLAST ONE?!
MTTR
I'm con-fiscating that!
HEY...!! YOU CAN'T BRING VIDEO GAMES TO SCHOOL...!
MTTR
I THINK I'LL UNLEASH ONE... A RONPA, AS PART OF MY SELF-INTRO...
HEY, TEACHER ...

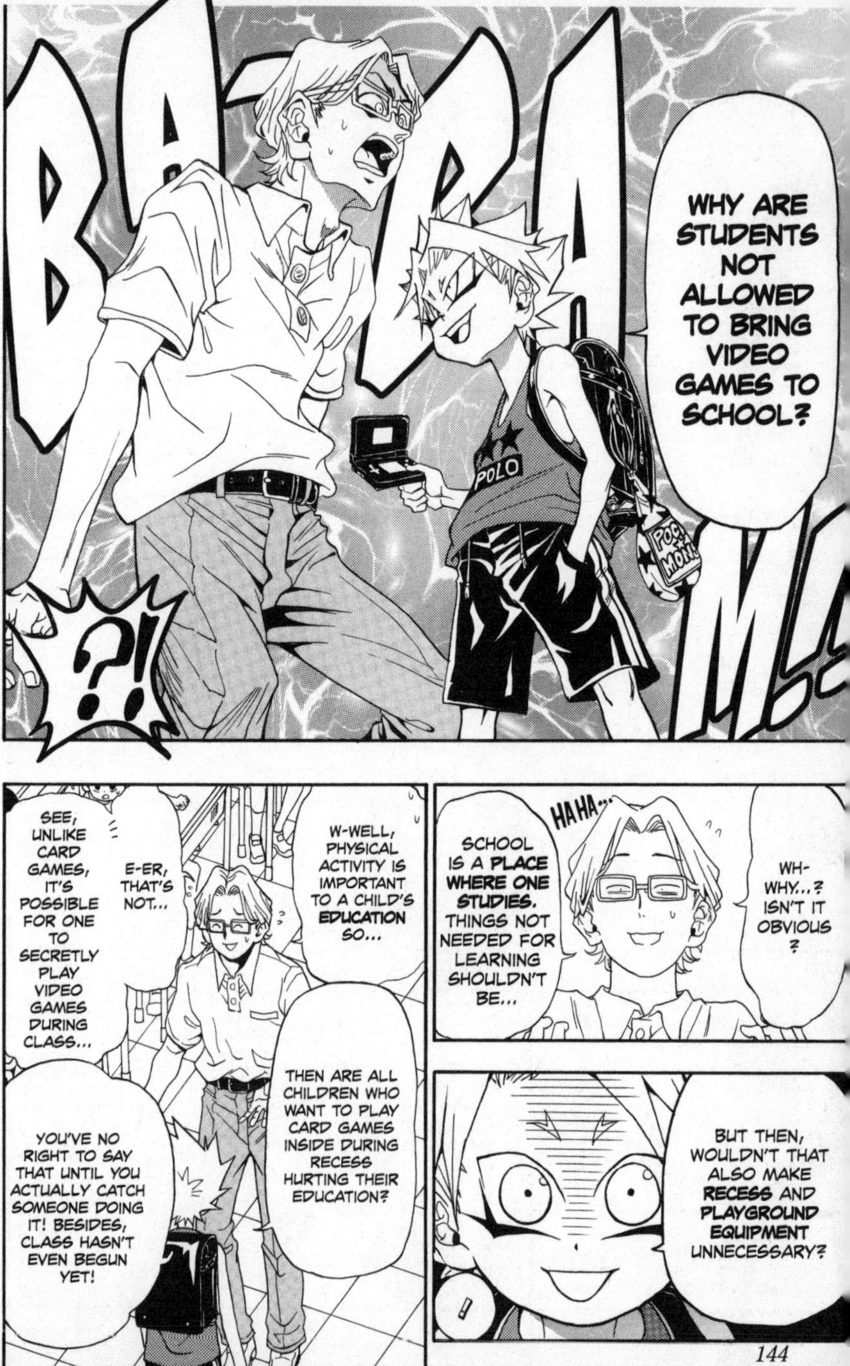
WHY ARE STUDENTS NOT ALLOWED TO BRING VIDEO GAMES TO SCHOOL?
?!
WH- WHY...? ISN'T IT OBVIOUS?
HAHA...
SCHOOL IS A PLACE WHERE ONE STUDIES. THINGS NOT NEEDED FOR LEARNING SHOULDN'T BE...
BUT THEN, WOULDN'T THAT ALSO MAKE RECESS AND PLAYGROUND EQUIPMENT UNNECESSARY?
!
W-WELL, PHYSICAL ACTIVITY IS IMPORTANT TO A CHILD'S EDUCATION SO...
THEN ARE ALL CHILDREN WHO WANT TO PLAY CARD GAMES INSIDE DURING RECESS HURTING THEIR EDUCATION?
E-ER, THAT'S NOT...
SEE, UNLIKE CARD GAMES, IT'S POSSIBLE FOR ONE TO SECRETLY PLAY VIDEO GAMES DURING CLASS...
YOU'VE NO RIGHT TO SAY THAT UNTIL YOU ACTUALLY CATCH SOMEONE DOING IT! BESIDES, CLASS HASN'T EVEN BEGUN YET!

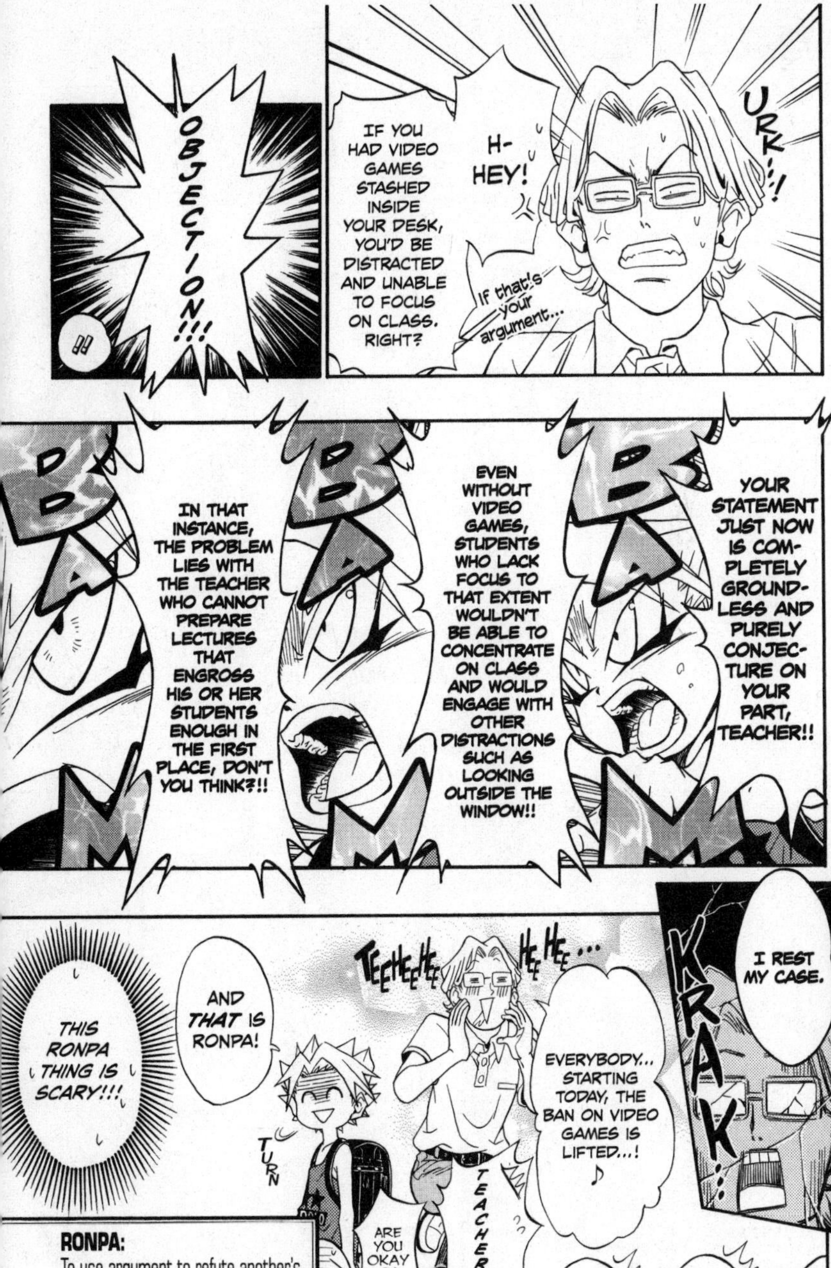
URK...!
H-HEY!
IF YOU HAD VIDEO GAMES STASHED INSIDE YOUR DESK, YOU'D BE DISTRACTED AND UNABLE TO FOCUS ON CLASS. RIGHT?
If that's your argument...
OBJECTION!!!
!!
BAM
YOUR STATEMENT JUST NOW IS COMPLETELY GROUNDLESS AND PURELY CONJECTURE ON YOUR PART, TEACHER!!
BAM
EVEN WITHOUT VIDEO GAMES, STUDENTS WHO LACK FOCUS TO THAT EXTENT WOULDN'T BE ABLE TO CONCENTRATE ON CLASS AND WOULD ENGAGE WITH OTHER DISTRACTIONS SUCH AS LOOKING OUTSIDE THE WINDOW!!
BAM
IN THAT INSTANCE, THE PROBLEM LIES WITH THE TEACHER WHO CANNOT PREPARE LECTURES THAT ENGROSS HIS OR HER STUDENTS ENOUGH IN THE FIRST PLACE, DON'T YOU THINK?!!
I REST MY CASE.
KRAK...
EVERYBODY... STARTING TODAY, THE BAN ON VIDEO GAMES IS LIFTED...! ♪
TEEHEEHEE HEE HEE...
TEACHER!!!
ARE YOU OKAY?!
AND THAT IS RONPA!
TURN
THIS RONPA THING IS SCARY!!!

RONPA:
To use argument to refute another's theories; to verbally defeat someone.

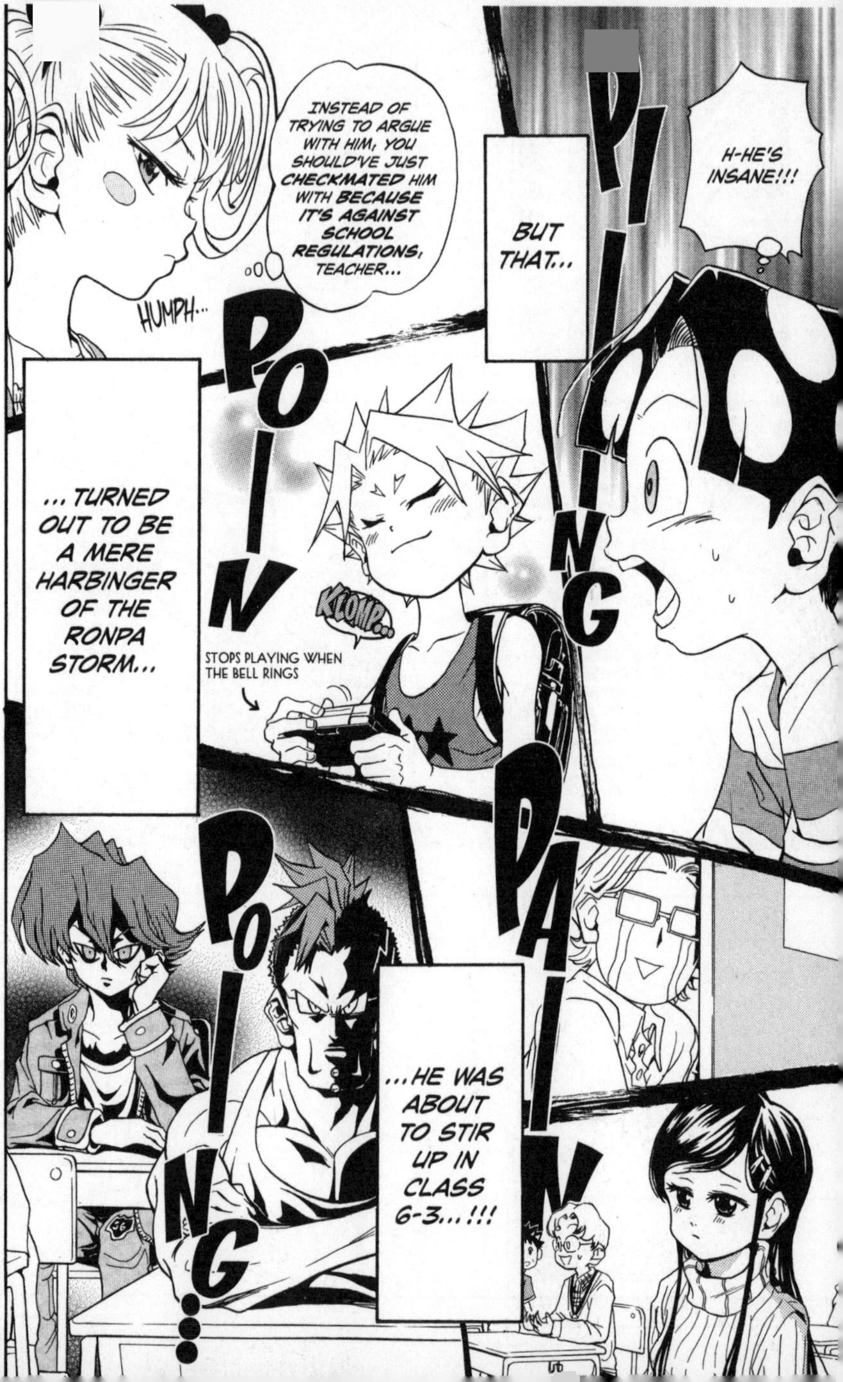
H-HE'S INSANE!!!
BUT THAT...
PIIING
INSTEAD OF TRYING TO ARGUE WITH HIM, YOU SHOULD'VE JUST CHECKMATED HIM WITH BECAUSE IT'S AGAINST SCHOOL REGULATIONS, TEACHER...
HUMPH...
POIIN
KLOMP...
STOPS PLAYING WHEN THE BELL RINGS
...TURNED OUT TO BE A MERE HARBINGER OF THE RONPA STORM...
PAIIN
...HE WAS ABOUT TO STIR UP IN CLASS 6-3...!!!
POIIING...

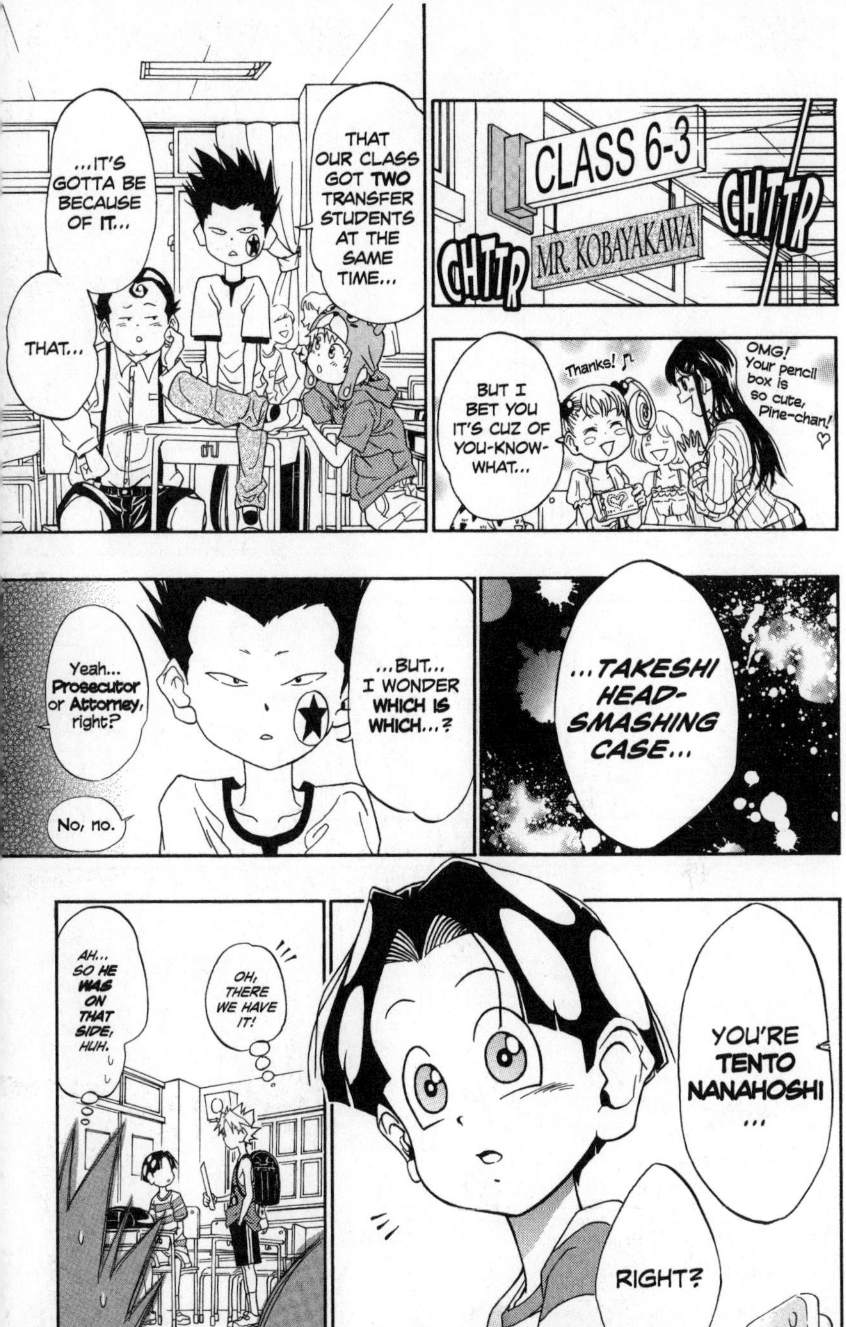
CLASS 6-3
MR. KOBAYAKAWA
CHTTR
CHTTR
OMG! Your pencil box is so cute, Pine-chan! ♡
Thanks! ♪
BUT I BET YOU IT'S CUZ OF YOU-KNOW-WHAT...
THAT OUR CLASS GOT TWO TRANSFER STUDENTS AT THE SAME TIME...
...IT'S GOTTA BE BECAUSE OF IT...
THAT...
...TAKESHI HEAD-SMASHING CASE...
...BUT... I WONDER WHICH IS WHICH...?
Yeah... Prosecutor or Attorney, right?
No, no.
YOU'RE TENTO NANAHOSHI...
RIGHT?
OH, THERE WE HAVE IT!
AH... SO HE WAS ON THAT SIDE, HUH.

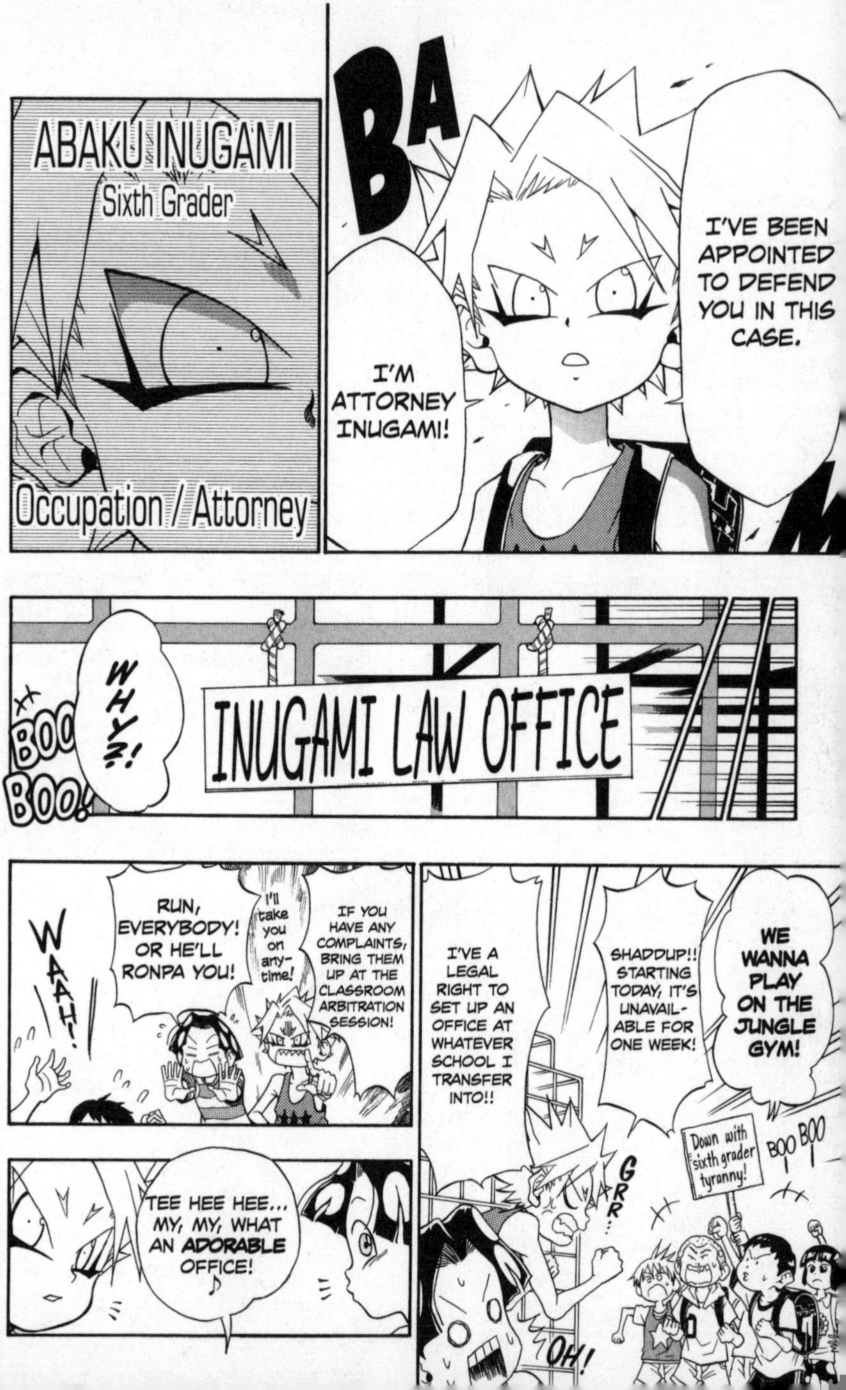
BAM
I'VE BEEN APPOINTED TO DEFEND YOU IN THIS CASE.
I'M ATTORNEY INUGAMI!
ABAKU INUGAMI
Sixth Grader
Occupation / Attorney
INUGAMI LAW OFFICE
WHY?!
BOO BOO!
WE WANNA PLAY ON THE JUNGLE GYM!
SHADDUP!! STARTING TODAY, IT'S UNAVAIL-ABLE FOR ONE WEEK!
I'VE A LEGAL RIGHT TO SET UP AN OFFICE AT WHATEVER SCHOOL I TRANSFER INTO!!
BOO BOO
Down with sixth grader tyranny!
GRR...
OH!
IF YOU HAVE ANY COMPLAINTS, BRING THEM UP AT THE CLASSROOM ARBITRATION SESSION!
I'll take you on any-time!
RUN, EVERYBODY! OR HE'LL RONPA YOU!
WAAAH!
TEE HEE HEE... MY, MY, WHAT AN ADORABLE OFFICE! ♪

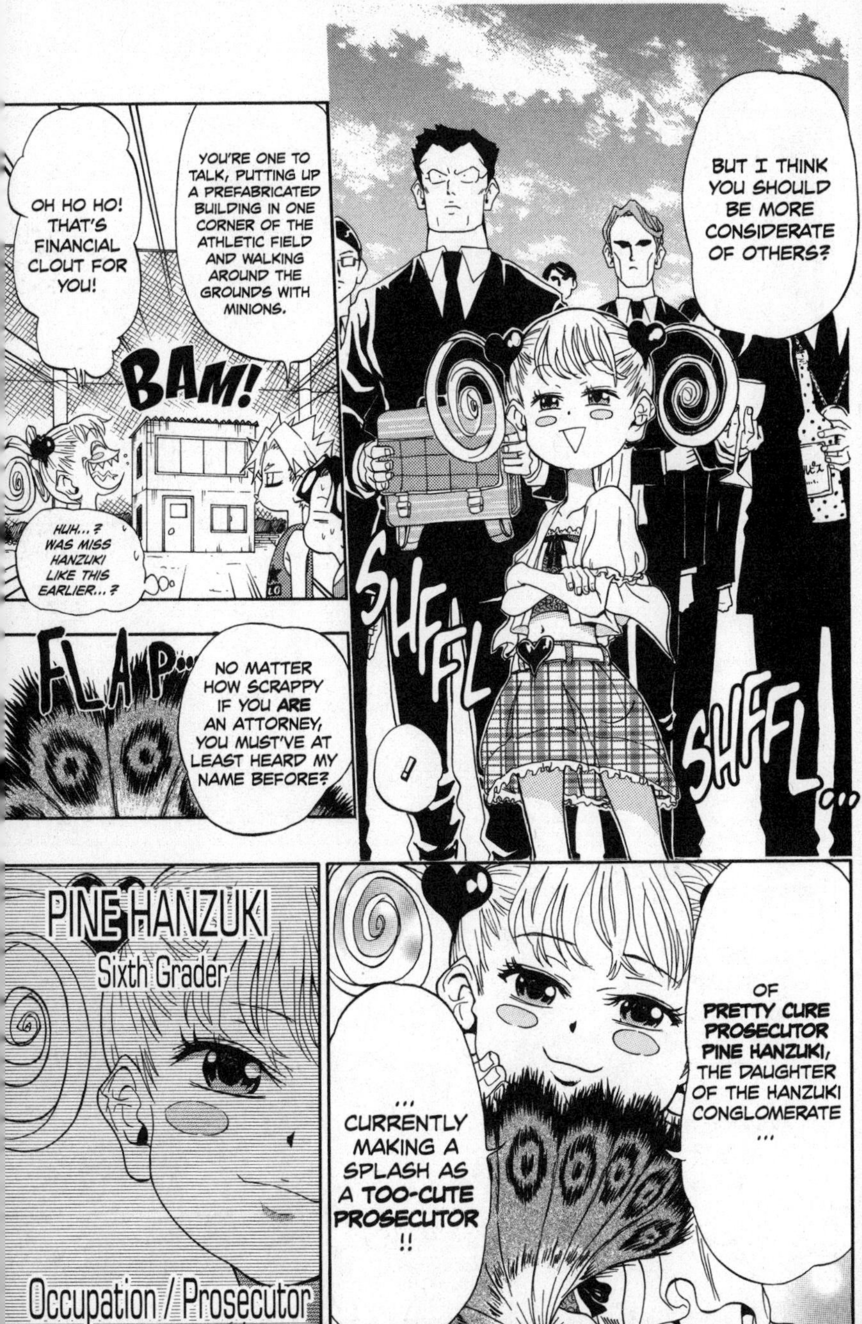
BUT I THINK YOU SHOULD BE MORE CONSIDERATE OF OTHERS?
SHFFL
SHFFL...
!
YOU'RE ONE TO TALK, PUTTING UP A PREFABRICATED BUILDING IN ONE CORNER OF THE ATHLETIC FIELD AND WALKING AROUND THE GROUNDS WITH MINIONS.
OH HO HO! THAT'S FINANCIAL CLOUT FOR YOU!
BAM!
HUH...? WAS MISS HANZUKI LIKE THIS EARLIER...?
NO MATTER HOW SCRAPPY IF YOU **ARE** AN ATTORNEY, YOU MUST'VE AT LEAST HEARD MY NAME BEFORE?
FLAP...
OF **PRETTY CURE PROSECUTOR PINE HANZUKI,** THE DAUGHTER OF THE HANZUKI CONGLOMERATE ...
... CURRENTLY MAKING A SPLASH AS A **TOO-CUTE PROSECUTOR** !!
PINE HANZUKI
Sixth Grader
Occupation / Prosecutor

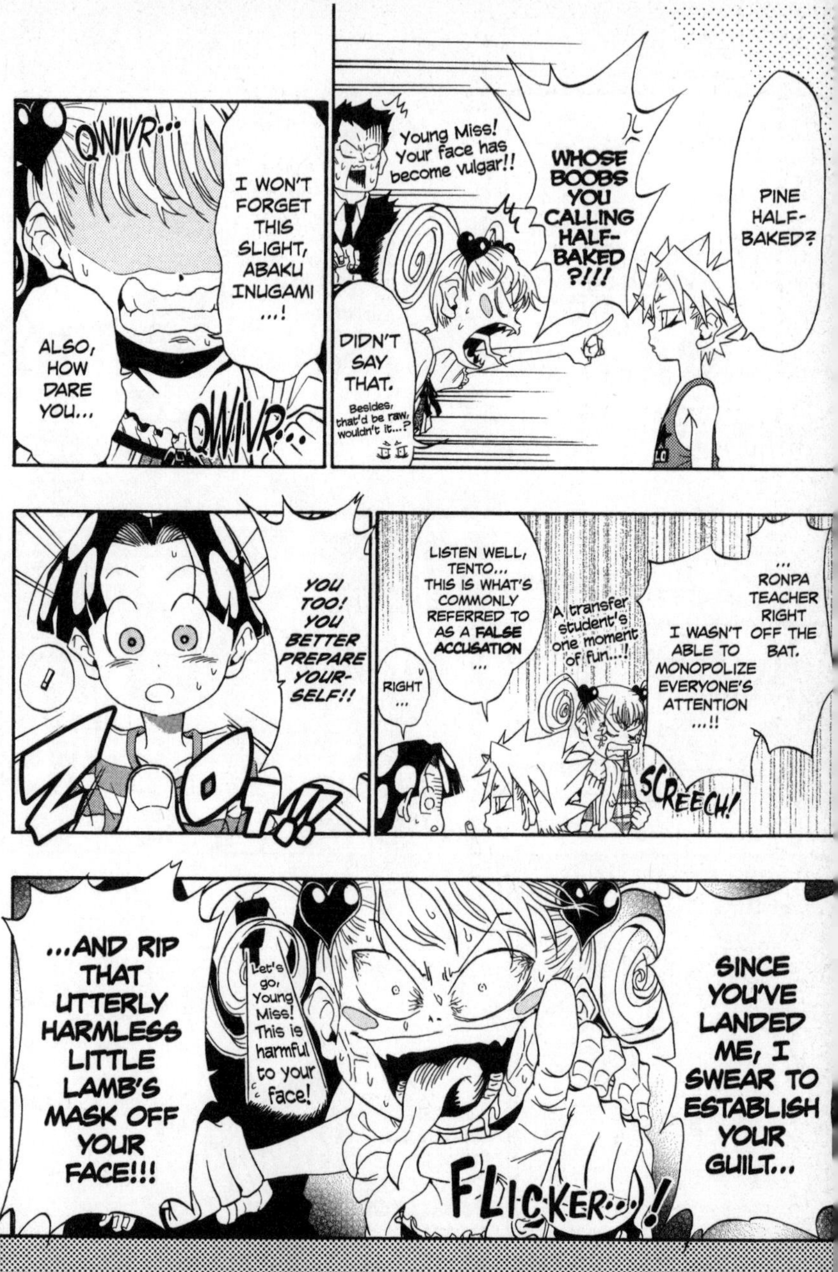
PINE HALF-BAKED?
WHOSE BOOBS YOU CALLING HALF-BAKED?!!!
Young Miss! Your face has become vulgar!!
DIDN'T SAY THAT.
Besides, that'd be raw, wouldn't it...?
QWIVR...
I WON'T FORGET THIS SLIGHT, ABAKU INUGAMI ...!
ALSO, HOW DARE YOU...
QWIVR...
... RONPA TEACHER RIGHT OFF THE BAT.
I WASN'T ABLE TO MONOPOLIZE EVERYONE'S ATTENTION ...!!
A transfer student's one moment of fun...!
LISTEN WELL, TENTO... THIS IS WHAT'S COMMONLY REFERRED TO AS A FALSE ACCUSATION ...
RIGHT ...
SCREECH!
YOU TOO! YOU BETTER PREPARE YOURSELF!!
!
ZOT!!
SINCE YOU'VE LANDED ME, I SWEAR TO ESTABLISH YOUR GUILT...
Let's go, Young Miss! This is harmful to your face!
...AND RIP THAT UTTERLY HARMLESS LITTLE LAMB'S MASK OFF YOUR FACE!!!
FLICKER...!

The School Judgment System...!!

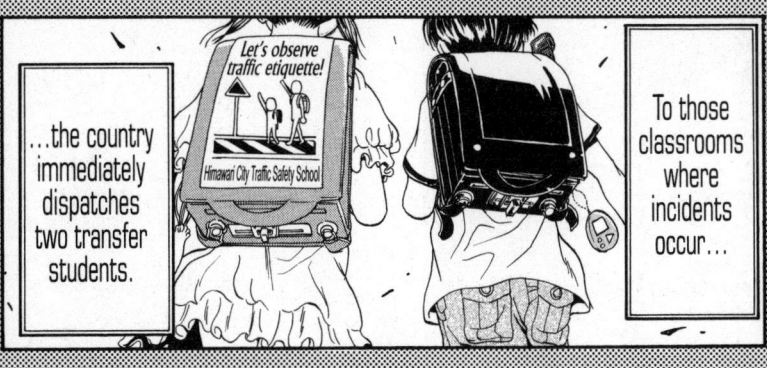

To those classrooms where incidents occur...
Let's observe traffic etiquette!
Himawari City Traffic Safety School
...the country immediately dispatches two transfer students.
One is a **prosecutor** (someone who tries to establish the guilt of the accused)
JUDGE (Dispatched a little later)
The other is an **attorney** (someone who proves the accused's innocence or seeks a reduced sentence)
PROSECUTOR
Accuses
Hands down the sentence.
ATTORNEY
Defends
THE ACCUSED
A student who did something wrong or is suspected of such.
WITNESSES
WITNESSES
Both are given a fixed amount of time to prepare evidence and testimony...
学
...after which they face off in **Classroom Arbitration Sessions** on Wednesdays during Sixth Period...
...where they attempt to shed light on the truth before an impartial court...!!!

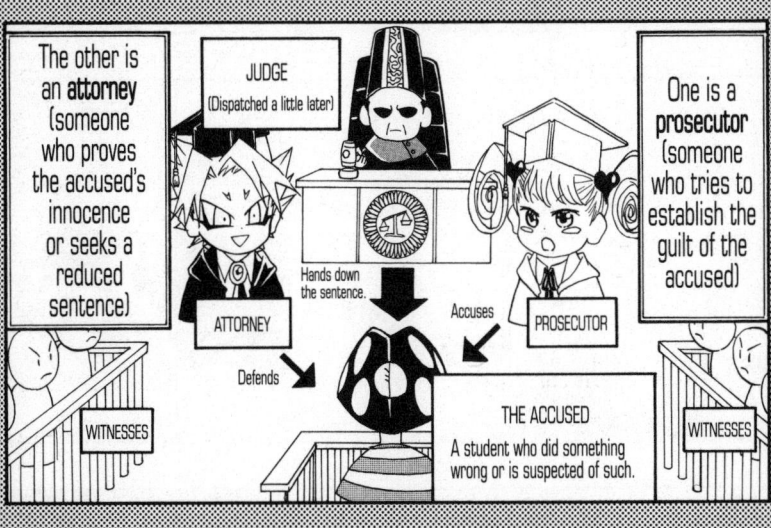

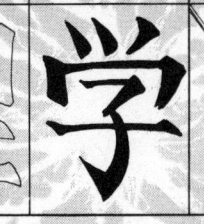

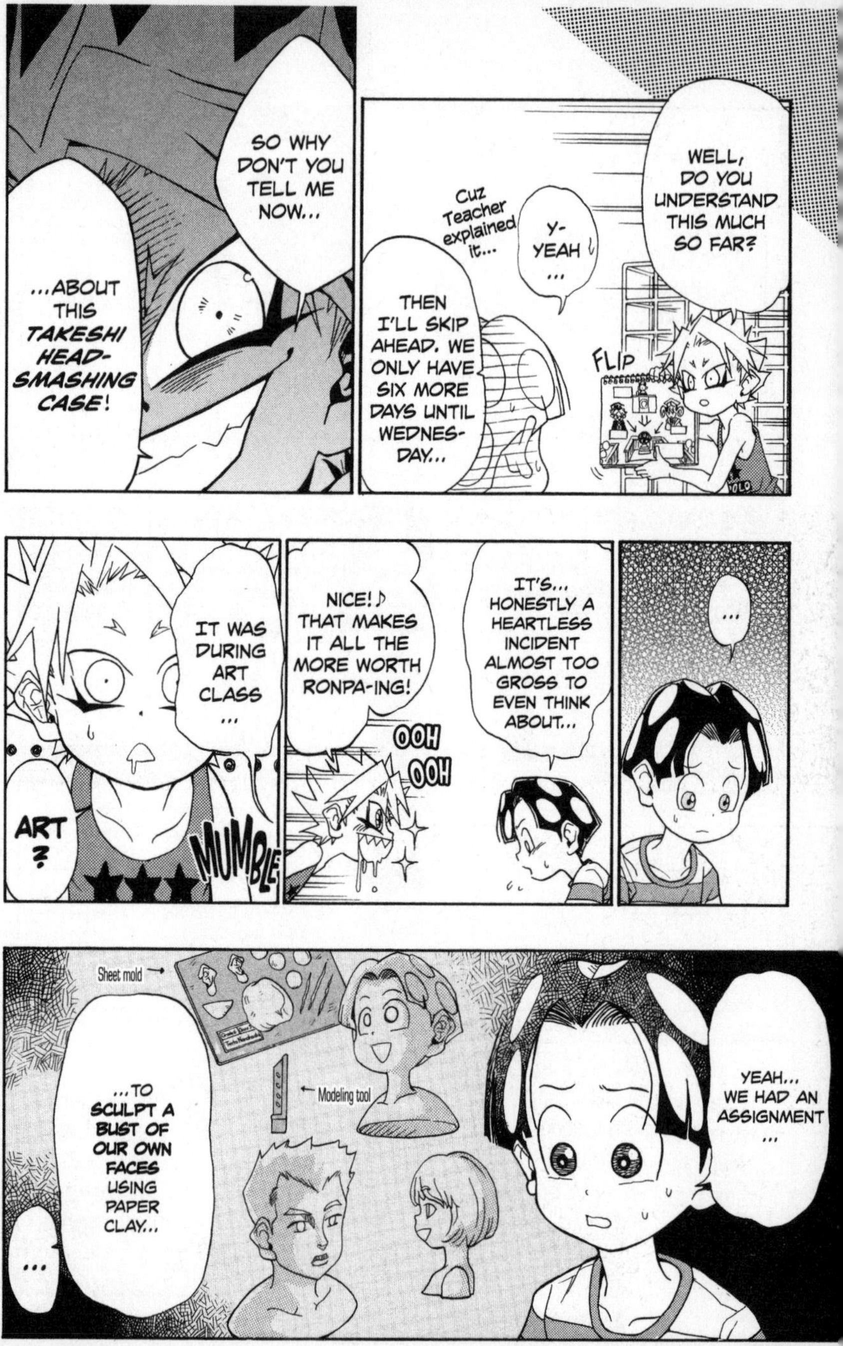
WELL, DO YOU UNDERSTAND THIS MUCH SO FAR?
Y-YEAH ...
Cuz Teacher explained it...
FLIP
THEN I'LL SKIP AHEAD. WE ONLY HAVE SIX MORE DAYS UNTIL WEDNES-DAY...
SO WHY DON'T YOU TELL ME NOW...
...ABOUT THIS TAKESHI HEAD-SMASHING CASE!
...
IT'S... HONESTLY A HEARTLESS INCIDENT ALMOST TOO GROSS TO EVEN THINK ABOUT...
NICE!♪ THAT MAKES IT ALL THE MORE WORTH RONPA-ING!
OOH OOH
IT WAS DURING ART CLASS ...
MUMBLE
ART?
YEAH... WE HAD AN ASSIGNMENT ...
Sheet mold
Modeling tool
...TO SCULPT A BUST OF OUR OWN FACES USING PAPER CLAY...
...

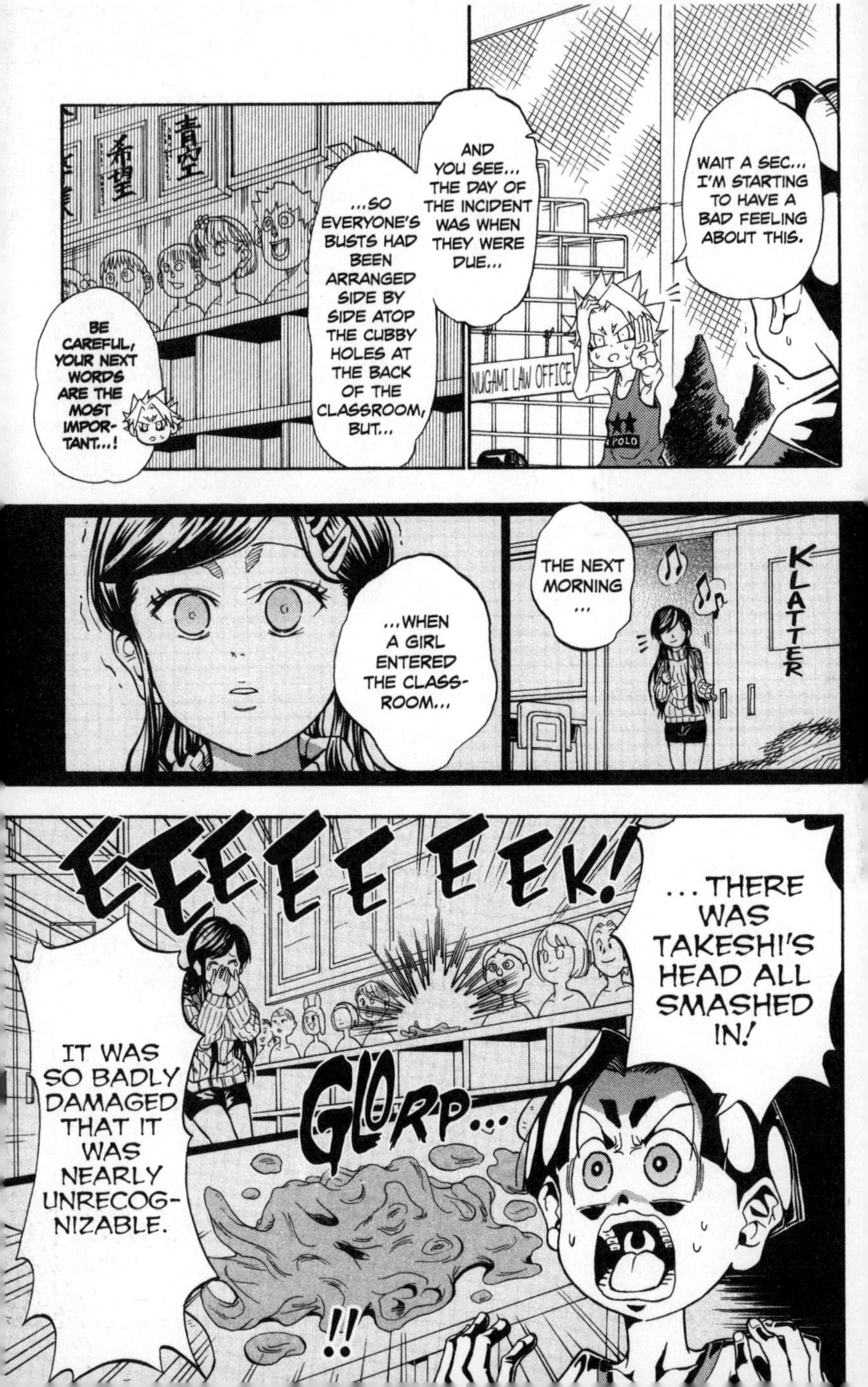
WAIT A SEC... I'M STARTING TO HAVE A BAD FEELING ABOUT THIS.
NUGAMI LAW OFFICE
AND YOU SEE... THE DAY OF THE INCIDENT WAS WHEN THEY WERE DUE...
...SO EVERYONE'S BUSTS HAD BEEN ARRANGED SIDE BY SIDE ATOP THE CUBBY HOLES AT THE BACK OF THE CLASSROOM, BUT...
BE CAREFUL, YOUR NEXT WORDS ARE THE MOST IMPORTANT...!
THE NEXT MORNING...
KLATTER
...WHEN A GIRL ENTERED THE CLASSROOM...
EEEEEEK!
...THERE WAS TAKESHI'S HEAD ALL SMASHED IN!
IT WAS SO BADLY DAMAGED THAT IT WAS NEARLY UNRECOGNIZABLE.
GLORP...
!!

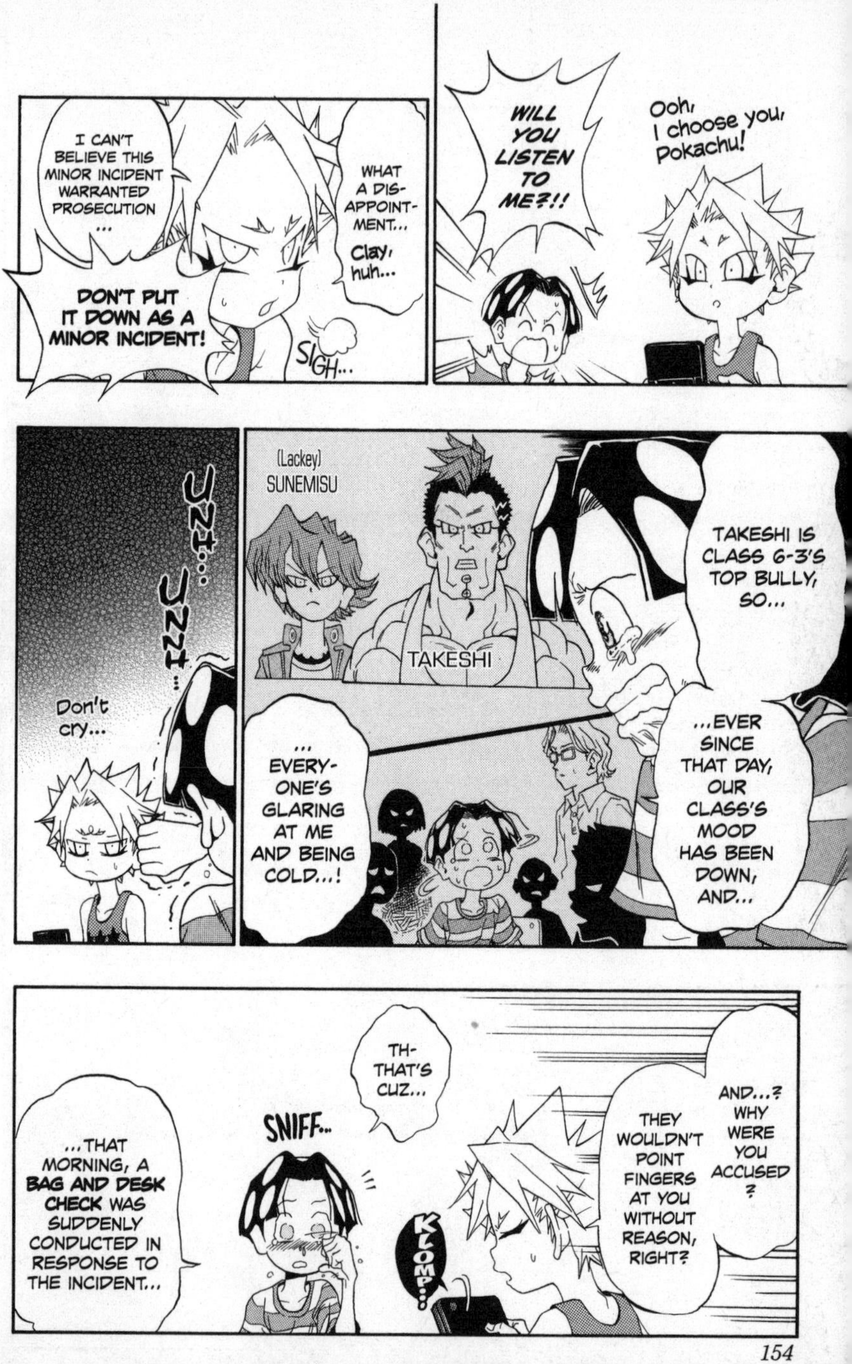
Ooh, I choose you, Pokachu!
WILL YOU LISTEN TO ME?!!
WHAT A DIS-APPOINTMENT... Clay, huh...
I CAN'T BELIEVE THIS MINOR INCIDENT WARRANTED PROSECUTION...
DON'T PUT IT DOWN AS A MINOR INCIDENT!
SIGH...
TAKESHI IS CLASS 6-3'S TOP BULLY, SO...
(Lackey) SUNEMISU
TAKESHI
...EVER SINCE THAT DAY, OUR CLASS'S MOOD HAS BEEN DOWN, AND...
...EVERYONE'S GLARING AT ME AND BEING COLD...!
UNH... UNNH...
Don't cry...
AND...? WHY WERE YOU ACCUSED?
THEY WOULDN'T POINT FINGERS AT YOU WITHOUT REASON, RIGHT?
KLOMP...
TH-THAT'S CUZ...
SNIFF...
...THAT MORNING, A BAG AND DESK CHECK WAS SUDDENLY CONDUCTED IN RESPONSE TO THE INCIDENT...

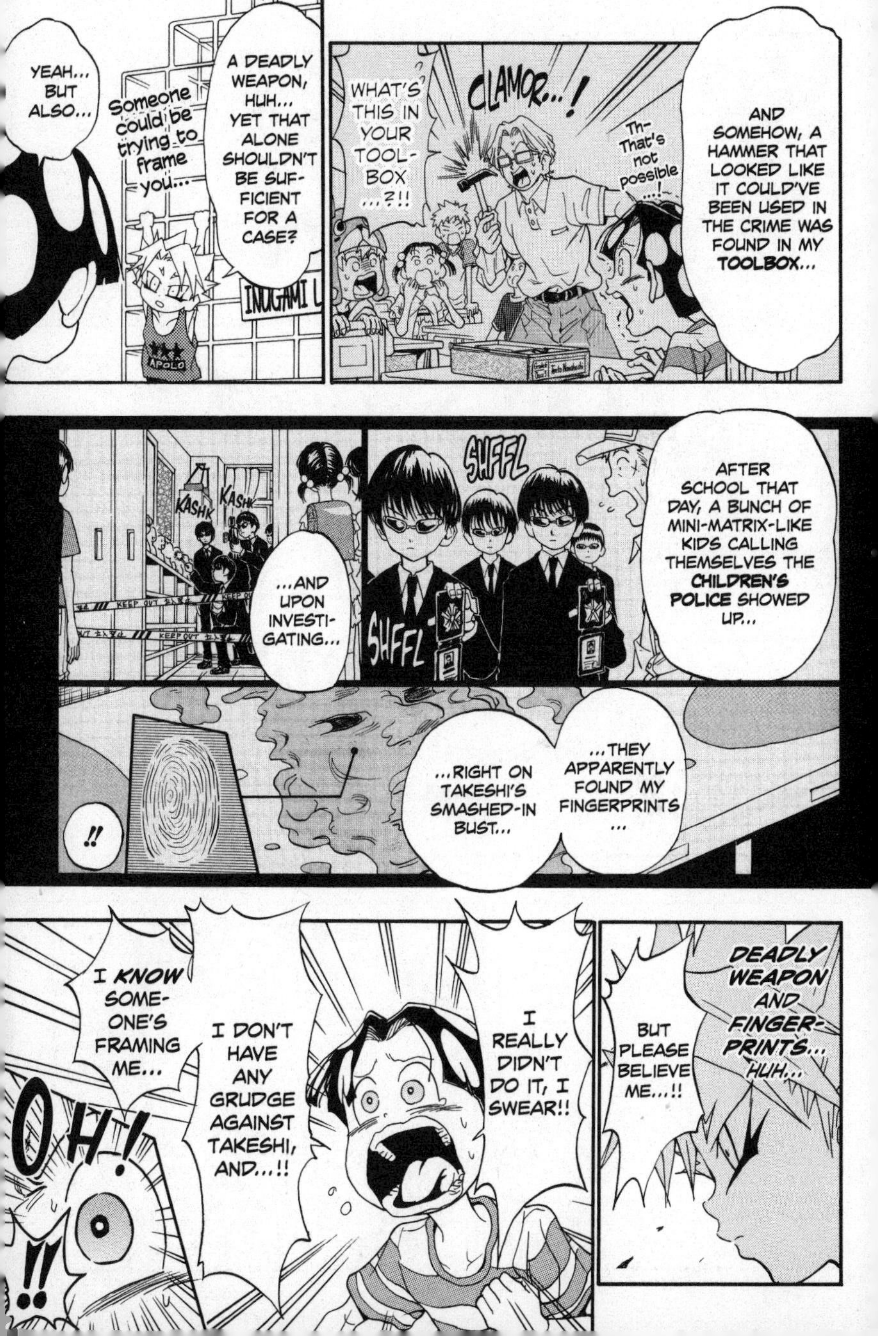
AND SOMEHOW, A HAMMER THAT LOOKED LIKE IT COULD'VE BEEN USED IN THE CRIME WAS FOUND IN MY TOOLBOX...
Th- That's not possible...!
CLAMOR...!
WHAT'S THIS IN YOUR TOOLBOX...?!!
A DEADLY WEAPON, HUH... YET THAT ALONE SHOULDN'T BE SUFFICIENT FOR A CASE?
Someone could be trying to frame you...
YEAH... BUT ALSO...
AFTER SCHOOL THAT DAY, A BUNCH OF MINI-MATRIX-LIKE KIDS CALLING THEMSELVES THE CHILDREN'S POLICE SHOWED UP...
SHFFL
SHFFL
...AND UPON INVESTIGATING...
KASHK
KASHK
...THEY APPARENTLY FOUND MY FINGERPRINTS...
...RIGHT ON TAKESHI'S SMASHED-IN BUST...
!!
DEADLY WEAPON AND FINGERPRINTS... HUH...
BUT PLEASE BELIEVE ME...!!
I REALLY DIDN'T DO IT, I SWEAR!!
I DON'T HAVE ANY GRUDGE AGAINST TAKESHI, AND...!!
I KNOW SOMEONE'S FRAMING ME...
OH!
!!

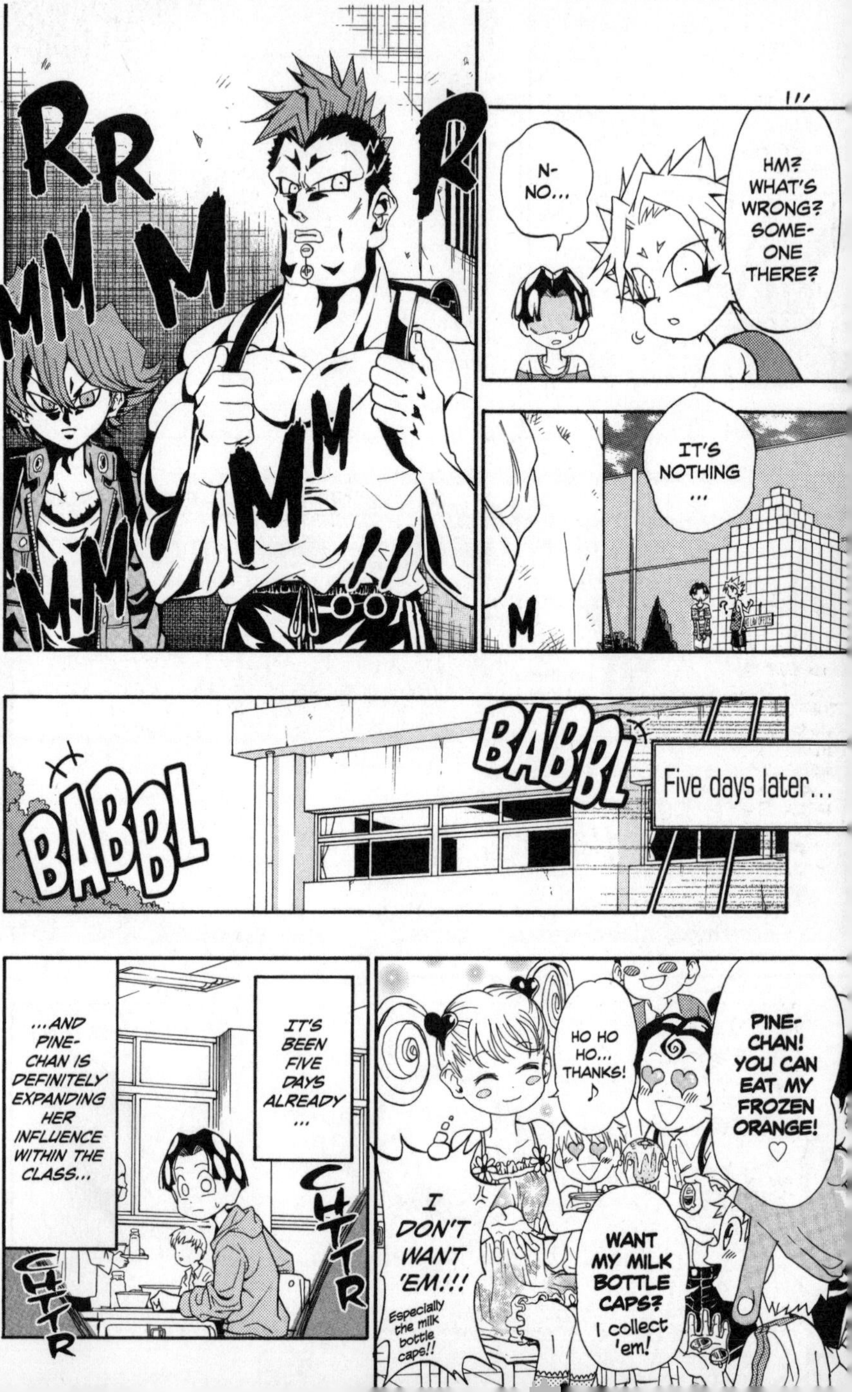
HM? WHAT'S WRONG? SOME-ONE THERE?
N-NO...
IT'S NOTHING...
M
RRMMMM
R
MMMM
MMM
Five days later...
BABBL
BABBL
PINE-CHAN! YOU CAN EAT MY FROZEN ORANGE! ♡
HO HO HO... THANKS! ♪
WANT MY MILK BOTTLE CAPS? I collect 'em!
I DON'T WANT 'EM!!!
Especially the milk bottle caps!!
IT'S BEEN FIVE DAYS ALREADY...
...AND PINE-CHAN IS DEFINITELY EXPANDING HER INFLUENCE WITHIN THE CLASS...
CHTTR
CHTTR

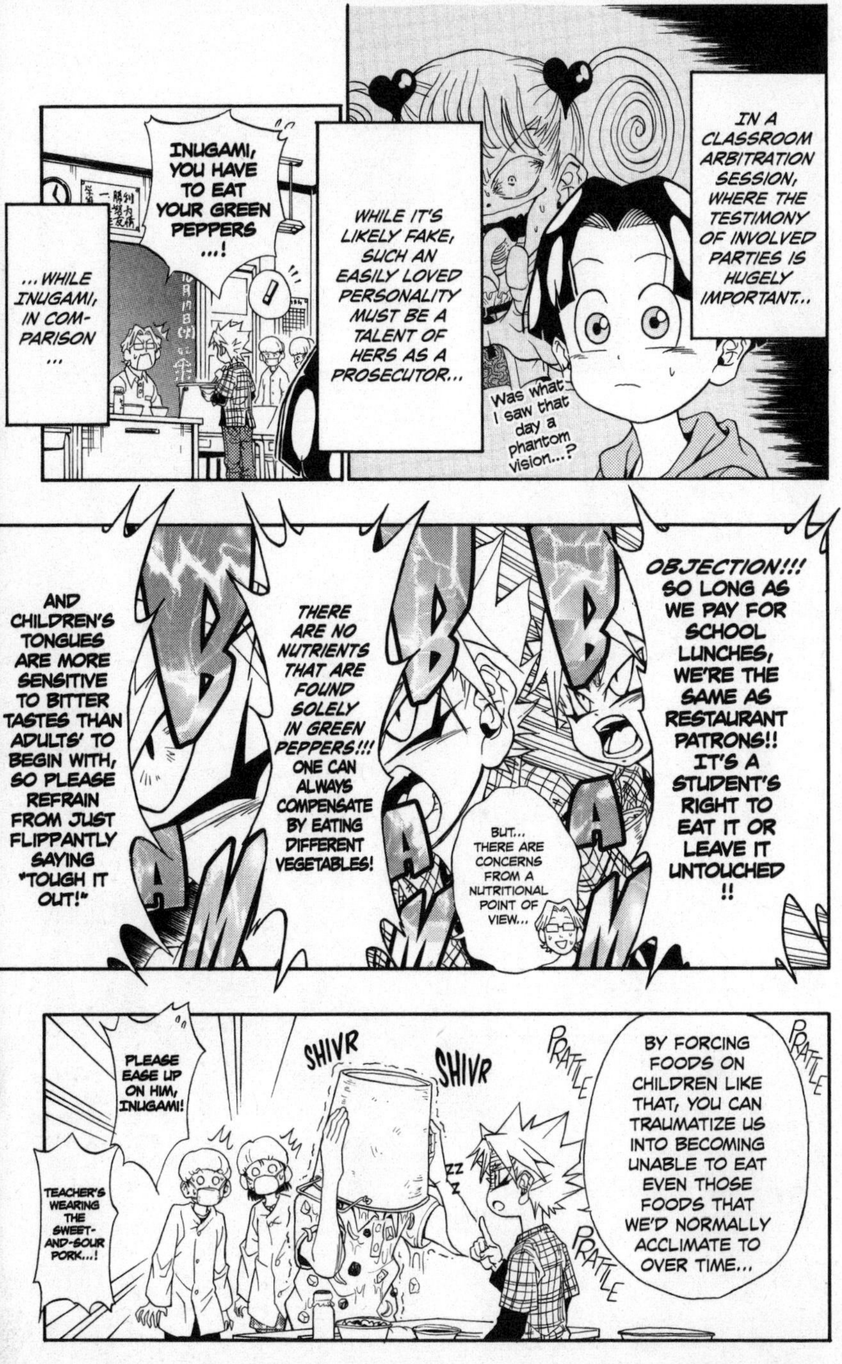
IN A CLASSROOM ARBITRATION SESSION, WHERE THE TESTIMONY OF INVOLVED PARTIES IS HUGELY IMPORTANT...
Was what I saw that day a phantom vision...?
WHILE IT'S LIKELY FAKE, SUCH AN EASILY LOVED PERSONALITY MUST BE A TALENT OF HERS AS A PROSECUTOR...
...WHILE INUGAMI, IN COMPARISON...
INUGAMI, YOU HAVE TO EAT YOUR GREEN PEPPERS...!
OBJECTION!!! SO LONG AS WE PAY FOR SCHOOL LUNCHES, WE'RE THE SAME AS RESTAURANT PATRONS!! IT'S A STUDENT'S RIGHT TO EAT IT OR LEAVE IT UNTOUCHED!!
BAM
BUT... THERE ARE CONCERNS FROM A NUTRITIONAL POINT OF VIEW...
THERE ARE NO NUTRIENTS THAT ARE FOUND SOLELY IN GREEN PEPPERS!!! ONE CAN ALWAYS COMPENSATE BY EATING DIFFERENT VEGETABLES!
BAM
AND CHILDREN'S TONGUES ARE MORE SENSITIVE TO BITTER TASTES THAN ADULTS' TO BEGIN WITH, SO PLEASE REFRAIN FROM JUST FLIPPANTLY SAYING "TOUGH IT OUT!"
PRATTLE
BY FORCING FOODS ON CHILDREN LIKE THAT, YOU CAN TRAUMATIZE US INTO BECOMING UNABLE TO EAT EVEN THOSE FOODS THAT WE'D NORMALLY ACCLIMATE TO OVER TIME...
PRATTLE
PRATTLE
SHIVR
SHIVR
PLEASE EASE UP ON HIM, INUGAMI!
TEACHER'S WEARING THE SWEET-AND-SOUR PORK...!

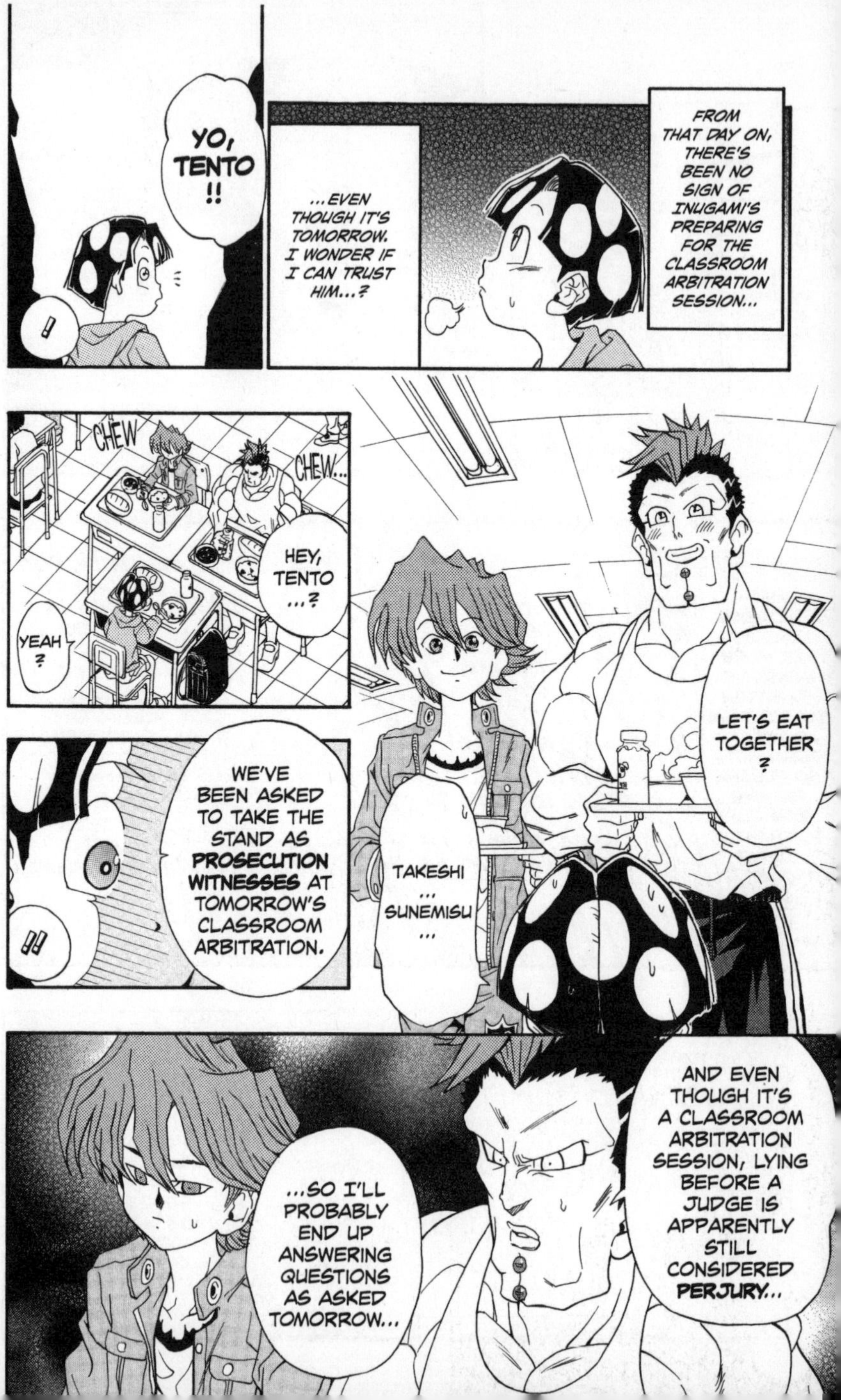
FROM THAT DAY ON, THERE'S BEEN NO SIGN OF INUGAMI'S PREPARING FOR THE CLASSROOM ARBITRATION SESSION...
...EVEN THOUGH IT'S TOMORROW. I WONDER IF I CAN TRUST HIM...?
YO, TENTO!!
!
LET'S EAT TOGETHER?
TAKESHI... SUNEMISU...
CHEW
CHEW...
HEY, TENTO...?
YEAH?
WE'VE BEEN ASKED TO TAKE THE STAND AS PROSECUTION WITNESSES AT TOMORROW'S CLASSROOM ARBITRATION.
!!
AND EVEN THOUGH IT'S A CLASSROOM ARBITRATION SESSION, LYING BEFORE A JUDGE IS APPARENTLY STILL CONSIDERED PERJURY...
...SO I'LL PROBABLY END UP ANSWERING QUESTIONS AS ASKED TOMORROW...

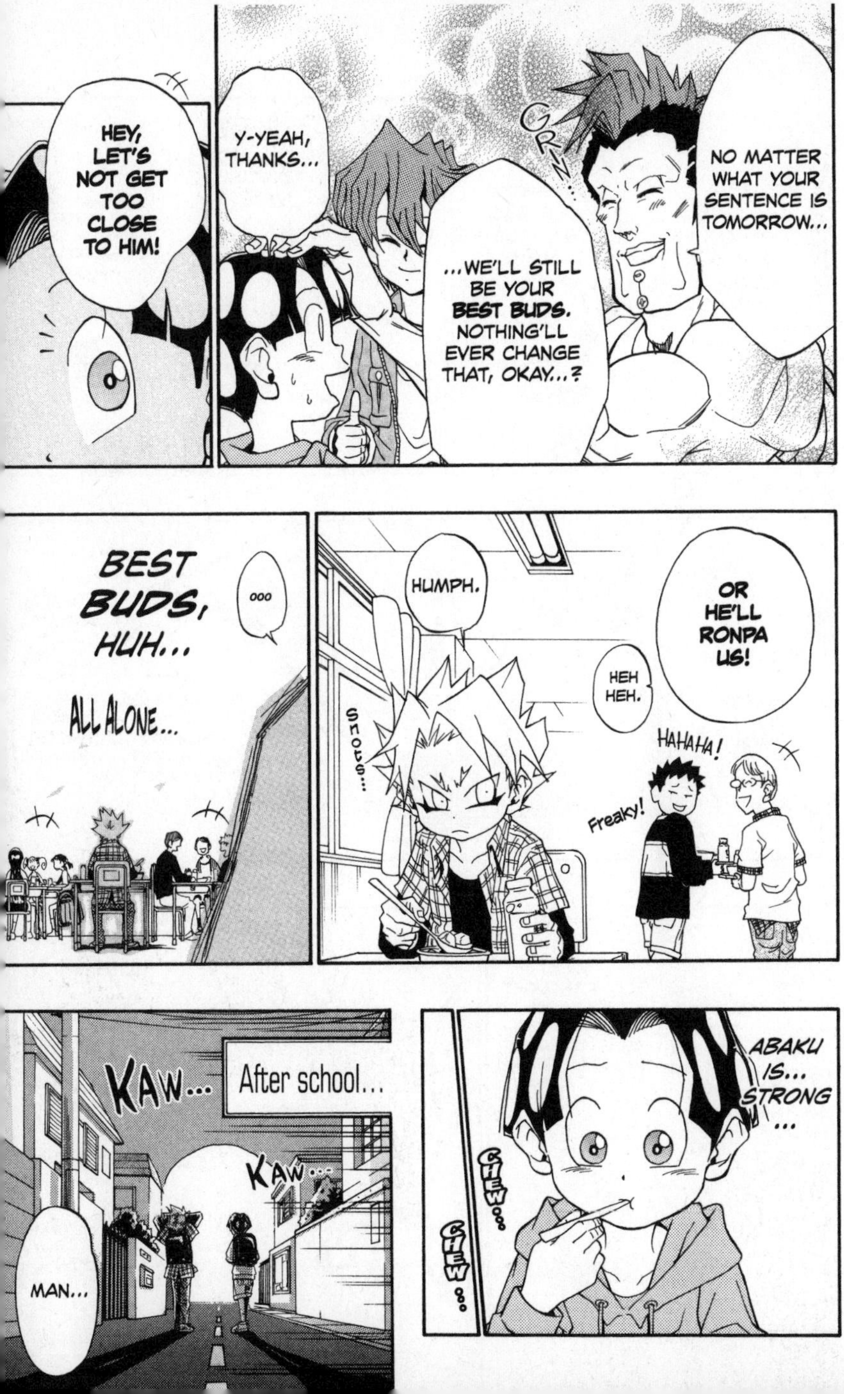
NO MATTER WHAT YOUR SENTENCE IS TOMORROW...
GRIN...
...WE'LL STILL BE YOUR **BEST BUDS.** NOTHING'LL EVER CHANGE THAT, OKAY...?
Y-YEAH, THANKS...
HEY, LET'S NOT GET TOO CLOSE TO HIM!
OR HE'LL RONPA US!
HEH HEH.
HAHAHA!
HUMPH.
Freaky!
Snots...
BEST BUDS, HUH...
...
ALL ALONE...
ABAKU IS... STRONG...
CHEW...
CHEW...
After school...
KAW...
KAW...
MAN...

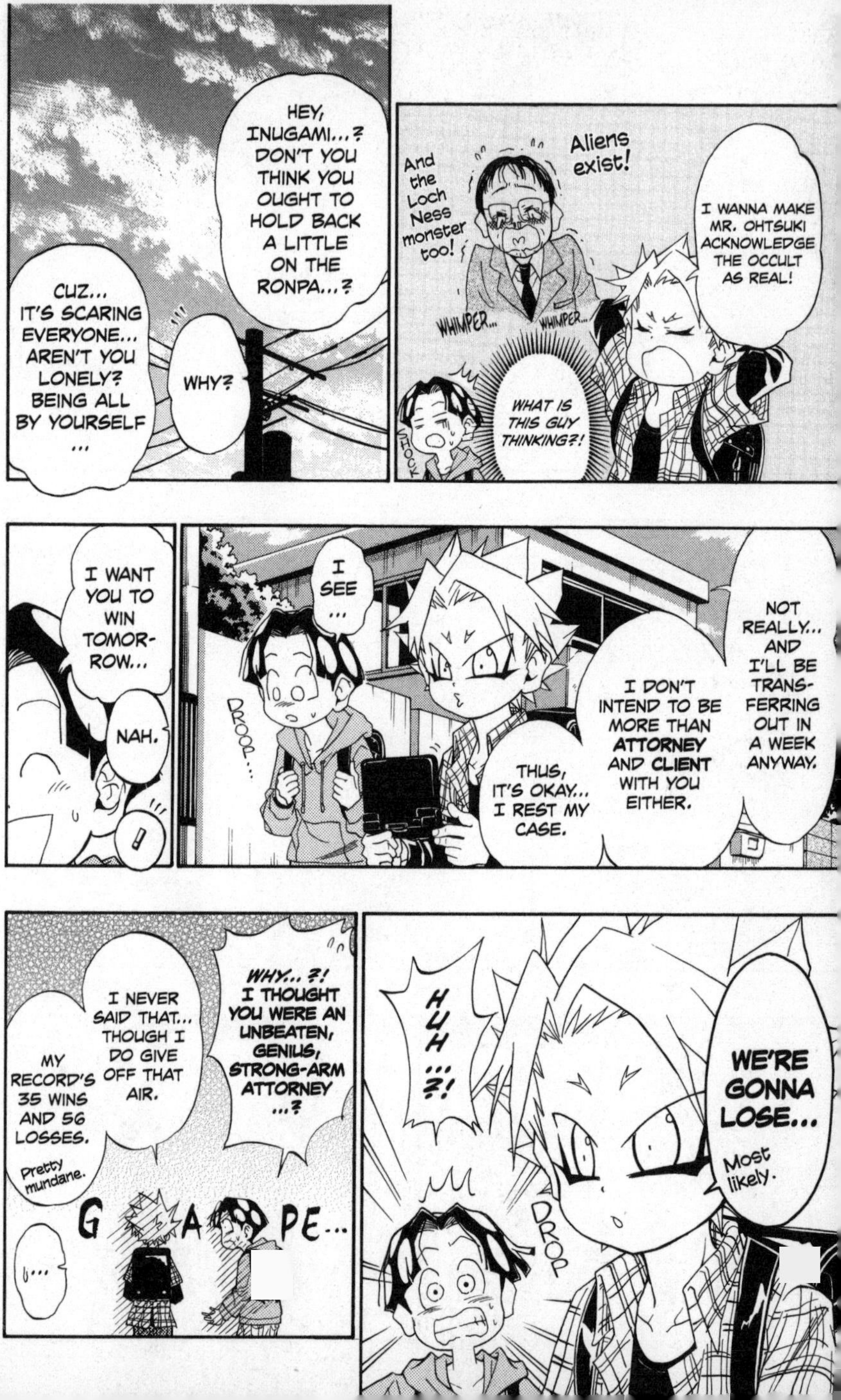
I WANNA MAKE MR. OHTSUKI ACKNOWLEDGE THE OCCULT AS REAL!
Aliens exist!
And the Loch Ness monster too!
WHIMPER...
WHIMPER...
WHAT IS THIS GUY THINKING?!
SHOCK
HEY, INUGAMI...? DON'T YOU THINK YOU OUGHT TO HOLD BACK A LITTLE ON THE RONPA...?
WHY?
CUZ... IT'S SCARING EVERYONE... AREN'T YOU LONELY? BEING ALL BY YOURSELF...
NOT REALLY... AND I'LL BE TRANSFERRING OUT IN A WEEK ANYWAY.
I DON'T INTEND TO BE MORE THAN ATTORNEY AND CLIENT WITH YOU EITHER.
I SEE...
THUS, IT'S OKAY... I REST MY CASE.
DROOP...
I WANT YOU TO WIN TOMORROW...
NAH.
!
WE'RE GONNA LOSE...
Most likely.
HUH...?!
DROP
WHY...?! I THOUGHT YOU WERE AN UNBEATEN, GENIUS, STRONG-ARM ATTORNEY...?
I NEVER SAID THAT... THOUGH I DO GIVE OFF THAT AIR.
MY RECORD'S 35 WINS AND 56 LOSSES.
Pretty mundane.
GAPE...
...

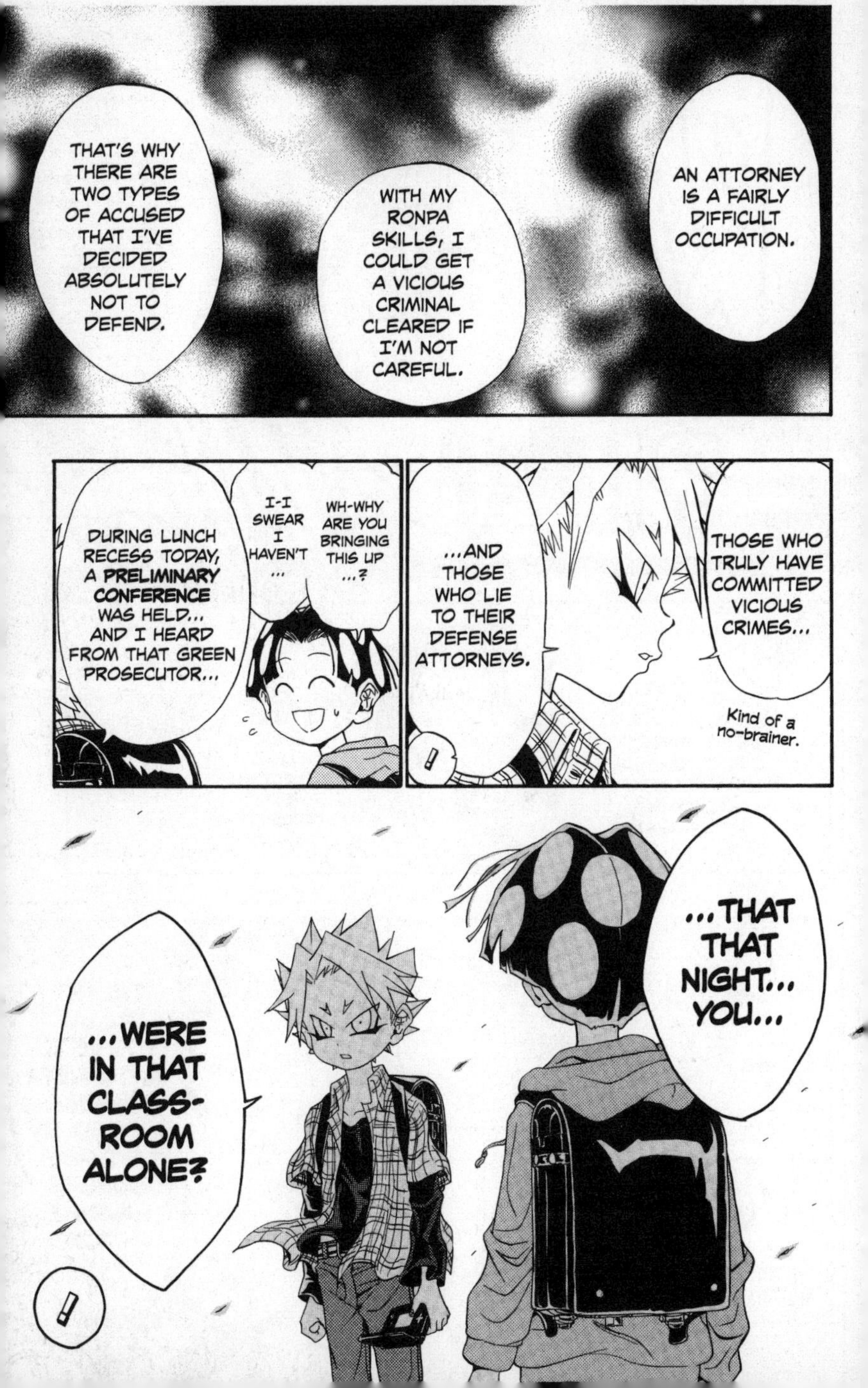
AN ATTORNEY IS A FAIRLY DIFFICULT OCCUPATION.
WITH MY RONPA SKILLS, I COULD GET A VICIOUS CRIMINAL CLEARED IF I'M NOT CAREFUL.
THAT'S WHY THERE ARE TWO TYPES OF ACCUSED THAT I'VE DECIDED ABSOLUTELY NOT TO DEFEND.
THOSE WHO TRULY HAVE COMMITTED VICIOUS CRIMES...
Kind of a no-brainer.
...AND THOSE WHO LIE TO THEIR DEFENSE ATTORNEYS.
!
WH-WHY ARE YOU BRINGING THIS UP...?
I-I SWEAR I HAVEN'T...
DURING LUNCH RECESS TODAY, A **PRELIMINARY CONFERENCE** WAS HELD... AND I HEARD FROM THAT GREEN PROSECUTOR...
...THAT THAT NIGHT... YOU...
...WERE IN THAT CLASS-ROOM ALONE?
!

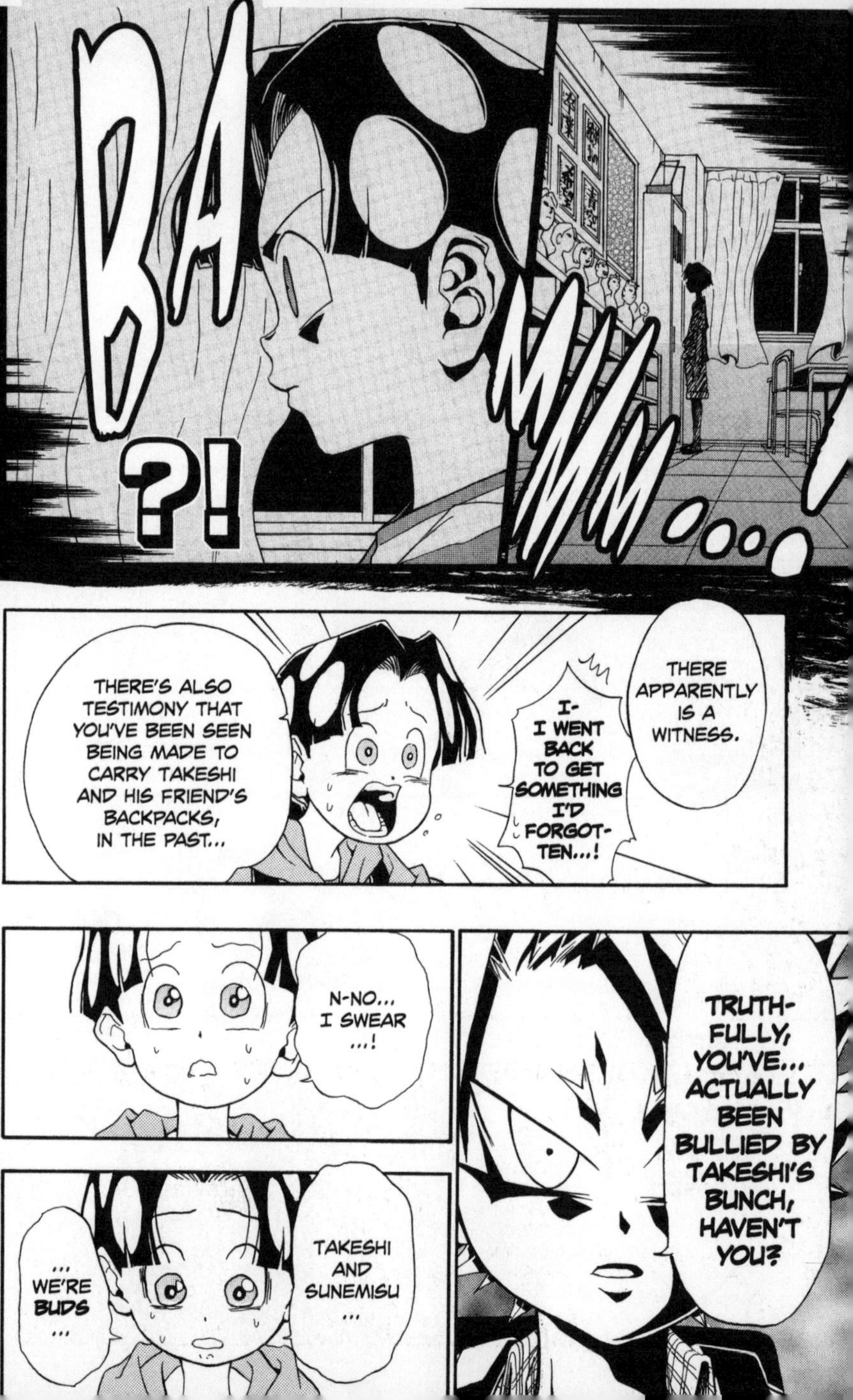
BA
?!
THERE APPARENTLY IS A WITNESS.
I- I WENT BACK TO GET SOMETHING I'D FORGOT-TEN...!
THERE'S ALSO TESTIMONY THAT YOU'VE BEEN SEEN BEING MADE TO CARRY TAKESHI AND HIS FRIEND'S BACKPACKS, IN THE PAST...
TRUTH-FULLY, YOU'VE... ACTUALLY BEEN BULLIED BY TAKESHI'S BUNCH, HAVEN'T YOU?
N-NO... I SWEAR ...!
TAKESHI AND SUNEMISU ...
... WE'RE BUDS ...

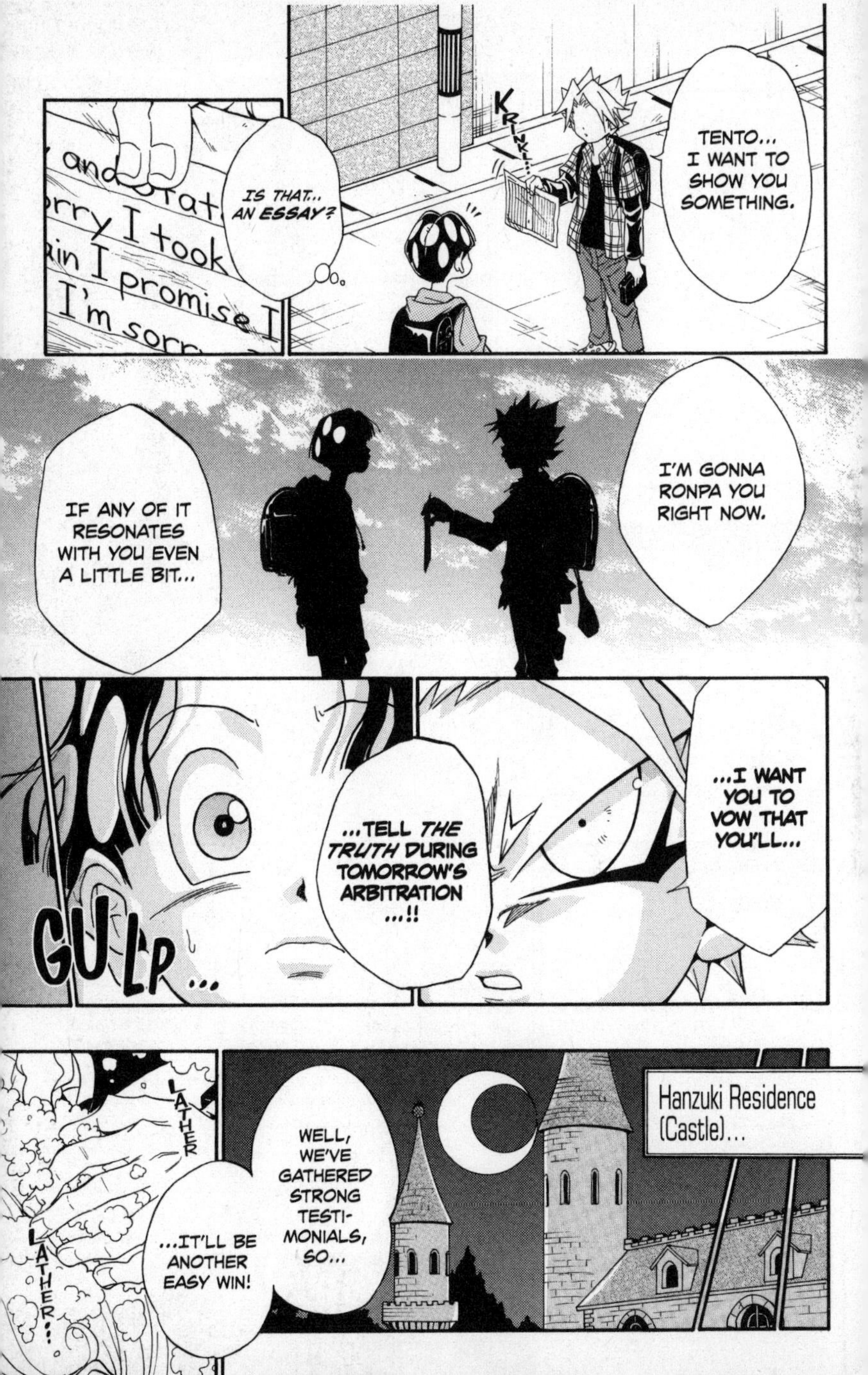
TENTO... I WANT TO SHOW YOU SOMETHING.
KRINKL...
IS THAT... AN *ESSAY*?
and stat
rry I took
in I promise I
I'm sorr
I'M GONNA RONPA YOU RIGHT NOW.
IF ANY OF IT RESONATES WITH YOU EVEN A LITTLE BIT...
...I WANT YOU TO VOW THAT YOU'LL...
...TELL *THE TRUTH* DURING TOMORROW'S ARBITRATION ...!!
GULP...
Hanzuki Residence (Castle)...
WELL, WE'VE GATHERED STRONG TESTI-MONIALS, SO...
...IT'LL BE ANOTHER EASY WIN!
LATHER
LATHER!!

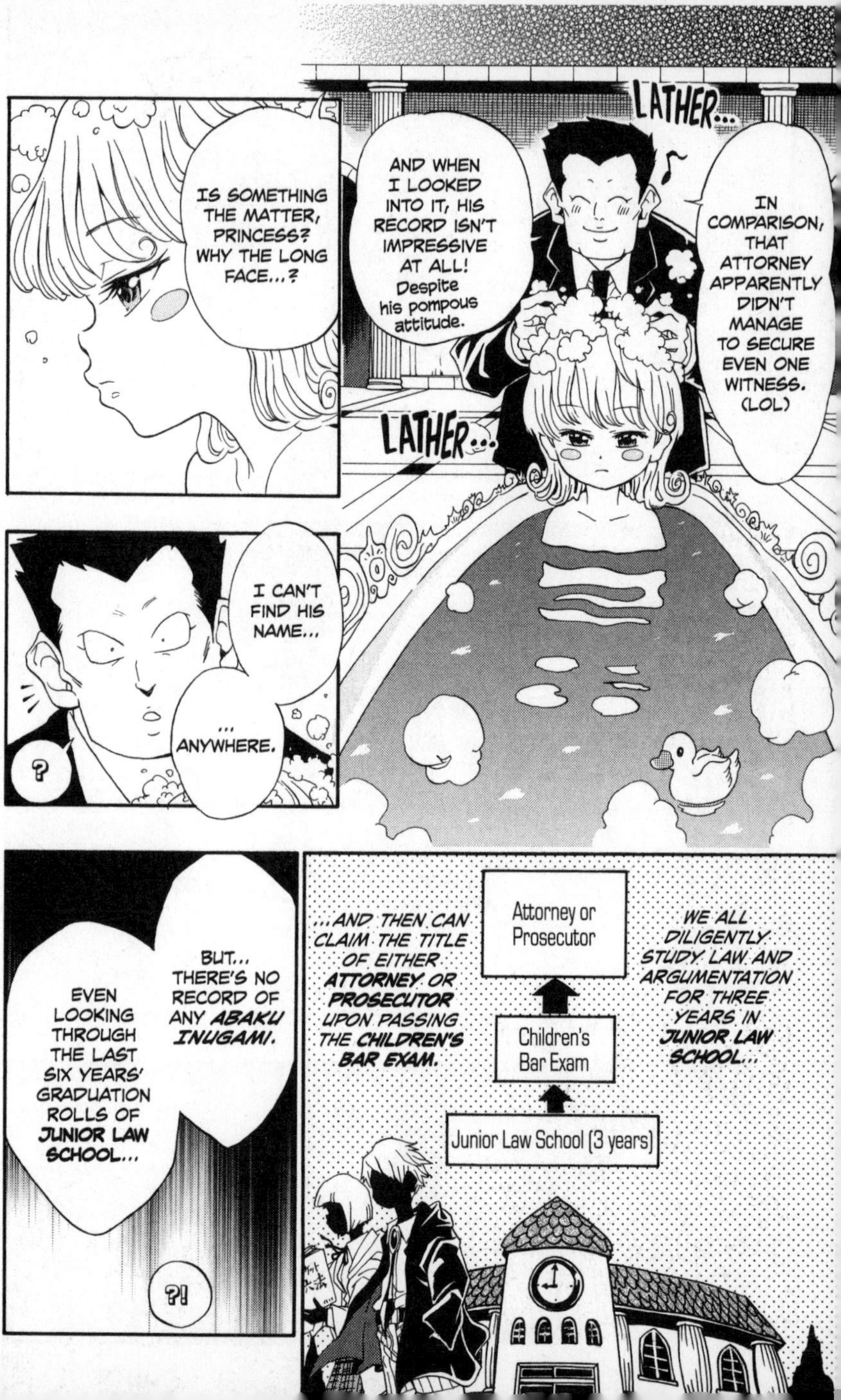
LATHER...
IN COMPARISON, THAT ATTORNEY APPARENTLY DIDN'T MANAGE TO SECURE EVEN ONE WITNESS. (LOL)
AND WHEN I LOOKED INTO IT, HIS RECORD ISN'T IMPRESSIVE AT ALL! Despite his pompous attitude.
LATHER...
IS SOMETHING THE MATTER, PRINCESS? WHY THE LONG FACE...?
I CAN'T FIND HIS NAME...
... ANYWHERE.
?
WE ALL DILIGENTLY STUDY LAW AND ARGUMENTATION FOR THREE YEARS IN JUNIOR LAW SCHOOL...
Attorney or Prosecutor
Children's Bar Exam
Junior Law School (3 years)
...AND THEN CAN CLAIM THE TITLE OF EITHER ATTORNEY OR PROSECUTOR UPON PASSING THE CHILDREN'S BAR EXAM.
EVEN LOOKING THROUGH THE LAST SIX YEARS' GRADUATION ROLLS OF JUNIOR LAW SCHOOL...
BUT... THERE'S NO RECORD OF ANY ABAKU INUGAMI.
?!

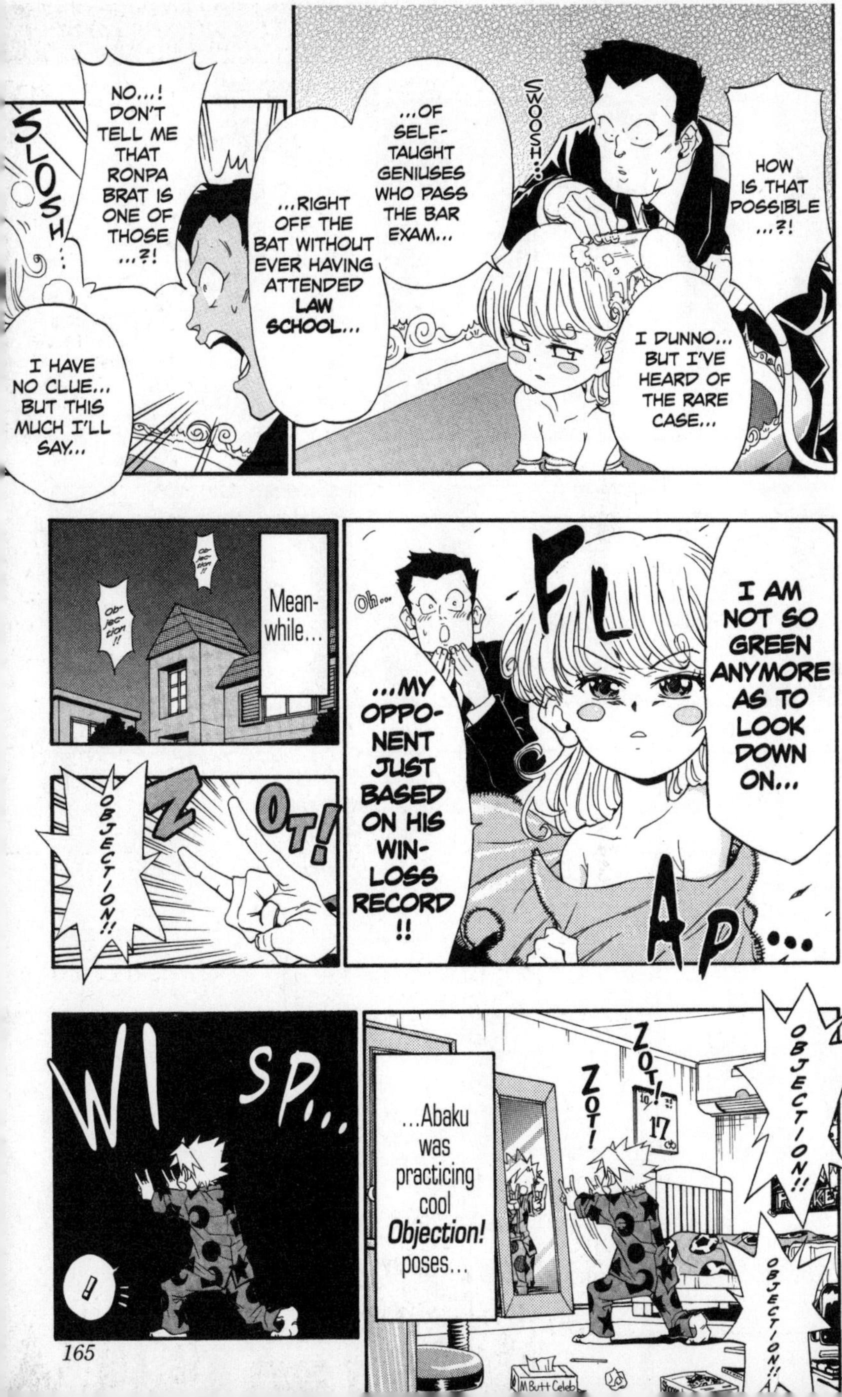
HOW IS THAT POSSIBLE...?!
SWOOSH...
I DUNNO... BUT I'VE HEARD OF THE RARE CASE...
...OF SELF-TAUGHT GENIUSES WHO PASS THE BAR EXAM...
...RIGHT OFF THE BAT WITHOUT EVER HAVING ATTENDED LAW SCHOOL...
NO...! DON'T TELL ME THAT RONPA BRAT IS ONE OF THOSE...?!
SLOSH...
I HAVE NO CLUE... BUT THIS MUCH I'LL SAY...
FLAP...
I AM NOT SO GREEN ANYMORE AS TO LOOK DOWN ON...
Oh...
...MY OPPONENT JUST BASED ON HIS WIN-LOSS RECORD!!
Mean-while...
Ob-jec-tion!!
Ob-jec-tion!!
ZOT!
OBJECTION!!
OBJECTION!!
ZOT!
ZOT!
...Abaku was practicing cool Objection! poses...
OBJECTION!!
WISP...
!

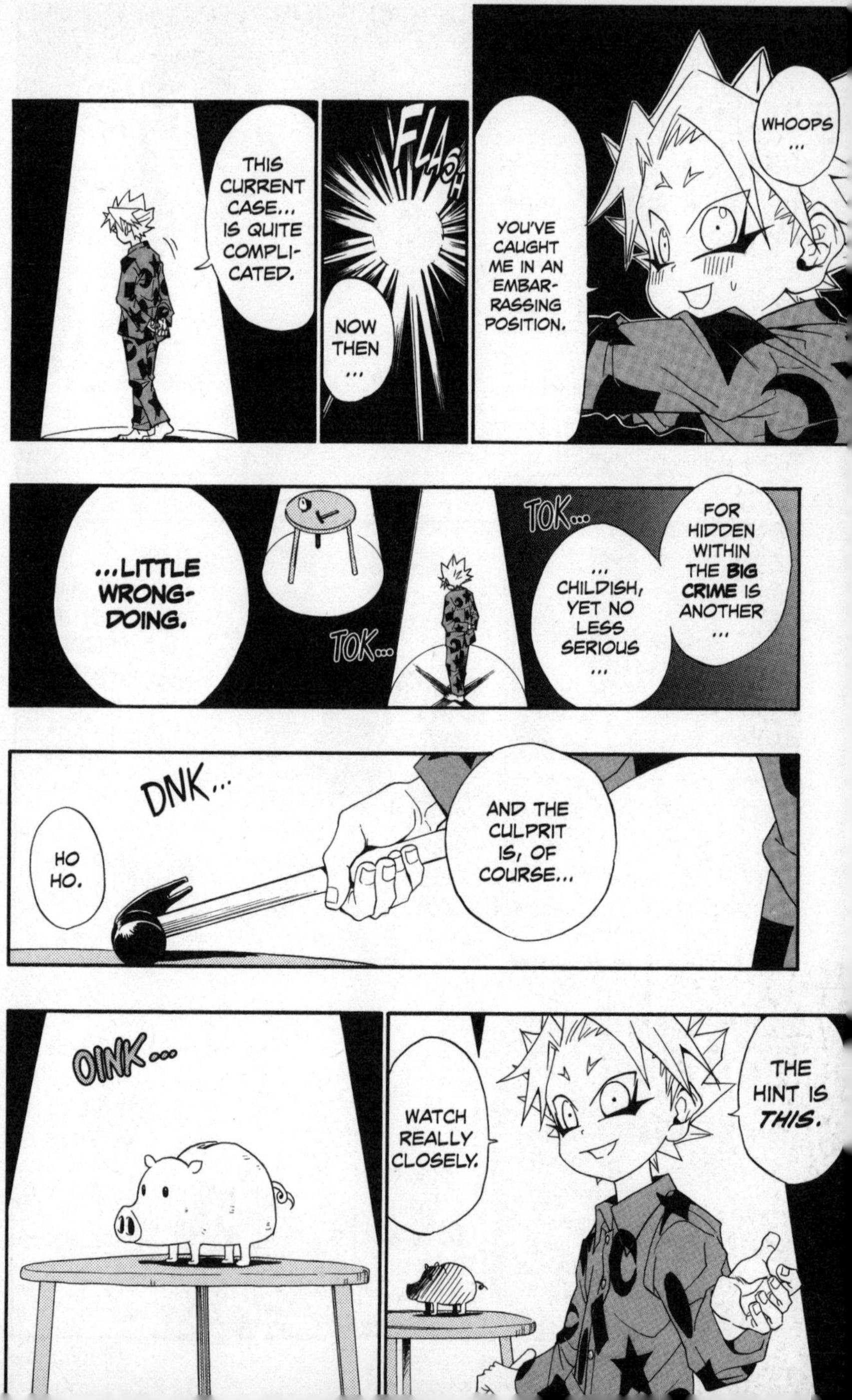
WHOOPS ...
YOU'VE CAUGHT ME IN AN EMBARRASSING POSITION.
FLASH
NOW THEN ...
THIS CURRENT CASE... IS QUITE COMPLICATED.
TOK...
FOR HIDDEN WITHIN THE **BIG CRIME** IS ANOTHER ...
... CHILDISH, YET NO LESS SERIOUS ...
TOK...
...LITTLE WRONGDOING.
AND THE CULPRIT IS, OF COURSE...
DNK...
HO HO.
THE HINT IS *THIS*.
WATCH REALLY CLOSELY.
OINK...

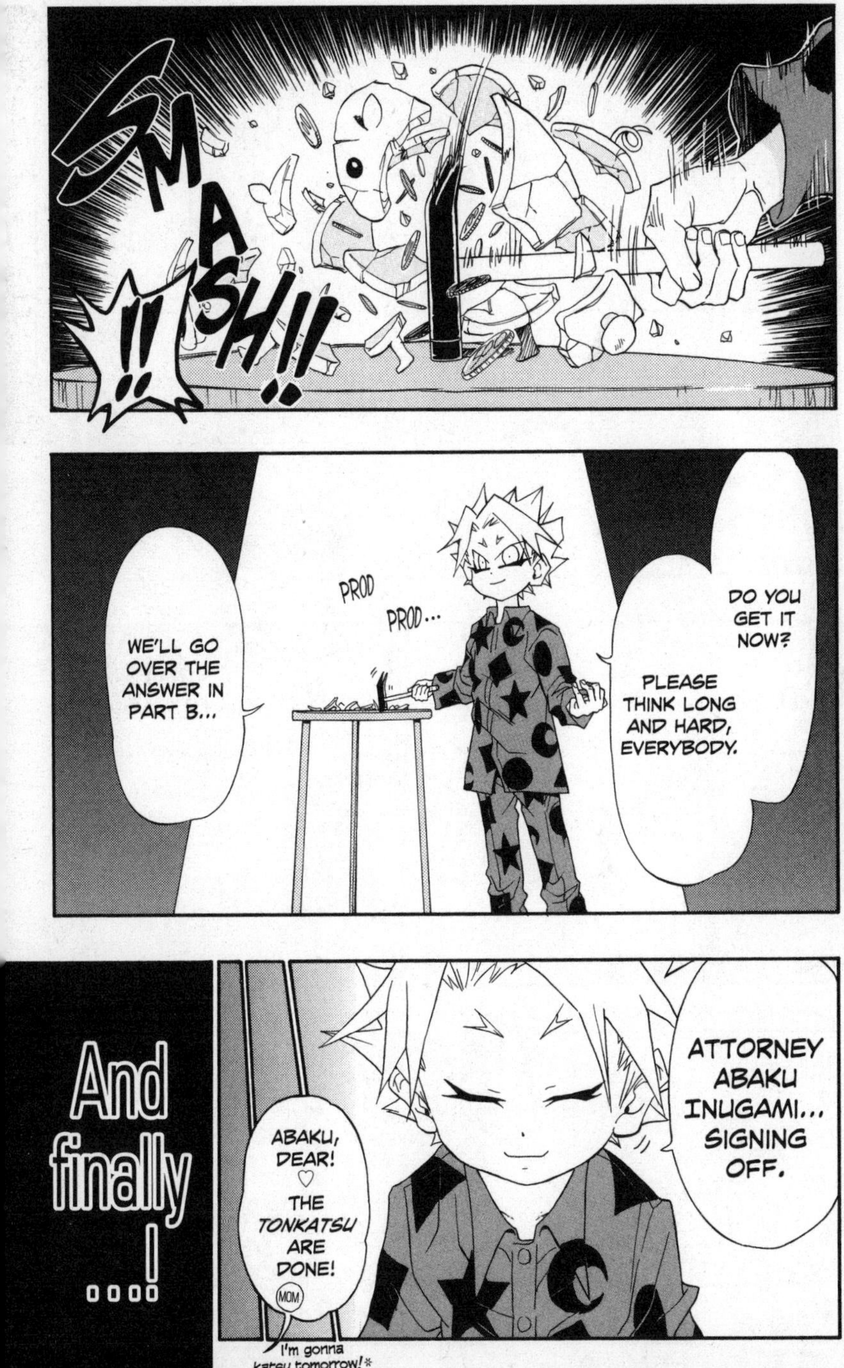
SMASH!!
!!
DO YOU GET IT NOW?
PLEASE THINK LONG AND HARD, EVERYBODY.
PROD
PROD...
WE'LL GO OVER THE ANSWER IN PART B...
ATTORNEY ABAKU INUGAMI... SIGNING OFF.
ABAKU, DEAR! ♡ THE *TONKATSU* ARE DONE!
MOM
I'm gonna katsu tomorrow!*
And finally!....

*SEE GLOSSARY ON PAGE 209.

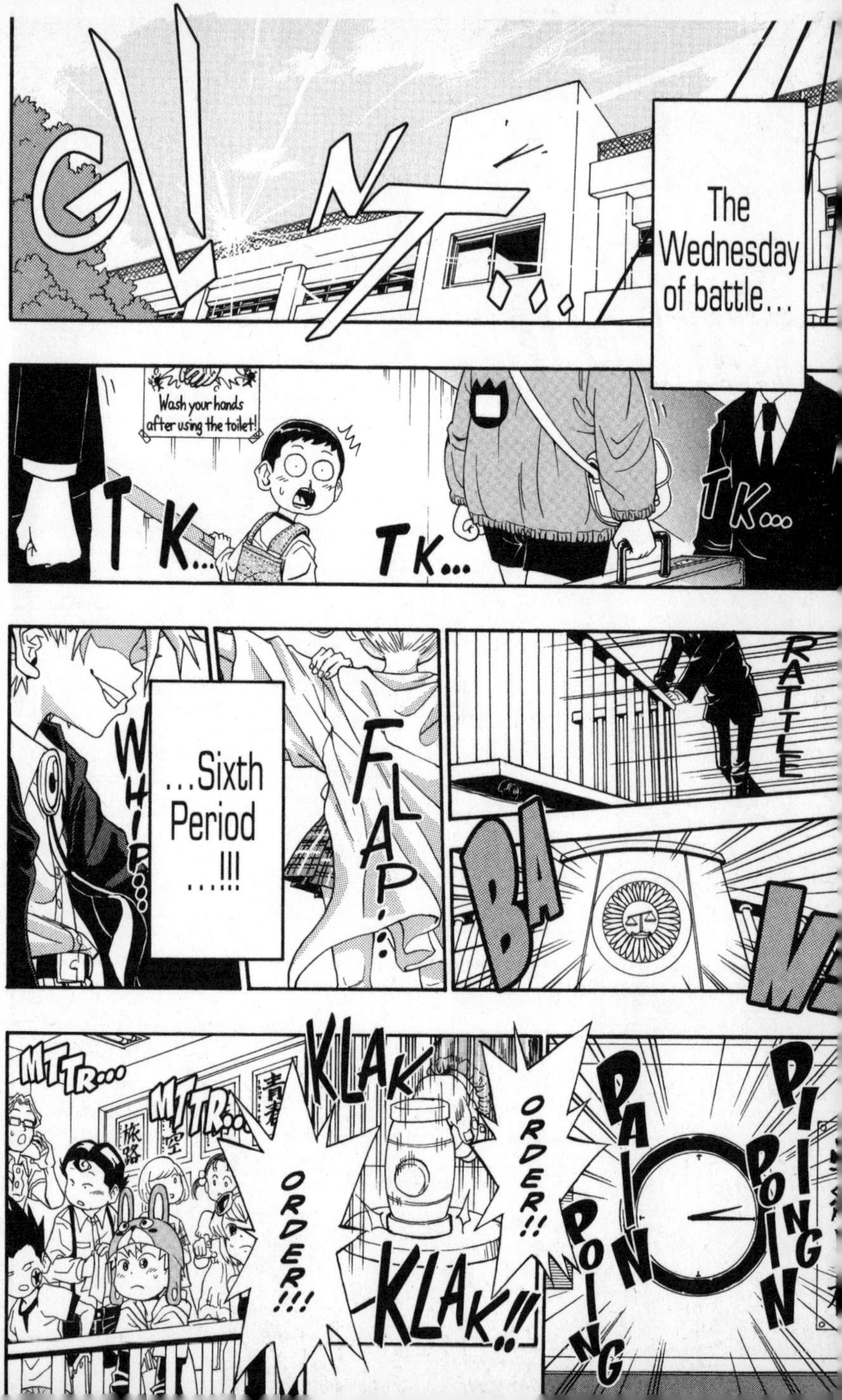
The Wednesday of battle...
GLINT...
TK...
TK...
Wash your hands after using the toilet!
TK...
RATTLE
BA
M
...Sixth Period ...!!!
FLAP...
WHIP...
PIIING
POIN
PAION
POING
ORDER!!
KLAK
ORDER!!!
KLAK!!
MTTTR...
MTTTR...

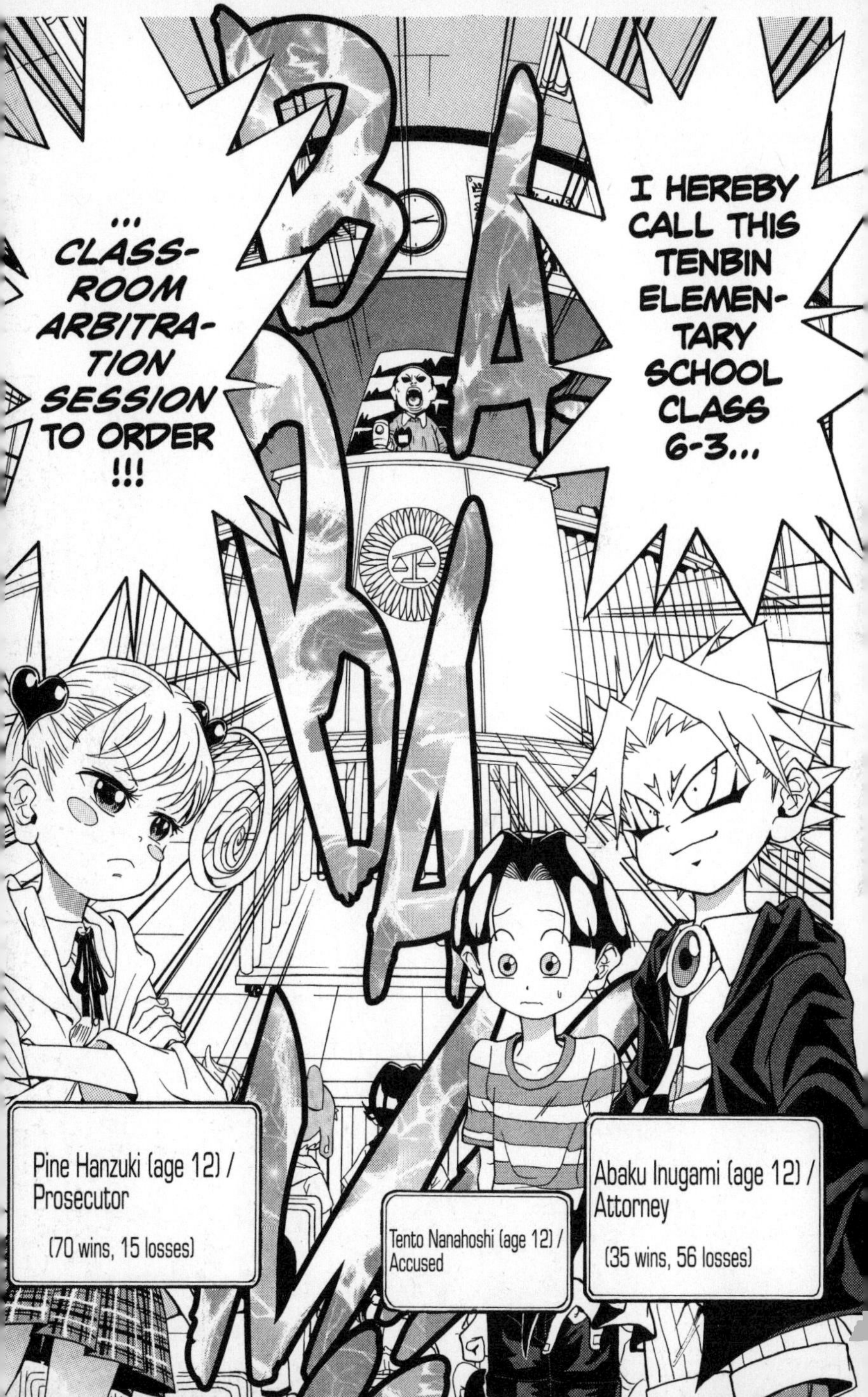
I HEREBY CALL THIS TENBIN ELEMENTARY SCHOOL CLASS 6-3...
...CLASSROOM ARBITRATION SESSION TO ORDER!!!
Abaku Inugami (age 12) / Attorney (35 wins, 56 losses)
Tento Nanahoshi (age 12) / Accused
Pine Hanzuki (age 12) / Prosecutor (70 wins, 15 losses)

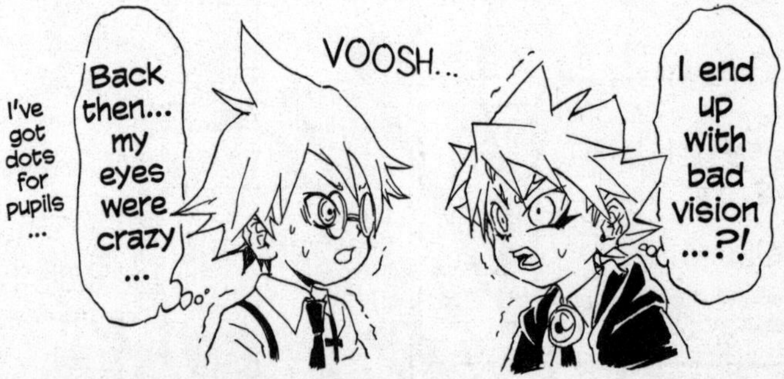
I end up with bad vision ...?!
VOOSH...
Back then... my eyes were crazy ...
I've got dots for pupils ...

SCHOOL JUDGMENT ONE-SHOT: PART B

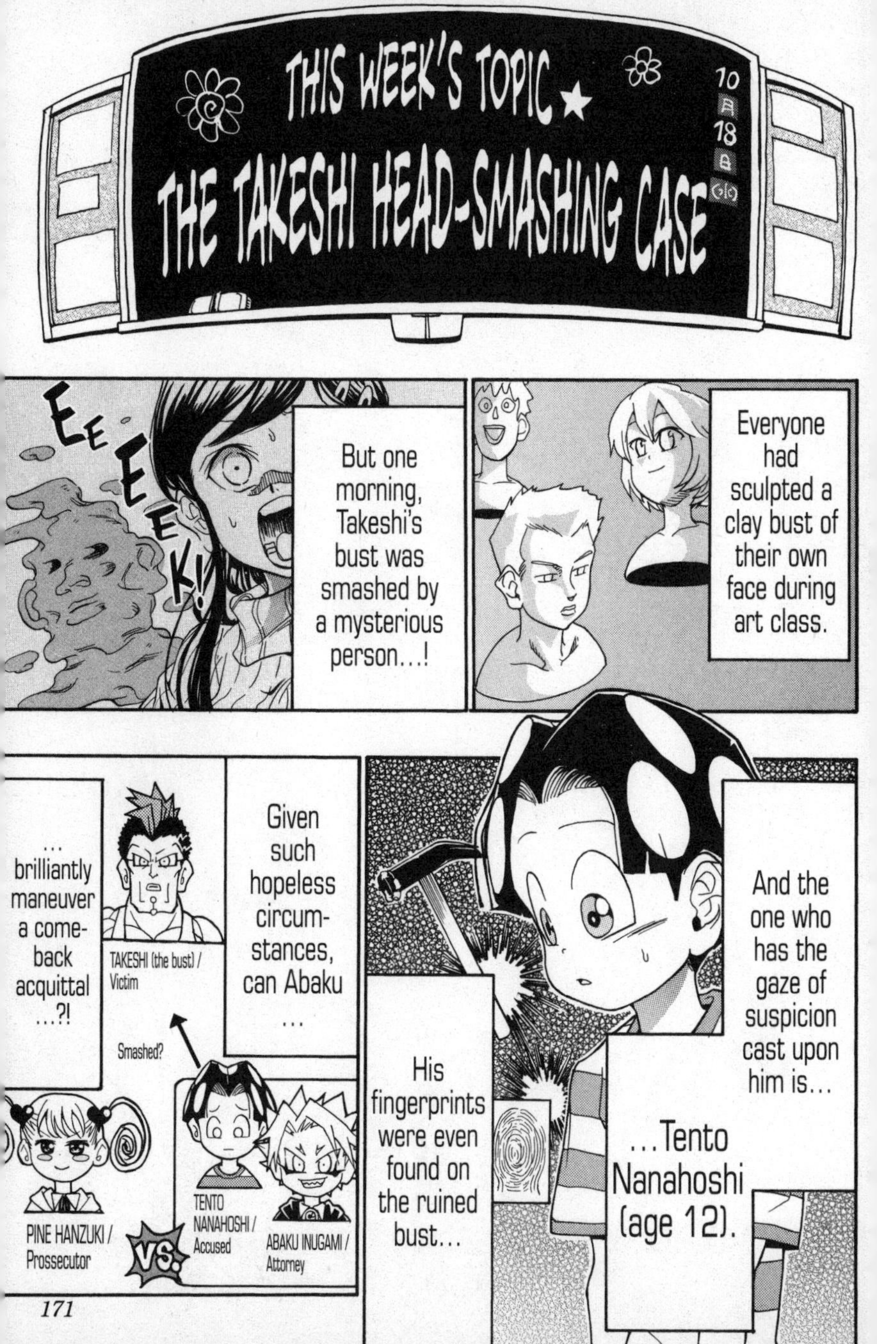

THIS WEEK'S TOPIC ★
THE TAKESHI HEAD-SMASHING CASE
Everyone had sculpted a clay bust of their own face during art class.
But one morning, Takeshi's bust was smashed by a mysterious person...!
EEEEEK!
And the one who has the gaze of suspicion cast upon him is...
...Tento Nanahoshi (age 12).
His fingerprints were even found on the ruined bust...
Given such hopeless circumstances, can Abaku ...
... brilliantly maneuver a come-back acquittal ...?!
TAKESHI (the bust) / Victim
Smashed?
PINE HANZUKI / Prossecutor
VS.
TENTO NANAHOSHI / Accused
ABAKU INUGAMI / Attorney

PART B ⟨COURTROOM ARC⟩

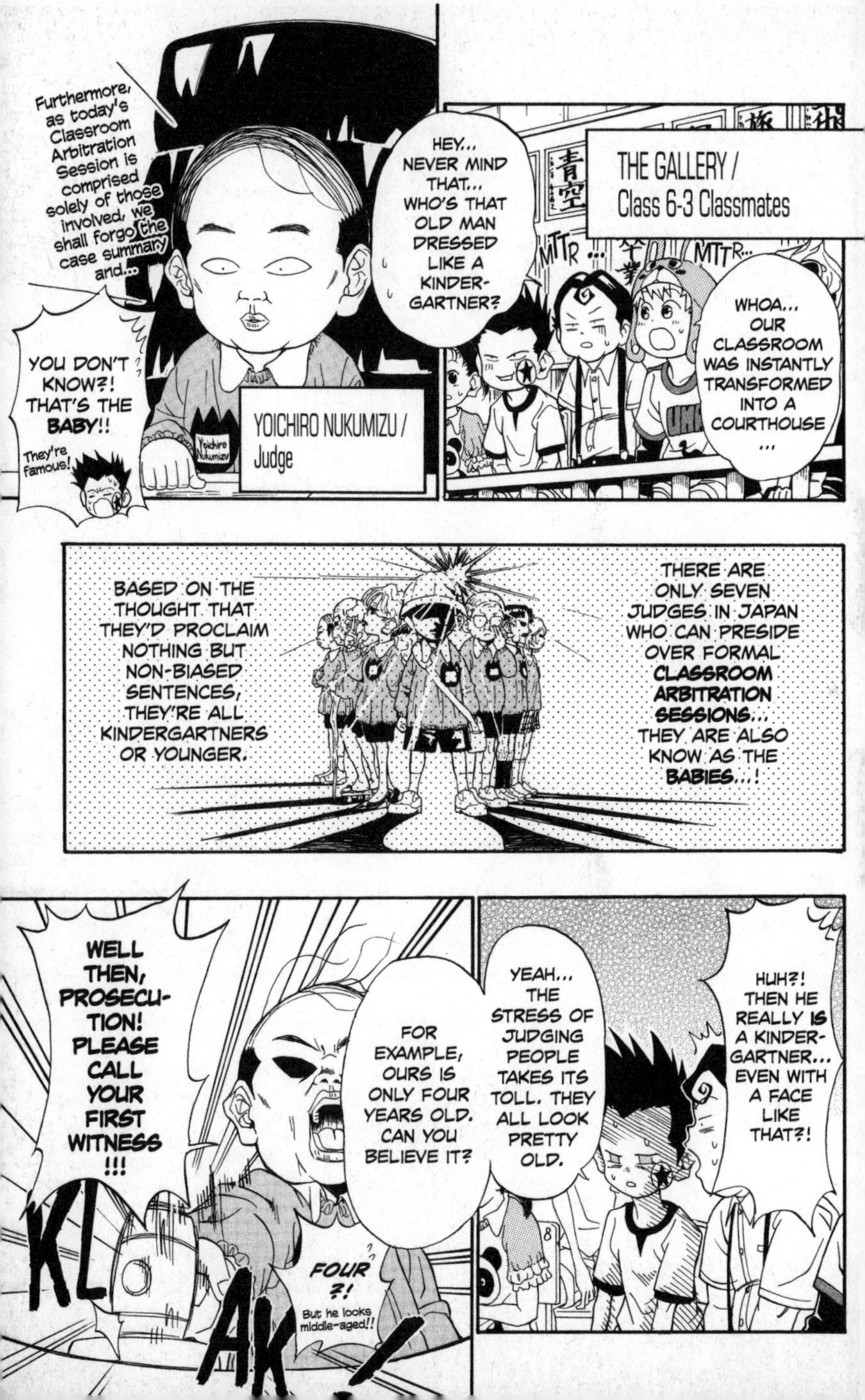
THE GALLERY /
Class 6-3 Classmates
MTTR... MTTR...
WHOA... OUR CLASSROOM WAS INSTANTLY TRANSFORMED INTO A COURTHOUSE...
HEY... NEVER MIND THAT... WHO'S THAT OLD MAN DRESSED LIKE A KINDER-GARTNER?
Furthermore, as today's Classroom Arbitration Session is comprised solely of those involved, we shall forgo the case summary and...
YOU DON'T KNOW?! THAT'S THE BABY!!
They're famous!
Yoichiro Nukumizu
YOICHIRO NUKUMIZU /
Judge
THERE ARE ONLY SEVEN JUDGES IN JAPAN WHO CAN PRESIDE OVER FORMAL CLASSROOM ARBITRATION SESSIONS... THEY ARE ALSO KNOW AS THE BABIES...!
BASED ON THE THOUGHT THAT THEY'D PROCLAIM NOTHING BUT NON-BIASED SENTENCES, THEY'RE ALL KINDERGARTNERS OR YOUNGER.
HUH?! THEN HE REALLY IS A KINDER-GARTNER... EVEN WITH A FACE LIKE THAT?!
YEAH... THE STRESS OF JUDGING PEOPLE TAKES ITS TOLL. THEY ALL LOOK PRETTY OLD.
FOR EXAMPLE, OURS IS ONLY FOUR YEARS OLD. CAN YOU BELIEVE IT?
FOUR?!
But he looks middle-aged!!
WELL THEN, PROSECUTION! PLEASE CALL YOUR FIRST WITNESS!!!
KLAK

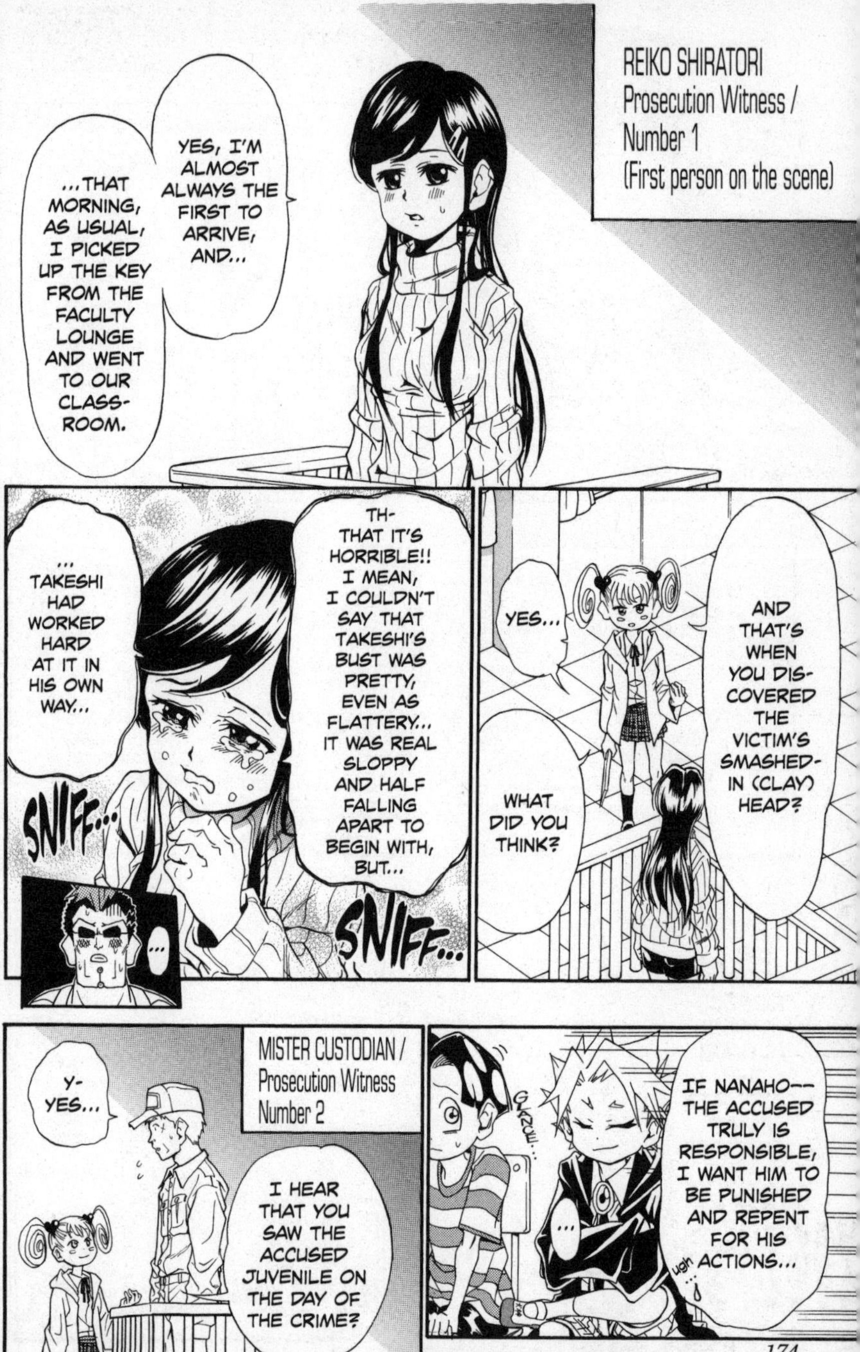
REIKO SHIRATORI Prosecution Witness / Number 1 (First person on the scene)
YES, I'M ALMOST ALWAYS THE FIRST TO ARRIVE, AND...
...THAT MORNING, AS USUAL, I PICKED UP THE KEY FROM THE FACULTY LOUNGE AND WENT TO OUR CLASS-ROOM.
AND THAT'S WHEN YOU DIS-COVERED THE VICTIM'S SMASHED-IN (CLAY) HEAD?
YES...
WHAT DID YOU THINK?
TH- THAT IT'S HORRIBLE!! I MEAN, I COULDN'T SAY THAT TAKESHI'S BUST WAS PRETTY, EVEN AS FLATTERY... IT WAS REAL SLOPPY AND HALF FALLING APART TO BEGIN WITH, BUT...
... TAKESHI HAD WORKED HARD AT IT IN HIS OWN WAY...
SNIFF...
SNIFF...
...
IF NANAHO-- THE ACCUSED TRULY IS RESPONSIBLE, I WANT HIM TO BE PUNISHED AND REPENT FOR HIS ACTIONS...
GLANCE...
...
ugh...
MISTER CUSTODIAN / Prosecution Witness Number 2
I HEAR THAT YOU SAW THE ACCUSED JUVENILE ON THE DAY OF THE CRIME?
Y- YES...

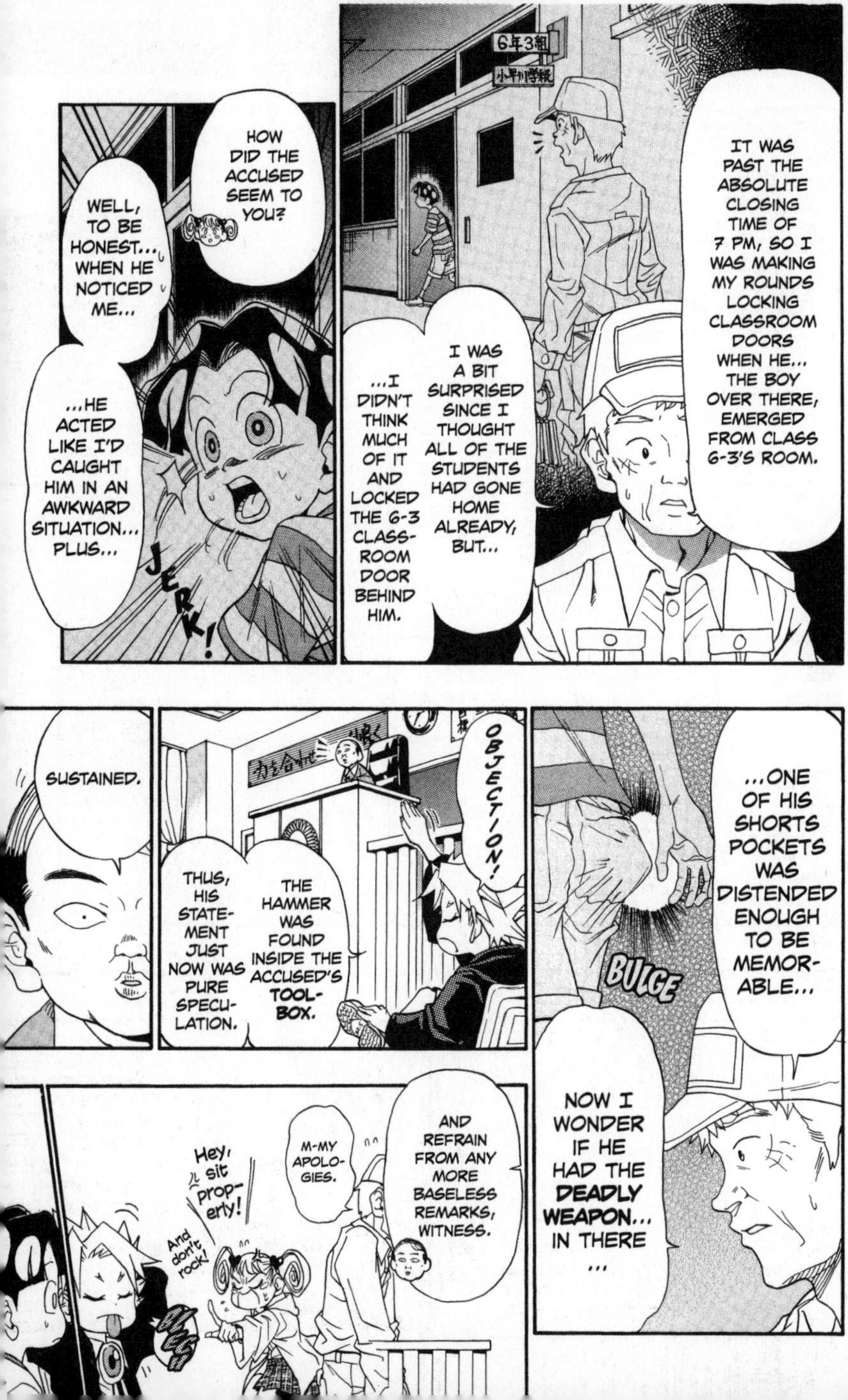
IT WAS PAST THE ABSOLUTE CLOSING TIME OF 7 PM, SO I WAS MAKING MY ROUNDS LOCKING CLASSROOM DOORS WHEN HE... THE BOY OVER THERE, EMERGED FROM CLASS 6-3'S ROOM.
I WAS A BIT SURPRISED SINCE I THOUGHT ALL OF THE STUDENTS HAD GONE HOME ALREADY, BUT...
...I DIDN'T THINK MUCH OF IT AND LOCKED THE 6-3 CLASSROOM DOOR BEHIND HIM.
HOW DID THE ACCUSED SEEM TO YOU?
WELL, TO BE HONEST... WHEN HE NOTICED ME...
...HE ACTED LIKE I'D CAUGHT HIM IN AN AWKWARD SITUATION... PLUS...
JERK!
...ONE OF HIS SHORTS POCKETS WAS DISTENDED ENOUGH TO BE MEMORABLE...
BULGE
NOW I WONDER IF HE HAD THE DEADLY WEAPON... IN THERE ...
OBJECTION!
THE HAMMER WAS FOUND INSIDE THE ACCUSED'S TOOLBOX.
THUS, HIS STATEMENT JUST NOW WAS PURE SPECULATION.
SUSTAINED.
AND REFRAIN FROM ANY MORE BASELESS REMARKS, WITNESS.
M-MY APOLOGIES.
Hey, sit properly!
And don't rock!

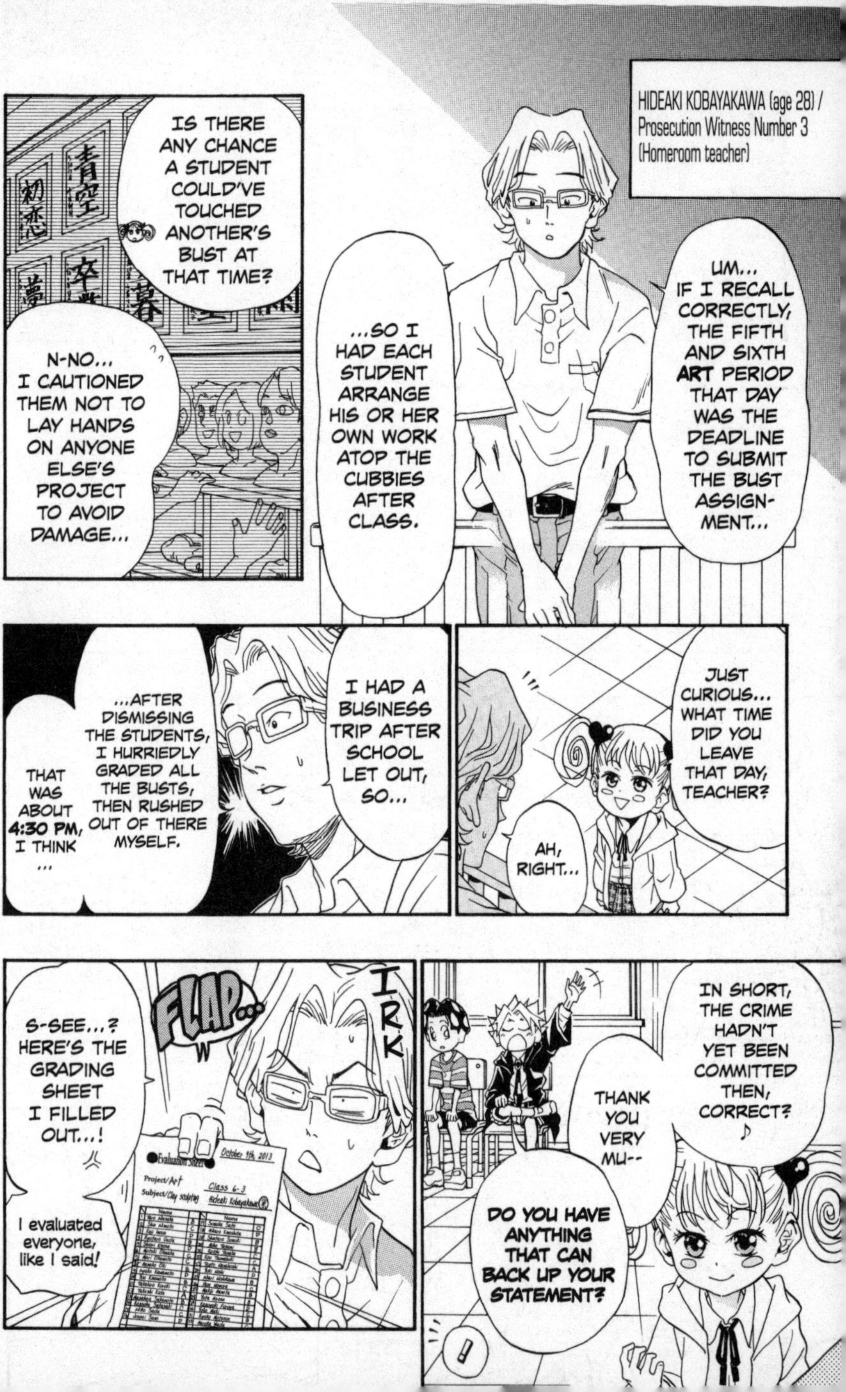
HIDEAKI KOBAYAKAWA (age 28) / Prosecution Witness Number 3 (Homeroom teacher)
UM... IF I RECALL CORRECTLY, THE FIFTH AND SIXTH ART PERIOD THAT DAY WAS THE DEADLINE TO SUBMIT THE BUST ASSIGNMENT...
...SO I HAD EACH STUDENT ARRANGE HIS OR HER OWN WORK ATOP THE CUBBIES AFTER CLASS.
IS THERE ANY CHANCE A STUDENT COULD'VE TOUCHED ANOTHER'S BUST AT THAT TIME?
青空
初恋
N-NO... I CAUTIONED THEM NOT TO LAY HANDS ON ANYONE ELSE'S PROJECT TO AVOID DAMAGE...
JUST CURIOUS... WHAT TIME DID YOU LEAVE THAT DAY, TEACHER?
AH, RIGHT...
I HAD A BUSINESS TRIP AFTER SCHOOL LET OUT, SO...
...AFTER DISMISSING THE STUDENTS, I HURRIEDLY GRADED ALL THE BUSTS, THEN RUSHED OUT OF THERE MYSELF.
THAT WAS ABOUT 4:30 PM, I THINK ...
IN SHORT, THE CRIME HADN'T YET BEEN COMMITTED THEN, CORRECT? ♪
THANK YOU VERY MU--
DO YOU HAVE ANYTHING THAT CAN BACK UP YOUR STATEMENT?
!
IRK
FLAP...
S-SEE...? HERE'S THE GRADING SHEET I FILLED OUT...!
Evaluation Sheet
October 11th, 2013
Project/Art
Subject/Clay sculpting
Class 6-3
Hideaki Kobayakawa
I evaluated everyone, like I said!

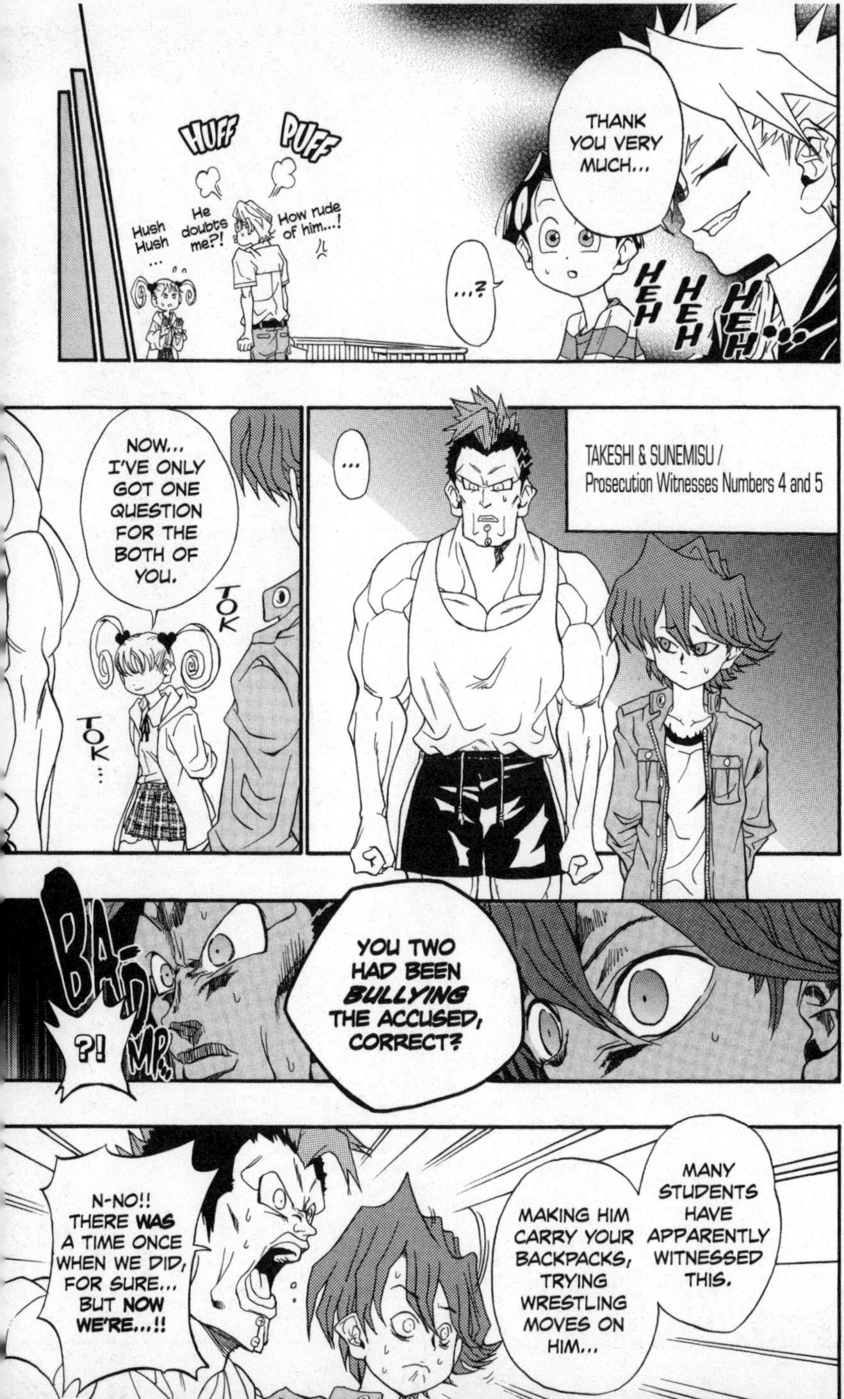
THANK YOU VERY MUCH...
HEH HEH HEH...
...?
How rude of him...!
PUFF
He doubts me?!
HUFF
Hush Hush ...
TAKESHI & SUNEMISU / Prosecution Witnesses Numbers 4 and 5
...
NOW... I'VE ONLY GOT ONE QUESTION FOR THE BOTH OF YOU.
TOK
TOK...
YOU TWO HAD BEEN BULLYING THE ACCUSED, CORRECT?
BA-DUMP
?!
MANY STUDENTS HAVE APPARENTLY WITNESSED THIS.
MAKING HIM CARRY YOUR BACKPACKS, TRYING WRESTLING MOVES ON HIM...
N-NO!! THERE WAS A TIME ONCE WHEN WE DID, FOR SURE... BUT NOW WE'RE...!!

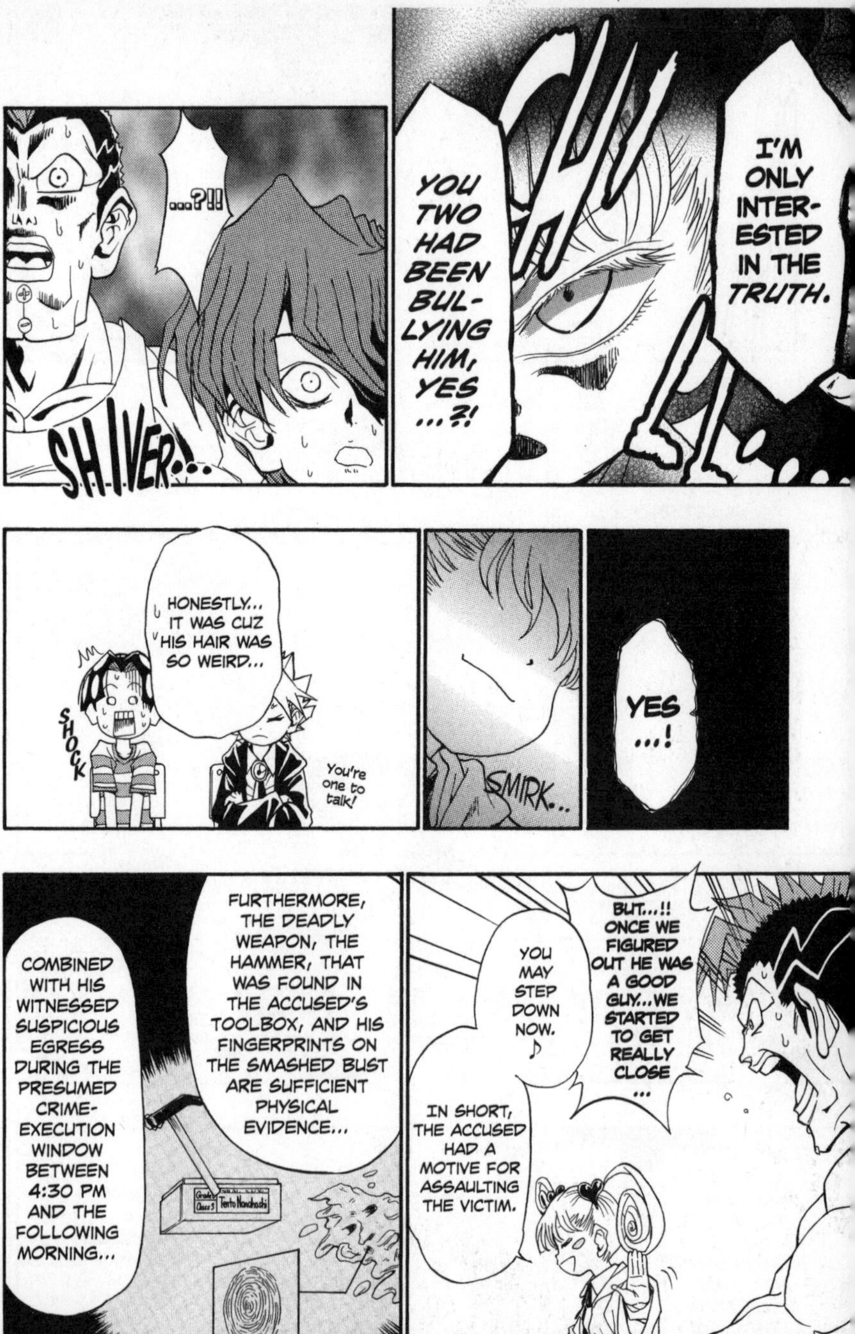
I'M ONLY INTER-ESTED IN THE TRUTH.
YOU TWO HAD BEEN BUL-LYING HIM, YES ...?!
...?!!
SHIVER...
YES ...!
SMIRK...
HONESTLY... IT WAS CUZ HIS HAIR WAS SO WEIRD...
SHOCK
You're one to talk!
BUT...!! ONCE WE FIGURED OUT HE WAS A GOOD GUY...WE STARTED TO GET REALLY CLOSE ...
YOU MAY STEP DOWN NOW. ♪
IN SHORT, THE ACCUSED HAD A MOTIVE FOR ASSAULTING THE VICTIM.
FURTHERMORE, THE DEADLY WEAPON, THE HAMMER, THAT WAS FOUND IN THE ACCUSED'S TOOLBOX, AND HIS FINGERPRINTS ON THE SMASHED BUST ARE SUFFICIENT PHYSICAL EVIDENCE...
Tento Nanohashi
COMBINED WITH HIS WITNESSED SUSPICIOUS EGRESS DURING THE PRESUMED CRIME-EXECUTION WINDOW BETWEEN 4:30 PM AND THE FOLLOWING MORNING...

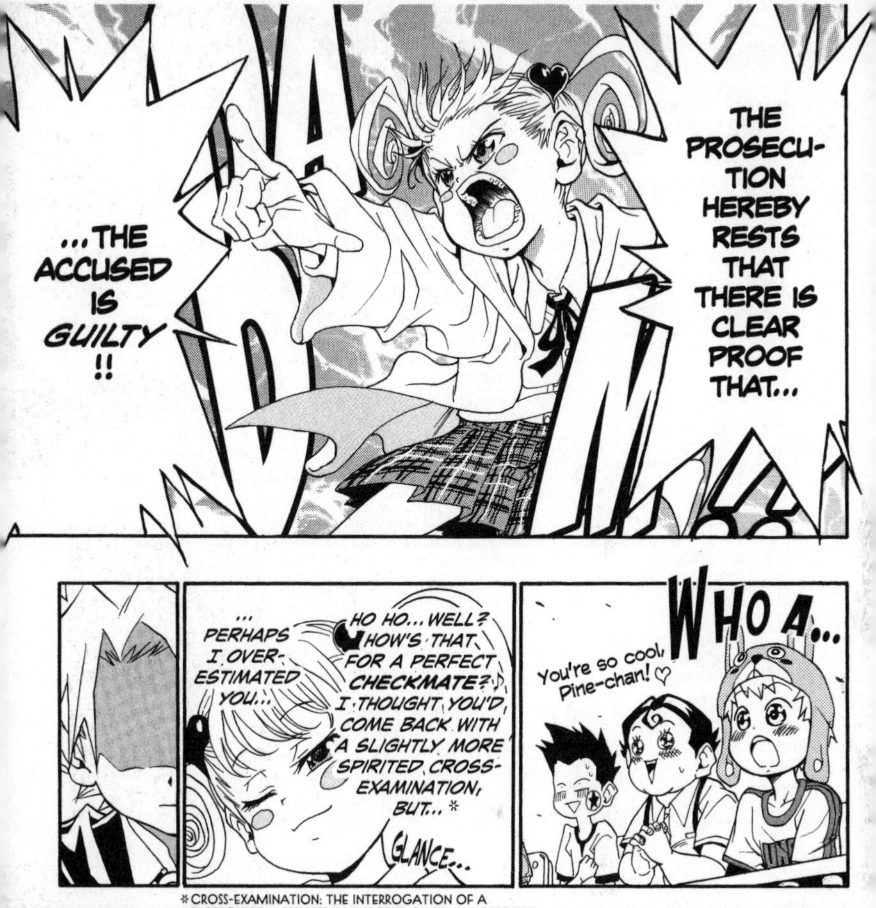
THE PROSECUTION HEREBY RESTS THAT THERE IS CLEAR PROOF THAT...
...THE ACCUSED IS GUILTY!!
WHOA...
You're so cool, Pine-chan! ♡
HO HO... WELL? HOW'S THAT FOR A PERFECT CHECKMATE? ♪ I THOUGHT YOU'D COME BACK WITH A SLIGHTLY MORE SPIRITED CROSS-EXAMINATION, BUT...*
GLANCE...
... PERHAPS I OVER-ESTIMATED YOU...

*CROSS-EXAMINATION: THE INTERROGATION OF A PROSECUTION WITNESS BY THE DEFENSE. OR THE OPPOSITE.

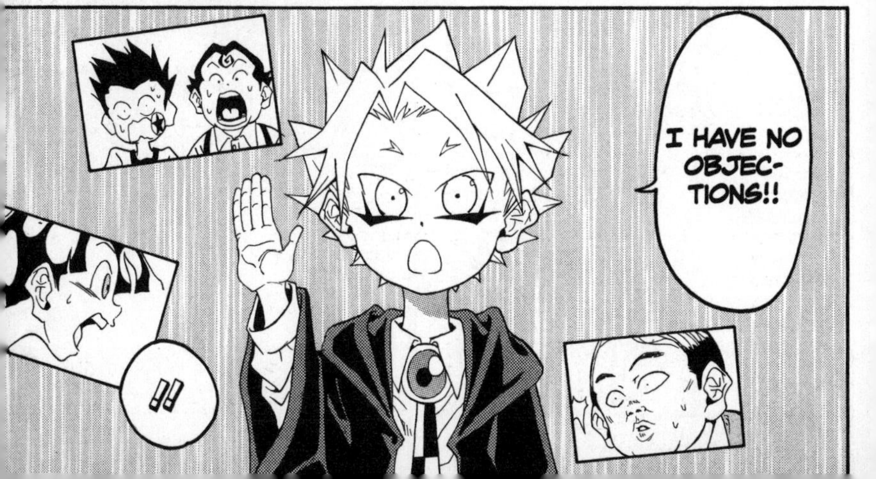
I HAVE NO OBJECTIONS!!
!!

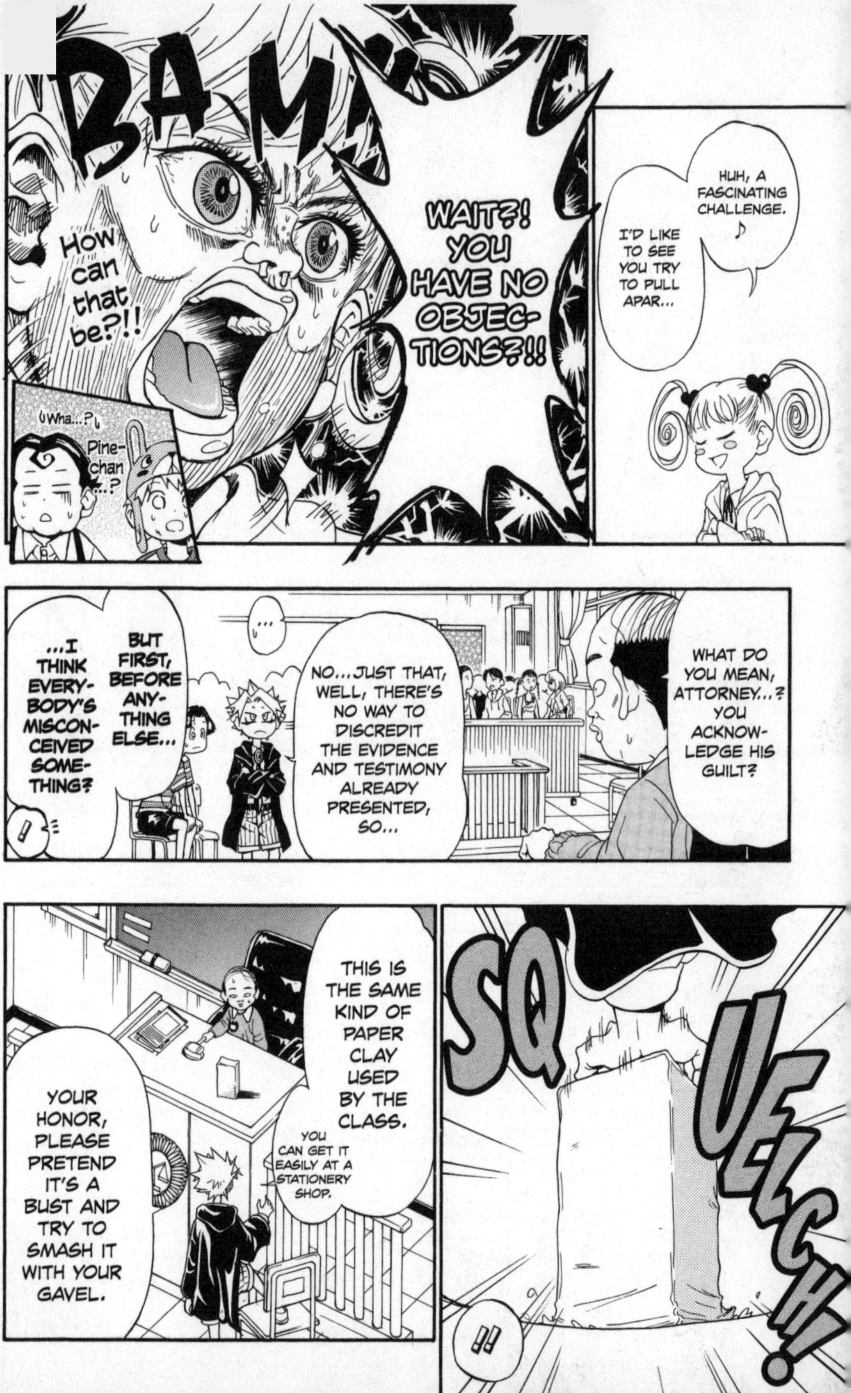
HUH, A FASCINATING CHALLENGE. ♪
I'D LIKE TO SEE YOU TRY TO PULL APAR...
BAM
WAIT?! YOU HAVE NO OBJECTIONS?!!
How can that be?!!
Wha...?
Pine-chan...?
WHAT DO YOU MEAN, ATTORNEY...? YOU ACKNOWLEDGE HIS GUILT?
...
NO... JUST THAT, WELL, THERE'S NO WAY TO DISCREDIT THE EVIDENCE AND TESTIMONY ALREADY PRESENTED, SO...
BUT FIRST, BEFORE ANYTHING ELSE...
...I THINK EVERYBODY'S MISCONCEIVED SOMETHING?
!
SQUELCH!
!!
THIS IS THE SAME KIND OF PAPER CLAY USED BY THE CLASS.
YOU CAN GET IT EASILY AT A STATIONERY SHOP.
YOUR HONOR, PLEASE PRETEND IT'S A BUST AND TRY TO SMASH IT WITH YOUR GAVEL.

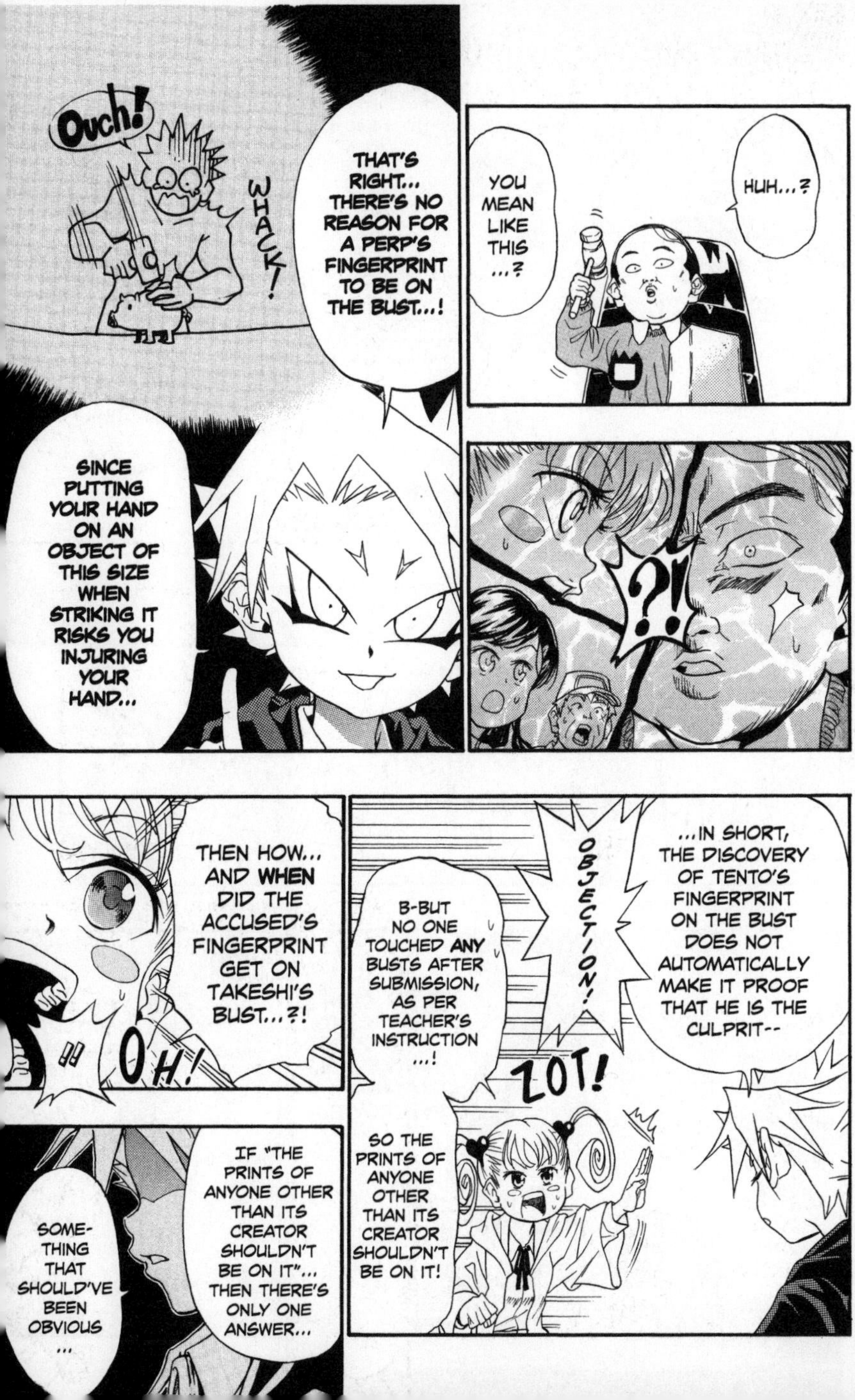
HUH...?
YOU MEAN LIKE THIS...?
?!
THAT'S RIGHT... THERE'S NO REASON FOR A PERP'S FINGERPRINT TO BE ON THE BUST...!
WHACK!
Ouch!
SINCE PUTTING YOUR HAND ON AN OBJECT OF THIS SIZE WHEN STRIKING IT RISKS YOU INJURING YOUR HAND...
...IN SHORT, THE DISCOVERY OF TENTO'S FINGERPRINT ON THE BUST DOES NOT AUTOMATICALLY MAKE IT PROOF THAT HE IS THE CULPRIT--
OBJECTION!
B-BUT NO ONE TOUCHED ANY BUSTS AFTER SUBMISSION, AS PER TEACHER'S INSTRUCTION...!
ZOT!
SO THE PRINTS OF ANYONE OTHER THAN ITS CREATOR SHOULDN'T BE ON IT!
THEN HOW... AND WHEN DID THE ACCUSED'S FINGERPRINT GET ON TAKESHI'S BUST...?!
OH!
!!
IF "THE PRINTS OF ANYONE OTHER THAN ITS CREATOR SHOULDN'T BE ON IT"... THEN THERE'S ONLY ONE ANSWER...
SOME-THING THAT SHOULD'VE BEEN OBVIOUS...

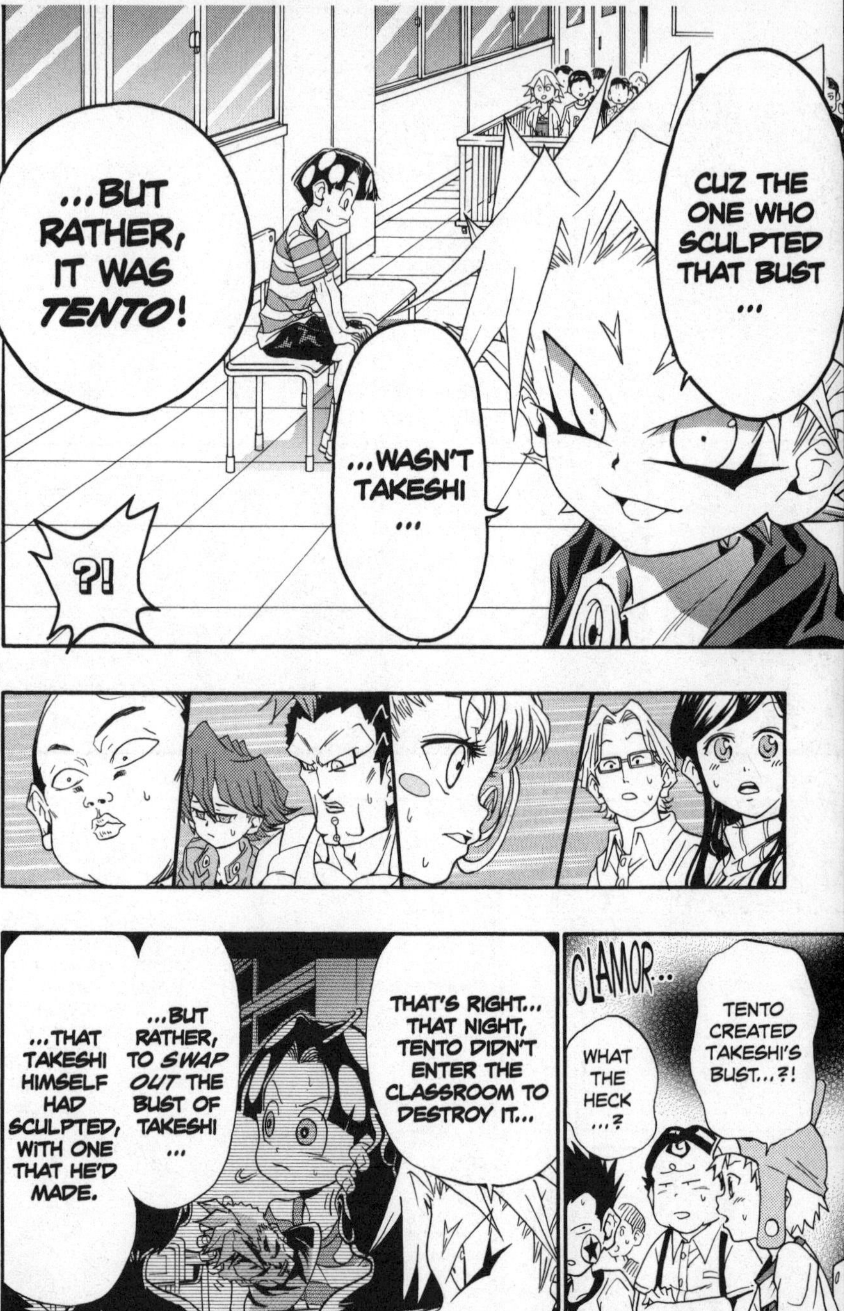
CUZ THE ONE WHO SCULPTED THAT BUST ...
...WASN'T TAKESHI ...
...BUT RATHER, IT WAS *TENTO*!
?!
CLAMOR...
TENTO CREATED TAKESHI'S BUST...?!
WHAT THE HECK ...?
THAT'S RIGHT... THAT NIGHT, TENTO DIDN'T ENTER THE CLASSROOM TO DESTROY IT...
...BUT RATHER, TO *SWAP OUT* THE BUST OF TAKESHI ...
...THAT TAKESHI HIMSELF HAD SCULPTED, WITH ONE THAT HE'D MADE.

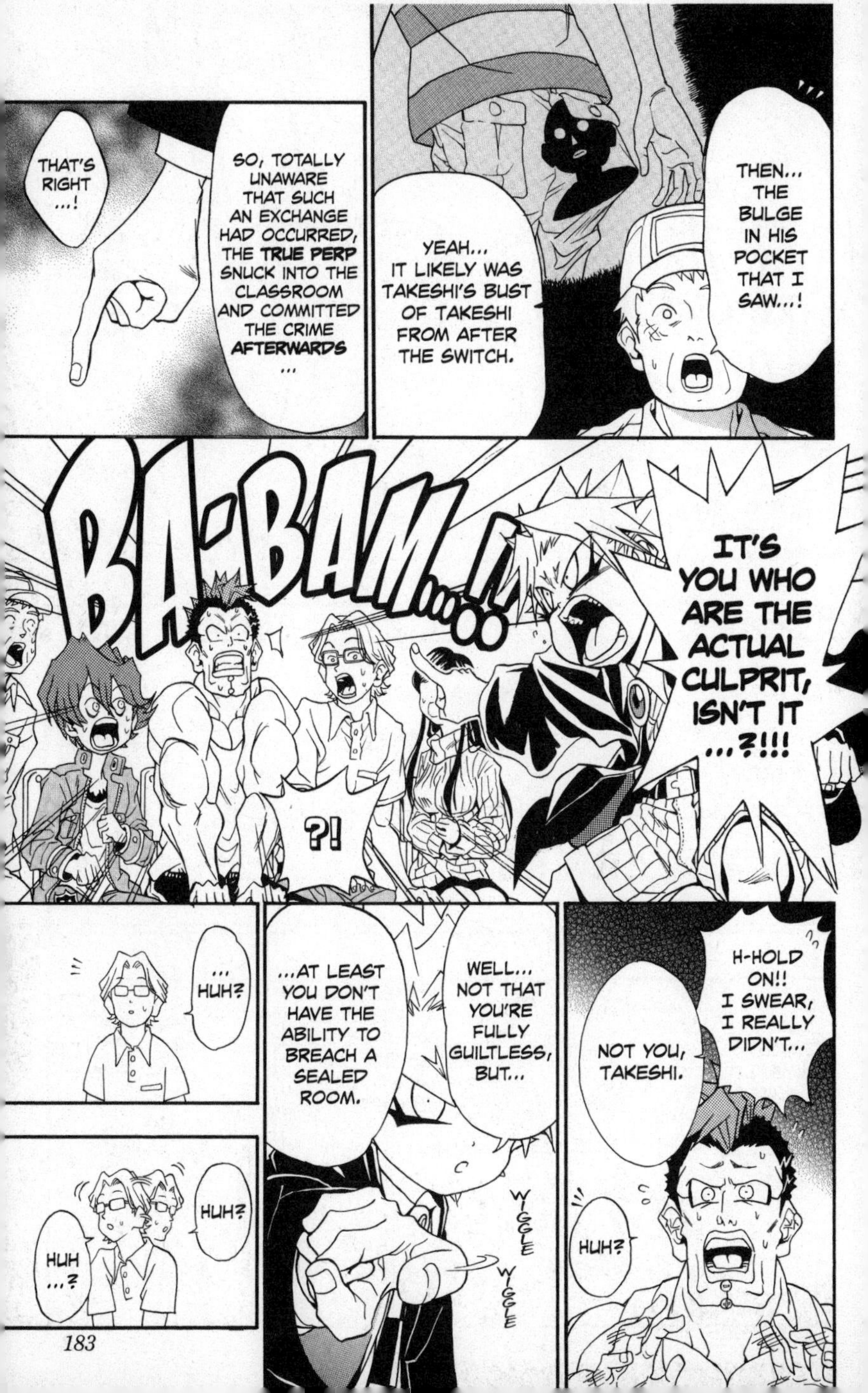
THEN... THE BULGE IN HIS POCKET THAT I SAW...!
YEAH... IT LIKELY WAS TAKESHI'S BUST OF TAKESHI FROM AFTER THE SWITCH.
SO, TOTALLY UNAWARE THAT SUCH AN EXCHANGE HAD OCCURRED, THE **TRUE PERP** SNUCK INTO THE CLASSROOM AND COMMITTED THE CRIME **AFTERWARDS** ...
THAT'S RIGHT ...!
IT'S YOU WHO ARE THE ACTUAL CULPRIT, ISN'T IT ...?!!!
BA-BAM...!!
?!
H-HOLD ON!! I SWEAR, I REALLY DIDN'T...
NOT YOU, TAKESHI.
HUH?
WELL... NOT THAT YOU'RE FULLY GUILTLESS, BUT...
...AT LEAST YOU DON'T HAVE THE ABILITY TO BREACH A SEALED ROOM.
WIGGLE
WIGGLE
... HUH?
HUH?
HUH ...?

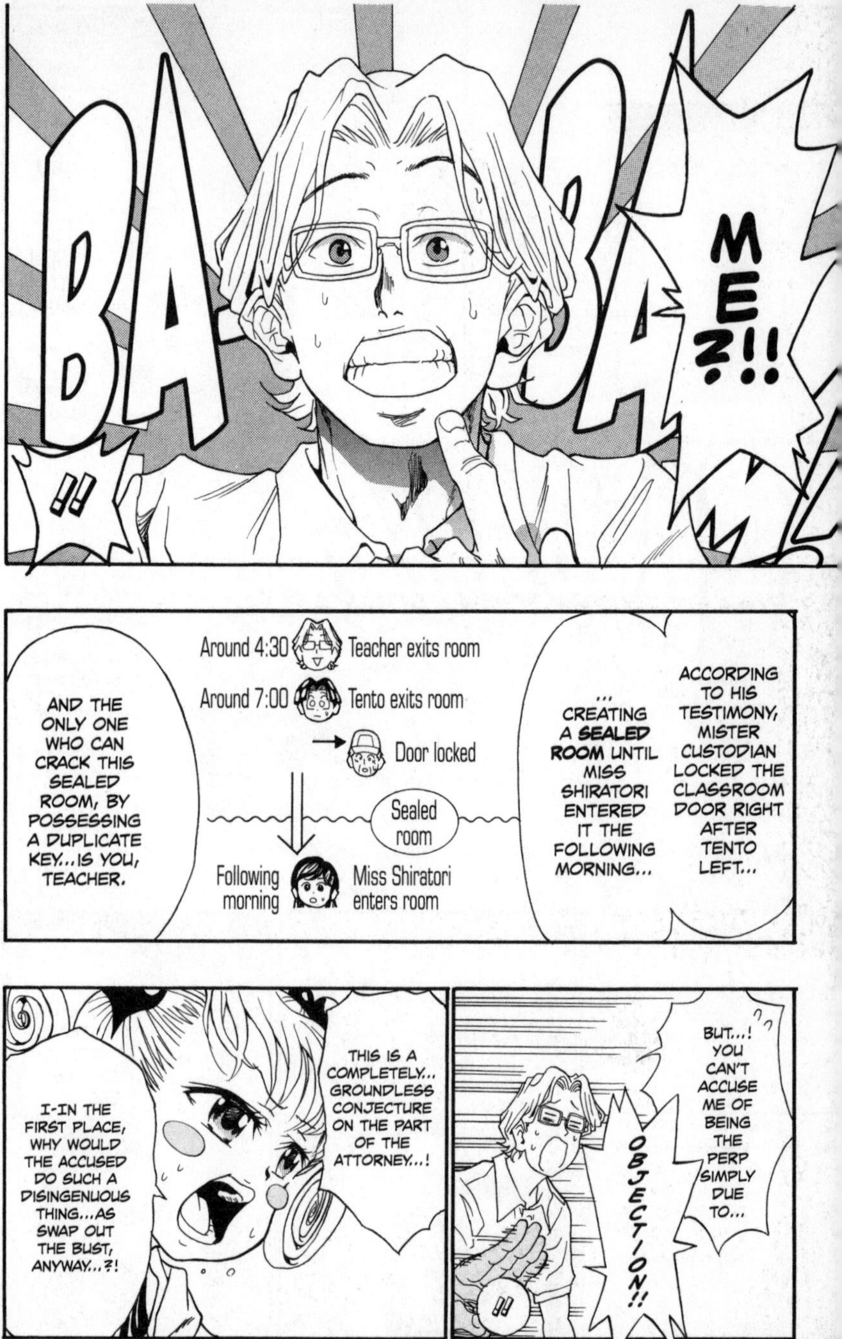

BA-
BA
ME?!!
!!
ACCORDING TO HIS TESTIMONY, MISTER CUSTODIAN LOCKED THE CLASSROOM DOOR RIGHT AFTER TENTO LEFT...
...CREATING A **SEALED ROOM** UNTIL MISS SHIRATORI ENTERED IT THE FOLLOWING MORNING...
Around 4:30 Teacher exits room
Around 7:00 Tento exits room
→ Door locked
Sealed room
Following morning Miss Shiratori enters room
AND THE ONLY ONE WHO CAN CRACK THIS SEALED ROOM, BY POSSESSING A DUPLICATE KEY...IS YOU, TEACHER.
BUT...! YOU CAN'T ACCUSE ME OF BEING THE PERP SIMPLY DUE TO...
OBJECTION!!
!!
THIS IS A COMPLETELY... GROUNDLESS CONJECTURE ON THE PART OF THE ATTORNEY...!
I-IN THE FIRST PLACE, WHY WOULD THE ACCUSED DO SUCH A DISINGENUOUS THING...AS SWAP OUT THE BUST, ANYWAY...?!

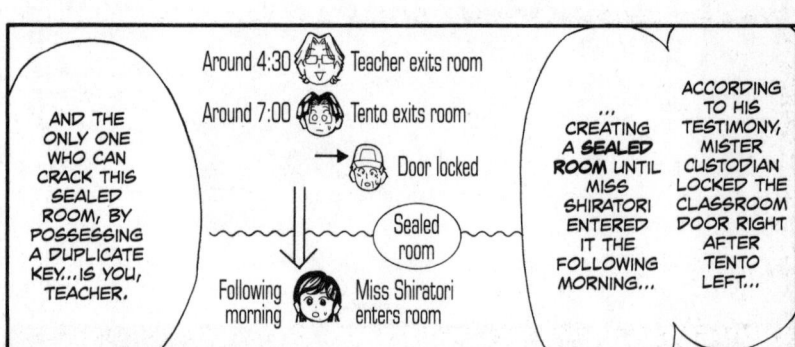

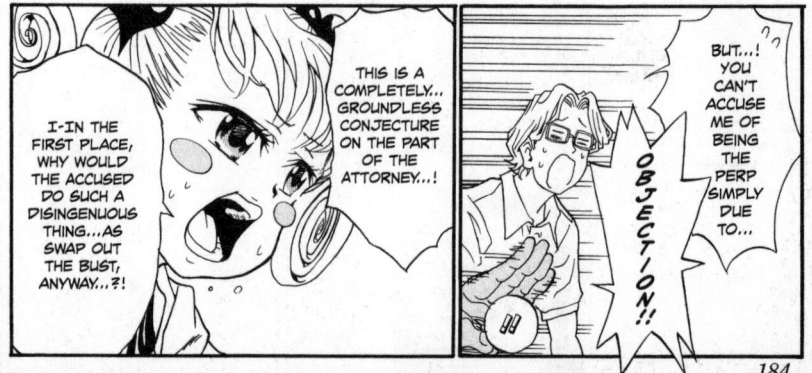

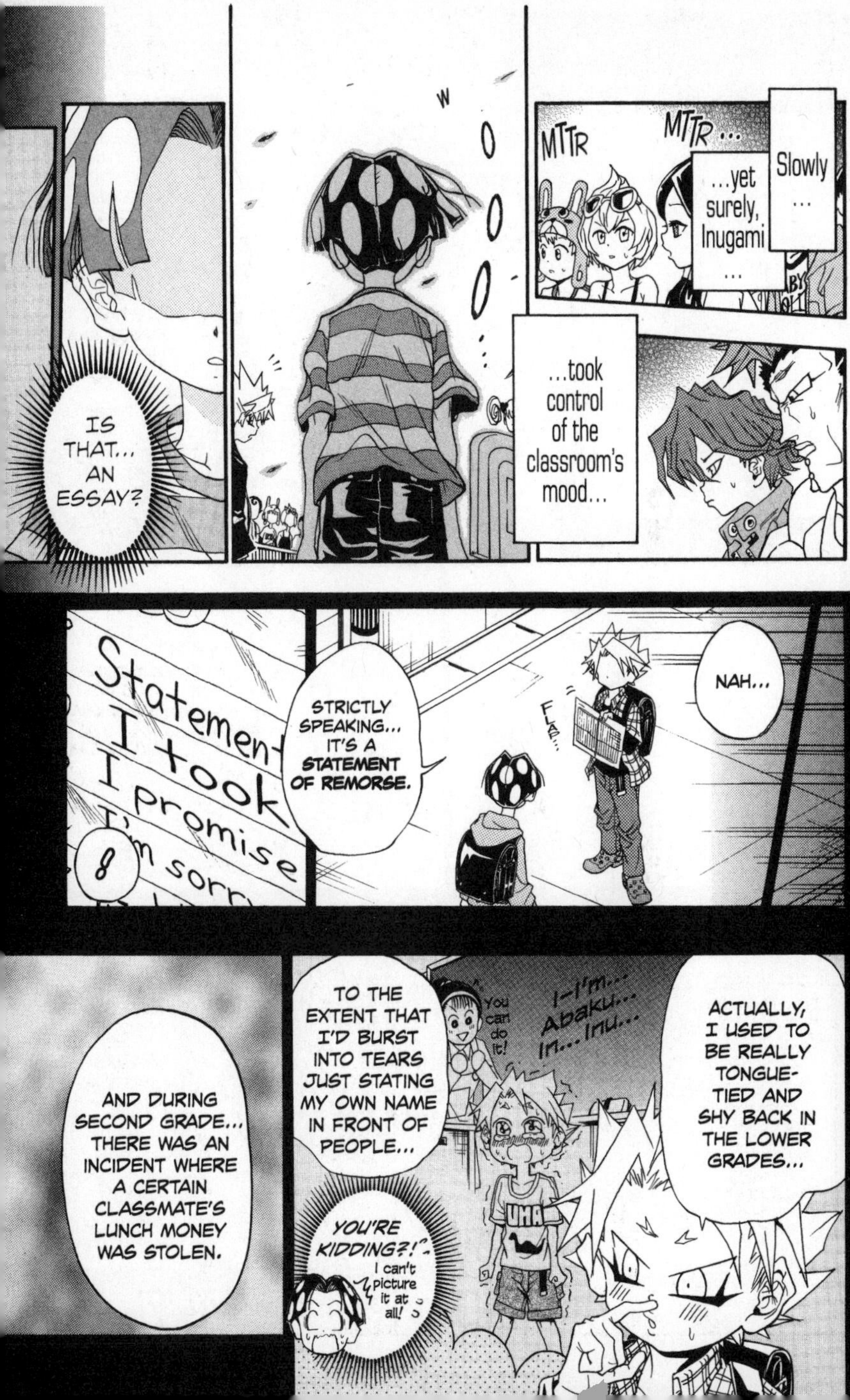
Slowly…
…yet surely, Inugami…
MTTR…
MTTR
…took control of the classroom's mood…
W
IS THAT… AN ESSAY?
NAH…
FLAP…
STRICTLY SPEAKING… IT'S A STATEMENT OF REMORSE.
Statement
I took
I promise
I'm sorr
ACTUALLY, I USED TO BE REALLY TONGUE-TIED AND SHY BACK IN THE LOWER GRADES…
I-I'm… Abaku… In… Inu…
You can do it!
TO THE EXTENT THAT I'D BURST INTO TEARS JUST STATING MY OWN NAME IN FRONT OF PEOPLE…
YOU'RE KIDDING?!
I can't picture it at all!
UMA
AND DURING SECOND GRADE… THERE WAS AN INCIDENT WHERE A CERTAIN CLASSMATE'S LUNCH MONEY WAS STOLEN.

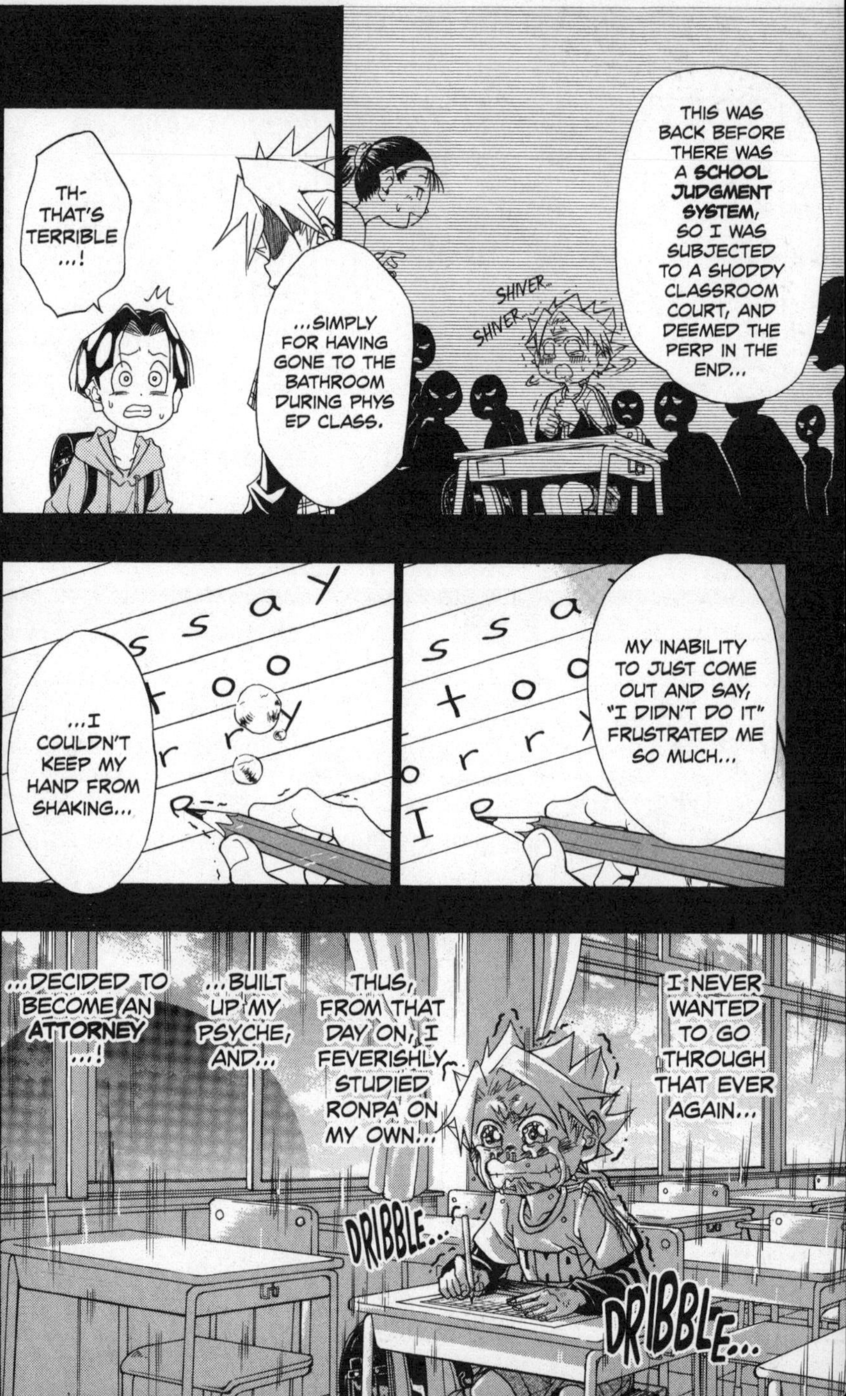
THIS WAS BACK BEFORE THERE WAS A **SCHOOL JUDGMENT SYSTEM**, SO I WAS SUBJECTED TO A SHODDY CLASSROOM COURT, AND DEEMED THE PERP IN THE END...
SHIVER... SHIVER...
...SIMPLY FOR HAVING GONE TO THE BATHROOM DURING PHYS ED CLASS.
TH- THAT'S TERRIBLE ...!
MY INABILITY TO JUST COME OUT AND SAY, "I DIDN'T DO IT" FRUSTRATED ME SO MUCH...
...I COULDN'T KEEP MY HAND FROM SHAKING...
I NEVER WANTED TO GO THROUGH THAT EVER AGAIN...
THUS, FROM THAT DAY ON, I FEVERISHLY STUDIED RONPA ON MY OWN...
...BUILT UP MY PSYCHE, AND...
...DECIDED TO BECOME AN **ATTORNEY** ...!
DRIBBLE...
DRIBBLE...

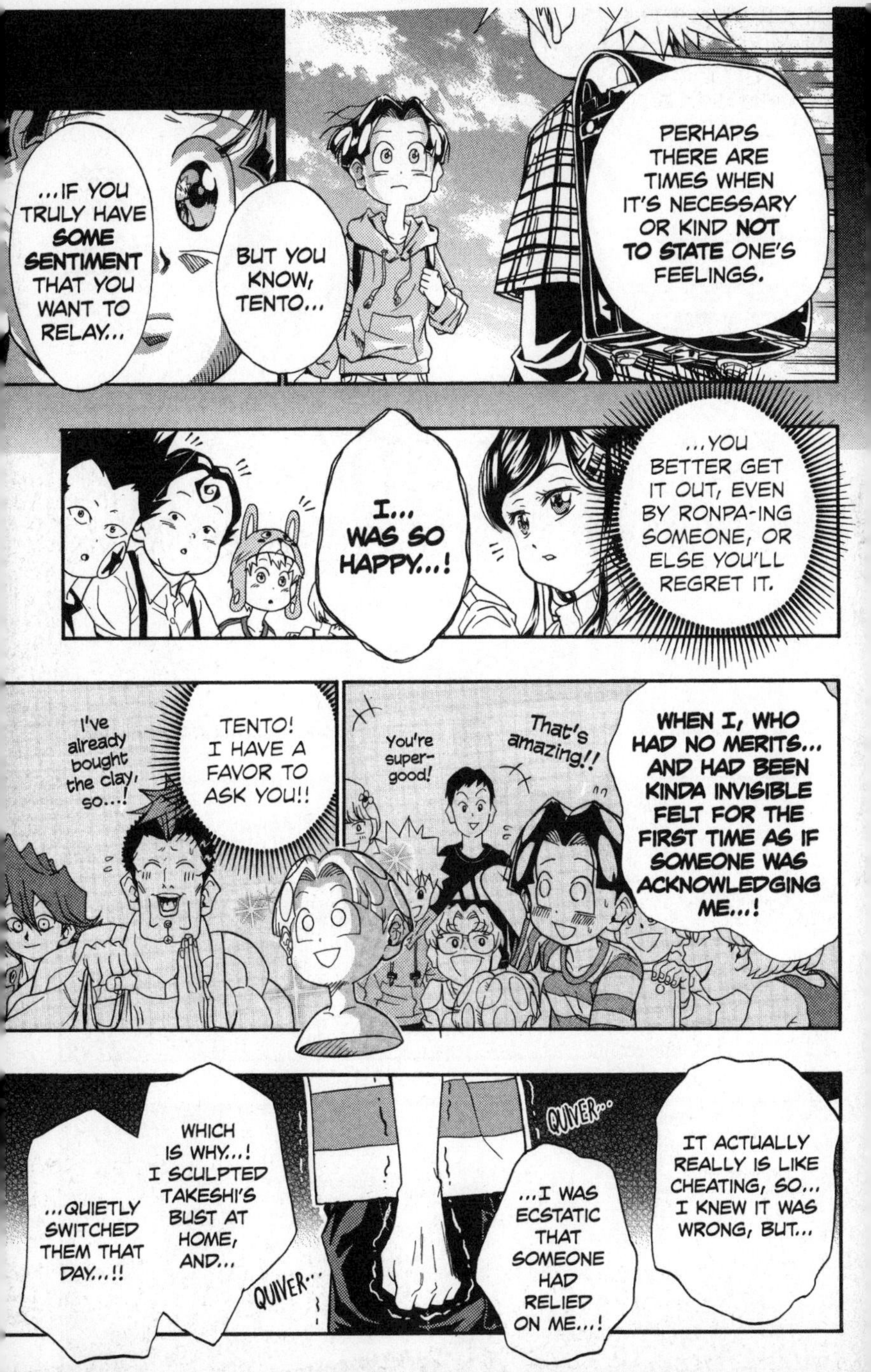
PERHAPS THERE ARE TIMES WHEN IT'S NECESSARY OR KIND NOT TO STATE ONE'S FEELINGS.
BUT YOU KNOW, TENTO...
...IF YOU TRULY HAVE SOME SENTIMENT THAT YOU WANT TO RELAY...
...YOU BETTER GET IT OUT, EVEN BY RONPA-ING SOMEONE, OR ELSE YOU'LL REGRET IT.
I... WAS SO HAPPY...!
WHEN I, WHO HAD NO MERITS... AND HAD BEEN KINDA INVISIBLE FELT FOR THE FIRST TIME AS IF SOMEONE WAS ACKNOWLEDGING ME...!
That's amazing!!
You're super-good!
TENTO! I HAVE A FAVOR TO ASK YOU!!
I've already bought the clay, so...!
IT ACTUALLY REALLY IS LIKE CHEATING, SO... I KNEW IT WAS WRONG, BUT...
QUIVER...
...I WAS ECSTATIC THAT SOMEONE HAD RELIED ON ME...!
WHICH IS WHY...! I SCULPTED TAKESHI'S BUST AT HOME, AND...
...QUIETLY SWITCHED THEM THAT DAY...!!
QUIVER...

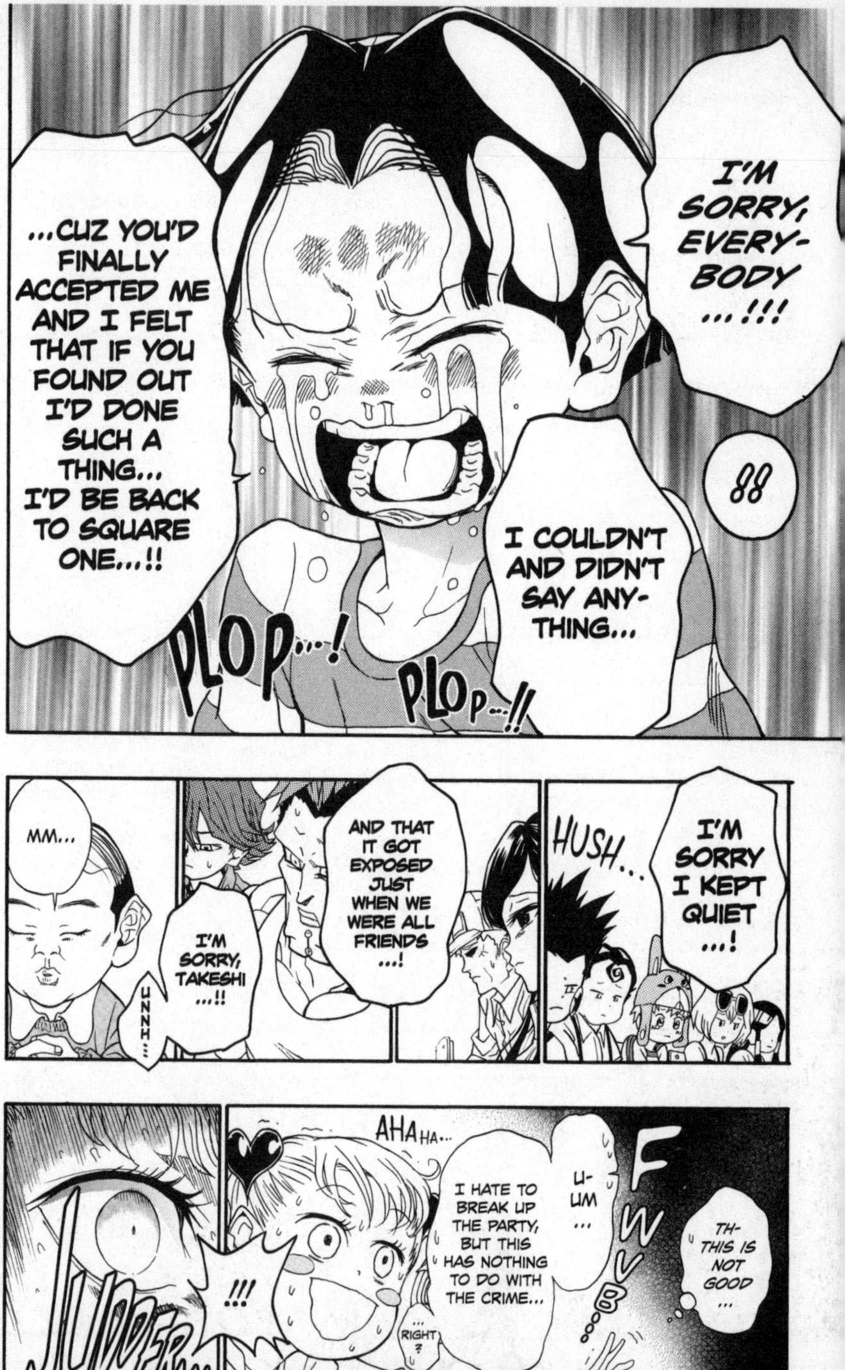
I'M SORRY, EVERY-BODY ...!!!
88
I COULDN'T AND DIDN'T SAY ANY-THING...
...CUZ YOU'D FINALLY ACCEPTED ME AND I FELT THAT IF YOU FOUND OUT I'D DONE SUCH A THING... I'D BE BACK TO SQUARE ONE...!!
PLOP...!
PLOP...!!
HUSH...
I'M SORRY I KEPT QUIET ...!
AND THAT IT GOT EXPOSED JUST WHEN WE WERE ALL FRIENDS ...!
I'M SORRY, TAKESHI ...!!
MM...
UNNH...
TH- THIS IS NOT GOOD ...
FWVBooo
U- UM ...
I HATE TO BREAK UP THE PARTY, BUT THIS HAS NOTHING TO DO WITH THE CRIME...
AHAHA...
... RIGHT ?
!!!
JUDDERoo

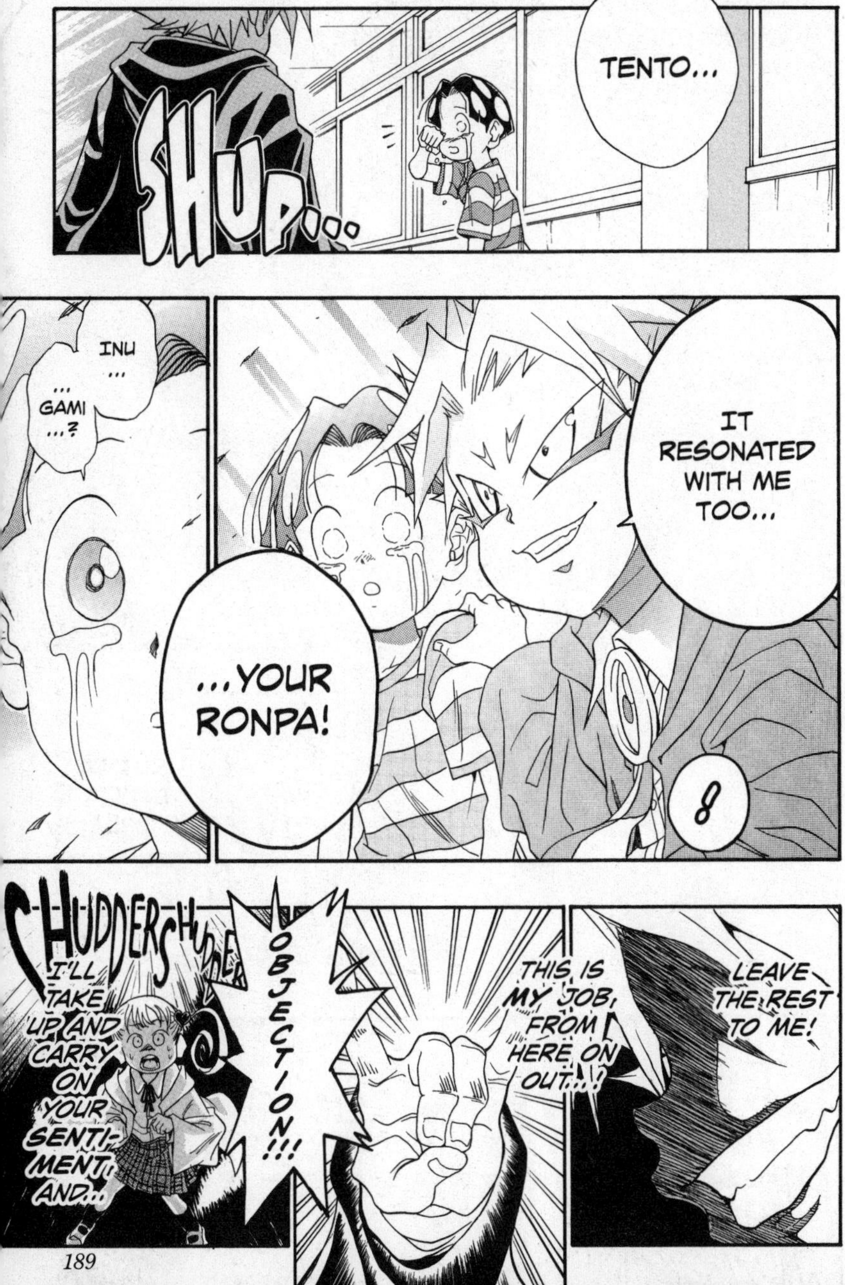
TENTO...
SHUP...
IT RESONATED WITH ME TOO...
...YOUR RONPA!
INU ...
...GAMI ...?
LEAVE THE REST TO ME!
THIS IS MY JOB, FROM HERE ON OUT...!
I'LL TAKE UP AND CARRY ON YOUR SENTIMENT AND...
OBJECTION!!!
CHUDDER SHUDDER

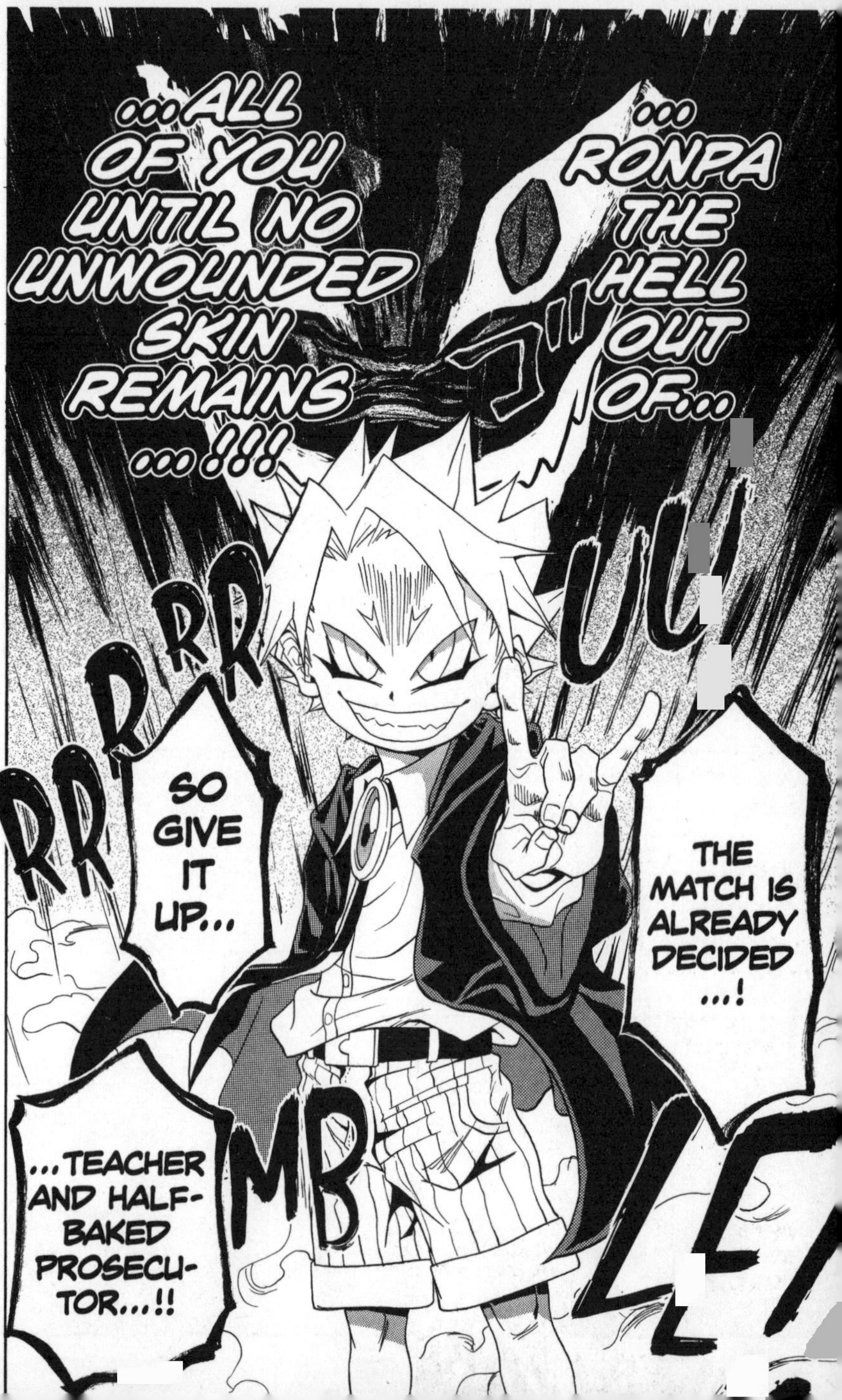
...RONPA THE HELL OUT OF...
...ALL OF YOU UNTIL NO UNWOUNDED SKIN REMAINS...!!!
THE MATCH IS ALREADY DECIDED...!
SO GIVE IT UP...
...TEACHER AND HALF-BAKED PROSECU-TOR...!!

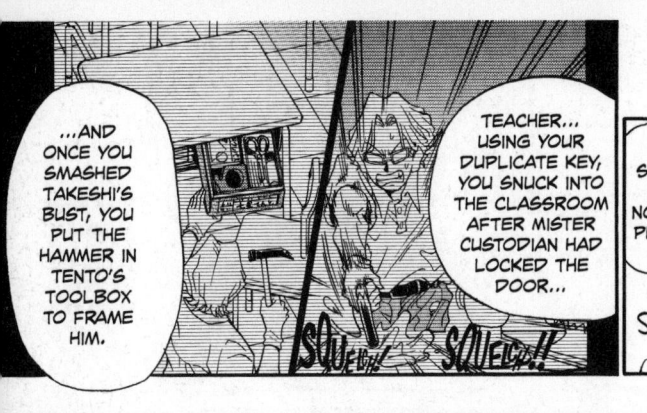

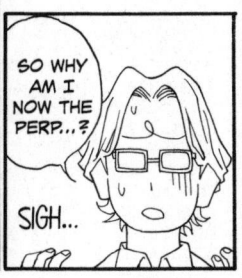

SO WHY AM I NOW THE PERP...?
SIGH...
TEACHER... USING YOUR DUPLICATE KEY, YOU SNUCK INTO THE CLASSROOM AFTER MISTER CUSTODIAN HAD LOCKED THE DOOR...
...AND ONCE YOU SMASHED TAKESHI'S BUST, YOU PUT THE HAMMER IN TENTO'S TOOLBOX TO FRAME HIM.
SQUELCH!!
SQUELCH!!
OBJECTION...!! TH-THAT'S JUST CONJECTURE! THERE'S NO EVIDENCE THE ACCUSED EVEN SWITCHED THE BUSTS...
OBJECTION!
THAT EVIDENCE HAS ALREADY BEEN PRESENTED...
BY TEACHER HIMSELF...!
?!
DANGLE
Project/Art
Subject/Clay sculpting
Class 6-3
Hideaki Kobayakawa
MY GRADING SHEET...?!
WHAT'S THAT GOT TO DO...
BEFORE WE GET TO THAT...
YOUR HONOR, I DID NOT APPLY IN ADVANCE, BUT I'D LIKE TO ASK EVERYONE IN THE GALLERY TO ATTEST TO ONE THING?
I'LL OKAY IT.
HEY, CLASS 6-3!
TURN
PLEASE ANSWER HONESTLY!

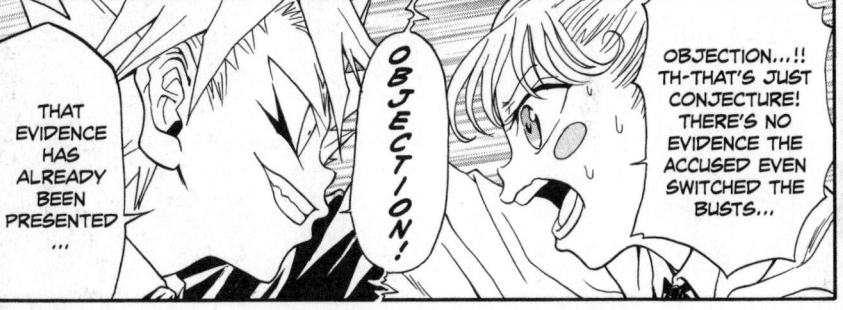

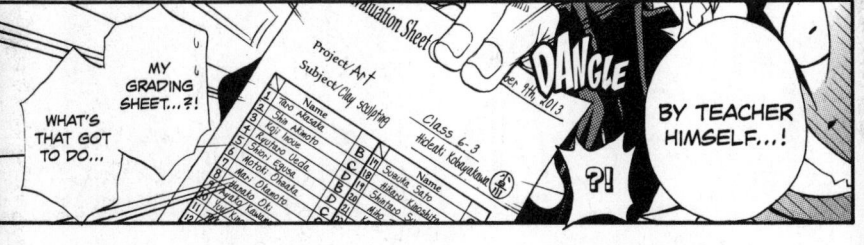

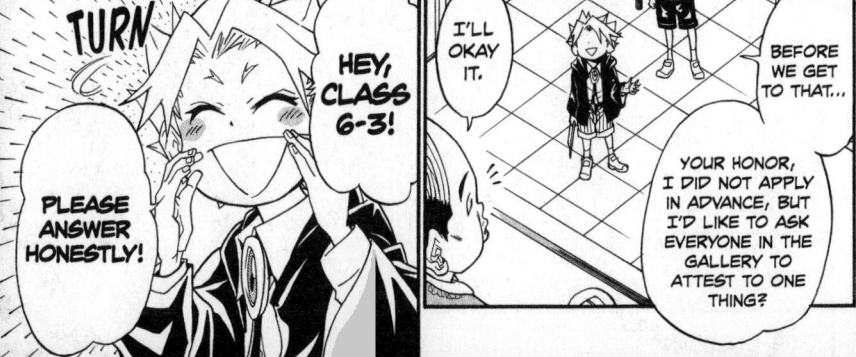

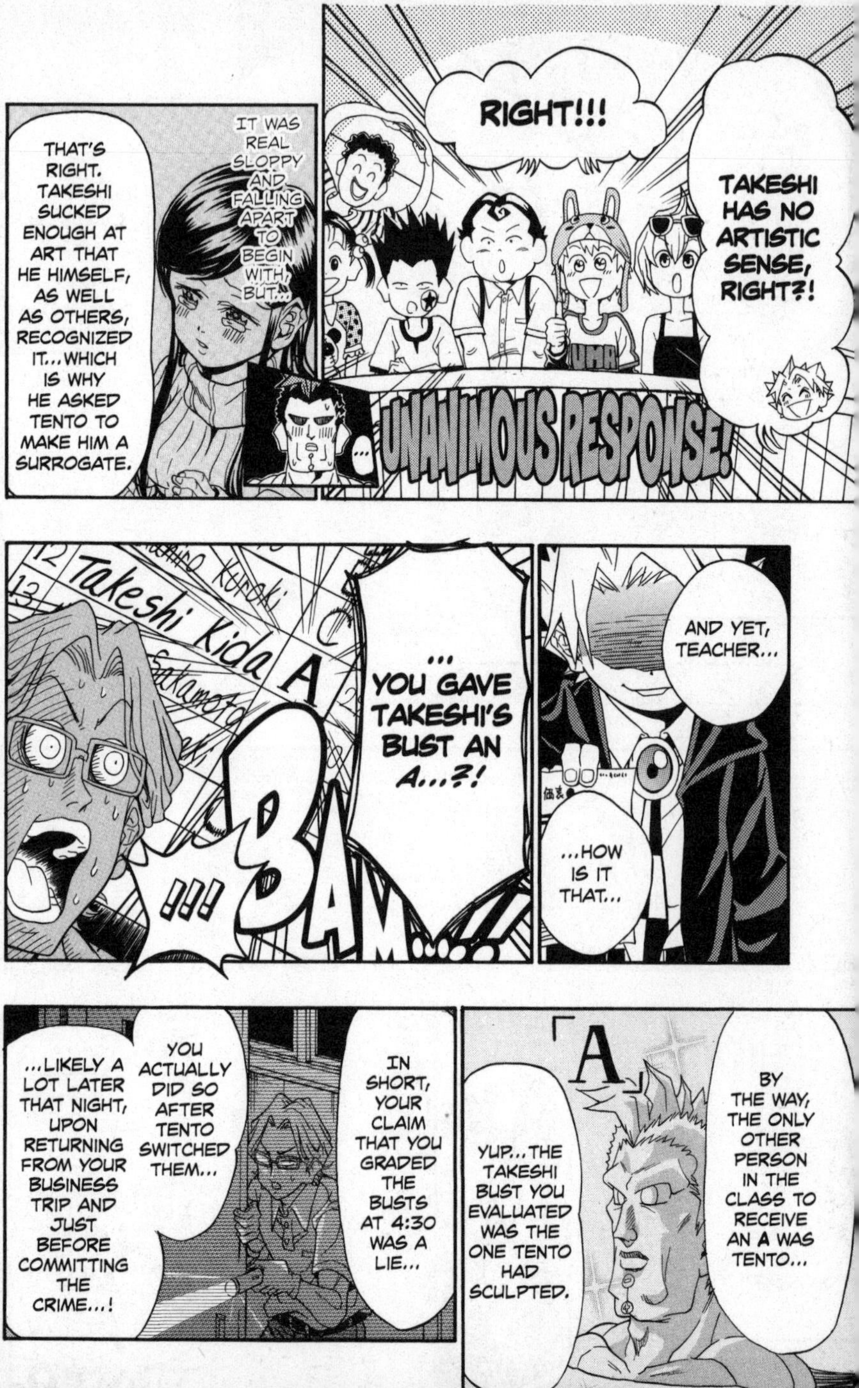
TAKESHI HAS NO ARTISTIC SENSE, RIGHT?!
RIGHT!!!
...
UNANIMOUS RESPONSE!
IT WAS REAL SLOPPY AND FALLING APART TO BEGIN WITH, BUT...
THAT'S RIGHT. TAKESHI SUCKED ENOUGH AT ART THAT HE HIMSELF, AS WELL AS OTHERS, RECOGNIZED IT...WHICH IS WHY HE ASKED TENTO TO MAKE HIM A SURROGATE.
AND YET, TEACHER...
...HOW IS IT THAT...
... YOU GAVE TAKESHI'S BUST AN A...?!
Takeshi Kida
A
BAM...
!!!
BY THE WAY, THE ONLY OTHER PERSON IN THE CLASS TO RECEIVE AN A WAS TENTO...
「A」
YUP...THE TAKESHI BUST YOU EVALUATED WAS THE ONE TENTO HAD SCULPTED.
IN SHORT, YOUR CLAIM THAT YOU GRADED THE BUSTS AT 4:30 WAS A LIE...
YOU ACTUALLY DID SO AFTER TENTO SWITCHED THEM...
...LIKELY A LOT LATER THAT NIGHT, UPON RETURNING FROM YOUR BUSINESS TRIP AND JUST BEFORE COMMITTING THE CRIME...!

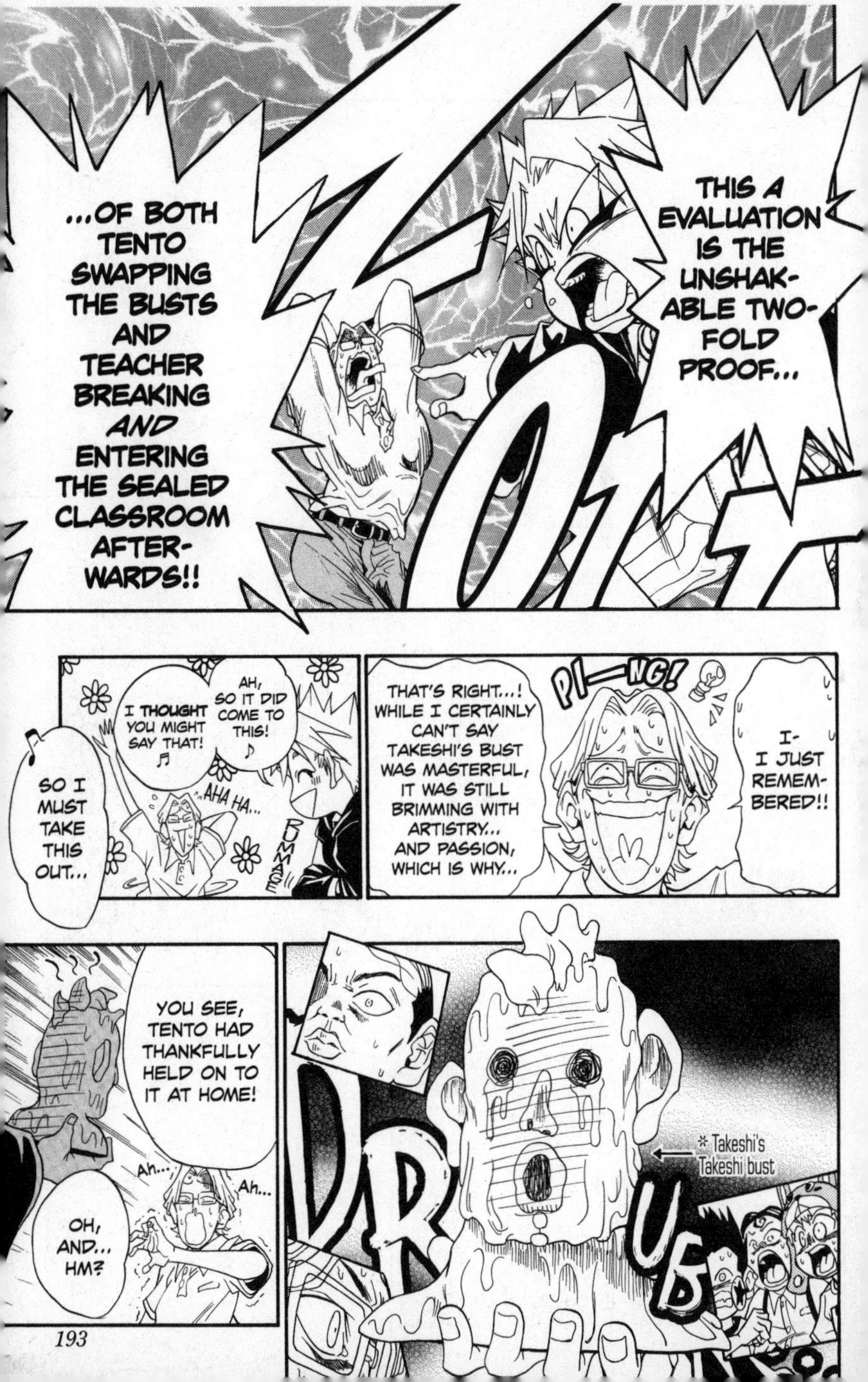
THIS A EVALUATION IS THE UNSHAKABLE TWO-FOLD PROOF...
...OF BOTH TENTO SWAPPING THE BUSTS AND TEACHER BREAKING *AND* ENTERING THE SEALED CLASSROOM AFTERWARDS!!
I- I JUST REMEMBERED!!
PI—NG!
THAT'S RIGHT...! WHILE I CERTAINLY CAN'T SAY TAKESHI'S BUST WAS MASTERFUL, IT WAS STILL BRIMMING WITH ARTISTRY... AND PASSION, WHICH IS WHY...
AH, SO IT DID COME TO THIS! ♪
I THOUGHT YOU MIGHT SAY THAT! ♬
AHA HA...
RUMMAGE
SO I MUST TAKE THIS OUT...
* Takeshi's Takeshi bust
YOU SEE, TENTO HAD THANKFULLY HELD ON TO IT AT HOME!
Ah...
Ah...
OH, AND... HM?

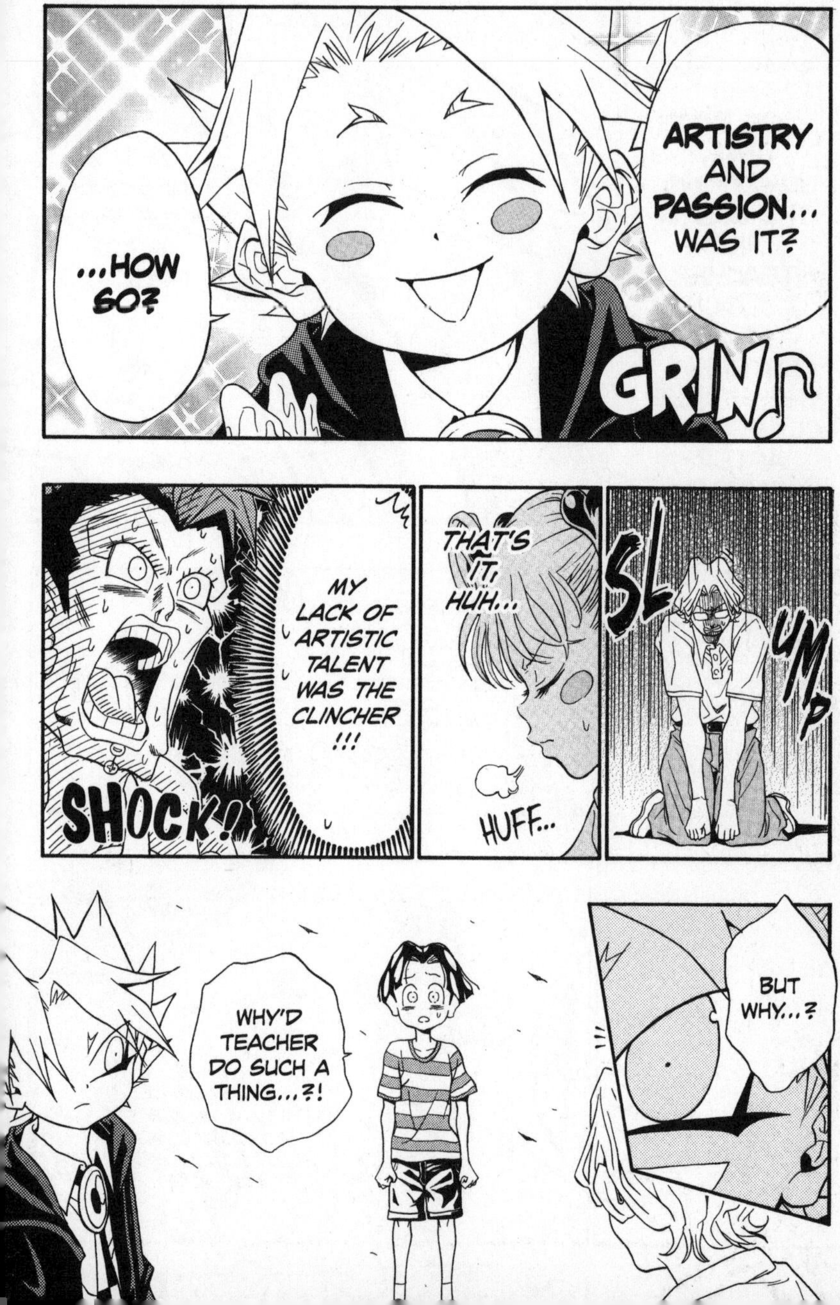
ARTISTRY AND PASSION... WAS IT?
GRIN♪
...HOW SO?
SLUMP
THAT'S IT, HUH...
HUFF...
MY LACK OF ARTISTIC TALENT WAS THE CLINCHER!!!
SHOCK!
BUT WHY...?
WHY'D TEACHER DO SUCH A THING...?!

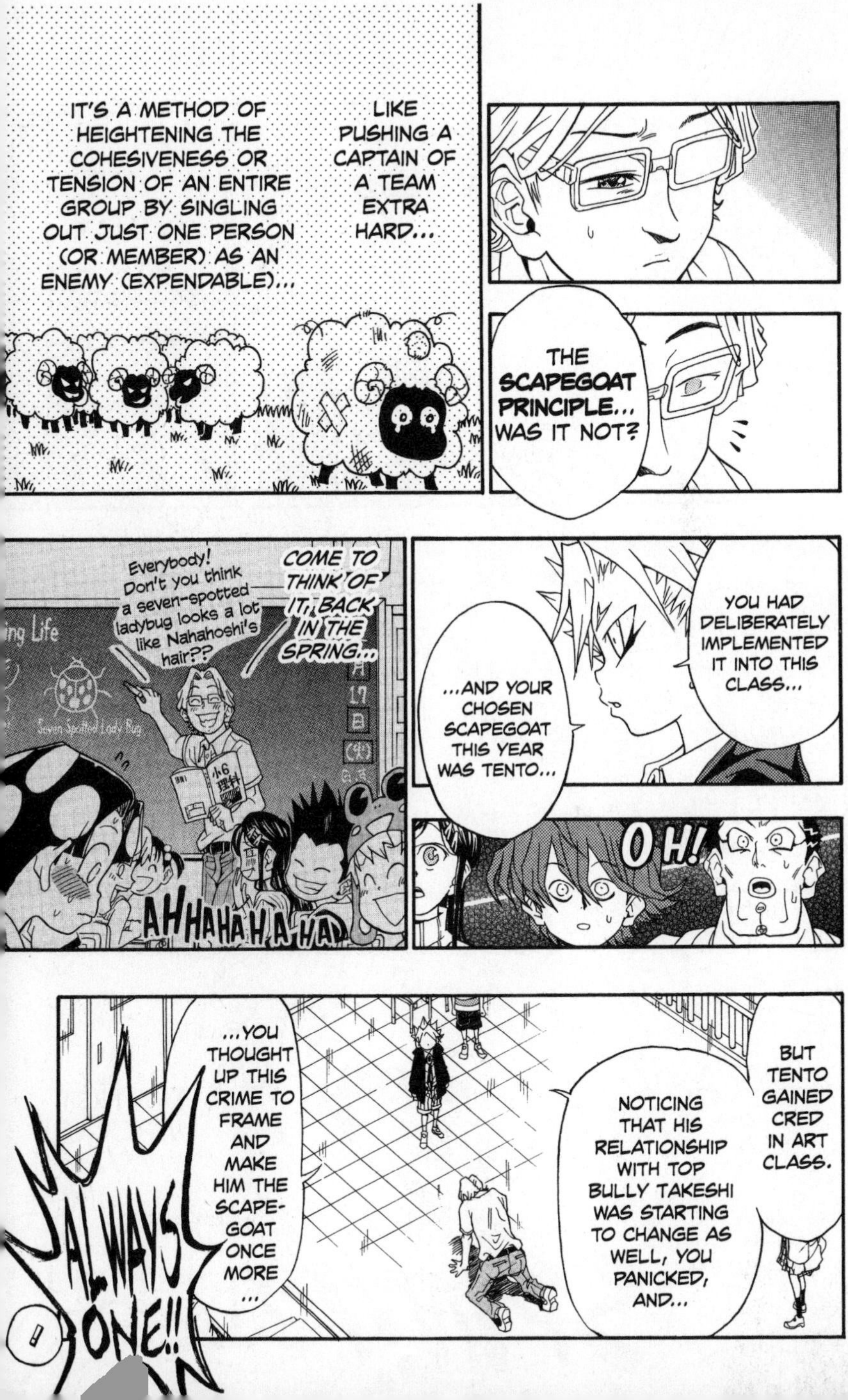
THE SCAPEGOAT PRINCIPLE... WAS IT NOT?
IT'S A METHOD OF HEIGHTENING THE COHESIVENESS OR TENSION OF AN ENTIRE GROUP BY SINGLING OUT JUST ONE PERSON (OR MEMBER) AS AN ENEMY (EXPENDABLE)...
LIKE PUSHING A CAPTAIN OF A TEAM EXTRA HARD...
YOU HAD DELIBERATELY IMPLEMENTED IT INTO THIS CLASS...
...AND YOUR CHOSEN SCAPEGOAT THIS YEAR WAS TENTO...
OH!
COME TO THINK OF IT, BACK IN THE SPRING...
Everybody! Don't you think a seven-spotted ladybug looks a lot like Nahahoshi's hair??
Seven Spotted Lady Bug
AHHAHAHAHAHA
BUT TENTO GAINED CRED IN ART CLASS.
NOTICING THAT HIS RELATIONSHIP WITH TOP BULLY TAKESHI WAS STARTING TO CHANGE AS WELL, YOU PANICKED, AND...
...YOU THOUGHT UP THIS CRIME TO FRAME AND MAKE HIM THE SCAPE-GOAT ONCE MORE...
ALWAYS ONE!!

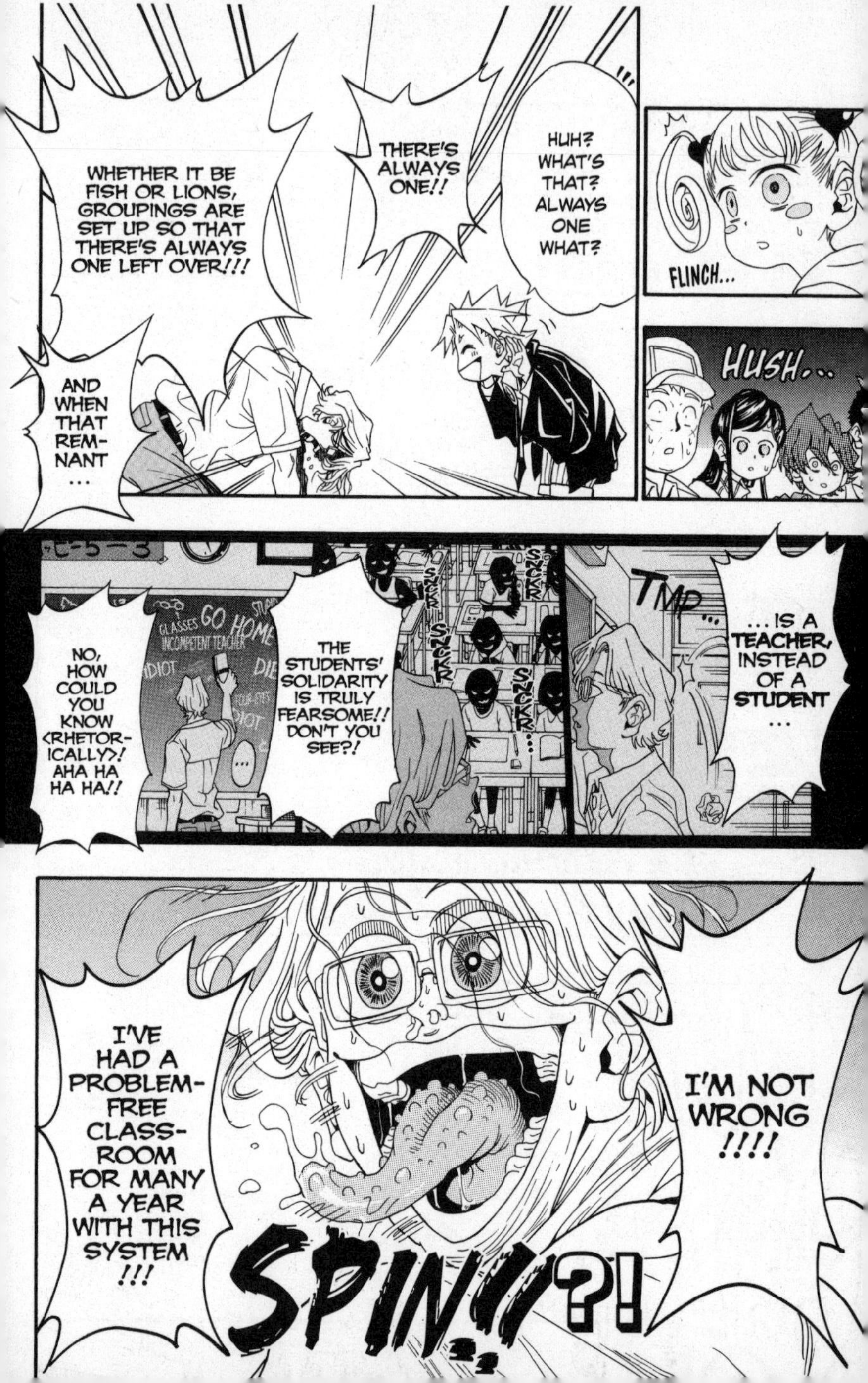
FLINCH...
HUSH...
HUH? WHAT'S THAT? ALWAYS ONE WHAT?
THERE'S ALWAYS ONE!!
WHETHER IT BE FISH OR LIONS, GROUPINGS ARE SET UP SO THAT THERE'S ALWAYS ONE LEFT OVER!!!
AND WHEN THAT REMNANT...
TMP...
...IS A TEACHER, INSTEAD OF A STUDENT...
SNCKR
SNCKR
SNCKR
SNCKR...
THE STUDENTS' SOLIDARITY IS TRULY FEARSOME!! DON'T YOU SEE?!
GLASSES
GO HOME
INCOMPETENT TEACHER
IDIOT
DIE
FOUR-EYES
NO, HOW COULD YOU KNOW <RHETORICALLY>?! AHA HA HA HA!!
I'M NOT WRONG !!!!
I'VE HAD A PROBLEM-FREE CLASSROOM FOR MANY A YEAR WITH THIS SYSTEM !!!
SPIN!?!

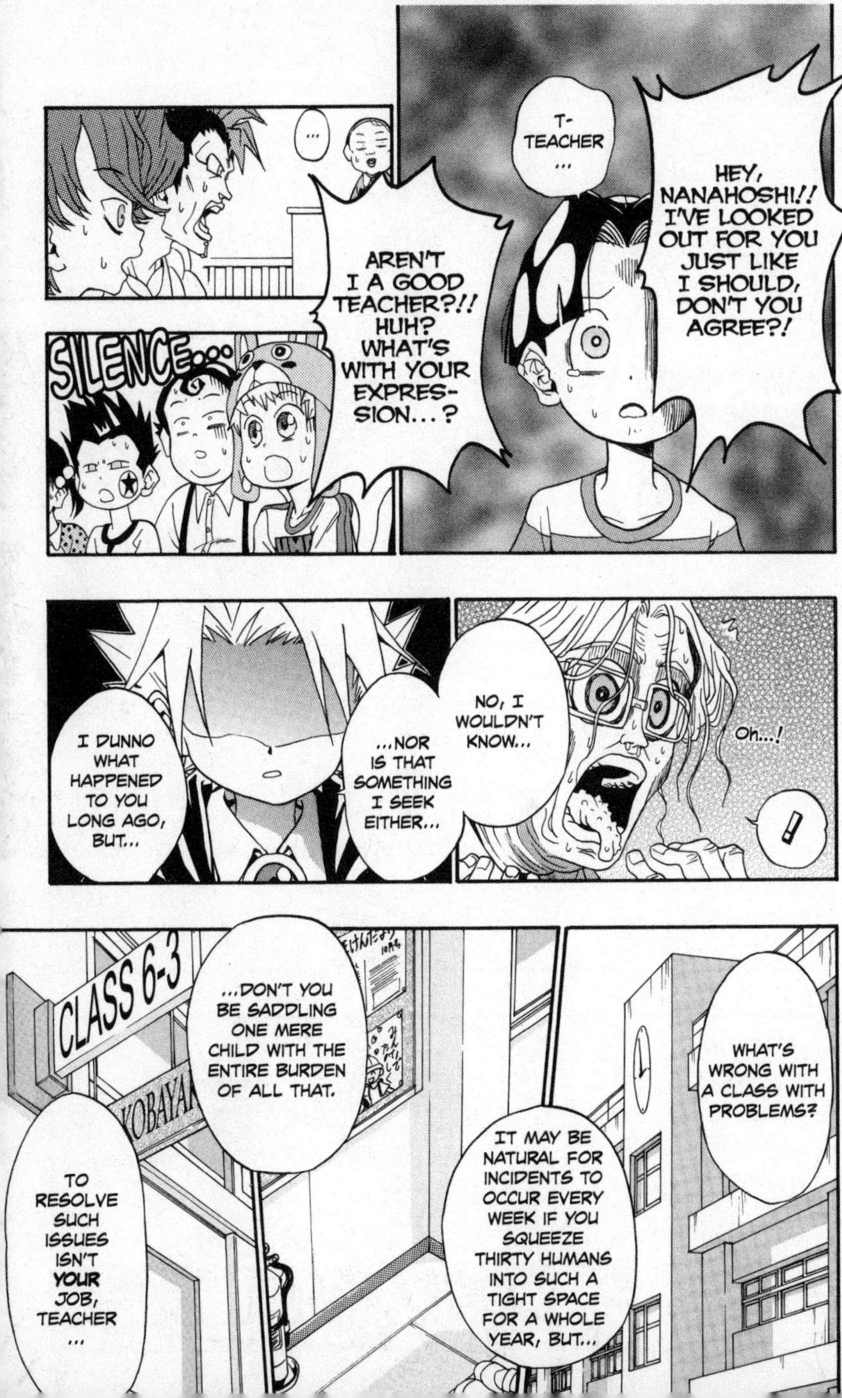
HEY, NANAHOSHI!! I'VE LOOKED OUT FOR YOU JUST LIKE I SHOULD, DON'T YOU AGREE?!
T-TEACHER...
AREN'T I A GOOD TEACHER?!! HUH? WHAT'S WITH YOUR EXPRESSION...?
...
SILENCE...
Oh...!
!
NO, I WOULDN'T KNOW...
...NOR IS THAT SOMETHING I SEEK EITHER...
I DUNNO WHAT HAPPENED TO YOU LONG AGO, BUT...
WHAT'S WRONG WITH A CLASS WITH PROBLEMS?
IT MAY BE NATURAL FOR INCIDENTS TO OCCUR EVERY WEEK IF YOU SQUEEZE THIRTY HUMANS INTO SUCH A TIGHT SPACE FOR A WHOLE YEAR, BUT...
CLASS 6-3
...DON'T YOU BE SADDLING ONE MERE CHILD WITH THE ENTIRE BURDEN OF ALL THAT.
TO RESOLVE SUCH ISSUES ISN'T **YOUR** JOB, TEACHER...

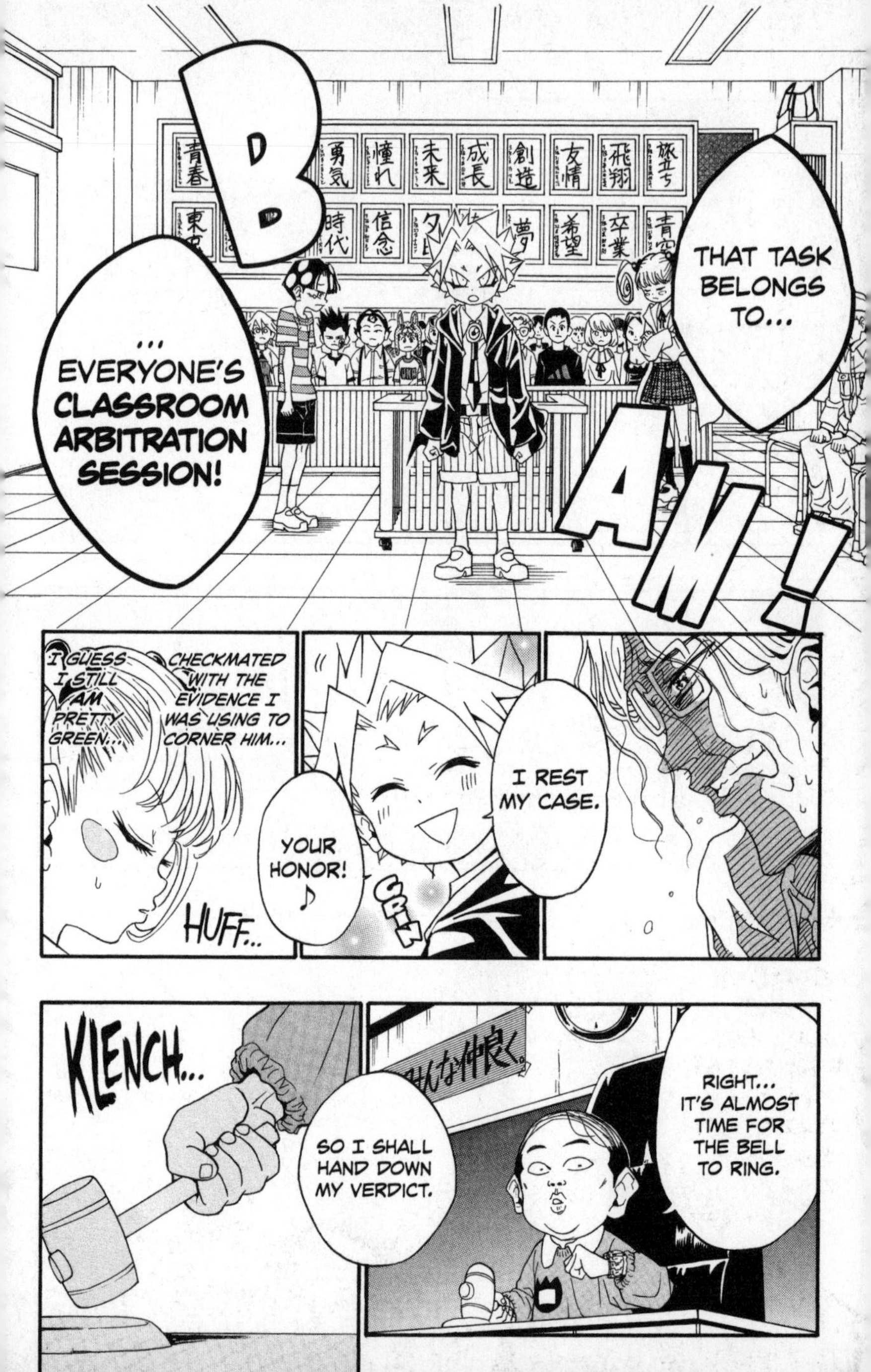
THAT TASK BELONGS TO...
...EVERYONE'S CLASSROOM ARBITRATION SESSION!
BAM!
I REST MY CASE.
YOUR HONOR! ♪
GRIN
CHECKMATED WITH THE EVIDENCE I WAS USING TO CORNER HIM...
I GUESS I STILL AM PRETTY GREEN...
HUFF...
RIGHT... IT'S ALMOST TIME FOR THE BELL TO RING.
SO I SHALL HAND DOWN MY VERDICT.
KLENCH...

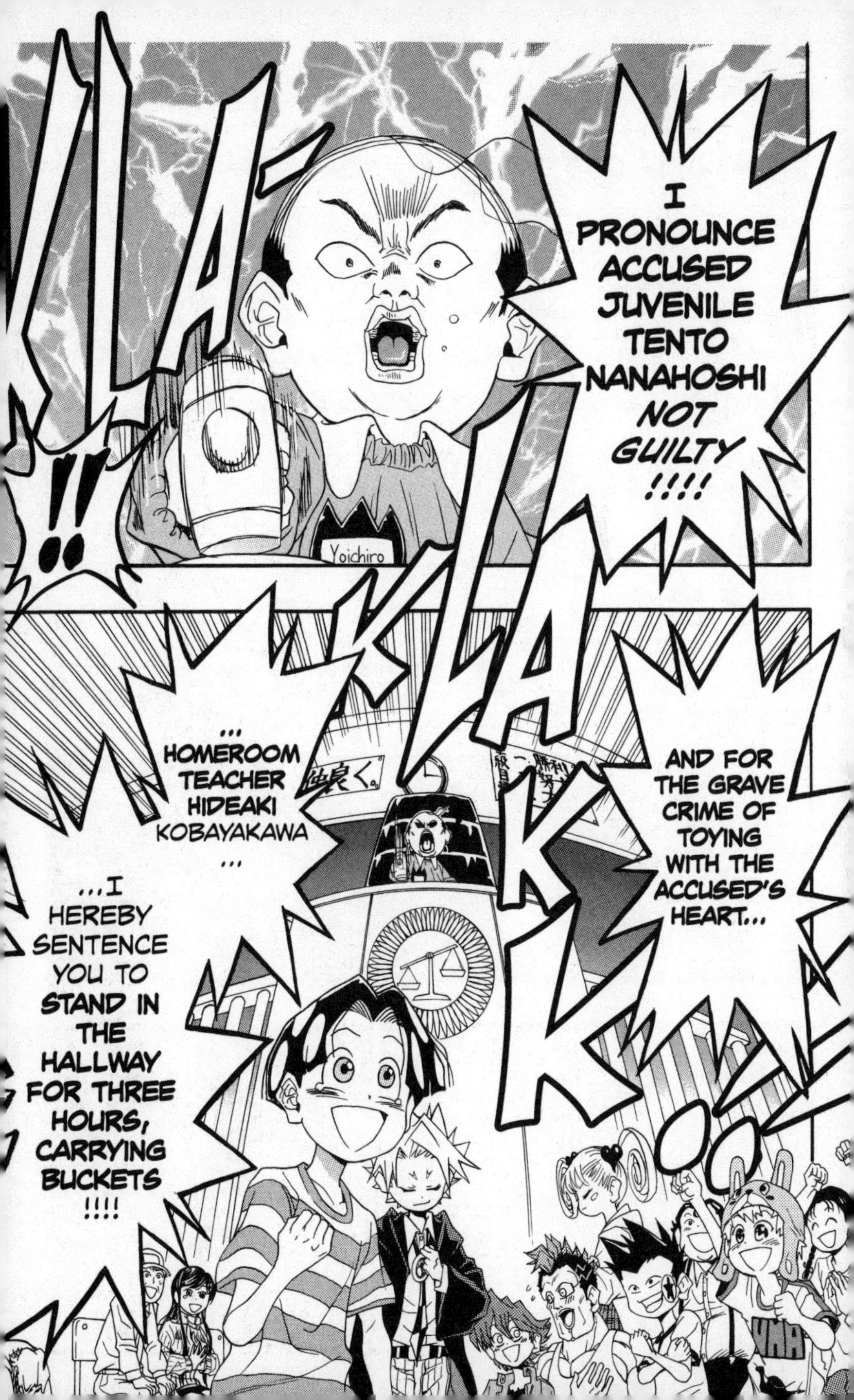
I PRONOUNCE ACCUSED JUVENILE TENTO NANAHOSHI NOT GUILTY!!!!
Yoichiro
AND FOR THE GRAVE CRIME OF TOYING WITH THE ACCUSED'S HEART...
...HOMEROOM TEACHER HIDEAKI KOBAYAKAWA...
...I HEREBY SENTENCE YOU TO STAND IN THE HALLWAY FOR THREE HOURS, CARRYING BUCKETS!!!!

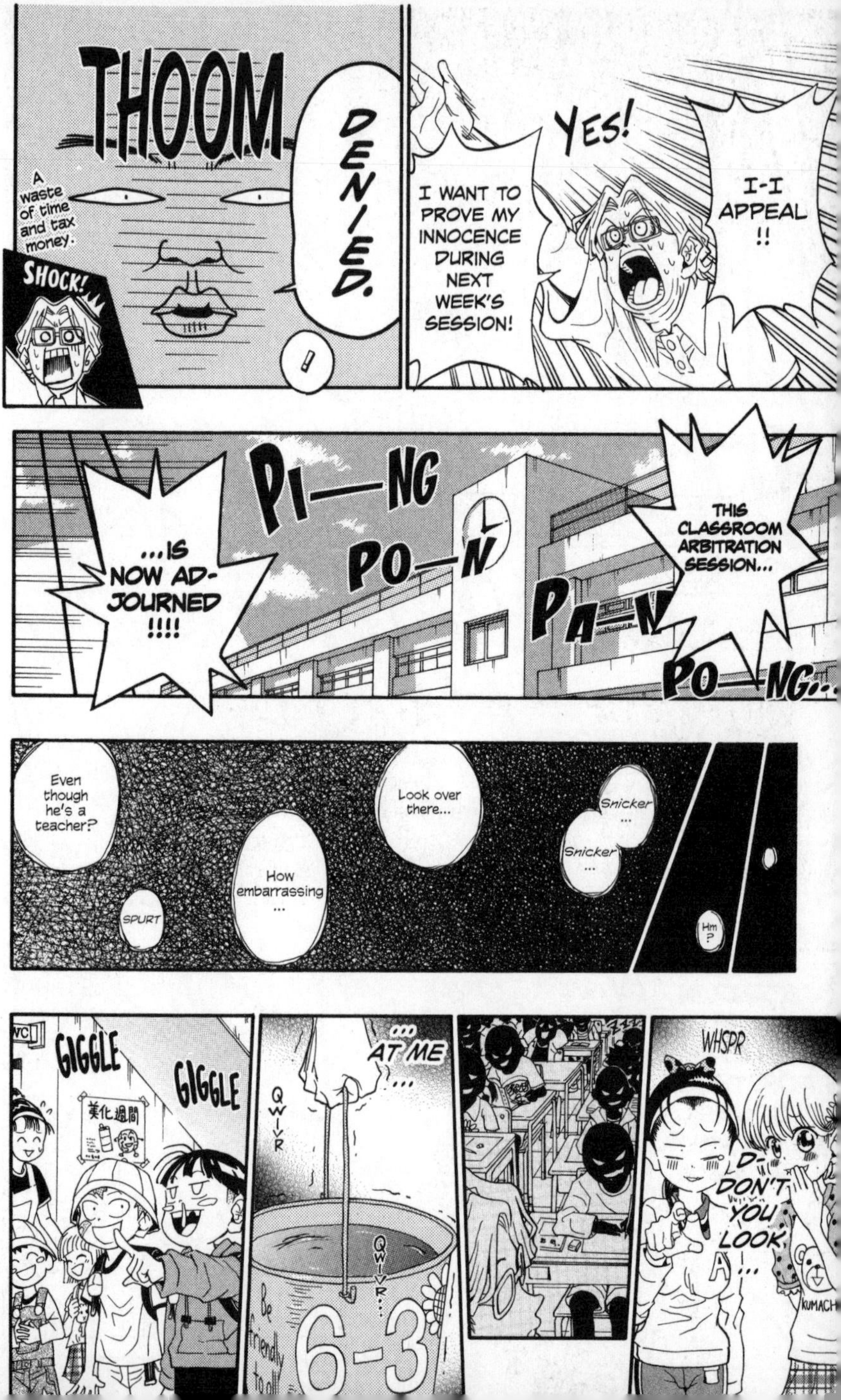
I-I APPEAL !!
YES!
I WANT TO PROVE MY INNOCENCE DURING NEXT WEEK'S SESSION!
!
DENIED.
THOOM
A waste of time and tax money.
SHOCK!
THIS CLASSROOM ARBITRATION SESSION...
PI—NG
PO—N
PA—N
PO—NG...
...IS NOW AD-JOURNED !!!!
Hm?
Snicker...
Snicker...
Look over there...
How embarrassing...
Even though he's a teacher?
SPURT
WHSPR
D-DON'T YOU LOOK A...
KUMACH
...AT ME...
QWIVR
QWIVR...
Be friendly to all!
6-3
WC
GIGGLE
GIGGLE
美化週間

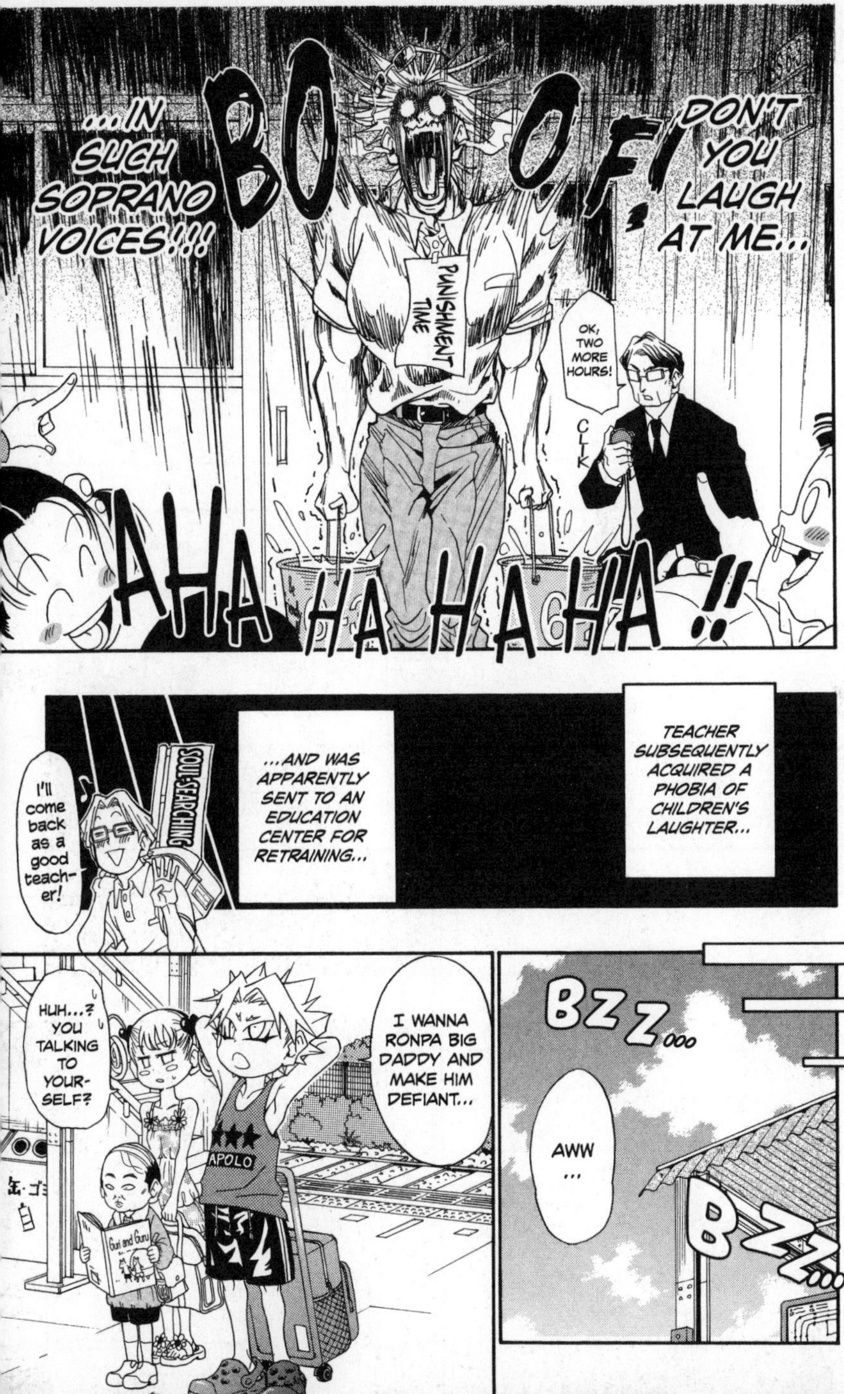
DON'T YOU LAUGH AT ME...
BOOF!
...IN SUCH SOPRANO VOICES!!!
PUNISHMENT TIME
OK, TWO MORE HOURS!
CLIK
AHAHAHAHAHA!!
TEACHER SUBSEQUENTLY ACQUIRED A PHOBIA OF CHILDREN'S LAUGHTER...
...AND WAS APPARENTLY SENT TO AN EDUCATION CENTER FOR RETRAINING...
SOUL-SEARCHING
I'll come back as a good teacher!
BZZ...
AWW...
BZZZ...
I WANNA RONPA BIG DADDY AND MAKE HIM DEFIANT...
HUH...? YOU TALKING TO YOURSELF?
APOLO
Guri and Guru

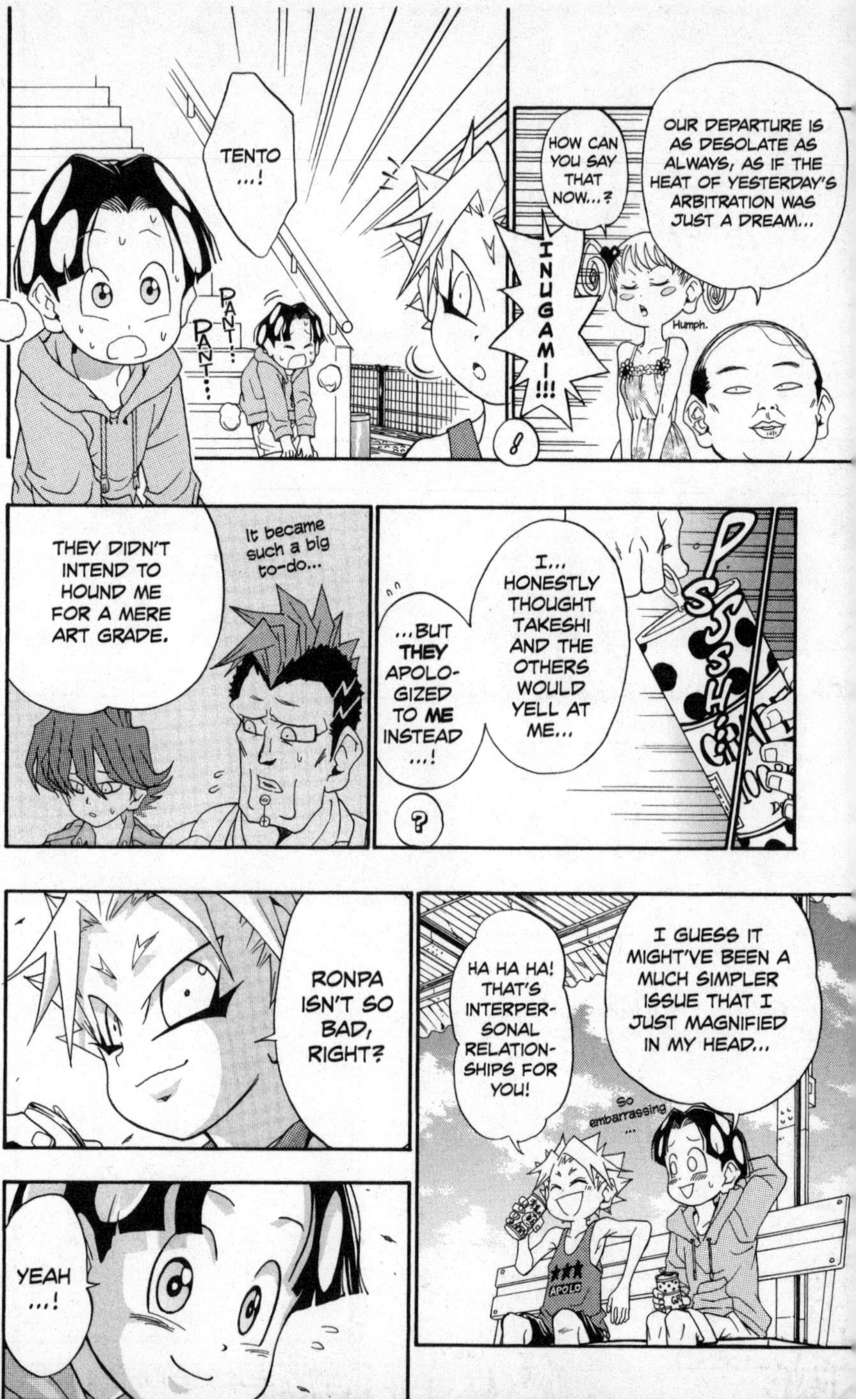
OUR DEPARTURE IS AS DESOLATE AS ALWAYS, AS IF THE HEAT OF YESTERDAY'S ARBITRATION WAS JUST A DREAM...
Humph.
HOW CAN YOU SAY THAT NOW...?
INUGAMI!!!
TENTO ...!
PANT! PANT...
I... HONESTLY THOUGHT TAKESHI AND THE OTHERS WOULD YELL AT ME...
...BUT THEY APOLOGIZED TO ME INSTEAD ...!
PSSSH
It became such a big to-do...
THEY DIDN'T INTEND TO HOUND ME FOR A MERE ART GRADE.
I GUESS IT MIGHT'VE BEEN A MUCH SIMPLER ISSUE THAT I JUST MAGNIFIED IN MY HEAD...
HA HA HA! THAT'S INTERPERSONAL RELATIONSHIPS FOR YOU!
So embarrassing ...
RONPA ISN'T SO BAD, RIGHT?
YEAH ...!

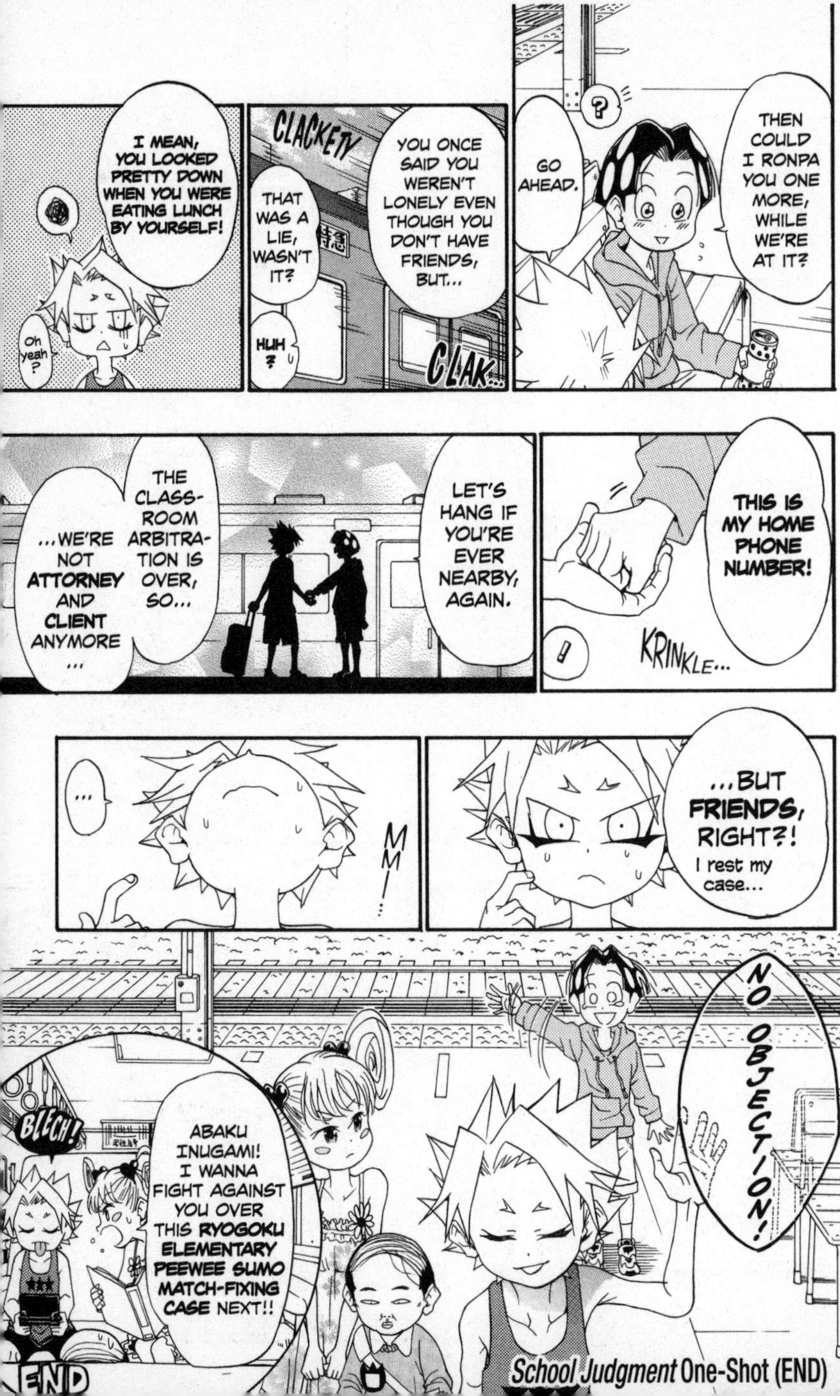
THEN COULD I RONPA YOU ONE MORE, WHILE WE'RE AT IT?
?
GO AHEAD.
YOU ONCE SAID YOU WEREN'T LONELY EVEN THOUGH YOU DON'T HAVE FRIENDS, BUT...
CLACKETY
THAT WAS A LIE, WASN'T IT?
HUH?
CLAK...
I MEAN, YOU LOOKED PRETTY DOWN WHEN YOU WERE EATING LUNCH BY YOURSELF!
Oh yeah?
THIS IS MY HOME PHONE NUMBER!
!
KRINKLE...
LET'S HANG IF YOU'RE EVER NEARBY, AGAIN.
THE CLASSROOM ARBITRATION IS OVER, SO...
...WE'RE NOT ATTORNEY AND CLIENT ANYMORE...
...BUT FRIENDS, RIGHT?! I rest my case...
MM!...
...
NO OBJECTION!
ABAKU INUGAMI! I WANNA FIGHT AGAINST YOU OVER THIS RYOGOKU ELEMENTARY PEEWEE SUMO MATCH-FIXING CASE NEXT!!
BLECH!
END
School Judgment One-Shot (END)

Manga: Nobuaki Enoki

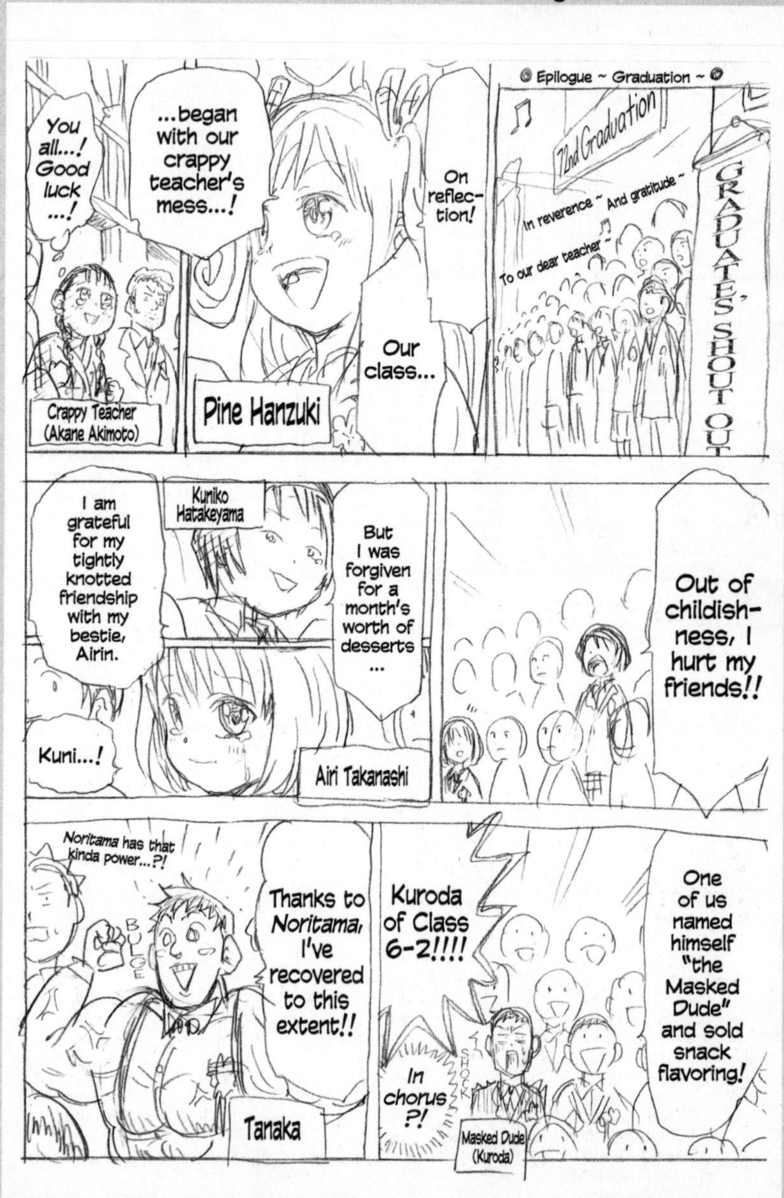
Epilogue ~ Graduation ~
72nd Graduation
In reverence ~ And gratitude ~
To our dear teacher ~
GRADUATES' SHOUT OUT
On reflection!
Our class...
...began with our crappy teacher's mess...!
Pine Hanzuki
You all...! Good luck...!
Crappy Teacher (Akane Akimoto)
Out of childishness, I hurt my friends!!
Kuniko Hatakeyama
I am grateful for my tightly knotted friendship with my bestie, Airin.
But I was forgiven for a month's worth of desserts...
Kuni...!
Airi Takanashi
One of us named himself "the Masked Dude" and sold snack flavoring!
Kuroda of Class 6-2!!!!
In chorus?!
SHOCK
Masked Dude (Kuroda)
Thanks to Noritama, I've recovered to this extent!!
BULGE
Noritama has that kinda power...?!
Tanaka

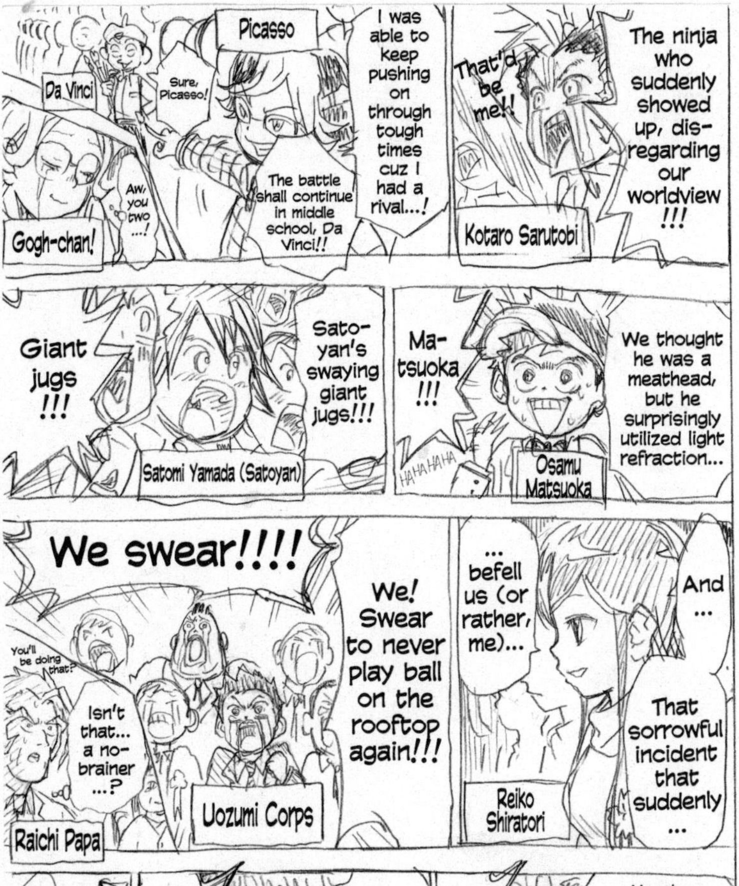
The ninja who suddenly showed up, dis-regarding our worldview!!!
That'd be me!!
Kotaro Sarutobi
I was able to keep pushing on through tough times cuz I had a rival...!
Picasso
The battle shall continue in middle school, Da Vinci!!
Sure, Picasso!
Da Vinci
Aw, you two ...!
Gogh-chan!
We thought he was a meathead, but he surprisingly utilized light refraction...
Ma-tsuoka!!!
HAHAHAHA
Osamu Matsuoka
Sato-yan's swaying giant jugs!!!
Giant jugs!!!
Satomi Yamada (Satoyan)
And ...
That sorrowful incident that suddenly ...
... befell us (or rather, me)...
Reiko Shiratori
We! Swear to never play ball on the rooftop again!!!
We swear!!!!
Uozumi Corps
Isn't that... a no-brainer ...?
You'll be doing that?
Raichi Papa
He who brought a smart phone and a weird mecha-like backpack to school despite telling everyone to not break regulations...
... Higa-shide!!
Forgive me...!
Shuichi Higashide
He abruptly zapped a classmate with his recorder ...
... Higa-shide!!!!
Forgive me...!
And ...!
SHUP

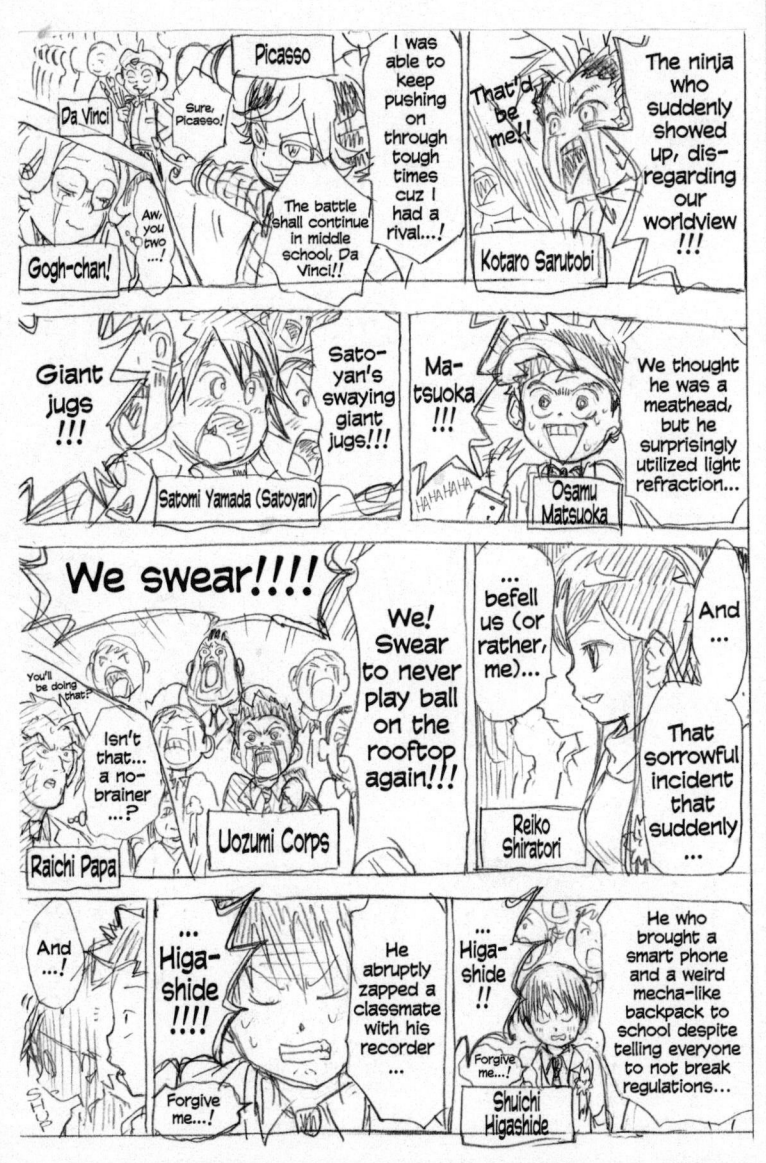

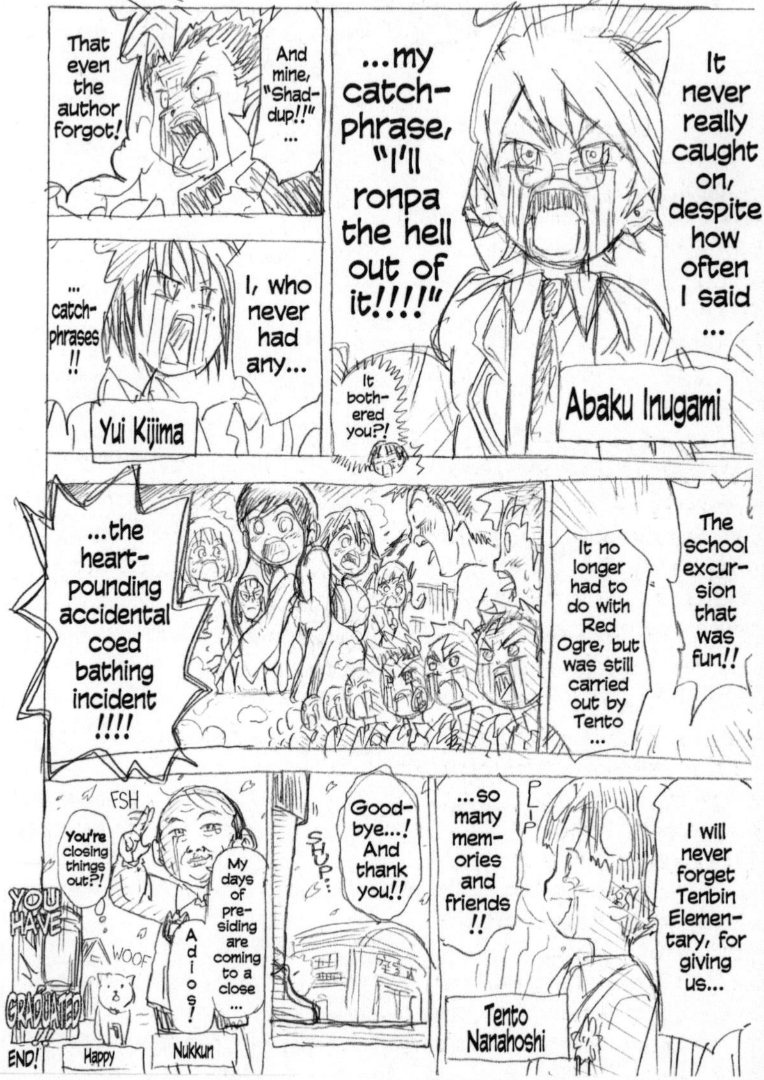
It never really caught on, despite how often I said ...
...my catch-phrase, "I'll ronpa the hell out of it!!!!"
Abaku Inugami
It bothered you?!
And mine, "Shaddup!!" ...
That even the author forgot!
I, who never had any...
... catch-phrases !!
Yui Kijima
The school excursion that was fun!!
It no longer had to do with Red Ogre, but was still carried out by Tento ...
...the heart-pounding accidental coed bathing incident !!!!
I will never forget Tenbin Elementary, for giving us...
...so many memories and friends !!
FLIP
Tento Nanahoshi
Good-bye...! And thank you!!
SHUP...
My days of presiding are coming to a close ...
Adios!
FSH
You're closing things out?!
WOOF
Nukkun
Happy
YOU HAVE GRADUATED!!
END!

AFTERWORD

First, I must apologize.
In order to draw the ending that I wanted, I needed to have the final chapter, "The Session That Started It All," appear in *Shonen Jump+* because I was one chapter short. Hence, there were many readers who only read the main magazine and got the gut-wrenching cliff-hanger, "Tento...you're Red Ogre, aren't you?!" and I'm truly sorry for that. I hope this book will provide you closure.

That being the said, this ending *is* exactly what I pictured from the very beginning. *School Judgment* was always a tale of these *four* characters. In terms of plot or deeper meaning, I feel like it would be tasteless for me to go into it myself, so in place of those various things I included the FYI notes I gave Obata Sensei for the final chapter here.

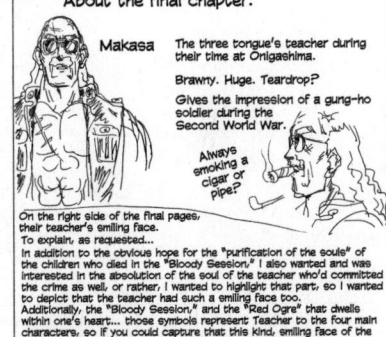

About the final chapter.

Makasa — The three tongue's teacher during their time at Onigashima.

Brawny. Huge. Teardrop?

Gives the impression of a gung-ho soldier during the Second World War.

Always smoking a cigar or pipe?

On the right side of the final pages, their teacher's smiling face.
To explain, as requested...
In addition to the obvious hope for the "purification of the souls" of the children who died in the "Bloody Session," I also wanted and was interested in the absolution of the soul of the teacher who'd committed the crime as well, or rather, I wanted to highlight that part, so I wanted to depict that the teacher had such a smiling face too.
Additionally, the "Bloody Session," and the "Red Ogre" that dwells within one's heart... those symbols represent Teacher to the four main characters, so if you could capture that this kind, smiling face of the Teacher is not aimed just at the four as first graders, but simultaneously turned toward the current sixth graders who have reunited as a single flower, I think it would provide proof that the four have been able to graduate and move on from that tragedy.
The cleansed teacher's soul benevolently watches over the current four...I intend to have put in such a dream-like or illusionary nuance, so if you could please not color the area outside the panels black like the usual flashbacks. However, to avoid it being unclear and result in readers mixing it up with the left-hand panel containing the current four, I'd be thrilled if you could apply a hazy white screentone so that it's easy to tell left and right apart. Though this is the final chapter of my inadequacy and inability to assist more...

I continue to be indebted to you until the very end.

Finally, I'd like to offer my gratitude once more. First, to Obata Sensei and all of his staff, who took this novice's shoddy *storyboards* every week and elevated them into brilliant *manga*, thank you very much! I shall treasure this experience for the rest of my life. Next, to my editor Mr. Saito, who has patiently looked at my manga since my teens and guided it to serialization, thank you.
And to everyone who has supported me all this time...thanks! To everybody who has faithfully read this manga—thank you!!
Thank you so very much...!!!
I am going to keep studying and training hard in order to bring you an even more enthralling manga someday. If you happen to catch sight of it, please read it.
Well then, with hopes that we shall meet again when effort leads to a season of full bloom... Ahem...

"Court is hereby adjourned!!"

Nobuaki Enoki

COURT IS NOW IN SESSION

Hi! Thank you for reading *School Judgment: Gakkyu Hotei*! There are quite a few instances in this series where knowledge of the Japanese language is a key part of understanding the cases and extra pages, so I would like to take the time to explain some of this to you!

Sign (p. 7)	The sign reads, "Public Prosecutor's Office."
Puppy-gami (p. 14)	Pine refers to Inugami as a dog or puppy on multiple occasions. While it sounds like she is doing it just to be mean, Inugami's name is written with the kanji 犬神, which mean "dog" and "god," respectively. So when she is calling him a puppy, she is actually making a joke about his name.
Pine Half-Baked (p. 14)	Pine's last name, Hanzuki, is written with the kanji for "discriminate" and "moon." The way that Abaku says it here, however, implies that she is half-baked or physically underdeveloped.
Chalkboard (p. 21)	The writing on the chalkboard says, "Friday, July 8th. Classroom helpers: Sumiyoshi and Minagawa."
Momotaro (pgs. 51–52)	The Three Tongues, Inugami, Sarutobi and Kijima, are all named after characters from the legend of Momotaro. Inugami is the dog (*Inu*), Sarutobi is the monkey (*Saru*) and Kijima is the pheasant (*Kiji*). Their teacher picked them to play these parts in the play since their names fulfilled the roles in the story.
裁 (*sai*) (kanji on judge's stand, p. 70)	This kanji comes from the word 裁判所 (*saibansho*), which means "courthouse."
学 (*gaku*) (kanji on board, pgs. 139, 151)	This kanji appears in multiple places throughout *School Judgment*, including in the Japanese title. The kanji can mean "education," "study," "learn" or "school," depending on the context.

Katsu vs. Katsu (p. 167)	In the Japanese language, there are many words that are homonyms. The *katsu* (**カツ**) in "tonkatsu" is literally "fried pork cutlet," which is what Abaku's mom serves him for dinner. However, Inugami uses crafty wordplay to say that he will *katsu* (**勝つ**) the case, which in Japanese means "to win."
Chalkboard (p. 171)	The writing on the chalkboard says, "Thursday, October 18th."
Ladybug (p. 195)	The teacher makes a joke that Tento's hair looks a lot like the seven-spotted ladybug. Tento Nanahoshi's name is a direct reference to this bug. "Ladybug" in Japanese is *tentomushi*. Additionally, Tento's last name is Nanahoshi, which means "seven stars." This is most likely a reference to the seven spots on a ladybug.

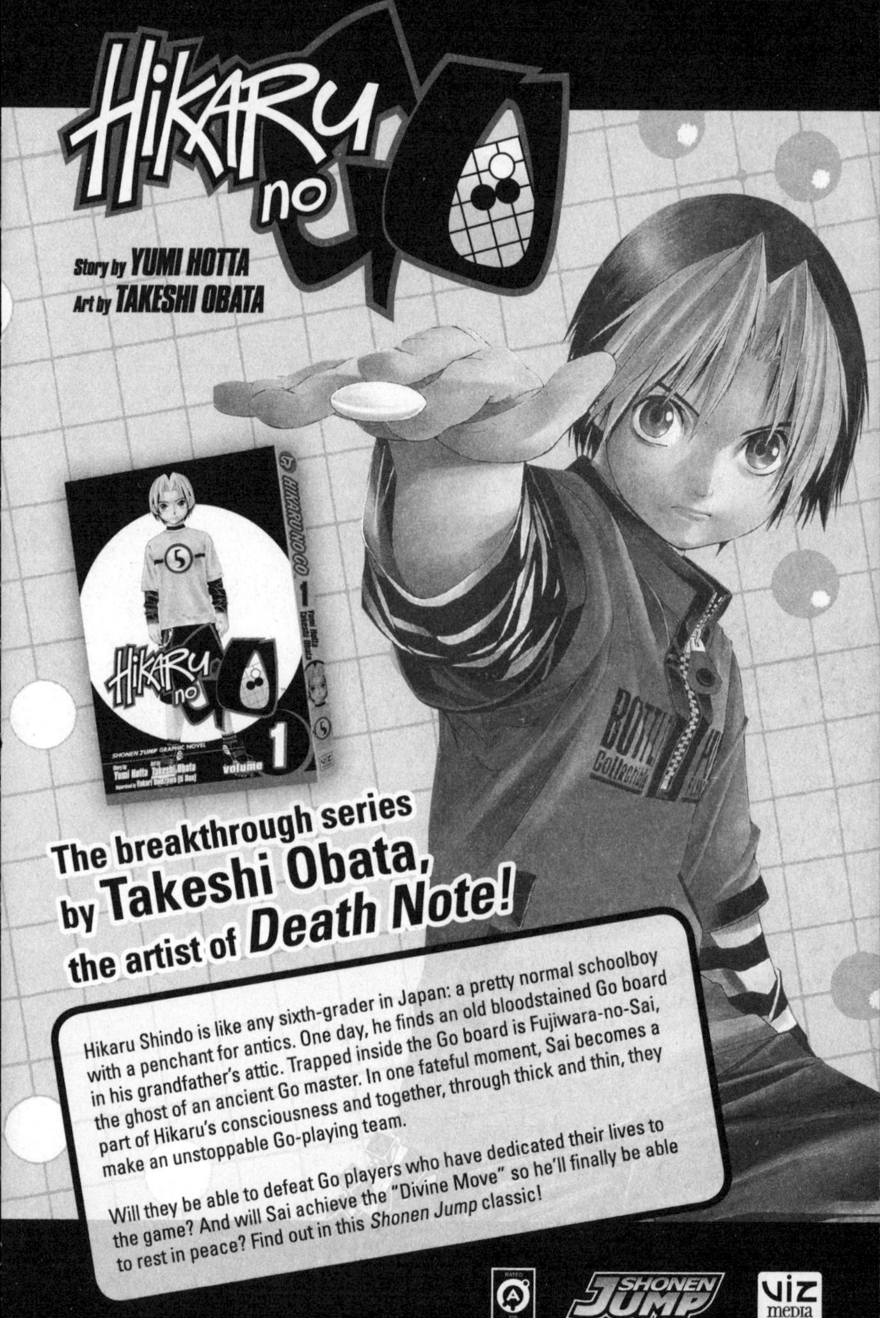
Hikaru no Go
Story by YUMI HOTTA
Art by TAKESHI OBATA
The breakthrough series by Takeshi Obata, the artist of Death Note!
Hikaru Shindo is like any sixth-grader in Japan: a pretty normal schoolboy with a penchant for antics. One day, he finds an old bloodstained Go board in his grandfather's attic. Trapped inside the Go board is Fujiwara-no-Sai, the ghost of an ancient Go master. In one fateful moment, Sai becomes a part of Hikaru's consciousness and together, through thick and thin, they make an unstoppable Go-playing team.
Will they be able to defeat Go players who have dedicated their lives to the game? And will Sai achieve the "Divine Move" so he'll finally be able to rest in peace? Find out in this Shonen Jump classic!
RATED A FOR ALL AGES ratings.viz.com
SHONEN JUMP
www.shonenjump.com
VIZ media
www.viz.com

A KILLER COMEDY FROM *WEEKLY SHONEN JUMP*

ASSASSINATION CLASSROOM

STORY AND ART BY
YUSEI MATSUI

Ever caught yourself screaming, "I could just kill that teacher"? What would it take to justify such antisocial behavior and weeks of detention? Especially if he's the best teacher you've ever had? Giving you an "F" on a quiz? Mispronouncing your name during roll call...*again*? How about blowing up the moon and threatening to do the same to Mother Earth—unless you take him out first?! Plus a reward of a cool 100 million from the Ministry of Defense!

Okay, now that you're committed... How are you going to pull this off? What does your pathetic class of misfits have in their arsenal to combat Teach's alien technology, bizarre powers and...*tentacles*?!

BAKUMAN。

STORY BY TSUGUMI OHBA
ART BY TAKESHI OBATA

From the creators of *Death Note*

The mystery behind manga making REVEALED!

Average student Moritaka Mashiro enjoys drawing for fun. When his classmate and aspiring writer Akito Takagi discovers his talent, he begs to team up. But what exactly does it take to make it in the manga-publishing world?

Bakuman。 Vol. 1
ISBN: 978-1-4215-3513-5
$9.99 US / $12.99 CAN *

The mystery behind *manga-making* revealed!

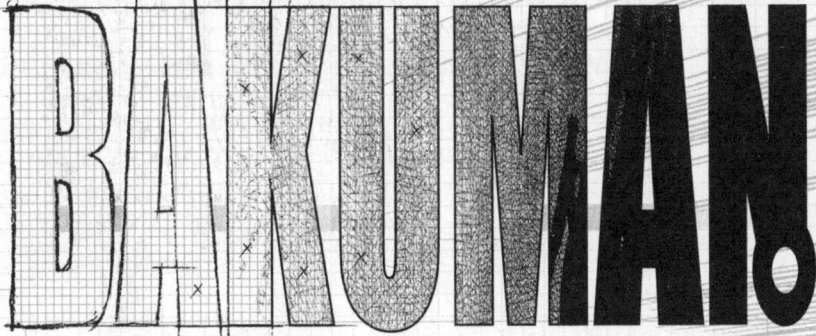

BAKUMAN。

Story by **TSUGUMI OHBA** ✦ *Art by* **TAKESHI OBATA**

From the creators of **Death Note**.

BAKUMAN。 COMPLETE BOX SET

Comes with a *two-sided poster* and the *Otter No. 11* mini-comic!

Average student Moritaka Mashiro enjoys drawing for fun. When his classmate and aspiring writer Akito Takagi discovers his talent, he begs Moritaka to team up with him as a manga-creating duo. But what exactly does it take to make it in the manga-publishing world?

This *bestselling series* is now available in a COMPLETE BOX SET!

A 20% SAVINGS OVER BUYING THE INDIVIDUAL VOLUMES!

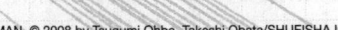

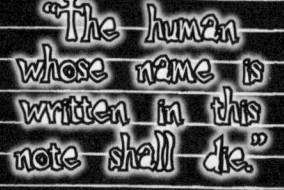

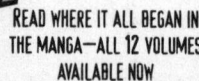

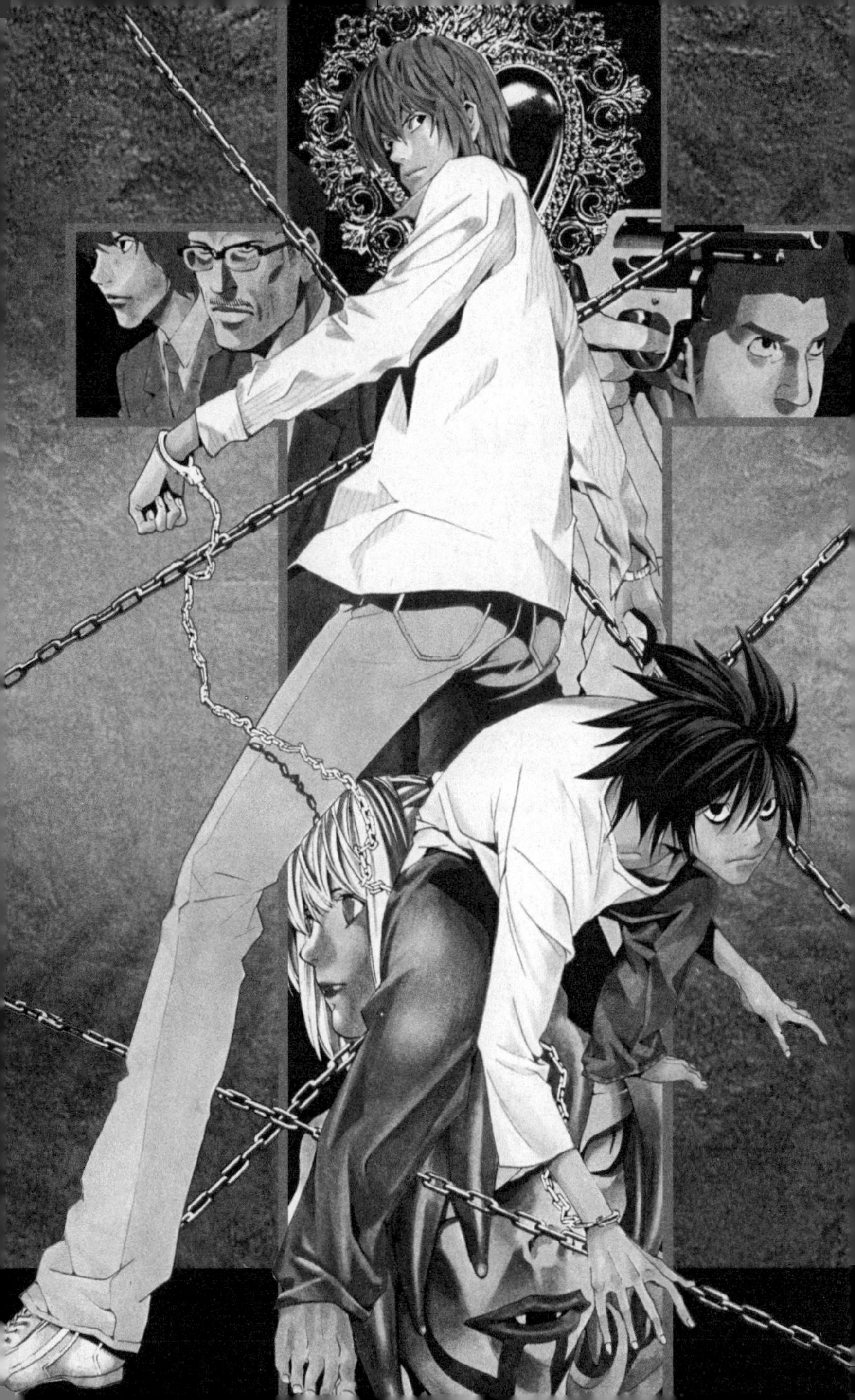

YOU'RE READING THE WRONG WAY!

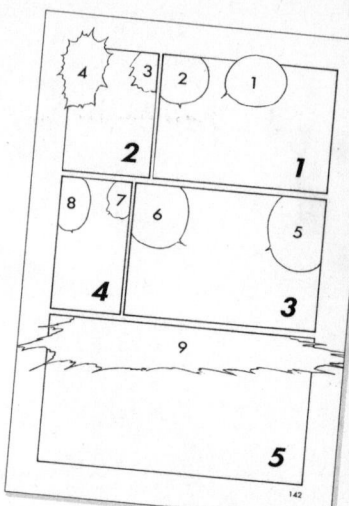

School Judgment: Gakkyu Hotei

reads from right to left, starting in the upper-right corner. Japanese is read from right to left, meaning that action, sound effects and word-balloon order are completely reversed from English order.